The General Method of
Social Work Practice

FOURTH EDITION

The General Method of Social Work Practice

McMahon's Generalist Perspective

Elizabeth March Timberlake
The Catholic University of America

Michaela Zajicek Farber
The Catholic University of America

Christine Anlauf Sabatino
The Catholic University of America

Allyn and Bacon

Boston • London • Toronto • Sydney • Tokyo • Singapore

Series Editor: *Patricia Quinlin*
Editor in Chief, Social Sciences: *Karen Hanson*
Editorial Assistant: *Alyssa Pratt*
Marketing Manager: *Jackie Aaron*
Editorial-Production Administrator: *Annette Joseph*
Editorial-Production Coordinator: *Holly Crawford*
Editorial-Production Service: *Lynda Griffiths, TKM Productions*
Photo Researcher: *Katharine S. Cook*
Artist: *Asterisk, Inc.*
Composition Buyer: *Linda Cox*
Electronic Composition: *Publishers' Design and Production Services, Inc.*
Manufacturing Buyer: *Suzanne Lareau*
Cover Administrator: *Linda Knowles*
Cover Designer: *Kristina Mose-Libon*

Copyright © 2002 by Allyn & Bacon
A Pearson Education Company
75 Arlington St., Ste. 300
Boston, MA 02116

Internet: www.ablongman.com

Previous editions were written by Maria O'Neil McMahon and published under the title *The General Method of Social Work Practice: A Generalist Perspective*, copyright © 1996, 1990, 1984 by Allyn & Bacon.

Library of Congress Cataloging-in-Publication Data

Timberlake, Elizabeth M.
    The general method of social work practice : McMahon's generalist perspective / Elizabeth March Timberlake, Michaela Zajicek Farber, Christine Anlauf Sabatino.—4th ed.
        p. cm.
    Rev. ed. of: The general method of social work practice / Maria O'Neil McMahon. 3rd ed. c1996.
    Includes bibliographical references and index.
    ISBN 0-205-29816-8
    1. Social work education.   2. Social work education—Curricula.   3. Social service.
4. Holism.   I. Farber, Michaela Zajicek.   II. Sabatino, Christine Anlauf.   III. McMahon, Maria O'Neil. General method of social work practice. IV. Title.

HV11 .M374 2001
361.3—dc21

                                                                                00-051092

Printed in the United States of America
10 9 8 7 6 5 4 3 2 1   RRD-VA   06 05 04 03 02 01

Photo credits: p. 1: Nubar Alexanian/Stock, Boston; p. 18: Jim Estrin/New York Times Pictures; p. 38: Stone/Loren Santow; p. 80: Michael Newman/PhotoEdit; p. 116: Tony Freeman/PhotoEdit; p. 156: James Shaffer/PhotoEdit; p. 201: Stone/Jon Bradley; p. 253: Will Hart; p. 308: Will Hart; p. 339: Charles Gupton/Stock, Boston.

CONTENTS

IN MEMORIAM
MARIA JOAN O'NEIL McMAHON, D.S.W. (1937–1996)

Maria Joan O'Neil McMahon, friend and colleague, died of cancer on October 26, 1996. For her, social work represented a calling of service to others and provided a sense of meaning and fulfillment in life's purpose. Throughout her lifetime, she evidenced her commitment to social justice and the enhancement of human life through both social action and direct social work practice.

During her tenure as a Sister of Mercy of Connecticut, Sr. Maria Joan O'Neil earned her M.S.W. and D.S.W. at The Catholic University of America. Upon completion of her graduate study, she worked in a residential treatment center for children with emotional disturbances, taught in and chaired the undergraduate social work program at Saint Joseph College, and developed a degree program in child welfare at the college. At East Carolina University, Sr. Maria Joan was instrumental in working with faculty to achieve the initial accreditation of the M.S.W. program and the transformation of the undergraduate and graduate social work programs into an autonomous School of Social Work. She served as the school's first dean and later as a tenured professor of social work.

After almost three decades, she left the order to follow a different Catholic faith commitment and service path. Later, she met Dennis McMahon, who became her life partner in marriage, in sharing her commitment to serving the poor and vulnerable, and in carrying out faith-based volunteer work.

Throughout her career as a social work educator, Dr. McMahon demonstrated sensitivity and responsiveness to the needs of students and served as a model of professional excellence through her teaching, community service, and scholarship. She taught many courses in generalist practice, human behavior, cultural diversity, and social welfare policy and services to multiple generations of undergraduate and graduate social work students. She was an active member of numerous social work organizations, including the National Association of Social Workers, the Council on Social Work Education, and the National Association of Deans and Directors. She served as a commissioner of the Commission on Accreditation of the Council on Social Work Education. Her consultations with new and established social work programs extended throughout the United States and around the world. Dr. McMahon's community involvement included, among others, serving on the Permanent Standing Committee on Social Services of the National Conference of Catholic Charities, on the Advisory Board of Catholic Charities Indochinese Resettlement Program, as the Board Chair of Eastern North Carolina Poverty Committee, and as the Board Chair of Catholic Social Ministries of the Diocese of Raleigh. She received multiple honors and awards, including Outstanding Social Worker of the Year in Connecticut and distinguished alumna of the National Catholic School of Social Service of The Catholic University of America.

Dr. McMahon's refereed articles, practice monographs, and books focused on poverty, child welfare, families, the general method of social work practice, social work education, and social work personnel issues. Her books include *The General Method of Social Work Practice* (today in its 4th edition) and *Advanced Generalist Practice with an International Perspective*. Her international professional presentations encompassed social work educational issues, social development, and social rights. Her national presentations covered rural social work, poverty, child welfare, the general method of social work practice, and social work education.

IN HER OWN WORDS
A COMMITMENT TO SERVICE TODAY

(The following excerpts are from a 1990 talk delivered to social workers in public social services by Maria Joan O'Neil McMahon, D.S.W.)

It is very fitting that at least once a year social workers take a little distance from the pressures, demands, policies, and procedures to reflect and recommit ourselves to what, in fact, we are all about. We know that there was a time when our country went through a depression. We were in trouble and people were going under. At that time, our nation decided that it was not going to be a society built on survival of the fittest and instituted a means to care and help people meet their needs through the rough times so that they could once again become productive members of society. Thus, the 1935 Social Security Act reflects the highest value of our nation—that is, the value of the potential and worth of every human being. To demonstrate that value and to serve the institution of public assistance, government officials looked at many disciplines and people. They did not choose individuals from psychology or psychiatry who deal primarily with the individual. They did not choose people from the fields of sociology or social planning who deal primarily with the social environment. They sought people who understood both, because they knew that the purpose of the Social Security Act was to help individuals function effectively in society. They chose social work as the primary discipline to carry out the job, because social workers have always had the dual person and environment perspective.

So even with your pressures, your stresses, and your often difficult jobs, what keeps you going and what keeps so many other noble, seasoned, wonderful people in public sector jobs has been the fact that there is meaning and purpose to what these jobs are about and the fact that they and you have a commitment—a commitment to human service. What does *commitment* mean? Dictionaries (*Webster's*, 1990) define it as a "declaration of adherence to an ideal or doctrine" or as a "decisive moral choice for a definite course of action." Commitment is a decisive choice. What about *service?* The definition of *service* is "to meet the needs of others" or "to repair or provide maintenance for others." Within the public social service system, there is the need for a decisive choice or declaration of adherence to the ideal and a definite course of action in serving, in meeting the needs of others, and in repairing or providing maintenance for others. So often, the larger the service system gets, the less social workers realize how important they are. And yet, the larger the service gets, the more important every single link is, because that chain has gotten so large that if one link weakens, the whole thing breaks down. Thus, no matter what your role is, if you are a member of a public social service department, you are in a public service role and you are needed.

What's going on today? Have you noticed that in the literature we now hear about homeless families? People out on the streets are no longer called bums or bag ladies. Today in America, we have children and mothers and fathers walking our streets because they are homeless. Do we as a society realize that when we decrease opportunities for people, pull back on our programs and services for those in need, there is a corresponding increase in crime, suicide, drug addiction, and family breakdown? We see that result in society today where there is obviously a pulling back of basic opportunities for food, clothing, and shelter for people in need. Who is there to be a voice? Who is there to hold on to those high values that say, yes, we care; yes, we are going to meet needs and provide opportunities? Who is there, as the Bible says, "When I was hungry, you fed me. When I was homeless, you found a place for me to live. When I was anxious, you calmed my fears. When I was naked, you clothed me"? Who is there today to feed, clothe, and find homes for others? You know who's doing it. You are.

Our poor and our needy have a real problem called poverty, and it is a multifaceted problem that involves the health system, the education system, the social service system, transportation, housing, unemployment, and more. There is no simple answer to poverty. You are not to blame and your service system is not to blame because poor people are dependent on you. The sad thing is that there are not enough resources to give you the basics of what the poor need or the opportunities to go beyond that bare subsistence. To truly serve today, we have to grow in our knowledge and skills, to become more sophisticated ourselves in doing justice to what social work is all about. Just as one of the key messages we have learned is that poverty is not a simple problem, one of the things we have also learned is that there's a need for teamwork, holistic understanding, and commitment. Everybody is called to care.

Now where do we begin? We begin with a sense of unity in our own services—teamwork—we're in it together. Shared commitment is what brings us together. As we work together toward our goal, we grow in seeing that it is not enough. Others are needed. Well, come to us, schools of social work committed to the same goals, because commitment and caring are what bring us together. If we are preparing students to get out there, to take responsible leadership roles in human services, then they had better be taught what it is really all about out there. How are we going to teach them today's reality if we practiced 20 years ago and have been in academia ever since? We need you to keep us informed about what is going on. We need your field placements; we need your data; we need your information; we need your communication. What do you need from us? You need someone with the time to take a more distant view, to research and document human needs and practice issues, to share in spreading the news of the needs of people today. For example, you have people coming to you without housing, who are hungry, who are drowning. You're meeting those immediate needs. Some of us in this audience have the time and expertise to gather information, to do research on the causes, effects, and interventions, and to publicize our findings. We are needed to teach and prepare people to work with you, to join you when you need more people coming into your agencies who know what it is all about, or to take over when you are ready to retire.

Yes, we need each other—the servers and the academics. Yes, it is a team effort and not just for social workers and agencies or educators and schools of social work but we need political support and power. How do we get it? I'll tell you how. It involves a story about a man who was awakened in the night by some-one who was hungry. The man said, "I have a neighbor who has bread. Let us go and get some for you." So he knocked at the door, but the neighbor didn't answer. He kept knocking, and the neighbor came to the top window and said, "Who is it? Go away, I'm sleeping." You know that story? The man didn't swear and curse; he just said, "We have someone here who is hungry." The neighbor said, "I'm sleeping. Don't bother me," and went back to bed. What did the man do? He kept knocking. So the neighbor came again to the window and said, "I told you to leave me alone." The man said, "We have someone here who is hungry." You know that story? The neighbor went back to bed. The man kept knocking. Finally, what happened? The neighbor said, "I can't get any sleep; for God's sake here is the bread." That is a story in the Bible and that is who we are. We are the people who keep knocking, who don't go away, because if we do, what's going to happen? Who will be there? What would happen in an uncaring, survival-of-the-fittest society? What keeps us going so that we don't give up, burn out, get tired of knocking? What keeps us going is what was brought out by John Steinbeck in *The Grapes of Wrath* or by Abraham Maslow when he described how people become self-actualized. What keeps us going is the recognition that we have meaning and purpose in our lives. Yes, we have our goals and we have our dreams and we have our past experiences. But most of all, what keeps us going is the belief in human life and our commitment to human service. We know we can't do it all. But we sure can do something, and that's what keeps us going. We are doing what we can to make a difference, and that gives us purpose and meaning. That makes us more than just alive; it truly helps us live.

But most of all, we find meaning here and now in the present moment, and that's what it is all about—to live the present fully. No matter what you're doing when you work within the human service system, you have meaning and purpose within the present moment for persons currently in need. Whether these human beings know it or not, we value them and believe in the potential of human life. Think about your call to really live the gift of the present moment. To quote Buechner (1983, p. 86), "Listen to your life. See it for the fathomless mystery that it is. In the boredom and pain of it, no less than in the excitement and gladness: touch, taste, and smell your way into the holy and hidden of it because in the last analysis, all moments are key moments, and life itself is a grace."

My parting words are: Know that you are a grace to many in your own way. You might be the *only* grace to many. My hope is that through your recommitment, you will continue to do the marvelous job that those of you in public social services, and those of you who stay in public social services, are really doing today.

PREFACE

As Dr. McMahon noted in the third edition of *The General Method of Social Work Practice: A Generalist Perspective* (1996, p. xi), "The value of social work generalists who can work at multiple levels with diverse populations, problems, policies, and environments is becoming increasingly recognized." This statement is especially relevant for entry-level practitioners in today's era of uncertainty, managed care cost controls, and fragmented service systems.

An organizing theme throughout this fourth edition is preparation for competent, accountable, entry-level generalist practice in social work with client systems evidencing more and more serious problems-in-living in increasingly complex environments. This edition of Dr. McMahon's book updates text and references in a way that retains her holistic philosophical orientation, generalist perspective, and General Method of social work practice. The conceptual framework of the generalist perspective, however, has been reframed and expanded to include an ecological-systems perspective, a problem focus, a strengths/needs orientation, a multilevel approach, an open selection of theories and interventions, and a problem-solving process. Careful attention has been paid throughout this edition to the influences of multiculturalism, social pluralism, and socio-demographic diversity on individual and collective functioning, client systems' perception and definition of problems and needs, and client systems' patterns of seeking and using help.

The book's "how to" approach at the micro, mezzo, and macro levels of practice has been maintained throughout the presentation of the basic social work processes and stages of the General Method. Skills and techniques associated with each stage and appropriate for the entry-level practitioner are described and illustrated by practice vignettes and longer practice exemplars. These applications highlight the micro, mezzo, and macro levels of generalist practice with client, action, and target systems in seven field settings: child welfare, gerontology, public social welfare, community services, education, corrections, and a homeless shelter. Figures and tables are used throughout to clarify concepts and practice examples. Learning exercises facilitate the development of self-awareness and practice skills.

Chapter 1 presents social work's philosophical valuing of persons as whole human beings who are individually unique and self-determining as they reveal their needs and strengths, seek services, and solve problems within the context of their environmental life-space. The chapter describes the five elements of purpose, sanction, values, knowledge, and methods that form the foundation for social work practice. Chapter 2 explores the six elements in generalist practice: an ecological-systems perspective, a problem focus, a strengths/needs orientation, a multilevel approach, an open selection of theories and interventions, and a problem-solving process. The chapter defines the General Method of social work practice and distinguishes entry-level and graduate-level practice using the General Method as a basic problem-solving procedure with a variety of client, action, and target systems at the micro, mezzo, and macro levels of practice.

Chapter 3 presents a knowledge paradigm for exploring and understanding the major variations in worldview among human beings by virtue of their cultural, social, and socio-demographic group membership. Instead of in-depth profiling of multiple groups, however, selected exemplars of similarities and differences among and within groups are used to illuminate focal concepts and principles inherent in strengths-oriented, culturally competent generalist practice with an empowerment orientation.

Chapters 4 through 9 present the practice stages and processes of the General Method. Chapter 4, Engagement, identifies three focal points of problems, feelings, and goals in the initial interactions between the social worker and the client system. Chapter 5, Data Collection, directs inquiry to gathering subjective and objective information about the problems presented, the persons involved in the problems, and the potential and actual resources and barriers in the environment that may affect the person-problem-environment situation. Chapter 6, Assessment, appraises the person-in-environment configuration in order to prioritize problems, plan and contract interventions, and set the structure for evaluating outcomes. Assessment involves the intellectual activity of interpreting and drawing inferences derived from collected data and formulating a plan of action through framing solutions to identified problems.

Chapter 7, Intervention, clusters the various helping activities of the entry-level generalist under the four major headings of direct intervention, information and referral, case management and teamwork, and indirect intervention. With each of these activities, particular techniques and skills are used to work with different problems, age groups, and types of systems at various levels of practice.

Chapter 8, Evaluation, presents methodology and tools for assessing the results of the actions taken. It focuses on documenting practice effectiveness and analyzing the level of goal attainment. Chapter 9, Termination, comprises the time taken and the process used in planning to cease contact. The closure process in micro, mezzo, and macro practice involves five tasks: integrating earlier work and consolidating gains, supporting personal and collective resourcefulness, creating a sense of accomplishment and hope, strengthening a client system's ability to function within an enhanced environment, and building a bridge linking present and future. The losses in this ending stage are acknowledged and examined, but attention is also given to the celebratory elements of ending as graduation and beginning anew.

Chapter 10 discusses the scope of the General Method and advocates its use in addressing the multiple needs of the poor. It examines the basic identity of the generalist practitioner and shows how, over time and with practice experience, the knowledge base and practice skills deepen and expand to bring about a higher level of micro, mezzo, and macro practice expertise for the seasoned social work generalist.

We gratefully acknowledge the comments and suggestions from the following reviewers: Freddie Avant, Stephen F. Austin State University; Jan Black, California State University, Long Beach; Valire Carr Copeland, University of Pittsburgh; and Eleanor Tolson, University of Illinois at Chicago. Thank you, also, to Alyssa Pratt at Allyn and Bacon and to Lynda Griffiths at TKM Productions.

ABOUT THE AUTHORS

Elizabeth March Timberlake, D.S.W., LICSW, LCSW-Clinical, is an Ordinary Professor of social work at The Catholic University of America. She has taught social work practice model development and advanced research for doctoral students, taught social work theory and practice with children and their families for master's students, and served as field instructor for undergraduates in a school setting. A senior clinician, Dr. Timberlake has specialized in direct and indirect practice with children and their parents and has worked with them and on their behalf for 40 years in child welfare, family service agencies, mental health centers, school settings, and private practice. She has worked to empower families in housing projects and on the streets and has served on the governing boards of social agencies such as United Way, Associated Catholic Charities, Christ Child Society School Counseling Program, Good Shepherd Center, and Christ Child Institute. Dr. Timberlake is currently Director of The Catholic University of America's National Research Center for Child and Family Services. Her extensive research and scholarship have focused on children's coping and adaptation in the face of various life stressors, families' coping with homelessness, physical and mental illness of children and adults, treatment process and outcome, improving social work practice and social service delivery for children and youth, the impact of federal law on school social work practice, and current trends in social work practice.

Michaela Zajicek Farber, D.S.W., LCSW-Clinical, is a Faculty Research Associate of the National Research Center for Child and Family Services and a Lecturer at The Catholic University of America. She has taught basic research, program and practice evaluation, and context of practice with children and families. Dr. Farber has earned master's and doctoral degrees in social work. She has practiced social work for 15 years with children and adults coping with development disabilities, physically challenging conditions, and mental illness. She has worked through research to understand and empower families of infants and toddlers in Early Head Start, conducted needs assessments to strengthen the ability of social agencies to respond to changing client needs and resources, and conducted social agency program evaluations to improve client service delivery. Her scholarship focuses on children's services and practice/program evaluation.

Christine Anlauf Sabatino, D.S.W., LICSW, LCSW-Clinical, is an Associate Professor of social work at The Catholic University of America. She has taught the general method of social work practice at the baccalaureate and master's levels, the integrative senior field seminar, human behavior and the social environment, and school social work. Dr. Sabatino has earned baccalaureate, master's, and doctoral degrees in social work. She has 28 years of social work practice as a school social worker, consultant, group home social worker, and clinical social worker and has served as program director and clinical supervisor of a private inner-city school counseling program. Her research and scholarship have focused on school social work practice, the impact of federal policies on social work and pupil personnel services, research issues in school social work, homeless children, and social work personnel issues.

The General Method of Social Work Practice

CHAPTER

1

The Foundation for Generalist Practice in Social Work

Given societal changes and the evolving nature of the social work profession, achieving precision in identifying and unifying social work's values, knowledge, and methods remains an ongoing challenge. In undertaking this task, this book draws on the rich written and oral traditions of twentieth-century social work as the point of departure for (1) integrating the various dimensions of the profession into a unified whole and (2) providing a comprehensive conceptual framework for understanding and practicing entry-level professional social work in the twenty-first century. Building on McMahon's (1996) generalist perspective, this book depicts an entry-level professional social worker whose practice with client, target, and action systems is framed within a holistic ecological-systems perspective, grounded in various theories and social work practice concepts, and guided by general problem-solving methodology and social work precepts. Trained in social work programs accredited by the Council on Social Work Education and usually termed *B.S.W.s* (whether the actual degree is Bachelor of Social Work [B.S.W.] or Bachelor of Arts [B.A.] in social work, or another variation), these professionals are employed in settings such as public social welfare and human service agencies, child welfare agencies, youth and family service settings, vocational rehabilitation programs, criminal justice programs, hospitals and health care settings, community action agencies, neighborhood centers, social planning agencies, international service organizations, and caregiving settings for children, adults, and seniors with special needs.

Holism and Social Work

In social work, there is a philosophical valuing of persons as whole human beings who are individually unique and self-determining as they reveal needs, set goals, seek services, and solve problems within the context of their environmental life-space. Persons and populations are viewed holistically when the focus is on (1) the total person and the interdependent dimensions of body, spirit, mind, and feelings; (2) the person nested within and transacting with the environment; and (3) the environment as consisting of social, physical, economic, psychological, and political forces that support and impede individual and collective social functioning and well-being. Thus, the family, culture, physical surroundings, community, and society of the individual are seen as essential parts of a holistic view of person-in-environment.

In considering the needs and resources of human beings holistically, the focus is on the whole hierarchy of needs and the necessary relationship of each to the others and to the resources that are available, accessible, and acceptable. Maslow (1970), for example, identifies the needs of a person as crossing over the physical (bodily needs), intellectual (cognitive needs), socio-affective (social/emotional needs), and spiritual (aesthetic needs) dimensions of persons. In this context, a *need* is something crucial for a reasonable level of living, human development, and psychosocial functioning. A *want*, by contrast, is a desire for something beyond basic survival needs and includes those desires and aspirations that motivate human beings toward goal achievement, enhance human satisfaction, and promote a sense of well-being (Wall, Timberlake, Farber, Sabatino, Liebow, Smith, & Taylor, 2000). Some common human needs (Towle, 1957) are universal across all environments; other needs and wants are influenced by the transactions between persons and their environments and by persons' goals and aspirations for their lives. In Maslow's (1970) tradition, needs and wants are intertwined with aspirations and form a hierarchical pyramid that progresses from a wide base of physical survival needs in most environments toward a peak of creative self-actualization that reflects individual goals in particular environments. This holistic view highlights the interdependence of human needs and goals and the personal and environmental resources for meeting them.

Within the broad resource network of human services, social workers and other providers become increasingly aware of the interdependence of the community service network as they strive to apply a holistic helping approach. During service delivery, the interrelationships of various professionals with one another and with the family, culture, community, and organizations of their client systems may evolve smoothly, but more often, working together requires conscious effort. Thus, case coordination and teamwork with their group building, collaboration, mediation, negotiation, and management processes become essential professional tools for effective holistic service delivery. Although persons, families, groups, organizations, and communities with particular needs and resources may come to the attention of individual practitioners or single agencies, holistically minded helpers do not lose sight of the fact that each is very much a part of other persons, families, groups, organizations, and communities; that each need and goal is strongly related to other needs and goals; and that a single service can meet neither all the needs and goals of any one entity nor one need and goal for all entities.

In considering different methods of social work practice, Baer and Federico (1979, p. 5) note that the emphasis in generalist approaches is on a "holistic assessment and intervention at the level of both people and systems." Brieland, Costin, and Atherton (1985, p. 146) concur in viewing generalist practice as providing a holistic perspective on practice situations, stating, "The small voluntary agency finds that it cannot afford a variety of specialists, and the large public agency has learned that to be effective it cannot separate individual and family improvement from societal change. For those who seek the world in holistic terms, the generalist has come to represent a promising solution."

Generalist Practice in Social Work

Professional social workers engaged in *generalist practice* may be entry-level or graduate-level practitioners. Within the profession, there has been confusion over the use of the concepts *general* and *generic*. Although by definition, both terms may be used to describe "what is characteristic of a whole group" (*Webster's*, 1990, p. 378), the concept of *generic* is used mainly to refer to what is at the core or root of all practice, and *general* or *generalist* is used to refer to a type of practice that is "not confined by specialization or careful limitation" (*Webster's*, 1990, p. 379). Today, the commonly accepted characteristics of the generalist practice model cluster into the following four major dimensions, which are elaborated on in Chapter 2 and throughout this book:

1. A professional knowledge, value, and skill base that is
   - built on liberal arts knowledge
   - built on a holistic conceptualization of the foundation for social work practice
   - anchored in an ecological-systems perspective and a strengths/needs orientation
   - transferable between and among multiple practice contexts (fields of practice), practice settings (primary social work and multidisciplinary agencies or institutions), and social problems of person-in-environments

- applicable to diverse client systems (individual, family, group, organization, community) across multiple levels of practice (micro, mezzo, macro)
2. A multidimensional conceptual framework that reflects
   - an open selection of theories and interventions
   - a problem focus
   - a person-in-environment focus that reflects the interrelatedness of human problems, life situations, and social conditions
3. Versatile assessment that
   - attends to the uniqueness and diversity of client systems and environments
   - draws from an ecological-systems perspective and a strengths/needs orientation
   - is not constricted by particular theoretical frameworks, intervention models, or client systems
4. Intervention roles and strategies based on the
   - client system's unique problems/needs, resources, goals, and environmental circumstances
   - client system's environmental factors targeted for change
   - size and level of the client system targeted for change

Thus, to practice effectively, a social work generalist is expected (1) to have acquired a basic core of knowledge for professional social work, (2) to operate from a holistic philosophical perspective, and (3) to have integrated this core social work knowledge with the four essential dimensions of generalist practice.

Undergraduate social work programs accredited by the Council on Social Work Education (CSWE) offer a generalist professional curriculum that builds on a liberal arts base in preparing students for entry-level social work practice. Generalist practice is also found in the curriculum of graduate programs, along with various concentrations for advanced or graduate-level practice. In master's degree programs, a generalist curriculum in the first year of study serves as a stepping stone for second-year study in selected concentrations characterized by in-depth attention to type of clients served, methods used, practice level addressed, or primary role assumed.

The Foundation of Social Work Practice

As described in the classic working definition of the social work profession (Commission on Social Work Practice, NASW, 1956, as cited in Bartlett, 1958), the five elements of purpose, sanction, values, knowledge, and methods that are rooted in the identity of all social workers form the common base for their practice within the holistic perspective of person-in-environment. Whereas the fundamental elements of purpose and values generally remain the same today, the sanction, knowledge, and methods of contemporary social work practice have been greatly influenced by legal regulatory trends, the exponential explosion of knowledge, and changing needs and goals of various client systems.

Purpose

The twofold purpose of social work continues to be (1) enhancing the social functioning of individuals, families, and groups in their social environments (Richmond, 1917) and (2) modifying environmental conditions associated with population need, limited resources, and risk factors (Addams, 1910). That is, social workers enable individuals, families, groups, organizations, and communities to function more effectively within their various environments (Lundblad, 1995; Meyer, 1993; Miley, O'Melia, & DuBois, 1998). They also work to improve environmental conditions for vulnerable populations (Gutierrez & Cox, 1998; Homan, 1999; Tropman, Erlich, & Rothman, 1995). The ways in which social workers implement their purpose take different forms, approaches, roles, and methodologies. For example, social workers engage in direct practice with persons in such roles as counselor, enabler, broker of services, and case manager and in indirect practice with persons in such roles as advocate, consultant, team member, and administrator. They engage in direct practice with environments in such roles as consultant, organizer, advocate, group facilitator, mediator, and administrator and in indirect practice with environments in such roles as researcher, analyst, planner, programmer, and fund-raiser. On the one hand, they work to prevent, remediate, or minimize human problems and risk factors while enhancing human strengths, resources, and protective factors. On the other hand, they work to prevent, ameliorate, and minimize environmental conditions associated with population need, limited resources, and risk factors while enhancing population strengths and protective factors. In sum, social workers' mission is directed toward the development of the maximum potential of individuals and environments in order that client systems might improve their social functioning and achieve the highest quality of individual and collective well-being. As stated in the *Code of Ethics* (NASW, 1996, p. 1):

> The primary mission of the social work profession is to enhance human well-being and help meet the basic human needs of all people, with particular attention to the needs and empowerment of people who are vulnerable and oppressed, and living in poverty. A historical and defining feature of social work is the profession's focus on individual well-being in a social context and the well-being of society. Fundamental to social work is attention to the environmental forces that create, contribute to, and address problems in living.

Sanction

Philosophically, the profession's tradition of social responsibility may be traced back to such early socio-political and religious writings as the 1750 B.C. Babylonian Code of Hammurabi, the sixth-century B.C. writings of Confucius, the writings of the Greco-Roman empires, and the various codifications of the Judeo-Christian traditions (Reamer, 1993). As a societal philanthropical endeavor, social work is rooted in the Elizabethan Poor Law of 1601 and seventeenth-century human welfare measures in the American colonies. As a societally sanctioned profession, however, social work in the United States did not come of age until the twentieth century.

Being a societally sanctioned profession simply means having governmental authorization to perform designated tasks and activities in carrying out the profession's explicit mission and purpose. Specifically, federal, state, and local governments authorize social work practice through legislation that:

- Creates social programs and social work role positions in multidisciplinary service programs
- Allocates funding for social work programs, role positions, and practice activities
- Legally incorporates and licenses agencies, organizations, and institutions that employ social workers to establish programs and serve client systems
- Regulates or licenses individual social work professionals

Since 1992, for example, all 50 states, as well as the District of Columbia (D.C.), Puerto Rico, and the U.S. Virgin Islands, have had some form of governmental sanctioning of social work practice through licensing or certification of individual professionals.

Employing agencies provide authority and permission for social workers to engage in practice within the service boundaries specified in their legal charters of incorporation. Client systems and consumers of social work services further authorize social workers to serve them in order to enhance specified aspects of their social functioning and modify specific environmental conditions. As a collective body, social workers come together and act through professional organizations such as the National Association of Social Workers (NASW), Council on Social Work Education (CSWE), and Federation of Clinical Social Workers to name a few.

Thus, the authority and permissions that sanction the practice of social workers in society come from several different sources. These include (1) the clients served; (2) human service agencies under public, private, or religious auspice; (3) the organized profession; and (4) governmental agency boards with the responsibility for legal regulation.

Values

Values in social work form three interrelated dimensions, which include preferred ways of thinking about persons and society, preferred instrumentalities for dealing with people-in-environment, and preferred goals and outcomes (Levy, 1973). Social work's preferred view of persons as inherently good and possessing worth, dignity, and capacity for change and society as containing resources, opportunities, and barriers forms the ideological foundation of the profession. Specifically, social workers recognize that every human being possesses the potential for fulfillment and greatness but acknowledge that human beings are fallible, with needs and goals that may necessitate protection, support, and resources from their environments. They also recognize that a just and caring society is both a resourceful system with open doors and a social environment that, at times, needs influence and direction by responsible, compassionate professionals. This value foundation guides social workers' preference for outcomes that mobilize environmental resources and opportunities and enhance human dignity and social functioning. These outcomes are attained through the preferred instrumentalities or tools—such as the professional self, social work knowledge, and intervention methods and skills—that social workers use in working with people and their environments.

Although the profession's values draw heavily from the Judeo-Christian ideological traditions, some principles such as that of compassion for vulnerable persons are also central tenets in other spiritual traditions, including Islam and Buddhism (Bullis, 1996; Canda & Furman, 1999). Thus, social workers' commitment to engage in activities that promote the potential of both persons and environments may flow not only from the profession's value base but also from their own personal beliefs and spiritual traditions that are congruent with the profession's core values.

As a profession, social work is guided by explicit values, a moral commitment, and a written code of ethics (NASW, 1996; Reid & Popple, 1992; Shardlow, 1989; Timms, 1983). Social work's values are rooted in the fundamental ideals of belief in the inherent dignity and worth of every human being and recognition of the need for a democratic and caring society. This ideological base is identifiable in social welfare policies, programs, and practices that (1) seek to preserve the right of all persons to experience a sense of safety and well-being in everyday life and (2) are set into motion through democratic participatory government in which equality of rights is enforced and social justice becomes the norm (Drower, 1996; Pray, 1991; Tropman, 1989). That is, social workers strive to modify, develop, and sustain the capabilities of individuals and the resources of societies so that together they may promote improved social functioning and the highest quality of well-being for communities and persons. Not surprisingly, these ideals emphasize the centrality and interrelatedness of person and environment for carrying out social work's mission.

Social work values reflect the ultimate goal of the profession and have been formally organized into a code of ethics and practice principles. As first identified by Biestek (1957), the basic prescriptive principles of social work practice were conceptualized as individualization, purposeful expression of feelings, controlled emotional involvement, acceptance, nonjudgmental attitude, self-determination, and confidentiality. Although initially framed as principles for casework, more recent authors have noted their generic applicability for practice with systems of any size (Biestek, 1957; McMahon, 1996; Piccard, 1988). Essentially, these principles guide the social worker in:

- Recognizing that every client system is unique and deserving of consideration and respect (individualization)
- Understanding the human need to express one's feelings and the value in this expression as a means of fostering growth (purposeful expression of feelings)

- Using one's feelings and emotions appropriately for the service of others (controlled emotional involvement)
- Demonstrating that human beings have a right to be accepted as they are (acceptance)
- Avoiding passing judgments on people (nonjudgmental attitude)
- Respecting the right of client systems to choose for themselves as much as possible (self-determination)
- Keeping information obtained from or about clients confidential (confidentiality)

The National Association of Social Workers (NASW, 1996, pp. 5–6) has promulgated a similar but somewhat different listing of core professional values together with corresponding ethical principles:

- *Service:* "Social workers' primary goal is to help people in need and to address social problems."
- *Social justice:* "Social workers challenge social injustice."
- *Dignity and worth of the person:* "Social workers respect the inherent dignity and worth of the person."
- *Importance of human relationships:* "Social workers recognize the central importance of human relationships."
- *Integrity:* "Social workers behave in a trustworthy manner."
- *Competence:* "Social workers practice within their areas of competence and develop and enhance their professional expertise."

These values and principles comprise the rules of conduct and ethical standards for professional responsibility, decision making, and conduct that are set forth in the NASW *Code of Ethics* (1996).

As further codified, these standards include social workers' ethical responsibilities to clients, colleagues, practice settings, and the profession. More specifically, the NASW *Code* identifies a range of professional responsibilities to client systems, including commitment, self-determination, informed consent, competence, cultural competence and social diversity, conflicts of interest, privacy and confidentiality, access to records, appropriate maintenance of boundaries, safeguarding interests and rights, and interruption and termination of services (section 1). In addition, the *Code* identifies the need for social workers to maintain appropriate boundaries in their professional relationships (sections 1.09–1.13) and not to allow "personal problems, psychosocial distress, legal problems, substance abuse, or mental health difficulties" to interfere with their professional performance (section 4.05). Also stressed is the need for social workers with personal difficulties that do interfere with professional performance to "immediately seek consultation and take appropriate remedial action by seeking professional help, making adjustments in workload, terminating practice, or taking any other steps necessary to protect clients and others" (section 4.05). In addition, the *Code* speaks to social workers' collegial responsibility for the profession. That is, any social worker who is aware of a colleague with personal difficulties is expected to consult with the person and assist him or her in "taking remedial action" (section 2.10). Thus, working within agencies, society, and the profession and with client and related systems, the social worker is able to draw on the *Code of Ethics* for direction and support.

Knowledge

Standing at the interface of person and environment with a dynamic two-sided value base, social workers simultaneously relate to both person and environment. To carry their value commitment forward into professional action, they need to possess empirical and theoretical knowledge of persons, environments, their interdependence, and their transactions. Whereas values form the ideological basis for professional action, knowledge forms the objective basis for practice principles (Linzer, 1999; Reamer, 1993). Therefore, the foundation knowledge base of professional social work has been purposefully selected to provide a theoretically framed and empirically grounded understanding of:

- The thoughts, feelings, behaviors, needs, resources, and goals of human systems within the context of their strengths, risks, multiple cultures, social pluralism, and socio-demographic variance
- The structures and processes of the environment that influence human development and biopsychosocial functioning, organizational and community functioning, and the planned change process
- The transactions occurring between persons and environments
- Hypotheses, principles, and processes associated with change in client, target, and action systems
- Transactions among the various systems and hierarchical levels that constitute their work environments

Empirically grounded knowledge refers to substantive matter that has been subjected to systematic inquiry in order to discover or check facts. Empirical explanations of practice phenomena and intervention methods are assumed to represent known truth—that is, information derived from actual experience, experimentation, or observation. By contrast, *theoretically framed knowledge* refers to a coherent group of abstract propositions used in a systematic explanation of particular practice phenomena and intervention methods. Theoretical explanations both derive from and inform practice. They represent a way of organizing ideas, thoughts, and information in order to understand professional issues, practice phenomena, and intervention goals and plans, and they guide intervention with client, action, and target systems. Without organizing theoretical frameworks, social work knowledge simply becomes an overwhelming array of disparate facts, ideas, and assumptions about the many facets of helping found in professional practice. Without the order imposed by theory, it is not possible for social workers to function professionally.

The source of this empirically grounded and theoretically framed knowledge is twofold. Much of it is drawn from the disciplines of biology, anthropology, psychology, sociology, political science, and economics as well as the profession of medicine. Increasingly, however, knowledge is being generated from within the social work profession in such areas as social welfare policies and services, social work practice methods, the social work relationship, person-in-environment, and individual, family, group, organizational, and community dynamics, to name a few. Much of today's emerging knowledge from outside and within the profession is interrelated and relevant to social work practice. Yet, when viewed as a whole, the huge amount of contemporary knowledge appears overwhelming and unmanageable. To counter this, social workers systematically organize and present established and emerging knowledge in relation to their triplex classification schema of (1) person, (2) environment, and (3) the transactions between them (see Table 1.1). Since the categories of this classification schema are not mutually exclusive, however, the items in the table are grouped according to their predominant focus.

For example, to understand the *person,* a social worker calls on the assorted information that collectively provides a comprehensive, dynamic view of the ever-evolving total person, complete with strengths, needs, and aspirations. This knowledge includes the psychological, biological, social, sexual, cognitive, moral, and spiritual dimensions of the human person, which are conceptualized according to subsystems, developmental stages, and life course developmental milestones. It also includes understanding the common human needs and basic goals for human development and self-actualization. Knowledge about the *person* is presented both as aggregate commonalities and individual uniqueness.

Information about the numerous systems that constitute the *environment* for each person includes resources and barriers to opportunity in relation to family, kinship networks, informal and formal social structures, professionals and institutions, and policy matters. It also includes knowledge about cultures, economics, politics, organizations, and communities as social systems.

The middle, or *In,* category of Table 1.1 lists knowledge that focuses on the *transactions* that take place as persons and environmental systems interface. These transactions are explored in terms of their functional relationship over time to the characteristics and processes of both the environment and the developing person. Throughout life, for example, people grow and mature through the progressively more complex and reciprocal processes actively taking place between them and the individuals, objects, and symbols in their immediate and distant environments (Bronfenbrenner, 1999). Indeed, these influences on the person are at the center of theories such as psychodynamic, psychosocial, behavioral, and cognitive and interventive approaches such as crisis and empowerment. Similarly, communities grow and develop through complex transactional processes between environmental resources, personal needs and goals, and barriers and opportunities in relation to resource availability, acceptability, and accessibility. These influences on the environment are at the center of such theories as symbolic interaction, learning, exchange, and conflict.

TABLE 1.1 Foundation Knowledge for Social Work

Social Work		
Person	*In*	*Environment*

Holistic Analytic Paradigm

Well-being	Goodness-of-fit	Just and fair society
Resilience, strengths	Coping	Access to opportunity
Needs, wants, aspirations	Role fulfillment	Resource utilization
Appraisal	Exchange/stress/conflict	Resource allocation
Diversity	Variability	Diversity
Risk factors	Barriers	Risk factors
Protective factors	Support	Protective factors
Empowerment	Problem solving	Access to resources

Unit of Attention

Individuals	Interaction	Groups
Children	Intrapersonal	Organizations
Adolescents	Interpersonal	Communities
Adults	Familial	Societal institutions
Older adults	Communal	National
Couples	Societal	International
Traditional	Behavioral actions	Culture as context
Nontraditional	Relationship formation	Social policies
Families	Continuing education	Legislative
Nuclear	Work, employment	Economic
Nontraditional	Role fulfillment	Health
Blended	Play, recreation	Education
Extended	Communication	Social welfare
Foster	Verbal	
Adoptive	Nonverval	
	Symbolic	

Concepts	**Theories**	**Concepts**
Human development	Psychodynamic	System development
Biology	Psychosocial	Barriers to resources
Neurology	Behavior	Access to opportunity
Genetic, heredity	Cognitive	Risk, protective factors
Physical motor	Social learning	Social justice
Cognitive	Role	Nurturing, sustaining institutions
Language, communication	Symbolic interaction	Support systems
Emotional, affective	Social exchange	Informal
Nutritional	Conflict	Formal
Sexual, intimacy	Family	Open/closed systems
Moral	Group	
Spiritual	Organization	
	Community	
	General systems	

Although Table 1.1 does not provide an exhaustive list of all the knowledge used in social work, the categories do form an organizing framework both for social work's existing knowledge and for building its future knowledge base. When the items in the three categories are juxtaposed, the result enables social workers to gain a holistic perspective and acquire greater understanding of the person-in-environment.

Methods and Skills

For social workers' actions to be more than an expression of values and mere technical application of information about person-in-environment, their professional intervention must be directed by critical thought and disciplined application of the knowledge base to specific client, target, and action systems under particular circumstances. Therefore, guided by purpose, sanction, values, and knowledge, social workers execute a series of activities within the framework of a specific method to achieve identified goals with client, target, and action systems. These activities constitute the methods and skills of the social worker (see Table 1.2). For example, social workers are known for using interpersonal relationships in a helping process. Sensitivity to feelings and disciplined use of self with various client systems have been consistently recognized as an essential part of the professional repertoire, as have problem solving, goal setting, and task defining. That is, through an open, supportive professional relationship, social workers help clients identify tasks and proceed toward problem resolution and goal accomplishment. Thus, in a list of practice skills, relational and problem-solving skills obviously would be included (see the *Person* and *In* columns of Table 1.2).

Sometimes in environmental work, however, there are occasions when social workers need to interact with systems, organizations, and communities that are not client systems (Pincus & Minahan, 1973, p. 63). In this sense, *client system* refers to individuals, families, groups, organizations, or communities "who sanction or ask for the change agent's [social worker's] services, who are the expected beneficiaries of service, and who have a working agreement or contract with the change agent." Thus, in addition to working with client systems, a social worker often joins with others to form action systems to bring about changes in particular target systems. That is, *action systems* are formed when a social worker joins with clients and other professionals, agencies, organizations, and community members to work with and through them in order to influence a particular target system and accomplish specific goals. An example would be joining with a group of welfare mothers to address the quality of preschool care provided by a housing project. In exploring causes of problems or sources for meeting needs, social workers may identify target systems in either the immediate or distant environment as needing change in order to achieve goals.

When an environmental *target system* is dysfunctional and refuses to accept the change efforts of social workers and clients, the use of a supportive, enhancing relationship, together with problem-solving skills, is inappropriate and ineffective. An example would be a housing or social service program that rejects applicants on

TABLE 1.2   **Foundation Methods/Skills for Social Work**

Social Work		
Person	*In*	*Environment*
Professional interviewing skills	Client-centered method	Socio-political skills
Ethnographic interviewing skills	Problem solving	Advocacy
Empathic responding skills	Problem identifying	Social action
Relationship bonding skills	Data collecting	Giving testimony
Skill in enhancing client strengths	Assessing/goal setting	Bargaining
Skill in empowering clients	Planning/task defining	Organizing
	Selecting/implementing intervention	Publicizing
	Evaluating	Demonstrating
	Terminating	Mediating
	Case management	Consciousness raising
	Crisis intervention	Uncovering
	Family preservation	Locality development skills
	Social worker-centered skills	Educating
	Skill in disciplined use of professional self	Facilitating
	Skill in disciplined application of foundation knowledge	Brokering
	Skill in ethical decision making	Empowering
	Professional skills	Social planning skills
	Time management	Technology
	Teamwork	Fact gathering
	Documentation	Analysis
	Research	

the basis of marital status. In such instances, the social worker stands at the interface of person and environment and uses research, political, and advocacy skills in goal-directed work to change the environmental target system. In addition to the basic relational and problem-solving skills of micro- and mezzo-level practice, therefore, social workers need a range of macro-level practice skills and strategies, such as the ability to conduct needs assessments, document evidence, build coalitions, advocate for particular points of view, publicize issues, bring legal action, organize demonstrations, and seek legislative action (see the *Environment* column in Table 1.2).

Besides working with client systems and environmental target systems, social workers are expected to perform certain activities as employees within their agencies and as members of their profession. Thus, professional responsibility requires such skills as keeping records; maintaining confidentiality; using supervision, collaborating with multiple disciplines, and building teams; and managing time effectively and efficiently. Research skills—particularly for monitoring client system progress, evaluating outcomes, and identifying trends in their own agency practice—are equally important.

In summary, the person-in-environment perspective provides a comprehensive framework for conceptually organizing the many complex foundation methods and skills of social workers today. In turn, this framework clearly conveys that a whole array of methods and skills is available for responsible choice and flexible individualized selection, depending on the circumstances of a given situation.

Holistic Conceptualization of the Foundation of Social Work Practice

Table 1.3 offers a comprehensive paradigm of the foundation of social work practice. This paradigm uses the traditional person-in-environment perspective that has prevailed throughout social work's history as the means for systematically organizing the elements of purpose, sanction, values, knowledge, and methods/skills and integrating them through a holistic conceptualization. As demonstrated

TABLE 1.3   A Holistic Conceptualization of the Foundation for Social Work Practice

Social Work		
Person	*In*	*Environment*

Purpose
- To enhance the social functioning of individuals, families, and groups in their social environments
- To modify environmental conditions associated with population need, limited resources, and risk factors

Sanction
Clients, social and human service agencies, the profession, government (laws)

Values		
Dignity and worth of person	Practice principles *Code of Ethics*	Democratic, caring society

Knowledge		
	Holistic Analytic Paradigm	
Well-being	Goodness-of-fit	Just and fair society
Resilience, strengths	Coping	Access to opportunity
Needs, wants, aspirations	Role fulfillment	Resource utilization

TABLE 1.3 Continued

	Social Work	
Person	*In*	*Environment*
Appraisal	Exchange/stress/conflict	Resource allocation
Diversity	Variability	Diversity
Risk factors	Barriers	Risk factors
Protective factors	Support	Protective factors
Empowerment	Problem solving	Access to resources

	Unit of Attention	
Individuals	Interaction	Groups
Children	Intrapersonal	Organizations
Adolescents	Interpersonal	Communities
Adults	Familial	Societal institutions
Older adults	Communal	National
Couples	Societal	International
Traditional	Behavioral actions	Culture as context
Nontraditional	Relationship formation	Social policies
Families	Continuing education	Legislative
Nuclear	Work, employment	Economic
Nontraditional	Role fulfillment	Health
Blended	Play, recreation	Education
Extended	Communication	Social welfare
Foster	Verbal	
Adoptive	Nonverbal	
	Symbolic	

Concepts	*Theories*	*Concepts*
Human development	Psychodynamic	System development
Biology	Psychosocial	Barriers to resources
Neurology	Behavior	Access to opportunity
Genetic, heredity	Cognitive	Risk, protective factors
Physical motor	Social learning	Social justice
Cognitive	Role	Nurturing, sustaining
Language, communication	Symbolic interaction	institutions
Emotional, affective	Social exchange	Support systems
Nutritional	Conflict	Informal
Sexual, intimacy	Family	Formal
Moral	Group	Open/closed systems
Spiritual	Organization	
	Community	
	General systems	

(continued)

TABLE 1.3   Continued

	Social Work	
Person	*In*	*Environment*
	Methods/Skills	
Professional interviewing skills	Client-centered method	Socio-political skills
Ethnographic interviewing skills	Problem solving	Advocacy
Empathic responding skills	Problem identifying	Social action
Relationship bonding skills	Data collecting	Giving testimony
Skill in enhancing client strengths	Assessing/goal setting	Bargaining
Skill in empowering clients	Planning/task defining	Organizing
	Selecting/implementing intervention	Publicizing
	Evaluating	Demonstrating
	Terminating	Mediating
	Case management	Consciousness raising
	Crisis intervention	Uncovering
	Family preservation	Locality development skills
	Social work-centered skills	Educating
	Skill in disciplined use of professional self	Facilitating
	Skill in disciplined application of foundation knowledge	Brokering
	Skill in ethical decision making	Empowering
	Professional skills	Social planning skills
	Time management	Technology
	Teamwork	Fact gathering
	Documentation	Analysis
	Research	

in this table, the foundation values, knowledge, and methods/skills for generalist practice are viewed collectively under the triplex of *person, in,* and *environment*. The social worker is positioned in the center, *where the action is* and *where all the parts are held in balance for use or redistribution*. Their change efforts may pull from or be directed toward either the person or the environment, depending on the need. In this position, the social worker actualizes the basic dimensions of the profession through dynamic interactions with his or her work environment. The General Method of practice, as set forth in this book, contains the various elements depicted in this holistic conception of foundation and organizes the content needed for the processes of helping and taking action.

Conclusion

As social work generalists work with a variety of systems, they use problem-solving and other planned change processes and their professional selves to activate foundation knowledge, values, and methodological skills. As presented here, the foundation of social work practice is the common base not only for entry-level social workers but also for graduate-level social workers whose education has provided them with additional specialized knowledge and skill competencies. An overview of the key elements that characterize generalist practice, with emphasis on the General Method, will be presented in the next chapter. A paradigm for exploring and understanding multiculturalism and socio-demographic variability will be presented in Chapter 2 as a central feature or core element of the General Method. In the remainder of the book, each phase of the General Method will be addressed in depth.

CHAPTER

2

The Generalist Perspective and the General Method of Social Work Practice

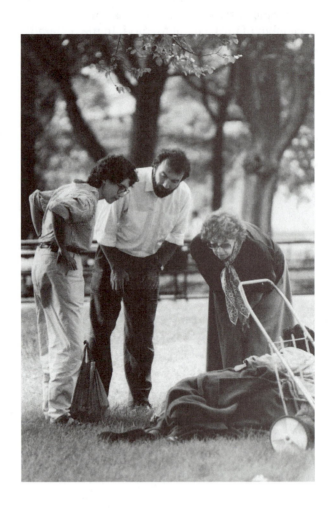

Entry-level social workers bring to their practice a professional identity grounded in a holistic social work foundation that is built on a liberal arts base. As noted in Chapter 1, this professional foundation provides social workers with a sense of professional purpose and sanction as well as the knowledge, values, and skills for competent practice with client, action, and target systems of all sizes. The liberal arts base provides social workers with a well-rounded view of the world and enables them to think critically about people and their strengths, uniqueness, and problems; society and its diverse social conditions; and culture and its varied expression in human behavior, social environments, art, music, dance, literature, science, history, and philosophy.

Although not addressing method, Baer and Federico's (1979; pp. 86–89) classic listing of professional social work competencies in the early days of entry-level generalist practice by baccalaureate social workers clearly remains applicable to contemporary social work in the twenty-first century. As abstracted from their report, these competencies include the ability to:

1. Identify and assess situations where the relationship between people and social institutions needs to be initiated, enhanced, restored, protected, or terminated.
2. Develop and implement a plan for improving the well-being of people based on problem assessment and exploration of obtainable goals and available options.
3. Enhance the problem-solving, coping, and developmental capacities of people.
4. Link people with systems that provide them with resources, services, and opportunities.
5. Intervene effectively on behalf of populations most vulnerable and discriminated against.
6. Promote the effective and humane operation of the systems that provide people with services, resources, and opportunities.
7. Participate actively with others in creating new, modified, or improved service, resource, and opportunity systems that are more equitable, just, and responsive to consumers of services, and work with others to eliminate those systems that are unjust.
8. Evaluate the extent to which the objectives of the intervention plan were achieved.
9. Evaluate one's own professional growth and development continually through assessment of practice behavior and skills.
10. Contribute to the improvement of service delivery by adding to the knowledge base of the profession as appropriate and by supporting and upholding the standards and ethics of the profession.

In relation to practice method, Baer and Federico (1979, p. 155) conclude, "All efforts in the generalist unitary approach to practice are based on the premise that all of a person's needs involve a variety of systems and that the social worker functions at the interface of people and social systems or societal institutions."

In clarifying what constitutes the general method that guides the action of the generalist practitioner, this chapter addresses four questions: What is the generalist perspective? What is generalist social work practice? What is the method used in generalist practice? How do entry-level (B.S.W.) and graduate-level (M.S.W.) practice differ?

The Generalist Perspective

In generalist practice, the social work foundation—which consists of purpose, sanction, values, knowledge, skills, and the person-in-environment perspective—is developed and expanded through an overlay and integration of six additional practice elements (see Figure 2.1):

1. An ecological-systems perspective
2. A problem focus
3. A strengths/needs orientation
4. A multilevel approach
5. An open selection of theories and interventions
6. A problem-solving process

These practice elements interrelate and overlap as the generalist provides services to individuals, families, groups, organizations, and communities. Together, the social work foundation (Chapter 1) and the practice elements (this chapter) highlight the meaning of generalist practice and contribute to the development of an integrated picture that may be called the *generalist perspective*. By definition, a *perspective* means a "broad view of events or ideas in their true nature and relationships" (*Webster's*, 1990, p. 677).

In other words, generalist practice assumes that the foundation is rudimentary to all social work practice and that the conceptual frameworks, focus, and methodology identified in the six practice elements are essential means for using foundation knowledge, values, and skills. Whereas the generalist perspective refers to a view of what a social worker *brings* to a problem(s)-person(s)-situation(s), generalist practice refers to what a social worker *does* in a problem(s)-person(s)-situation(s) in micro-, mezzo-, and macro-system practice. Thus, entry-level generalists are prepared to work directly with a variety of people, populations, and problems as well as the families, groups, organizations, and communities that comprise their environments. Over and above this common foundation for all social work practice, the intervention of graduate-level social workers is described according to the theoretical frameworks, focus, and methodology used in various specialized intervention models, such as clinical social work, developmental play therapy, family therapy, community organization, program administration, and social planning and policy.

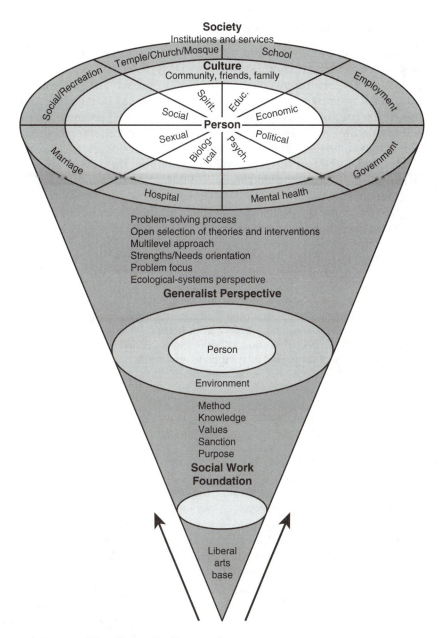

FIGURE 2.1   The Generalist Perspective

Ecological-Systems Perspective

To address the interactions and transactions of person and environment, generalist practice combines general systems, social systems, and ecological concepts and processes. The resulting ecological-systems approach portrays human and environmental systems at the micro (individual), mezzo (family, small group), and macro (large group, organization, community) levels as open, self-organizing, self-regulating, and adaptive functional units of action, interaction, and transaction and as comprised of intricate, interdependent subsystems (Robbins, Chatterjee, & Canda, 1998). In support of this combination, Kirst-Ashman and Hull (1999, p. 16) note that "both systems theory and the ecological perspective provide major tools for social work."

To understand the ecological-systems perspective as a central element in generalist practice, however, definitions of *systems* and *ecology* are essential:

> A system is a dynamic order of parts and processes standing in mutual interaction. (von Bertalanffy, 1968, p. 208)

> Social systems attempt to protect their survival through *adaptation* and *self-preservation* and are interrelated and *interdependent;* human systems and their environments are intimately connected to one another. Thus, *people* and their *environments* are involved in a process of continued adaptation to one another and must be viewed holistically. (Robbins, Chatterjee, & Canda, 1998, pp. 27–28)

> Ecology is the science concerned with the adaptive fit of organisms and their environments and with the means by which they achieve a dynamic equilibrium and mutuality. (Germaine, 1973, p. 326; Mattaini, Lowery, & Meyer, 1998, p. 5)

Thus, in an ecological-systems perspective, *systems* and *ecology* are integrated by viewing the *person(s)* as a *system(s)*, the *environment(s)* of the person as a *system(s)*, and the *fit* and *transactions* between person(s) and environment(s) *ecologically*. As depicted in Figure 2.2, the person is seen as a system with various interdependent parts that include biological, psychological, political, economic (occupational), educational, spiritual, social, and sexual, to name a few (see Table 1.1). The environment is viewed as a system consisting of two major parts that nurture (family, friends, groups, community) and sustain (institutions, organizations, programs in society at large) (Bronfenbrenner, 1999). In sum, the ecological-systems perspective enhances understanding of person-in-environment by highlighting the actions, interactions, and transactions that may take place among the various parts and at the boundary where the person (organism) and environment interface.

A precursor for the application of the ecological-systems perspective to social work practice is found in William Gordon's (1969) writings on boundary work. Just as ecology concerns itself with the adaptive fit of organisms and their environments, Gordon's seven basic ideas constitute extensive consideration of what

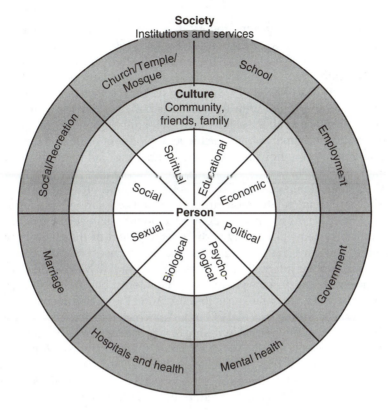

FIGURE 2.2   An Ecological-Systems Perspective of Person in Environment

occurs at the boundary between a client system and its environment. As summarized by Hearn (1979, pp. 350–351):

1. Social work has a simultaneous dual focus . . . upon the person and . . . situation, upon the system and its environment.
2. It occurs at the interface between the human system and its environment. . . .
3. The phenomenon which occurs at the interface is a transaction between system and environment. . . .
4. Transaction is a matching effort, whose focus is the coping behavior of the organism on the system side, and the qualities of the impinging environment on the environmental side. . . .
5. An encounter between the organism and the environment leaves both changed. . . .
6. The best transactions are those which promote the growth and development of the organism while at the same time being ameliorative to the environment. . . .
7. Unattended systems proceed . . . toward disorder, . . . disorganization, . . . or . . . a positive increase in entropy. . . . Thus, for growth . . . , there has to be a continuous redistribution of entropy between organism and environment.

Rooted in general systems theory, Gordon's boundary work provides the branch for the ecological-systems perspective to bear fruit in social work. Although they evolved over a 30-year period, the similarities between the early ideas of Gordon (1962) and the more recent ideas of Germaine and Gitterman (1979, 1995) and Mattaini, Lowery, and Meyer (1998) as they define *ecology* are readily seen: "Ecology is a science concerned with the relations between living organisms—in this case, human beings and all the elements of their environments. It is concerned with how organisms and environments achieve a goodness-of-fit or adaptive balance and equally important, how and why they sometimes fail to do so" (Germaine & Gitterman, 1979, p. 362).

An ecological perspective also notes transactional processes and serves as a "metaphor for human relatedness through mutual adaptation" (Mattaini, Lowery, & Meyer, 1998, p. 6). As a way of integrating or synthesizing elements into a whole, the ecological-systems perspective "directs the vision of the client [system] and social worker toward the complex transactions in cases, helping connect them, and recognizing their interactions" (Mattaini, Lowery, & Meyer, 1998, p. 6).

In the ecological-systems perspective, the interactions, transactions, and interdependence between the organism (subsystem) and the environment (macrosystem) are seen as crucial for the survival of both. Any change in one may have a positive or negative effect on the other (Germaine & Gitterman, 1996). The complexity and diversity among people and the various systems that constitute their immediate and distant environments as they act, exchange, interact, and transact continuously for survival are highlighted. In the most recent revision of his original 1943 conceptualization of the ecological model, Bronfenbrenner (1999) added the prefix *bio*, with the result that his revised dynamic model incorporated the role of the environment into the processes of human development and change throughout the life cycle. That is, his revised bio-ecological model defines environmental process in terms of its functional relationship to and reciprocal transaction with various characteristics of the environment and the developing person. In other words, both person and environment are constantly, mutually, and actively exchanging with and influencing each other for better or worse at the boundaries of their existence.

For social workers, the ecological-systems perspective and its newer bio-ecological variant help reinforce the holistic perspective of person-in-environment. This perspective is clear that it is not enough to look at or work with either people or environments alone or in isolation from each other. Rather, the emphasis needs to be on the critical nature of the lifeline between person and environment, because it is at the boundary where the two meet that many stresses and problems occur and resources are found.

A Problem Focus

In social work, the word *problem* is often used in describing the purpose, definition, focus, and process of the profession. Multiple authors over the past 50 years, for example, have asserted that social work is a problem-solving process (Bisman, 1994; Hepworth, Rooney, & Larsen, 1997; Levy, 1973; Perlman, 1957; Siporin, 1975, 1993).

Indeed, the classic 1956 "Working Definition of Social Work Practice" states the purpose of the profession: "To assist individuals and groups to identify and resolve or minimize problems arising out of disequilibrium between themselves and their environment" (Commission on Social Work Practice, NASW, 1956, as cited in Bartlett, 1958, p. 6).

Some years later, Siporin (1975, p. 3) refers to *social problems* in his definition of *practice:* "Social work is defined as a social institutional method of helping people to prevent and resolve their social problems, to restore and enhance their social functioning." More recently, Bisman (1994, p. 27) adds the social agency as a dimension of problem focus, noting that "what has been called the dual perspective of person and environment actually has three components. Person and environment mean the consideration of individuals within the context of the community and its resources, social policies and regulations, and the service delivery of the organization."

On the one hand, the meaning and use of the concept *problem* in social work have been debated and criticized as too limiting and tied to pathological or negative situations and conditions. The concept has also been criticized as too general a term for distinguishing the essence of social work from other professions that describe their work as problem solving. On the other hand, *problem* has been defined as any "question proposed for solution or discussion" (*Webster's,* 1990, p. 721). In social work, the question is: What does this client system need for problem resolution? When defined in this manner, the concept has room not only for pathological conditions, risk factors, and negative situations but also for the strength, resilience, and protective factors and micro and macro resources essential to the prevention, maintenance, restoration, and enhancement functions of social work.

Perlman (1970, p. 133) normalized the term *problem* for social workers when she wrote that "living is a problem-solving process" and noted that the goal for social workers was to enhance problem-solving capacities. In clarifying problems as a source of difficulty in everyday person-to-person or person-to-task relationships, Perlman (1970, pp. 146–148) pointed out that the problem identified by a client system is not necessarily *the problem* (meaning the basic causative agent in the person's difficulty, the problem of major importance). "It is simply a problem in the helpseeker's current life situation which disturbs or hurts him in some way, and of which he would like to be rid." She saw the social worker's task with the client as collaborative and focused on identifying what the client needs in order to cope with or be rid of the focal problem. She also noted that for the majority of people seeking help from social workers, the problem is based on forces outside of themselves and within their social role transactions.

Following Merton's (Merton, 1957; Merton & Nisbet, 1971) theoretical tradition, Germaine and Gitterman (1979, p. 371) conceptualized *problems* in terms of *dysjunction* and *stress* between the person and environment:

> In the Life Model, therefore, human problems and needs are conceptualized as outcomes of transactions between the parts of that whole. Thus they are defined as problems in living which have created stress and taxed coping abilities. Within the interface where person and environment touch, the problem or need reflects a dysjunction between coping needs and environmental nutriments.

For a social situation to be defined as a problem implies that it has been evaluated by someone as undesirable. That is, there must be an evaluator or definer for a problem to exist as such (Pincus & Minahan, 1973).

In generalist practice, *the problem* is the initial focus and pervasive issue attended to throughout a problem-solving procedure with individuals, families, groups, organizations, and communities. As an essential element of generalist practice, problem focus is a broad concept referring to the issue, need, question, or difficulty brought to the generalist's center of attention for study and action at any given time.

In the past, the focus of attention for study and intervention by social workers was often determined according to their method of practice. The traditional methods were casework, group work, and community organization. Today, in generalist practice, however, the focal problem presented to generalists directs the

1 = Engagement
2 = Data collection
3 = Assessment
4 = Intervention
5 = Evaluation
6 = Termination

FIGURE 2.3   The Problem as Seen in the General Method of Social Work Practice

conceptual explanations of both the problem and the interventions used in general problem-solving methodology (Turner & Jaco, 1996). That is, depending on the problem and related goals, the social worker selects the most appropriate explanations for problem assessment and the most appropriate interventions for problem resolution. The problem thus becomes the pivotal point of the spiraling six-stage problem-solving process to be explained further throughout this book (see Figure 2.3).

A Strengths/Needs Orientation

From a strengths/needs orientation, the problem focus in generalist practice enables individuals, families, groups, organizations, and communities to "build something of lasting value from the materials and capital within and around them" (Saleebey, 1997, p. 233). This process involves joining with client systems in discovering and mobilizing the strengths, assets, and resources of both person and environment as key elements in seeking solutions, setting goals, meeting needs, and effecting change in problems and life trajectories.

As used in the General Method of social work practice, the strengths/needs orientation contains five assumptions:

1. Client systems at the micro, mezzo, and macro levels of practice have the inherent capacity for growth and change (Saleebey, 1997).
2. Each client system brings not only problems, adverse experiences, and needs but also a wide range of knowledge, beliefs, ordinary experiences, survival skills, capacity for resourcefulness, capabilities, resources, preferences, and aspirations to the problem-solving process (Fraser & Galinsky, 1997; Saleebey, 1996; Weick, Rapp, Sullivan, & Kisthardt, 1989).
3. Resources may be personal or communal, micro or macro level, and naturally occurring or formally constituted. They may include monetary and social capital. They may involve concrete realities—such as the physical environment, shelter, food, and instrumental supports—or more abstract realities—such as intrapersonal strengths, interpersonal relationships and support networks, environmental climate, and emotional supports.
4. Adversity may be experienced as both injurious and as a source of challenge and opportunity (McMillen, 1999; Wolin & Wolin, 1993).
5. The environment contains an ever-evolving mixture of demands and supportive resources, stresses and challenges, barriers and opportunities. The opportunities involve alternative options and choices, ways of being and doing, and routes to change (Friedman & Wachs, 1999; Saleebey, 1996).

Based on these strengths-oriented assumptions, the generalist practitioner joins with the client system in seeking solutions to problems, questions, and needs by

- Focusing on strengths, assets, and competencies while exploring problems and needs as catalysts for change, and creating opportunities for competencies to be displayed (Dunst, Trivette, & Deal, 1994)

- Strengthening the internal and external forces that serve to meet need and ameliorate or prevent risks (Fraser & Galinsky, 1997)
- Expanding resources, options, and choices that are available, acceptable, and accessible, and mobilizing strengths and competencies in the service of problem solving and goal achievement

In sum, the practice tasks involve problem solving, meeting needs, reducing risk factors, increasing protective factors, and stimulating generative factors in the service of the client system's strengths, needs, goals, and aspirations.

Integrating these strengths-oriented assumptions into the generalist perspective adds another dimension to the entry-level practitioner's way of thinking about and working with client, action, and target systems at the micro, mezzo, and macro levels. According to Saleebey (1997, p. 235), a strengths/needs orientation also changes the "nature of the contractual relationship . . . in the direction of power equalization, mutual assessment, and evolving agreements." Thus, the strengths/needs orientation of the General Method is closely linked to the concept of empowerment, which

> includes combining a sense of personal control with the ability to affect the behavior of others, a focus on enhancing existing strengths in individuals or communities, a goal of establishing equity in the distribution of resources, an ecological (rather than an individual) form of analysis for understanding individual and community phenomena, and a belief that power is not a scarce commodity but one that can be generated. (Gutierrez, 1990, p. 150)

That is, empowerment is a generative process through which the powerless and vulnerable are enabled to (1) mobilize personal, familial, organizational, and communal resources; (2) exercise greater control over their environment; and (3) meet their needs and attain their aspirations (Bailey, 1994; Cowger, 1997; Gutierrez, 1994, 1995; Lee, 1996; Pinderhughes, 1995).

> Client empowerment presupposes an existing condition of client disempowerment and marginality. Fitting subjects, therefore, of empowerment social work are socially despised persons, families, and groups. They may be poor in a country that values economic success, black in a culture that privileges white skin, chronically ill in a nation that equates health with productivity and productivity with merit, or old in a land that cherishes the vigor of youth and shuns symbolic and material reminders of human mortality. (Simon, 1994, pp. 24–25)

A Multilevel Approach

As noted earlier, generalists work with multiple client, target, and action systems. That is, their focus, conceptual framework, and methodology do not constrict their practice or expertise to working only, or mainly, with individuals, families, groups, organizations, or communities as *client systems* seeking help. Any one of these systems may also be seen as a target or action system. As a *target*, a system is viewed by the generalist as requiring change in order to meet the needs and goals of the client system. As a member of an *action* system, a social worker mobilizes that action system to work to bring about change in a target system and thereby accomplish the established goals (Pincus & Minahan, 1973).

Another way to categorize systems is according to the level of practice. As noted earlier, the *micro* practice level means one-on-one or individual work, *mezzo* refers to family and small group work, and *macro* refers to large-scale practice, such as with large groups, organizations, communities, institutions, or society (Brueggeman, 1996; De Hoyos, 1989; Zastrow, 1999). In generalist practice, social workers practice at whatever level is needed with whatever type system, depending on the problem in focus as assessed from an ecological-systems perspective. Thus, the generalist may be working at a particular practice level at a given time or with more than one level concurrently or sequentially. This *multilevel systems approach* connotes a readiness for variability in practice based on the problem in focus and the generalist's knowledge and skills for problem solving.

Open Selection of Theories and Interventions

Use of an *open selection of theories and interventions* means that generalists theoretically frame their practice but do not specialize in any one theoretical approach. Their use of theories and models to understand (assess) and to direct their actions (intervene) varies according to the problem in focus. Their only constriction may be due to their limited ability and experience in using particular theoretical frameworks and specialized models of interventions. When the situation and problem call for a more specialized approach, generalists make referrals.

The scope of attention for intervention by the generalist may extend from a person, to a family, to a group, to an organization, to a community, to society at large. In focusing on a problem, a whole range of possible causes, needs, and alternative solutions must be considered. Although generalists do not have depth of knowledge or specialized competence, entry-level social workers are expected to think with conceptual clarity and complexity, identify the particular client system and point of interface in need of attention, and use theory and other foundation knowledge to inform their practice. In summary, generalists are open to select the most appropriate conceptual explanation for an accurate assessment and planned intervention in the particular person-problem-situation.

Case Example
Peter, 18 years old, was referred to the community service center because of his withdrawn behavior and failing grades during his senior year in high school. Intake assessment revealed that he had cognitive abilities below age level and lacked physical stamina. He had always been a student with marginal grades. His withdrawal from school and neighborhood social activities was precipitated by increasing family demands to help with his father's business. According to his family's culture, the eldest son is expected to work in and eventually take over

the family business. At the point of seeking help, Peter was feeling rejected by his father and relatives and experiencing difficulty coping with the multiple pressures in his life.

The social worker in this case needs to be able to translate the *person-in-environment* framework into assessment via several knowledge pathways. For example, developmental theory would be used to assess Peter's potential for fulfilling developmentally appropriate life tasks and for securing a health evaluation of his physical capabilities. Cognitive theory would be used to assess Peter's attributed meanings to his problems as well as his cognitive potential for grappling with possible solutions. Role theory would be used to assess Peter's role (skills, expectations, and enactment) within the context of his family and community. The ecological-systems perspective would be used to identify the multiple systems impinging on Peter: his developmental self, family, school, and culture. A strengths/needs orientation would be used to assess his role performance competencies and social skills.

Figure 2.4 shows how the social worker uses Figure 2.2 and Table 1.3 in the application of knowledge. The lines of the circle in Figure 2.4 are the places where

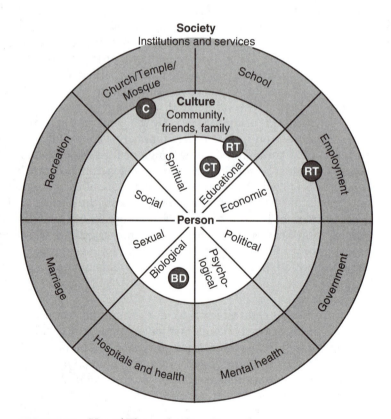

FIGURE 2.4   Use of Theory in Case Example

knowledge under the *in* category falls. Role theory is indicated as RT at the interfaces between person and family and between family and employment/society. The knowledge categorized under *person* or *environment* in Table 1.1 falls in the sections within the circles. For example, cognitive theory (CT) is in the *education* section; biological development (BD) is in the *biological* section; and knowledge about culture (C) is in the second circle with *community, friends,* and *family.* The application of this knowledge involves boundary work at the interfaces between Peter and his family and between his family and employment/society.

Thus, generalist practitioners selectively and collectively apply foundation knowledge to practice. They understand the meaning of this knowledge; grasp the concepts, statements, and sources for each theory; and selectively apply knowledge and theory to the person-environment situation. In addition, with the help of the ecological-systems framework, the generalist is able to view the relationships and complementarity among basic practice concepts and principles of foundation knowledge for collective application and more effective practice.

A Problem-Solving Process

Several writings describe the *how to* of practice in terms of a basic sequential process. Although the skills and stages of the processes may be stated in different words, similarities and overlap among writers are apparent. Four authors or author teams (Perlman, 1970; Shulman, 1999; Compton & Galaway, 1999; Hepworth, Rooney, & Larsen, 1997), for example, identify social work intervention as a multistage helping process and emphasize the importance of the professional helping relationship in problem solving with clients.

Perlman (1970) writes that her casework problem-solving process is actually applicable to any problem-solving efforts in the normal course of living and identifies several operations essential to the process. In her schema, the components of the process are study problem identification and feelings identification (client's); examination of causes and effects of the problem; search for means of solution, alternatives, and intervention planning; and treatment that involves making choices, decision making, and action to resolve problems. She sees the factors of *relationship* and *involvement with significant others* as necessarily present within the problem-solving process.

Shulman (1999) introduces a model of the helping process based on the work phases *beginning, work,* and *ending.* In the preliminary phase, social workers are concerned with empathy, communication, responding, and reporting. Central to the beginning phase is the art of developing a working relationship. It includes early contracting and clarification of boundaries. The work phase, according to Shulman, involves a series of skills, including elaboration, containment, and working with silences. The ending phase occurs when the separation process is carried out and skills for transition are utilized.

Compton and Galaway (1999) identify three basic phases with additional activities incorporated into the process. Their initial or *contact phase* includes problem identification, initial goal setting, and data collection. This phase also refers to joint assessments, goal setting, and planning. Their *middle phase* focuses on the implementation of the plan and on evaluation. Their *ending phase* includes referral, transfer, and termination.

Hepworth, Rooney, and Larsen (1997), too, agree that the helping process consists of three major phases but identify multiple areas for each stage: *Phase I—Exploration, engagement, assessment, and planning; Phase II—Implementation and goal attainment;* and *Phase III—Termination, planning maintenance strategies, and evaluation.* Each of these phases lays the groundwork for subsequent strategies and processes directed toward resolving problems and promoting problem-solving skills.

These authors note that the purpose of the social work intervention is to help clients cope more effectively with problems in living and thereby improve their quality of life. They agree that each phase or stage in the intervention process has distinct objectives and operations and note that these operations usually, but not always, proceed successively through the sequential stages. They also agree that the activities and skills used in each stage of the process differ more in prevalence, intensity, and purpose than in type.

Two different author teams (Lippitt, Watson, & Westley, 1958; Sheafor, Horejsi, & Horejsi, 1997), however, focus more on client systems and emphasize problem solving as a *planned change process.* From a more macro perspective, Lippitt, Watson, and Westley (1958, p. 130) were among the first to identify the problem-solving process as applicable to work with individuals, groups, organizations, and communities. Their seven phases include:

1. The development of a need for change
2. The establishment of a change relationship
3. The clarification or diagnosis of the client system's problem
4. The examination of alternative routes and goals, and establishing goals and intentions
5. The transformation of intentions into actual change efforts
6. The generalization and stabilization of change
7. Achieving a terminal relationship

Sheafor, Horejsi, and Horejsi (1997, p. 130) emphasize problem solving as planned change that usually requires the social worker and client system to:

- Identify the client [system's] problem, troublesome situation, or concern.
- Collect data and study the problem or situation (in context).
- Assess the problem (i.e., decide what needs to change, what can be changed, and how it might be changed).
- Establish goals and objectives for change.
- Formulate a plan on how to proceed.
- Take action based on the plan (i.e., intervention).
- Monitor progress and determine if the intervention is achieving the desired goals and objectives and, if necessary, modify the plan and try again.
- Once goals and objectives have been reached, terminate the intervention and evaluate the process to learn for future practice activities.

Sheafor, Horejsi, and Horejsi (p. 131) condense these processes into five phases with two central tasks for each phase: *Phase I—Intake and Engagement; Phase II—Data Collection and Assessment; Phase III—Planning and Contracting; Phase IV—Intervention and Monitoring; and Phase V—Termination and Evaluation.* These authors concur with the others that the progression of these sequential intervention stages is spiral, with frequent recycling or reworking of tasks and activities. That is, the cycle begins anew as problems are solved and new ones encountered (Lippitt, Watson, & Westley, 1958; Sheafor, Horejsi, & Horejsi, 1997).

Thus, a comparison of the different helping processes reveals that earlier and later authors with both micro and more macro emphases are in basic agreement in recognizing a general process for practice that consists of progressive stages leading to goal accomplishment. Most writers stress the need for flexibility in applying the process, with the expectation of overlap, recycling, and occasional inconsistency in the sequencing of phases. Building on these earlier works, this book describes a problem-solving process, called the *General Method,* that has characteristics similar to those stages and phases identified. The General Method includes six stages of engagement, data collection, assessment, intervention, evaluation, and termination that are applicable to social work with client systems at micro, mezzo, and macro levels of practice.

The General Method

In the "Working Definition of Social Work Practice," *method* is defined as "an orderly systematic mode of procedure" (Commission on Social Work Practice, NASW, 1956, as cited in Bartlett, 1958). According to Siporin (1975, p. 43), *method* refers to "the 'how' of helping, to purposeful, planned, instrumental activity through which tasks are accomplished and goals are achieved." Basically, *method* means an orderly process of action that connotes thought, purpose, and activity. In addition to reflection and action skills, the General Method incorporates the purpose, values, and knowledge of the profession into the *how* of intervention.

The first methods identified in social work practice focused on the way the social worker proceeded in working with an individual, running a group, or organizing a community. Those traditional methods of casework, group work, and community organization were seen as separate and distinct methodologies. Each method had its own integral set of knowledge and skills. Although some agencies and social workers primarily use only one of the traditional methods, there has been a growing acknowledgment of the need for social workers to be able to work with client systems of different sizes. Indeed, as brought out by Meyer (1966, p. 284) about 40 years ago, "The traditional separation of casework, group work, and community organization is no longer tenable."

At the entry level, there is a strong movement toward clarifying a social work procedure that is common to all methods. Although Gordon (1962, p. 5) discouraged "the dubious task of trying to extract from each [traditional method] what was common to all," he recognized "such broad stages as assessment, planning, taking action and evaluating [as] characteristic of any rationally based problem solving approach." Today, contemporary writers about entry-level social work practice have begun to describe a manner of proceeding that is orderly and systematized but refer to it as something other than a method. For many, the term *method* seems to be reserved for the three traditional methodological foundations of the profession (casework, group work, community organization).

Using the definition of *general* to mean what belongs to the "common nature" of a group and "not confined by specialization or careful limitation" (*Webster's*, 1990, p. 377) and the definition of *method* to mean "an orderly systematic mode of procedure" (*Webster's*, 1990, p. 570), it is possible to identify a general method of social work practice that is common to all the traditional methods, not bound by careful limitation, and consisting of a purposeful procedure ordered by six major stages—engagement, data collection, assessment, intervention, evaluation, and termination.

Within each of these six sequential stages, there are varying clusters of particular skills, such as communicating, using self purposively in professional relationships with client systems, collecting relevant information, contracting, evaluating, and saying a planned goodbye. In reality, these stages are not mutually exclusive and may even occur simultaneously or out of order. Yet the six-stage framework serves as a systematic guideline for organizing knowledge, thoughts, and actions of social workers as they interact with diverse systems.

The General Method may be utilized when working with individuals, families, groups, organizations, and communities. It is inclusive of work with environmental target and action systems as well as with client systems (Pincus & Minahan, 1973) and is built on the holistic base of the mission, purpose, knowledge, values, and skills social work presented earlier. Its main thrust is to serve as a guide for the professional actions of entry-level social workers.

The General Method, however, is more than the selection and sequencing of skills identified in the foundation of social work practice and more than a six-stage action chain. It is a professional problem-solving process carried out within the context of the generalist perspective. This means that throughout the process, the social worker focuses on identifiable problems, employs an ecological-systems perspective, problem solves from a strengths/needs orientation, selects openly from a range of theories and interventions, and readily practices at multiple levels of person-in-environment (that is, at the micro, mezzo, and macro levels of practice).

Entry-Level and Graduate-Level Practice

As noted earlier, entry-level generalists are guided by social work foundation knowledge, values, and skills when using the General Method as a basic problem-solving procedure with a variety of client systems. Within the ecological-systems perspective, generalist practitioners acknowledge human individuality, environmental variance, and client system diversity. Depending on the current reality of each unique problem situation, they move back and forth across practice levels and stages of the General Method.

The more advanced methods of graduate-level practitioners include much that is found in the General Method but also reflect the usage of specialized knowledge, skills, and procedures for work with particular client systems, problems, or populations. For example, the social worker with a graduate-level concentration in the area of children may employ a specialized method for working with children through developmental play therapy (Salladin & Timberlake, 1995; Timberlake & Cutler, 2001). The family specialist may employ a distinctive method of family preservation (Fraser, Nelson, & Rivard, 1997; Nelson & Landsman, 1992; Sandau-Beckler, Salcido, & Ronnau, 1993; Schwartz & AuClaire, 1995) or family therapy (Bardill, 1997; Kilpatrick & Holland, 1995; Nichols & Schwartz, 1995).

How do social workers decide the method of practice needed in a particular situation? To answer this question, they must consider several factors. Primarily, it is necessary to collect data on the severity of the problem or need being addressed and on the strengths and coping capacities of the client system in need. As depicted in Figure 2.5, there is a strong indication that a graduate-level social worker is needed when the severity of the problem or need is great and when the client system has few strengths and limited ability and motivation for dealing with the problem (see point 1 in Figure 2.5). To bring about the greatest possible improvement in these client situations, it is desirable that the social work practitioner have both general and specialized expertise. When the problem or need is of little severity and the client system has obvious strengths and coping capacities, the entry-level generalist will be able to intervene with a high expectancy for goal accomplishment (see point 2 in Figure 2.5).

As shown in Figure 2.5, some problem situations of clients may be serviced by either a graduate-level or entry-level general practitioner. That is, either the General Method or an advanced method could be used successfully. Where there is similarity in the assessed severity of the problem with the assessed strengths of

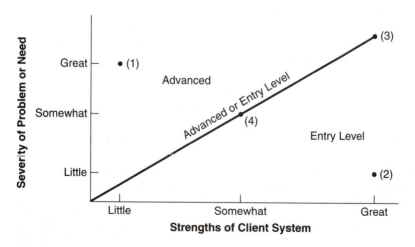

FIGURE 2.5 Entry-Level and Advanced Methodology

the client, a balance may result. In these cases, there is greater question as to whether advanced or entry-level generalist methods should be used for effective goal accomplishment. In other cases, there may be major life and death issues but the graduate-level practitioner is not needed because there are great strengths and few needs in the client system (see point 3 in Figure 2.5).

Some client-problem-need-strengths situations fall within a middle range of problem severity, entrenchment, and dysfunction. These client systems may be served successfully by either an entry-level social worker using the General Method or a graduate-level general practitioner using either the General Method or a specialized method. That is, in cases where the problem or need falls in the middle of the scale of severity and the client system's strengths are assessed as moderate, the selection of method may be arbitrary (see point 4 in Figure 2.5). For example, a community concerned with an increase in neighborhood crime may have some strengths for mobilizing itself to work on this emerging problem with the help of either an entry-level generalist or a graduate-level practitioner. The general problem-solving method or the specialized community-organization method could be effective. Or a team approach of both graduate-level and entry-level social workers could prove more efficacious.

Figure 2.5 may be a helpful tool for case assignment or planning. To use the tool, however, it is important to understand the meaning of the indicators of problem/need severity and of the client system's strengths and resources. A problem or need is assessed at little severity when it has recently emerged (time consideration) with limited scope (how many, how deeply involved) and when it has little life-or-death magnitude. When the client system is assessed as having little strength, it means that the persons or communities involved have very limited coping capacities, motivation, and resources. As the assessment moves higher on either scale, it means that there is evidence of a greater degree of client strength or problem severity. Owing to the human and artful nature of social work practice, it is difficult to identify scientific tools for measurement and prediction. Thus, decision making based on problem/need/strength is scientifically limited because it relies heavily on personal judgment and inconclusive data. It does, however, provide a framework for beginning conceptualization of distinctions in the use of the General Method.

Conclusion

The general method of social work practice involves a purposeful procedure. Respecting the right of a human system to self-determination, the generalist follows the lead of the client system receiving service and offers an approach that is a purposive, planned problem-solving approach. Sensitivity to client system variability enables the social worker to be skillful in timing the engagement, data collection, assessment, and intervention process and also in selecting methodology, tools, and techniques. With the identification of mutual goals, the social worker and the system of contact proceed with planned interactions that have the purpose of goal accomplishment. The General Method incorporates an ecological-systems perspective, an open selection of theories and interventions, and a multilevel approach. It is a strengths/needs–oriented problem-solving process consisting of six identifiable stages. Although the process generally follows these stages, it is dynamic in nature and not restricted to a set sequence with a rigid, fixed pattern. As pointed out earlier, elements of each stage are often observable in every stage. Frequently, there is a returning to an earlier stage for further work as problems or needs evolve. For clarity of conceptualization, however, the stages are presented in separate chapters as distinct and sequential.

In addition, the general nature of the method does not restrict a social worker to working with client systems of a particular size. It may be used with individuals, families, groups, organizations, and communities. Interventions are selected to match the individualized needs of the client system receiving service at a given time. A plan to work with members of a client system, for example, may include seeing them individually, as a family, and in groups. A plan to work with a community may include meetings with individual stakeholders and selected groups or communitywide meetings with stakeholders and politicians. The General Method blends communal and individual conceptualizations. A holistic perspective that recognizes individuality and interrelatedness is therefore fundamental to the General Method.

For entry-level social workers, the General Method is a guiding framework. Rather than learning about a variety of skills to be applied eclectically, the social worker who learns the General Method has a systematically organized body of knowledge and skills. He or she is enabled to be process-minded and to recognize movement in problem solving. The method guides the generalist and the client system receiving service in their collaborative effort toward goal attainment.

In sum, the *foundation of social work practice* consists of the elements of (1) purpose, (2) sanction, (3) values, (4) knowledge, and (5) method (skills). The major *elements of generalist practice* include (1) an ecological-systems perspective, (2) a problem focus, (3) a strengths/needs orientation, (4) a multilevel approach, (5) an open selection of theories and interventions, and (6) a problem-solving process. The social work foundation and the elements of generalist practice are depicted in Figure 2.1. Generalists call on this holistic perspective as they use the General Method in their social work practice. In addition to clarifying what constitutes the General Method that guides the actions of the generalist practitioner, the authors identify and articulate other central elements that characterize generalist practice. These elements and the General Method may be combined with the social work foundation presented in Chapter 1 to offer a holistic generalist perspective of social work practice.

CHAPTER

3

Human Diversity

Multiculturalism, Social Pluralism, and Socio-Demographic Variability

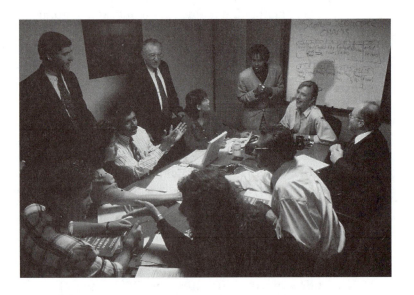

As noted earlier, the social work profession has a simultaneous dual commitment to social change in the interest of social justice and to social intervention in the enhancement of human life. The value base undergirding this commitment is a caring concern for the dignity, worth, and uniqueness of each and every human being. While certain common human needs are essential for all persons, individuals' frames of reference for thinking and feeling about these needs and seeking ways to fulfill them differ. These variations in frame of reference derive from:

- A person's membership in a particular cultural group (race, national origin, religion, ethnic group)
- Pluralizing social stratification influences (socioeconomic class, education, occupation, political power) and community environmental characteristics (urban, suburban, rural)
- Personal and socio-demographic variability in endowment, personality, age, gender, sexual orientation, health, and physical and mental ability

When social workers first enter the profession, they bring their own personal cultural values and vantage points for viewing client systems, problems and needs, strengths and vulnerabilities, and problem-solving approaches. Yet personal idiosyncratic frames of reference of person-in-environment are not sufficient tools for professional interaction with complex heterogeneous client systems. Indeed, multicultural population projections hold that, given existing birthrates and immigration patterns, one in every three residents in the United States by the year 2050 will be of nonwhite, non-European descent (Horwitz & Scheid, 1999). Therefore, this chapter seeks to promote awareness of, sensitivity to, and competence in working with multiculturalism, social pluralism, and socio-demographic human variability.

Social workers act in support of the oppressed to help them obtain freedom and growth. They respect the need of individuals to choose for themselves. They do not judge the choices and morality of others' behaviors as long as the choices or behaviors of one do not threaten or deprive others of life, choice, or expression. Social workers promote the tenets that to be human is to have choice and that people have a right to choose their own values, lifestyles, and behaviors. They recognize that, in addition to a commitment to uphold the values of life, choice, and individuality, a knowledge of human diversity is necessary to guide social workers' actions. Social workers exercise care to avoid stereotyping a member of any group. To *stereotype* means to attribute a uniform set of characteristics to a group of people and to deny their individual differences. In brief, *social workers demonstrate respect for and acceptance of the unique characteristics of diverse populations* (Council on Social Work Education, 1994).

To promote sensitivity and competence in working with diverse client systems, this chapter first presents a knowledge paradigm for exploring and understanding multiculturalism and ethnic group membership. It then addresses social pluralism and socio-demographic variability. Each section includes an exercise for self-assessment.

These knowledge areas and their accompanying self-awareness exercises serve two purposes. They help social workers organize their own personal and group membership value orientations, attitudes, assumptions, biases, and prejudices that may become barriers in understanding and communicating with others. Second, these knowledge areas set the stage for social workers' lifelong learning about their client systems and themselves in their professional roles. The purpose of this approach to human diversity is to build an inclusionary professional world view that

- Extends the professional self beyond the ethnocentrism and prejudice inherent in the boundaries and blinders of personal experience and own world view
- Respects and understands the protective role that multiculturalism, social pluralism, and socio-demographic variability play in adaptive social functioning and social enhancement
- Understands the impact of societal "isms" and human service delivery biases on individual and collective stress, risk, resilience, and well-being at the micro, mezzo, and macro levels of practice
- Uses the knowledge of multiculturalism, social pluralism, and socio-demographic variability to communicate clearly, interact respectfully, and act facilitatively with client, action, and target systems as well as human service providers in order to mobilize resources, solve problems, empower the vulnerable, and provide sensitive and competent services across diverse groupings of persons

Multiculturalism

Concepts and Terminology

In preparing to communicate with an individual, family, group, or community, a social worker takes time to study the cultural influences of the client system to be contacted. Cultural influences include goals and aspirations, patterns of resource utilization or help-seeking behaviors, self-concepts or identity, patterns of communication and emotional control, and ways of perceiving life events and social situations. To understand the full implications of cultural influences on practice, however, first requires an overview and definition of concepts central to ethnic-group membership and culturally competent service delivery.

Culture. *Culture* is the set of values, beliefs, and norms for socially acceptable language patterns, behaviors, and standards for ideal role types that represent the social structure of a given society. Culture is historically bound yet dynamic over time. It constructs a social reality that reduces the uncertainties in life by providing a means for understanding the world and for knowing the social location and expected behaviors for persons in this world. Cultural reality is apparent in (1) the societal structures of technology, laws and governance structures, religion and rituals, and social roles and rules (McGoldrick, Giordano, & Pearce, 1996) and (2) the cognitive, affective, and action realms associated with individual and collective values, beliefs, attitudes, ideas, and expectations in everyday life. It comprises a system of shared symbolic meanings rooted in the real and mental worlds of client, action, and target systems and is circumscribed by social factors in their environments, such as power and authority structures, access to opportunities, and institutional constraints. Through implicit and explicit group standards of behavior, culture influences personal thoughts, feelings, actions, and interactional patterns in community life. Cultural values affect the way people construe and evaluate problems, situations, and the actions taken in pursuit of important goals. Each culture has ideal role types, normative expectations, and shared symbolic interpretations that (1) give meaning to life experiences, (2) ground and identify a person's sense of self, and (3) generate a sense of individual well-being of persons-in-environment. Thus, in an individual sense, *culture* may be defined as a framework of assumptions for understanding self, making sense of the world, and communicating that understanding to others. Social workers encounter culture through the contexts of

- Client characteristics, behaviors, and life choices
- The social work profession's practices
- Work-environment agency practices
- Intervention-treatment standards of care practices
- Society's beliefs and ethnic-group memberships
- Their own characteristics, behaviors, and life choices

National Origin.   Persons who share a *place* or *nation of origin* and often common ancestry also share a sense of historical circumstances, continuity, and psychosocial referents that create a sense of social group identity. Individuals who identify with broader cultural traditions, such as the European American culture, however, also tend to identify strongly with a particular subculture(s) reflecting the specific country of family origin, family immigration patterns to the United States, and migration patterns and settlement location within the United States (specific cities, rural/urban, North/South/East/West). Recent war experiences of survivor groups may intensify the cumulative effect of the historic national past with frozen grief experiences, such as those associated with genocide, that have been passed along over the generations.

Intergenerational differences in identification with national origin wax and wane across generations as the focus shifts from who group members are by virtue of their life experiences in their nation of origin to what they have been taught about their national origin and the relationship between family teaching and life experiences in the United States. Over time, social identity defined by nation of origin as rooted in family traditions is likely to be maintained by leisure-time activities and festive traditions that reflect the voluntary enjoyable aspects of being an ethnic national, or, as classically termed, a symbolic national ethnic (Gans, 1979).

Race.   People who share a more or less distinctive combination of physical characteristics transmitted by their ancestors are said to be of the same *race*. Racial group members may or may not share the same sense of common group identity that ties an ethnic group together. *Racism* refers to the ideologies of superiority and negative attitudes involved in judging others solely on the basis of common physical characteristics, such as skin color, hair, body size, facial features, or language patterns. Racism also involves differential and detrimental treatment of racial group members by individuals and by social institutions. Internalization of the racist beliefs of a larger society by members of a racial group can be associated with negative self-evaluation, increased stress, and barriers to individual and communal well-being.

Ethnicity.   An *ethnic group* is a subculture within a society that has retained distinctive characteristics and traditions associated with categories of race, national origin, and/or religion. Ethnic group members, for example, share commonalities such as values, religious beliefs and practices, language, historical continuity, and place of origin or common ancestry. These commonalities, in turn, represent shared historical circumstances and psychosocial referents that, over time, create a sense of peoplehood, togetherness, and belongingness—that is, a common ethnic group identity. Ethnic group value systems function as those learned principles and rules that have evolved to help an individual choose between alternative courses of action, resolve conflicts, and make decisions in daily life. These value systems are useful in that they guide conduct in a variety of ways. They serve as standards for

- Taking positions on social issues
- Preferring one cultural, religious, or political ideology over another
- Guiding presentation of self to others
- Evaluating and judging self and others
- Comparing self and others
- Influencing or changing others
- Rationalizing beliefs, attitudes, and actions in order to maintain and enhance self-concept

Ethnic identity, the existence of a stable inner sense of who a person is, is formed by the successful integration of the various experiences of the self into a coherent self-image and refers to that part of personal identity that contributes to a person's image of self as an ethnic group member. Ethnic group socialization is intended to inculcate children with the cultural norms of behaviors, beliefs, and expectations of their subculture and thereby help them attach to their membership group. Ethnic assimilation and acculturation are the processes by which ethnic groups absorb characteristics of the dominant culture. The two processes, however, differ. In *assimilation,* members of an ethnic group are expected to abandon traditional ways and customs and adopt the new culture fully by completely changing their personal cultural identification, attitudes and beliefs, behaviors, language, marital expectations, parenting style and expectations, and sense of social responsibility so that they are congruent with the dominant culture. In *acculturation,* on the other hand, members of an ethnic group are expected to retain their original cultural heritage while learning about and adapting to new ways, beliefs, and behavioral expectations along the same seven dimensions. During acculturation (but not in assimilation), *ethnic conflict,* or ethnic group identity struggle over opportunities and resources, is expected as part of the group members' competition within themselves and with other groups over cultural maintenance, empowerment, and socioeconomic parity.

Experiencing *ethnocentrism,* or viewing another way of life as inferior to that of one's own culture, and *racism,* or devaluing others on the basis of their skin color, have always been a part of the ethnic adaptation process and experience of ethnic groups. The current beliefs about ethnic acculturation promote *multiculturalism,* or the ways, customs, and practices that respect and maintain ethnic cultural distinctiveness among different ethnic groups (Gutierrez, Alvarez, Nemon, & Lewis, 1997).

At the micro, mezzo, and macro levels of social work practice, the culturally competent generalist social worker is expected to do the following:

- Start where the particular client system is—that is, understand the client system's needs, strengths, and goals in respect to the client system's cultural beliefs, values, and perceptions.
- Know that the client system's beliefs, assumptions, and behaviors are rooted in the client system's cultural and acculturating experiences and that these may vary for different individuals (even within the same ethnic group).
- Avoid assuming that the client system will see the world the same way the social worker does (even when both share the same ethnic background).
- Assume that the client system will have different perceptions and find out the specific differences.
- Value the uniqueness and individuality of each client system.
- Use multicultural sensitivity in promoting individual, family, group, organizational, and community cooperative problem solving, collaborative facilitation, data collection, assessment, planning, intervention, action, research, and analysis of needs, strengths, and goals.
- Keep up with the professional literature about the effectiveness of policies and practices with different ethnic client systems.

Minority. *Minority* refers not to the particular cultural characteristics or the number of cultural group members but rather to the extent of a group's power and access to the resources and opportunities available in a society. Minority group members are likely to have less control over the circumstances of their lives than majority group members. That is, they are likely to experience economic, social, and political inequality, whereas the majority group tends to dominate society in the economic, social, and political realms. Although for some persons ethnic identity provides access and privilege, the social meaning of race/ethnicity for many members of minority groups often results in stigma, discrimination, and prejudice. Thus, minority status captures differential exposure to social, economic, and political stressors, variation in the social and personal resources available for coping with stress, and different value styles in coping and adaptation.

In the United States, four major racial/ethnic minority cultures with a combined population of 64.3 million people (O'Hare, 1992) have been identified: Native American, African American, Hispanic, and Asian/Pacific Islander. Although African Americans were by far the largest group several generations ago, today they account for less than half of all people of color in the United States. Hispanics and Asian Americans, by contrast, are the most rapidly growing groups (O'Hare, 1992).

For a social worker to be culturally sensitive and competent, knowing about the general characteristics of these four major U.S. cultures is not sufficient. For example, careful research has revealed great intragroup cultural variation and diversity apart from pluralizing social influences (socioeconomic class, education, occupation, political power, community environment) and personal and socio-demographic distinctions (endowment and personality, age and developmental stage, gender, sexual orientation, physical and mental ability). Specifically, 14 distinguishable subcultures have been identified among African Americans (Valentine, 1971; Williams, 1983); 98 subcultures are distributed across over 200 Native American tribes (Brown & Shaughnessy, 1979; Coggins, 1991); at least five Hispanic subgroups exist (Bean & Tienda, 1987; Marin & Marin, 1991); and there are 23 Asian/Pacific Islander subgroupings (Morales, 1976). Each of these subcultures has distinctive historical traditions, values, customs, attitudes, lifestyles, and languages or dialects. Although some common biological and social characteristics may exist among the members of a racial/ethnic minority group—such as the Samoan, Guamanian, Chinese, Japanese, Vietnamese, and Koreans of the Asian/Pacific cluster—a social worker needs to comprehend what it means for subgroup members to have a history and dynamic culture of their own and yet find themselves repeatedly linked to other subgroups that are similar but different.

In assessing the functioning of ethnic minority client systems, it is important for the social work generalist to consider the degree to which the client system has been socialized into the mainstream culture. Ethnic minority clients are members of two cultures. Thus, their functioning must be considered in relation to both their culture of origin and the majority culture. For example, first-generation minority clients adhere closely to their traditional beliefs, values, and patterns of behavior. By the third generation, clients have usually internalized many patterns of the dominant culture, although they typically maintain many traditional patterns of family relationships. Caution must be exercised, however, in considering the degree of acculturation of any client system, as errors can be easily made when the practitioner fails to recognize and attend to the uniqueness of each. The following factors have been identified as affecting the degree of bicultural socialization and interaction of ethnic minority client systems with mainstream society (DeAnda, 1984; Devore & Schlessinger, 1999; Norton, 1978, 1993; Pedersen, 1997) and have been recommended in carrying out ethnically sensitive and culturally competent social work services:

1. Assess the degree of commonality between the two cultures with regard to norms, values, beliefs, perceptions, and problem(s) being presented by the client system.
2. Consider the client system's command of language or bilingualism within each culture as related to educational and/or occupational achievement and fulfillment of daily tasks.
3. Assess the client system's degree of biculturalism or the degree to which the client system identifies with features of each culture in the pursuit of daily functioning.

4. Consider the degree of dissimilarity of the client system's physical appearance from the majority culture (facial features, skin color, body appearance), the degree to which this dissimilarity is valued or devalued by each culture, and the client system's response to such valuation.
5. Assess the client system's past and present experience with cultural role models (cultural translators and mediators) by identifying the importance and competence of significant persons who shaped their learning about the norms and expectations for each culture as related to the presenting problem.
6. Consider the client system's degree of ethnic identification through their affective perception and interpretation of the immigration experience, family narrative, and present generational standing.
7. Assess the degree to which the client system's conceptual and affective problem-solving style meshes and blends with the prevalent or valued style of the dominant culture as it pertains to the presenting problem.

Ethnic-Group Membership.   An ethnic group's historical experiences, cultural values, and world view influence the way its individual and collective members cognitively construe and affectively experience persons, situations, needs, problems, resources, and solutions. Thus, the social worker's cultural sensitivity can, in part, be fostered through a conceptual understanding of the role values play in everyday life experiences, knowledge of an ethnic group's particular history, and knowledge of its members' fundamental value orientations to various aspects of daily living.

At times, however, value clashes among ethnic groups and between particular ethnic groups and mainstream U.S. cultures become apparent. In these instances, the social worker has an obligation to go beyond cultural sensitivity and understanding and to become the interpreter of the value conflict. That is, the social worker helps the client system become aware that the two focal value systems are not congruent and syntonic in relation to selected life dimensions. Specifically, the social worker needs to

- Clarify how the two values of concern differ socially and culturally within the two cultural systems.
- Identify positive and negative social consequences for adhering to either value position.
- Identify legal consequences for either value position.
- Identify any value position and any legal obligations of the agency service delivery system.

Well-Being.   As values reflect people's general beliefs and prescribe desirable ways of being and behaving, they provide members with a sense of societal and family norms, expectations, and stability. They also provide standards for evaluating actions and outcomes, justifying opinions and conduct, planning and guiding behavior, deciding between alternative options, comparing self with others, influencing others, and presenting self to others. Only when exclusive identification labels, such as Jewish or AME (African Methodist Episcopal) values, are placed on particular cultural value systems do value orientations seem to stand on their own and be applicable by themselves with minimal reference to individuals, families, and peer groups (Tropman, 1989, 1999; Tropman, Ehrlich, & Rothman, 1995).

In each life area, cultural value systems provide living guides and usable frameworks for daily life choices and decision making. When an ethnic group value system is insufficient for an individual in a particular situation or life domain, the individual is likely to draw on his or her internal values that reflect (role) identification and sense of well-being as well as the family and significant peers. When these identifications are congruent, people experience a sense of support and well-being.

The value orientations of different ethnic groups may be assessed and understood through exploring the group's philosophical orientation toward nature and humanity, social orientation toward time and space, personal orientation toward self and others, life goals, and social responsibilities (Reid & Popple, 1992; Tropman, 1999; Wakefield, 1993):

1. Philosophical orientation toward nature in general and humanity in particular
   - Do the values reflect harmony with or mastery over nature?
   - Do the values reflect submissive sharing with or assertive achieving over nature?
   - Does the value orientation portray human nature as basically good and worthy or basically evil and unworthy?
2. Social orientation in time and space
   - Are the values congruent with a sense of societal clock time or a sense of personal time?
   - To what degree is the time orientation focused toward the past, the present, or the future?
   - To what degree is the spatial orientation focused toward personal space or communal space?
3. Personal orientation toward self and others
   - To what degree does the self-concept reflect the meaning of personal self-reliance versus reliance on family, neighborhood, and community?
   - To what degree is interaction with others reflected by values promoting assertive competition for scarce resources versus values reflecting cooperative interdependency?
   - Does social status reflect sharp boundaries between "us" and "them"?
   - To what degree is social mobility viewed as a permanent or a shifting status?
4. Personal orientation toward life goals
   - To what degree do the social rules of engagement reflect the concept of individualism and fair play versus communalism and fair share?
   - Does goal achievement reflect an attitude valuing personal optimizing and being first or an attitude valuing group affiliation and team achievement?

5. Personal orientation toward social responsibilities
   - Does the sense of social responsibility primarily attend to the causation of problems and sources of situational risks or to the conditions to be addressed and the issues to be resolved?
   - Are work, wealth, and material goods valued as part of self or as resources for self and others?

Cultures often interlock as individuals from varied backgrounds come together. An Anglo social worker, for example, with a future time perspective may become very annoyed with a Mexican American, present-oriented client who does not conserve her money to last throughout the month. This client, in turn, may become irritated with the social worker, who is seen as taking too much time to collect data before providing a direct service. A Pakistani American family oriented to the notion of extended family and collective family space may ignore the social worker's point that simultaneous and lengthy visits by grandparents, siblings, spouse, children, nieces, and nephews to a 35-year-old daughter in a semi-private hospital room are intruding on the personal space, health care expectations, and comfort level of the room's other occupant.

The well-being of ethnic group members, however, is contingent on more than the group's values and stability. It is dependent on economic and familial survival. It is also affected by the interactions of members' personal characteristics with cultural norms and expectations, the status of the ethnic subgroup, and the fit of the ethnic subgroup with the dominant culture. Cultural resources, such as family supports and religious affiliation, offer shields from adverse consequences of stress related to tensions in ethnic group membership. The common tension polarities that confront all minority group members have been identified as (1) oppression versus liberation, (2) powerlessness versus empowerment, (3) exploitation versus parity, (4) assimilation versus acculturation, and (5) stereotyping versus individuality (Lum, 1996, 1999; Pedersen, 1997). To work with minorities, social workers need to understand these existing tensions and provide the support necessary to empower minorities to speak, act, and assume responsibility for themselves as they organize to overcome particular tensions. Rather than expecting assimilation or conformity to exploitation, social workers demonstrate an understanding of each minority group and multicultural appreciation by supporting a client system's efforts to achieve cultural maintenance, empowerment, and parity.

Religion and Spirituality.   Religion, spirituality, and faith play important roles in different cultures. *Religion* refers to an "institutionalized pattern of beliefs, behaviors, and experiences, oriented toward spiritual concerns, shared by a community and transmitted over time in traditions" (Canda & Furman, 1999, p. 37). *Religious affiliation* refers to group membership in a formal institutional system of religious beliefs and practices. Although *spirituality* may be expressed through religious forms, it is understood as related "to a universal and fundamental aspect of what it is to be human—to search for a sense of meaning, purpose, and moral frameworks for relating with self, others, and the ultimate reality" (Canda & Forman, 1999, p. 37). As an essential human quality, spirituality is concerned with the development of meaning, moral values, and a relationship with a higher power. *Faith* refers to personal beliefs and relationship with a greater being. *Mystical experiences* transcend the human capacity for thinking and expression and involve "direct, personal encounters with aspects of reality that are beyond the limits of language and reason to express" (Canda & Furman, 1999, p. 40). Personal experience of the sacred mysteries may be part of faith.

Religion, spirituality, and faith each reflect multiple levels of religious identification and value commitments. At their core are the essential cultural beliefs and attitudes that comprise the central ideas and feelings to which value commitments are attached. At the next level, the outward form of this belief system is the ethic, or body of moral principles and spiritual beliefs, that reflects both core religious values and religiously influenced values on matters of daily living involving self and others, social roles and human interaction, achievement and work, and material goods and money. At the third or middle level, religious value orientations are embodied in the organizational structures of church, temple, synagogue, or sect. The codified policies of the fourth level reflect the formal institutionalized values of organized religion. The fifth and last level of religious identification and value commitments involves institutionally sanctioned religious practices (Tropman, 1999). At each of these five levels, members of a religious group may adhere to the essence of the cultural values and belief systems or to very specific and concrete ritualistic representations and procedures.

Increasingly, attention is being addressed to the impact of group membership in mainstream religions (Judaism, Christianity, Islam, Buddhism), alternative religions, and newer religious movements on the personal faith beliefs and the ordinary and extraordinary life experiences and choices of client, action, and target systems. This impact is apparent in the members' perceptions of their problems and needs, in their use of formal and informal support and advocacy systems, and in their actions to solve problems, achieve empowerment, overcome adversity, mobilize resources, meet needs, and achieve aspirations. Indeed, spiritual beliefs and values are often key determinants in client, action, and target systems' thinking, feeling, and acting in relation to environmental circumstances and major life events such as the following:

- Getting married, using reproductive technology, having children, rearing children, staying married
- Selecting an occupation, accepting certain kinds of employment, losing employment, changing jobs
- Coping with personal losses of family and friends, illness and trauma, community disasters
- Living in poverty, obtaining education and job training, finding housing, using day care

In addition, many of the larger social issues addressed in macro practice have religious dimensions. For example, societal provision of basic food, clothing, and shelter for the poor is tied up in centuries-old, value-laden issues of who is worthy to receive community aid. Similarly, today's capitation practices of managed care affect health care rationing and service provision to poor families as well as child welfare services to children most in need.

As noted in Chapter 1, social work and religion are connected historically and philosophically. At the operational level of practice method, however, the social work profession has not yet fully clarified the role of spirituality and faith in engagement, data collection, assessment, intervention, evaluation, and termination. Nor has the profession systematically addressed which spiritual or faith-based practices (such as religious literature, prayer, meditation, religious ritual, to name a few) are effective with which client, action, or target systems. A small cadre of scholars began to address these issues in the 1950s (Biestek, 1957; Spencer, 1956). A few more joined them in the 1970s and 1980s (Berl, 1979; Canda, 1983; Cornett, 1982; Joseph, 1975, 1987, 1988; Keith-Lucas, 1972, 1985; Loewenberg, 1988). More recently, this early cadre of scholars has expanded in number, productivity, and nuance of issues associated with policy and practice (Bullis, 1996; Canda, 1998; Canda & Furman, 1999; Cnaan, 1999; Derezotes, 1995; Garland & Conrad, 1990; Graham, Kaiser, & Garrett, 1998; Joseph, 1997; Siporin, 1990; Smith, 1995; Sullivan, 1994; Sullivan, 1992).

In problem-solving situations in which it is appropriate to address the underlying spiritual nature of the dilemma and inherent religiously based value conflicts, the social worker first gains an understanding of the client system's religious and spiritual beliefs, traditions, and ritual practices and then learns about any related federal laws or court rulings. For example, the natural hallucinogen of the peyote plant may be used in Native American ceremonials, animal sacrifices are part of Santeria faith practices, and religious cults may act to isolate members from the outside world (Bullis, 1996). These and other somewhat unusual religious practices and rituals are afforded First Amendment protection when they are central to the spiritual belief system of a particular organized religion. In all circumstances, however, the client system's spiritual beliefs are the major determinants in social work service provision in relation to a wide variety of life decisions. Each decision reflects client system choices that advance certain values at the expense of others. The rights guaranteed by the First Amendment and the social work ethic of the right of client systems to self-determination guarantee their right and responsibility in making their own value-based choices and being accountable for the consequences. It is clear that the social worker should not engage in professional practices that have the potential to harm client systems or their environments, convey the appearance of trying to convert a client system to the social worker's own religious beliefs, or employ professional practices that do not have demonstrated efficacy.

It is also clear that social workers in secular and sectarian settings have an obligation to work within and carry out agency policy concerning the role of spirituality in social service delivery in that agency and, in the case of public agencies, to follow the laws and judicial system rulings that govern the separation of church and state. Agency governing boards have a fiduciary right and responsibility to assure that agency funds are being spent as directed by explicit agency mission. These and other governing board policies have been upheld by the judicial system. The right of client systems to rely on the fit between explicit agency mission, social work services, and practice methods has also been supported by the social work profession. When a social worker ethically disagrees with an agency service delivery position based in a particular religious value orientation, she or he has a professional obligation to make an explicit decision and take one of the following courses of action:

- Seek to understand the reasons for and adhere responsibly and professionally to agency policy in day-to-day social work practice.
- Request and work for a policy change (which may not be possible if the issue in a sectarian agency is central to the mission or if the issue in a public agency is legally regulated).
- Register a complaint to administration, explain the professional/personal dilemma, and ask to be reassigned to a different service unit within the agency.
- Register a complaint to administration, explain the professional/personal dilemma, and resign.

Help-Seeking Behavior.   Distress is both a personal and a communal experience. It is shared when client systems want relief and help. Receiving and giving help are part of day-to-day caring experiences and involve preferences, choices, and decision making by client systems as to how they manage their lives. Help-seeking behavior involves (1) selecting specific others to provide assistance, confirm decisions, and offer advice; (2) communicating about needs, wants, and preferences; and (3) setting goals and problem solving.

Help-seeking attitudes are reflected in the client system's cultural values about self-sufficiency, type of help sought, and preferred patterns of problem solving and communicating. For example, Asian Americans of Japanese and Korean ancestry are likely to view persons with psychological problems as weaklings and the need to seek help for mental health problems as shameful (LeResche, 1992; Tamura & Lau, 1992). They attribute mental illness to supernatural forces (displeasure of ancestral spirits, spirit intrusion, somatic-natural condition) and tend to deal with such problems by internalizing them to avoid a loss of face. They are often distrustful of professional helpers (Duryea & Gundison, 1993). Such beliefs share much in common with those of Native Americans but the approach to treatment differs markedly. Whereas Native Americans often turn to indigenous folk healers (medicine men), Asians usually consider family care to be the most logical and effective treatment, as the cause is believed to be primarily interpersonal disharmony within the family. Jewish Americans, by contrast, freely seek help, including psychotherapy, as they view mental health problems as the result of individual unresolved intrapsychic forces (McGoldrick, Garcia-Preto, Hines, & Lee, 1989). African Americans (Boyd-Franklin, 1989), Asian and Pacific Americans (Yamashiro & Matsuoka, 1997), Caribbean Africans (Brice-Baker, 1996), and Latinos (Griffith & Villavicencio, 1985; McMiller & Weisz, 1996), on the other hand, prefer to seek help from family, friends, and churches. They may perceive questions as prying and intrusive, become belligerent and inarticulate, and require more time than Caucasian Americans to trust and become comfortable with a professional helper. European Americans usually prefer to seek help first from extended family members, religious organizations, and neighborhood clinic associations (Lee, 1996; McMiller & Weisz, 1996).

Different cultural communication styles may result in miscommunication and misunderstanding. In many Native American cultures, for example, direct eye contact is considered insulting and is avoided, whereas avoiding eye contact seems evasive and dishonest to European Americans. Many Asian cultures expect a period of polite conversation at the beginning of a visit to a professional. Rushing to the reason for the visit without some exchange of pleasantries is considered rude. Some cultures place importance on silence as a form of respect; others tend to be very expressive. Symbolic behaviors (such as time orientation, social distance, spacing, touching, facial expression, and gesturing) vary dramatically from culture to culture (Lefley & Pedersen, 1986; Pedersen, 1997).

Effective communication with client systems involves good verbal retention skills, high level of awareness of nonverbal behaviors, and an understanding of the cultural context of the language. Individuals learn their first or native language (or regional dialect) at an early age and at home. Thus, the first language is associated with intimacy, spontaneity, and informality. When speaking in their native language or dialect, client systems tend to be more emotionally open and expressive than in their second language or standard English (Kochman, 1981). A social worker's use of native language in conjunction with standard English directly affects a client system's perception of the social worker's credibility and the degree to which they demonstrate a change in attitudes and behaviors (Lum & Lu, 1999).

Social workers need to be aware that patterns of communication are bound in culture and experience and that client systems differ in the way they assign meanings to words, say things, and express themselves with gestures. Sensitivity to these differences is necessary in engaging people from different cultural backgrounds. Social workers, therefore, need to assess presenting problem(s) and need(s) based on the client system's

- Own language used to label a problem and express a need
- Symbolic meaning assigned to the problem and need
- Typical patterns of communication in presenting self and seeking help
- Prior experience with help seeking
- Expectation for self-sufficiency
- Orientation toward professional or indigeneous care and use of resources
- Own criteria for deciding whether satisfactory solution has been achieved

Self-Assessment of Cultural Sensitivity

In the General Method of social work practice, a sensitivity to cultural diversity may be demonstrated within each stage of the process. A social worker's sensitivity to the culture of a client, action, or target system is reflected in the way in which that social worker (1) engages the system of contact in identifying problems and needs, (2) collects data and makes an assessment and contract, (4) intervenes, (5) evaluates, and (6) terminates. Timing, communications, and actions show the extent to which a social worker realizes the value orientations of a culture. The social worker's attitude and approach also indicate an awareness of the pressures and problems that persist in the lives of persons from diverse ethnic cultures.

EXERCISE **3.1**

Cultural-Sensitivity Exercise

1. What is your cultural background?
2. Do you identify with a particular ethnic group?
3. Select an ethnic group you come the closest to identifying with, and describe the group's customary behaviors regarding each of the following:
   a. Role of father, mother, children, and extended family members
   b. Dating patterns
   c. Eating patterns
   d. Education
   e. Death and dying
4. How do you feel about your ethnic identity? What are the strengths and weaknesses you perceive in your ethnic group?
5. What ethnic groups lived in your home environment when you were growing up? How did your family relate to families of other ethnic groups (consider attitudes, experiences, power relationships; i.e., was one dependent on, or subordinate to, another)?
6. What are your earliest memories of meeting people of minority groups (i.e., African American, American Indian, Asian Pacific American, Hispanic)? How did your family relate to people of minority groups? (Consider attitudes, power relationships, experiences.)
7. Are your feelings about your own ethnic group related to any power relationship you experienced with other ethnic groups?
8. Are your feelings about *other* ethnic groups related to any power relationships you experienced with other ethnic groups?
9. With someone from a different ethnic background, compare your ethnic groups according to the factors given in item 3.
10. How do your feelings for your ethnic group compare with this person's feelings for his or her ethnic group?

For effective multicultural practice, a social worker needs to be consciously aware of his or her own culture as well as that of the client, action, or target system receiving service. Continued growth in self-awareness enables a social worker to recognize and appreciate the nuances within and among diverse cultures and begin to identify his or her own ethnocentric attitudes. As noted earlier, *ethnocentrism* is basically the belief that one's own ethnic group has the only appropriate and acceptable practices, values, and customary behaviors.

In Exercise 3.1, questions are proposed for reflection and discussion. The purpose of the exercise is to enhance cultural sensitivity and self-awareness. Through identifying, sharing, and comparing the facts, feelings, and experiences addressed in the exercise, social workers may gain a more empathic understanding of diverse groups.

Social Pluralism

Knowledge of multiculturalism alone, however, does not provide sufficient understanding of the world view and the value frame of reference of a client, action, or target system to be contacted. Within cultural groups, expressions of values and behavior vary along social structures that comprise systems of socialization, social control, social gratification, and social change. These social structural dimensions include socioeconomic class, poverty, political power, and community environment characteristics. Together, these social structures convey the social status or social worth of a person or group in the view of others.

Concepts and Discussion

Socioeconomic Class and Parity. The U.S. economy involves the production, distribution, and consumption of goods and services. The institutions that operationalize the U.S. economy are founded on principles of economic capitalism that include the pursuit of profit and private ownership. These principles evoke specific societal conditions and a dual labor market that includes (1) a primary labor market characterized by high wages, opportunities for advancement, benefits, and rules of due process that protect employment rights and (2) a secondary labor market characterized by low wages, little opportunity for advancement, few benefits, and minimal job protection. Although beginning to change, the primary labor market is dominated by white males; the secondary market consists primarily of women, minorities, and the working poor of all backgrounds. Apparent changes in the economic structure in the twenty-first century include new information technologies based on increasingly sophisticated computer hardware and software, increasing global economic interdependence, and the growing dominance of the information and service sectors over basic industrial manufacturing. These changes are associated with a high demand for increasingly specialized knowledge and skills and excellent wages. At the same time, however, there is structural unemployment, many low–income-generating employment options, and changes in the distribution pattern of jobs.

Although salaries and stock options together with a rising stock market have increased the wealth of those at the top, the wages of the majority have stagnated in comparison, and medical and pension benefits have declined. In addition, many U.S. workers have experienced a sharp slowdown in income with the advent of corporate downsizing, increased use of temporary workers, declining union membership and clout, fewer well-paid industry jobs, and increased difficulties in making an adequate living through farming. Together, these economic data trends suggest a shrinkage of the middle class and a narrowing of avenues for social mobility. Thus, these changes appear to be reinforcing the *status quo* and are not likely to enable the poor and working poor to achieve economic and social parity.

Socioeconomic class involves more than the amount of money and economic security available to a person, family, group, or community. It is a socially constructed perspective that reflects an understanding of the world, where a person fits within it, and a distinctive lifestyle. Social class is identified through such variables as income, occupation, education, residence, and group identification. Socioeconomic class is all encompassing and reflected in how a person thinks, acts, talks, looks, dresses, moves, and walks; in the shops, businesses, and restaurants patronized; in the friendships made; and in the schools attended, jobs attained, and neighborhoods lived in. It affects what persons have as available choices and what they perceive the choices to be (Farley, 1994). The social patterns attributed to groups on the basis of lower socioeconomic status or class level, however, may also be explained as a reaction to environmental conditions (Wright, 1985).

In the myth of a classless U.S. society, intelligence and ambition are highlighted as responsible for life success. Such a myth creates a false sense of hope or expectation that an individual and family can experience different life opportunities and get ahead. This hope and the occasional well-publicized success story tend to keep the hierarchical class structure in place and to place the blame for not moving up on the individual. Yet the reality is that class-based societal structures keep the poor and the working class locked into social positions of servitude. If class-oppressed people believe in equality of opportunity, they are likely to internalize the blame for their socioeconomic position and less likely to develop conscious awareness of socially imposed class limitations (Erikson & Goldthorpe, 1993).

Conversely, the myth of a classless society also keeps middle- and upper-class individuals and families entrenched in the socioeconomic privileges available. That is, the myth reinforces their beliefs that their privileges must be deserved due to their own personal merits and superiority and therefore are to be enjoyed and defended. In those instances in which their economic status may decline, they still have the language, thought, and behavior patterns to fall back on. Thus, they maintain the privilege of choice.

Personal well-being is contingent on economic survival and family and social stability. The accumulation of material goods and wealth provides a person with more options, opportunities, freedom, and leisure time. Accumulation of wealth is also associated with greater influence and power over others. Inequality of social resources brings with it a wide range of associated differences that may impact the social functioning of individuals, families, groups, organizations, and communities.

When people experience *classism*, it is both because they lack money, choices, and power and because of the way they think, talk, act, move, and make decisions.

The point where socioeconomic class and ethnicity intersect represents *ethnic reality*, or the socioeconomic cultural environment that influences the behaviors and dispositions of individuals, families, groups, and communities. These dispositions arise out of a group's (1) cultural values, as embodied in its history, rituals, and religion; (2) migration experiences; (3) encounters with mainstream culture; (4) approach to family organization; and (5) language adaptation (Erikson & Goldthorpe, 1993; Franklin, 1985). As ethnicity and socioeconomic class interlock, the client system experiences pressures and forces that arise from the incongruence between the two. For example, although a family may have moved into a higher social class (blue-collar to white-collar occupation, public to private school, smaller to bigger house, less well-off to wealthier neighborhood), family members may not be given full participation in the politics and activities of their new social environment because of their ethnicity and recently achieved socioeconomic strata. To the degree that the family's ethnicity is perceived as a devalued one by the majority of the community culture, the family may not to be accorded political power and access to environmental resources.

Consequently, social class is closely related to minority status because it addresses social stratification, or the hierarchical arrangement of persons based on economics, power, and status differences. Although people of color are often class-bound due to racial discrimination as well as socioeconomic differences, not all within a group are equally oppressed in respect to education, position in the occupational structure, and income. For example, although the adult Vietnamese community has fared poorly in California, their children's legendary success has become part of the common folklore (Caplan, Choy, & Whitmore, 1992; Jiobu, 1988).

Members of different ethnic groups with a history of poverty and discrimination move into segments of the middle class at varying rates. When the number of a particular group who make the upward transition is relatively small, those in the newfound position feel the lack of opportunity to interact with others like themselves. Consequently, the opportunity to share common experiences is limited and detrimental to all members of that particular ethnic group (Davis & Proctor, 1989).

Although ethnicity and culture provide motivation and a source of strength for individuals who draw on their ethnic identity and cultural beliefs, their minority status and social class struggles continually reinforce negative determinism in their move toward social equality and social justice. The culturally competent social worker must be aware of the dynamics of the prejudice and discrimination that accompany the ethnic acculturation process and the struggle for parity. *Prejudice* refers to a person's unfavorable beliefs and attitudes toward a particular group. *Discrimination*, by contrast, refers to behavioral actions that deprive a group of basic rights and opportunities. Prejudice does not always lead to discrimination. It is possible to discriminate against people without outright prejudice as, for example, when people act out of ignorance and insensitivity.

Prejudices tend to diminish or disappear when people have frequent personal contacts with each other. As people are subjected to the test of actual experience, supposed stereotypical beliefs or even real differences among people tend to shrink because people become much more aware of their similarities than their differences. Social workers themselves have, at times, been the objects of prejudice, stereotyping, and discrimination when they were labeled "do-gooders" or "flaming liberals" and paid less than other helping professionals in the human service field. Prejudice and stereotyping are antithetical to the value of affirming the uniqueness and individuality of people. Social work's commitment to promoting individuality and affirming the validity of individual experience are part of the essential components in any client system's gaining empowerment and parity.

Environment and Community Differences.   A knowledge of distinguishing characteristics of community environments helps social workers better understand the people of particular localities and the interactions and interrelationships that take place between different people and different environments. As brought out in the ecological-systems perspective, an environment is affected by the persons contained within it and, conversely, persons are affected by their environments. More specifically, an environment's growth is directly influenced by the endowment, personalities, values, and functioning of its residents. Interdependently, the growth and development of people are directly influenced by the nature, resources, values, and functioning of their environments. Thus, an understanding of rural, urban, and suburban localities can help a social worker become aware of diverse ways in which environments and persons may affect each other. If an individual, family, group, organization, or community is located in a rural environment, for example, their needs, experiences, values, resources, and development may be very different from those in urban or suburban areas.

Historically, the term *rural* has been used to refer to the country or to mean countrylike. Rural localities are often defined in terms of low population density (2,500–50,000 inhabitants) and relative isolation. *Urban* is a term that pertains to the city or things that are citylike. It is generally used to describe a highly populated area (over 50,000). Other factors that have been used to distinguish rural from urban areas include income sources and occupations (agriculture and agribusiness versus business and industry), lifestyle (simple versus complex), and structure and number of available human resources (highly structured and numerous versus informal and sparse) (Ginsberg, 1998). In 1995, 75.2 percent of the U.S. population lived in urban areas, as compared with 24.8 percent living in rural areas (U.S. Bureau of the Census, 1995).

The outlying regions of cities that often bridge urban and rural areas are called suburbs. Legally and demographically, a *suburb* is defined as an incorporated municipality within a standard metropolitan statistical area (SMSA) other than a central city (Lineberry, 1975). Although apparent changes are taking place in suburbia today, the definition traditionally has included a stereotypical conception of "familism, child-centeredness, single-family dwelling units, sharp segregation of workplace from residence, organizational consciousness . . . overlaid by a distinct touch of affluence" (Lineberry, 1975, p. 2).

General characteristics make urban, suburban, and rural localities distinguishable from one another. Urban locations, for example, generally offer various organized human services that are highly structured, with clearly stated policies and procedures. Rural areas may be devoid of formal, professional services but usually contain informal, natural helping networks that provide assistance. Whereas the power structure of an urban area may be described as pluralistic, with several complex interacting systems, the power structure of a rural area may be seen as elitist, with community decision makers often not holding formal positions of authority (see Figure 3.1). There is often a blurring of boundaries between political and sociocultural life in homogeneous rural communities (Ginsberg, 1998). The laws and procedures of an urban legal control system are more explicitly articulated and executed than those of a rural area; in the latter, informal means of regulation are frequently preferred for solving local problems (Johnson, 1993).

The central and distinguishing problems of rural areas often include generational poverty, rigid conservative mores and thinking, an increasing loss of youth from the area, and 60 percent of the nation's substandard housing (Conger & Elder, 1994; Farley, Griffiths, Skidmore, & Thackeray, 1982). By contrast, core problems for those who live in the city have been described in terms of depersonalization, loss of individuality, and inadequate housing options. From the Model Cities Programs of the 1960s War on Poverty to the present, federal programs to improve inner-city ghettoes have had only short-term success at best. By contrast, grass-roots community groups working to improve their surroundings have achieved some success. One exemplar is a public housing project in Macon, Georgia, in which the Housing Authority used community organization principles of self-help, empowerment, responsibility, and dignity to enable families to move toward self-sufficiency and to integrate public housing residents and their agendas into the mainstream political and social service policy-making circles of the community (Center for Visionary Leadership, 1998).

In recent years, urban development has led to the renovation of many old buildings in cities. These structures have been changed into upper- or upper-middle-class condominiums or apartments. As a result of such gentrification, poor and lower-middle-class city residents are often unable to find local housing. The absence of low-income housing in urban and suburban areas and the resistance by

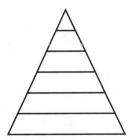 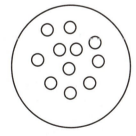

FIGURE 3.1   Power Structures

suburban residents to building such housing, along with the presence of restrictive zoning laws, have contributed to the contemporary housing crisis for the urban poor. Social workers have found that when low-income persons are relocated to surrounding areas, they often have problems locating transportation to and from their place of employment and needed human services.

People from rural areas discuss their problems and seek out professional help less readily than those from urban and suburban localities (Conger & Elder, 1994; Coward & Dwyer, 1993; Wijnberg & Colca, 1981). Spillover and conflicts from events of the past often run deep, affect the present-day behavior of rural residents, and create barriers to community problem solving and collaborative work. When informal networks are not providing the assistance needed, and social workers are not accepted by certain individuals in rural communities, a social worker may try to work cooperatively and collaboratively with the local power structure of community leaders and neighbors in order to connect the client system-in-need with a particular resource. For example, if a family is suffering because of problems such as mental illness or alcoholism and refuses to discuss its problems with a social worker, then the natural support systems of local clergy, doctor, or a friend may be willing to speak with the family to sanction the services of the social worker and to mobilize the network of nontraditional service providers such as informal caregivers, mutual self-help groups, church sisterhoods, or voluntary service groups.

In urban or suburban areas, a somewhat similar but more formal approach is used when indigeneous leaders or paraprofessionals are hired to serve as outreach workers to link services with persons-in-need. The generalist in the metropolis is usually better able to locate specialized services to help with problems such as those described in the earlier example (i.e., mental illness or alcoholism). In a rural area, however, the social worker may be the only professional resource available. It may be possible to work directly with the family, or it may be necessary to develop a program or write a grant to bring the needed service into the area. During the 1980s, severe economic losses in rural areas, particularly in farm communities, led to a decrease in informal social interactions and an increase in family breakdown. Major withdrawals of federal financial supports, soaring interest rates, declining prices, and rising surpluses have led to an increasing number of farm foreclosures and bankruptcies. Rural land values have declined up to 50 percent and more (Campbell, 1985; Fitchen, 1981). The economic crisis of farmers has been little understood; it has resulted in a high incidence of depression, family violence, and suicide. As stated by one farmer, "The loss of the land is not just the loss of one's job, it's the loss of one's life" (O'Neil & Ball, 1987, p. 2). This feeling exists especially when the land has belonged to a family for several generations. The farmer who experiences property foreclosure by a bank usually sees this as both a personal loss and a family disgrace.

Existing services in rural areas, such as Agricultural Extension Programs or Farm Bureaus, are often unable to cope effectively with the financial, social, and emotional crises facing poverty-stricken rural communities. Human service professionals and social service programs have made some efforts to join with such services in reaching out to farmers in crisis. They have helped farmers organize groups to advocate fairer policies and prices and locate other sources of income (Martinez-Brawley, 1980, 1987; Martinez-Brawley & Blundell, 1989). Although migrant workers or farm laborers and farm owners have frequently been adversaries in the past, the threat of losing the land has provided an opportunity to bring the two groups together to work for the common goal of keeping the farm operating and their livelihoods intact.

Whereas specialists are utilized in urban localities, generalists have been recognized as the most appropriate practitioners for rural communities (Ginsberg, 1998). In applying the General Method when working in a rural area, a social worker would find it helpful to have knowledge of rural economics (agriculture, mining, industry), regional planning and development, labor organizations, employment patterns, and relationships between public administration and services and also local rural governments and services (Conger & Elder, 1994; Martinez-Brawley & Blundell, 1989). In addition, a social worker in a rural area needs to be sensitive to local etiquette, folkways, values, the probable strong suspicion of outsiders, and the presence of natural helping networks. As Jenkins and Cook (1961, p. 415) point out:

> Agents of formal services often try to impose a program designed for an urban setting on rural people, ignoring rural values and attitudes. The professional worker frequently fails to respect the local residents who serve as natural helpers. Conversely, those in the natural helping network tend to reject the detached, professional behavior of the formal helper, preferring to "take care of their own."

A social worker in an urban or suburban area should have some understanding of the political struggles that take place in their localities over the metropolitan turf (Lineberry, 1975). As the subsystems in an urban or suburban area (whether they are organizations, cultural groups, churches, or geographic communities) compete for space and power in order to live out their values and aspirations, they frequently become involved with the complex political system. Political power, coalitions, public policy, and legal regulation are among the tools used in suburban and urban areas to secure and maintain land and resources.

Cities have been economically drained as people and many businesses have moved to suburbia. As suburbs have been incorporated with strict zoning, land-use restrictions, and population growth controls, the boundary lines between the suburbs and the central city have been tightened and the number and types of people allowed to enter suburban borders have been increasingly proscribed by suburban localities. While a decrease in suburban growth may result from existing discrimination, increasing growth controls, and resistance to growth, such a decrease may also reflect a depressed national economy or local energy shortage. Social workers need to be aware of attempts that have been made to consolidate or coordinate city and suburban governments. In some instances, consolidation has resulted in a loss of space and resources for particular groups. Through an understanding of urban politics, social workers are better able to assist and support local groups and individuals in organizing to advocate for fair distribution of finite resources within a locality.

EXERCISE 3.2
Value System Index

Assumptions	Totally Disagree 0	1	2	3	4	Totally Agree 5
1. Human beings are responsible for their own success or failure.						
2. Human nature is basically evil, but it can be overcome by an act of will.						
3. The primary purpose of society is to fulfill human needs, both material and emotional.						
4. If human needs were fulfilled, then we would attain goodness, maturity, adjustment, and productivity, and most of society's problems would be solved.						
5. Human beings are fallible but at the same time are capable of acts of great courage or unselfishness.						
6. People are capable of choice, in the "active and willing" sense, but may need help in making their choices.						
7. The primary purpose of life is the acquisition of material prosperity, which people achieve through hard work.						
8. The primary purpose of society is the maintenance of law and order, which make this acquisition possible.						
9. What hampers people from attaining fulfillment is external circumstance, not in general under their control.						
10. These circumstances are subject to manipulation by those possessed of sufficient technical and scientific knowledge, using the scientific method.						
11. Love is always the ultimate victor over force.						
12. The greatest good lies in terms of people's relationships with their fellows and with their creator.						
13. Unsuccessful or deviant individuals are not deserving of help, although efforts should be made up to a point to rehabilitate them or to spur them to greater efforts on their own behalf.						
14. Humanity and society are ultimately perfectible.						
15. Human beings are created beings; one of their major problems is that they act as if they were not and try to be autonomous.						
CP 1, 2, 7, 8, 13 HPU 3, 4, 9, 10, 14 JC 5, 6, 11, 12, 15						

Knowledge, skills, and experience beyond those of an entry-level generalist may be needed both by the social worker who becomes involved with urban or suburban politics or who works in a rural area with extensive problems, no formal service delivery system, and the limited natural helping networks. The rural social worker would very likely be expected to assume service roles in administration, teaching, program development, and policy formation in addition to direct practice. The urban social worker would need to have expertise in the use of the various political tools cited earlier.

The social worker with a sensitivity to diversity in environments comes to a geographic area with more realistic expectations and preparation. Social workers who are realistically prepared are then better able to help client systems, as well as to help themselves cope, develop professionally, and bring about change in the environment (Jones & Zlotnick, 1998).

Self-Assessment of Sensitivity
to Social Pluralism

Social workers and social welfare systems, as well as client systems and other work-related systems, may have contrasting values. On this point, Keith-Lucas (1972) identifies three major types of value systems found in U.S. society: (1) capitalist-puritan (CP), (2) humanist-positivist-utopian (HPU), and (3) Judeo-Christian (JC). Basic assumptions for each of these three value systems are given in Exercise 3.2. Capitalist-puritan value assumptions are described in items 1, 2, 7, 8, and 13 of the exercise. Humanist-positivist-utopian assumptions are given in items 3, 4, 9, 10, and 14. Assumptions of the Judeo-Christian system are indicated in items 5, 6, 11, 12, and 15. Completion of the instrument and summation of the item scores for each of the three major value assumptions provide a self-assessment of a social worker's underlying value orientations. Usually, a social worker is dominant in one but not totally identified with any value system. This exercise helps social workers grow in awareness of their own values and in sensitivity to the diversity of value systems that often conflict in human service delivery.

Socio-Demographic Variability

In addition to multiculturalism and social pluralism, human variability is influenced by endowment and personality as well as socio-demographic variance in age and developmental stage, gender, sexual orientation, and challenges in mental and physical ability.

Concepts and Discussion

Endowment and Personality.   *Endowment and personality* are additional diversity variables of *person*. The endowment of a person is a major contributor to his or her bio-psychosocial development and personality. *Endowment* refers to the natural gifts, talents, and abilities that a person has at birth. Genetic traits and characteristics, along with the innate mental, physical, and cognitive abilities of a person, are included. Genetic influences include mental and physical growth potential, ability to tolerate stress, and ways of responding to stress. Personality development takes place in human beings as they use endowment and interact with others in their environment. Basically, personality is influenced by (1) the endowment of a person, (2) the inherent qualities and opportunities found within a person's environment, and (3) the transactions that take place between person and environment. The personality of a human being consists of the combination and integration of characteristics and experiences that give a person his or her unique personhood. Social workers realize that a person's behavior and problems may relate to individual endowment and personality as well as to culture, class, sexual orientation, age, and developmental stage.

Age and Developmental Stage.   Human systems are in process and naturally go through various stages in their evolution. Human systems also form complex wholes with diverse functions that may progress independently of each other. The knowledge base of the social worker includes theories about the developmental processes that take place physically, socially, sexually, cognitively, spiritually, and morally in a person. Although an individual may be at one age chronologically, he or she may not be at a corresponding bio-psychosocial stage developmentally along one or all functioning dimensions. For example, a 12-year-old youngster may be operating at a 3-year-old level cognitively, or a 30-year-old may be functioning psychosocially at a developmental level similar to that of an adolescent.

Using knowledge of human development in the social environment, the social worker considers the bio-psychosocial and spiritual developmental level at which a person is functioning from the multidimensional perspective of *person*. In Table 3.1, conceptualizations for considering stages of development according to complementary theories are outlined and juxtaposed. When a lag is observed in any dimension of development, the social worker may have a beginning idea of the needs, problems, and tasks confronting the person at that time. A social worker should keep in mind that each person's development is unique and that a number of interrelated and interacting factors contribute to and direct development. These factors include endowment, culture, and gender.

Sensitivity to age and developmental stage helps the social worker find the most appropriate way to communicate with a client, action, or target system and to understand the problems and challenges each may be facing. There are distinct communication approaches that are more effective than others when working with particular age groups. For example, small children (approximately up to age 3) have been helped through directly involving the child's parents or significant others in providing the service. The social worker supports the parent figure, who works directly with the child. Children from approximately ages 4 through 11 often find it difficult to carry on a verbal conversation with a new adult. They are used to having adults teach, direct, or parent them. Social workers are usually more effective with children at this age when they communicate through the use of play. For adolescents (ages 12 to 17), a challenging type of play—such as sports,

TABLE 3.1   A Multidimensional Perspective of Human Development

Age	Physical	Psychosexual	Psychosocial	Cognitive	Moral	Spiritual
0–3	Marked growth; teething (6–8 months); crawling (9–12 months); self-feeding; walking (1–); bowel and bladder control (2–1)	Oral stage (0–1) Anal stage (1–3)	Trust versus mistrust (0–1) Autonomy versus shame and doubt (1–3)	Sensorimotor stage (0–18 months) Object permanence (18 months)	Preconventional level Stage 1: Punishment and obedience	Sensing oneness, being cared for
3–6	First permanent teeth; stronger voice; receptive; alert brain; manual and motor power	Phallic (Oedipal stage)	Initiative versus guilt	Preconceptual stage (2–4)	Stage II Naive instrumental hedonism—conformity for reward	Beginning sense separateness, self-will
6–12	Increased muscular ability and coordination; girls' growth rate exceeds boys'	Latency stage	Industry versus inferiority	Intuitive stage (4–7) Concrete-operational stage (7–11)	Conventional level Stage II: "Good boy/good girl" conformity to avoid disapproval Stage IV: Authority, maintaining law and order	Experiencing God's attributes through parents and environment; beginning to hear and use religious words Social responses: formal religious education ritual; loyalty to faith of parents; anthropomorphic religious concepts

(continued)

TABLE 3.1 Continued

Age	Physical	Psychosexual	Psychosocial	Cognitive	Moral	Spiritual
13–18	Girls: Development of breasts, pubic hair, complexion changes, onset of menstruation Boys: Development of pubic hair, sperm, voice changes, complexion changes	Adolescence (genital stage)	Identity versus identity diffusion	Formal-operational (11–15)	Postconventional level Stage V: Morality of contract; standards of society; individual rights	Religious questioning; religious awakening; varying sense of faith; rebelliousness
18–35	Leveling off of growth	Maturity—to love and to work	Intimacy versus isolation		Stage VI: Morality of individual principles of conscience; universal ethical principles	Crisis/conversion experience Affiliation with (or withdrawal from) organized religious sect
35–65	Change in weight distribution; metabolism and sensory abilities slow down; menopause—women		Generativity versus stagnation or self-absorption			Search for and deepening of personal religious experience; active church participation
65–	Marked decrease in motor coordination; taste buds decline; organs begin to dysfunction		Ego integrity versus despair			Deepening of personal religion; finding religion to give meaning and support for death

Note: The primary theorists who have conceptualized the processes and stages identified above are: physical—Theodore Litz; psychosexual—Sigmund Freud; psychosocial—Erik Erikson; cognitive—Jean Piaget; moral—Lawrence Kohlberg; spiritual—Gordon Allport and Maria Joan O'Neil. Specific references for each would be too numerous to print here.

chess, or other game activities—may help reduce their apprehensions. Using peer groups is also an effective way to reach adolescents, as hearing from peers rather than adults is generally more acceptable. The adult, on the other hand, functions in a verbal world. Here, too, however, the social worker needs to be sure that the language and vocabulary used are appropriate for the particular adult client system receiving service. Those who may be considered elderly (over age 65) often feel more secure when the social worker comes to them in their own homes. Yet here, too, depending on need and attitude toward social workers who may be much younger, those who are older may be helped through meeting with elderly colleagues with whom they share common concerns and experiences.

Just as individuals pass through developmental stages, so do human systems containing more than one person (couple, family, group, organization, community). In general, there are six basic stages to this group developmental process: (1) testing/tunneling in, (2) role clarifying, (3) working, (4) reformulating, (5) accomplishing, and (6) terminating. In the beginning stage of testing, system members usually observe and conform. As there is movement for role clarification, power struggles may become apparent. With the acceptance of positioning, purpose, rules, and guidelines, these human systems move into the work stage. As tasks and goals begin to be accomplished, members of the system grow in confidence and may venture out into new behaviors and goals. Reformulating roles and responsibilities may cause tensions and conflicts among members. If communication is open and members are able to change, a more mature, equal, or democratic type of functioning may be reached with a high level of system accomplishment. Eventually, individual members of the group may terminate as a whole. Members often join with outside individuals or human systems to form new functioning units.

Just as a social worker recognizes diversity in the human developmental process, they also recognize the different growth levels of families, groups, organizations, and communities. Such knowledge and sensitivity help a social worker in problem assessment, progress evaluation, and ongoing facilitation of growth and development within various size systems.

Gender

Women.   The predominant patriarchal ideology found in United States society and in other societies fosters institutional sexism through which women have long experienced inequality and victimization. *Sexism* means the subjugation of one sex to another. When the term is used today, it basically refers to women being subordinate to men and to the existing attitudes, policies, and practices that demonstrate this discrimination. The unequal treatment of women and the acceptance of male dominance in society are due to differences in gender roles rather than to physiological differences between the sexes. The definitions of *masculinity* and *femininity* identified by society dictate the expected behavioral patterns for men and women. These behavioral patterns prescribed by society are called *gender roles* (Davis & Proctor, 1989; Romero, 1977). If social workers are to be helpful to women, it is important that they understand the nature and scope of the female gender role as it has evolved within a sexist society.

The socialization, sex-typed life experiences, and role expectations of women differ from those of men. The traditional gender role imposed on a woman as a dependent, long-suffering, conforming, emotionally nurturing, and sweet female has not been a satisfying and health-promoting role for many. Women have often felt constricted and ineffective in this role. They have experienced tensions and conflict that are due to lack of privilege and power. Some women have internalized society's image of themselves and have accepted a self-concept in which they are helpless, inadequate, and submissive. These women often need help to reject their negative self-attributes and to become resocialized as competent and whole persons (Jordan, Kaplan, Miller, Stiver, & Surrey, 1991).

Problems such as rape, incest, battering, and harassment have been concealed and even condoned in society. Women have been found to avoid experiencing success in order to prevent the negative consequences they expected as a result of their accomplishments (Belenky, Clinchy, Goldberger, & Tarule, 1986). In addition, the majority of the U.S. poor are women (Goldberg & Kremen, 1990; Mahaffey, 1976). Evidence shows that employment and promotion opportunities for women are not comparable to those for men. Also, women do not have equal opportunity in the decision-making structures of the job market (Goldberg & Kremen, 1990).

In addition to these problems, some women suffer personally from drinking, drugs, and depression. Although various psychological, physical, economic, and social factors may have an impact on their lives, women with these problems have often expressed strong sentiments of failure as women or helpless feelings of being trapped in a situation where there is no way out (Belle, 1982; Dominelli & McLeod, 1989). Often, a relationship can be found between the personal and social problems of women and the negative societal beliefs and practices against women that exist in their culture and environments.

In the past, service providers worked to help women adjust to their feminine role. Today, however, there is an increasing recognition of the need for social workers to help women become consciously aware of how they have been socialized and to find ways for them to grow in self-actualization. Social workers need to realize that difficulties that in the past may have been identified as individual, personal problems of women are actually a social problem, with a social cause and possible political solution. As a woman discusses her problems with a social worker, she may be surprised and supported in learning that other women have had similar experiences and that, collectively, they are victims of sexism in society (Gutierrez & Lewis, 1999). Through joining together, women have begun to develop a sense of empowerment and to expose the destructive forces they experience. Organized movements—such as the Suffrage Movement, the Women's Trade Union, the National Consumer's League, and the National Organization for Women—have greatly contributed to improving the status of women in U.S. society.

Social workers can help women develop additional coping skills in assertiveness, self-confidence, self-reliance, expression of anger, confrontation, organization, and leadership. A sense of independence can be enhanced if the social worker assumes the role of a facilitator more than that of expert. In the General Method, a collaborative approach is used in which the social worker and the client system engage in a shared problem-solving process. Thus, this method aptly lends itself to working with women in a sensitive responsive manner.

Men.   Whether men are responsible for the development and maintenance of sexism in society can be debated endlessly. However, it is more important for women and for men to become involved in searching out the positives and the potential for both as they go through the process of redefining gender roles. These issues are currently affecting the basic foundation and institutions of U.S. society. Men may struggle with accepting changes in the feminine gender role because such acceptance necessitates their letting go of power and privilege. Nevertheless, there are possible advantages for men if the results of women's liberation include a change in the demands and expectations for men in a sexist society (David & Proctor, 1989).

In essence, men also may be seen as victims of sexism. Having to assume the strong, dominant, breadwinning, protector role has had negative and sometimes fatal effects on men. They have been expected to perform with total success at work and at home. A man's occupation has been seen as his primary status determinant and basic identity. As a result, failure in work is perceived as failure in personhood for many men.

The drive to succeed has also influenced men's suicidal actions. The instruments used by men to commit suicide are more certain to complete the task successfully than those used by women. Over 70 percent of all completed suicides are committed by men (Davis & Proctor, 1989; Goldberg, 1978; Horwitz & Scheid, 1999).

Being cast in the role of a strong male has restricted men's freedom to acknowledge and express emotions. Supportive relationships have been generally limited to a man's wife, with few sustained peer friendships. Even emotional displays with children have been considered out of character for a man. The stress and tensions felt by men and left unexpressed have resulted in stress-related illnesses and an earlier death rate for men than for women. Such problems, directly related to the masculine gender role, can now begin to be identified and possibly resolved if men join in the movement to overcome existing sexism in society. As pointed out by Goldberg (1978, p. 1), "The social revolutions of recent years can lessen the male's time-honored burdens, help him reclaim denied emotion, expand his sensual responsiveness, bring new dimensions of honesty and depth to his heterosexual relationships, as well as alert him to the self-destructive compulsions within him."

Rather than respond openly and hopefully to women's liberation, some men are feeling extremely threatened by the changes they witness in their wives, daughters, friends, and associates. They experience shock, hurt, and fear as women change, compete, and achieve in the workplace, the political field, and the family. Some fight the movement; others react by withdrawal from encounters with women. Although it may be difficult for a man to seek help with his feelings, a sensitive social worker can help him understand and express what he is experiencing. With support, men may begin to see some value in letting go of social norms and moving into a more adult level of collaborative sharing with women.

Contemporary social changes have resulted in a variety of significant problems for men. These may include problems in areas such as custody battles, male single parenting, and fathering after divorce when children remain with their mothers or when parents have joint custody. Social workers are able to help men with these problems through such efforts as counseling and establishing support groups for single fathers.

Although sexism has a direct effect on men and women in U.S. society, the problems of racism and poverty overshadow and compound the situation for minority men and women. Nonwhite males have a shorter life expectancy than all females and all other males (Gary & Leashore, 1982; Horwitz & Scheid, 1999). Black males, in particular, have the highest rate of being victimized by crime and robbery, of experiencing job injuries, of being in low-status service jobs, and of being unmarried. Black male prisoners have stated their desire to be able to care for and to protect their partners and children as others do (O'Neil, 1980–83). The lack of opportunities in society has frequently led them to try to improve their economic status by participating in illegal activities. Social workers can demonstrate sensitivity to the high-risk status of black men through such efforts as promoting community groups to serve as support networks for black males and through advocating social policies that are responsive to their employment and economic needs. Unless efforts to overcome racism and poverty are sustained and achieved, success in gender egalitarianism will be of little significance for poor minority men and women (Davis & Proctor, 1989; Gutierrez & Lewis, 1999).

It is possible that the changes taking place in gender roles may result in new, ongoing problems for men and women in general. Women may go to such an extreme in their efforts to prove their equality with men that they may become engrossed in competition and power struggles. They, too, may develop stress-related illnesses and a lower life expectancy pattern as they suppress feelings and stress achievement. With men changing their masculine role, one development may be a shift toward their demonstrating strength through interpersonal and intellectual skills. This change, however, may prove to be equally stressful for men as they strive for success and mastery in these skill areas.

Instead of evolving into new problems, the movement for change in gender roles can be a reciprocal process that produces growth and gains for both sexes. Social workers may contribute to making this a reality by helping men and women clarify who they are, why they are the way they are, and where they are in the process of becoming. As men and women strive for wholeness, a beneficial goal to work for is the separation of role and status from gender. Emphasis needs to be placed on individuality with an acceptance of flexible roles as appropriate to each situation. Social workers can help men and women develop a definition of self and role that is individualized and sensitive to the person's as well as others' needs and growth. The General Method of social work practice is based on the practice principle of *individuality*. In applying the method to gender issues, a social worker keeps in mind the unique needs and circumstances of each client system.

Self-Assessment of Gender Sensitivity.   As with other types of human diversity, social workers need to be aware of their own personal attitudes and possible stereotypical ideas regarding gender roles. A simple exercise that may assist a student or social worker to grow in self-awareness in this area is found in Exercise 3.3.

Sexual Orientation.   A *homosexual* person has been defined as "one who is motivated in adult life by a definite preferential erotic attraction to members of the same sex and who usually (but not necessarily) engages in overt sexual relations with them" (Marmor, 1980, p. 85). McNaught (1981) describes two primary types of homosexuals: (1) *transitional*—an individual who is basically heterosexual but engages in homosexual behavior when no one of the opposite sex is available (as in prisons or military service) and (2) *constitutional*—an individual whose sexual orientation toward the same sex is set at around the ages of 3 to 5 years.

Basically, *homosexuality* is a general term used to describe men or women. Many homosexual men prefer to be referred to as *gay* and many homosexual women prefer the term *lesbian*. To be gay or lesbian involves psychological and

---

EXERCISE **3.3**

Gender-Sensitivity Questions

1. What would be your immediate reaction when hearing about a 40-year-old woman marrying a 20-year-old man?
2. How do you feel about having a woman in charge of
    a. Your bank (president)
    b. Your place of employment
    c. The military
    d. Your church
    e. The executive branch of the government (president of the United States)
3. Who did the cooking, cleaning, and shopping in your house when you were growing up?
4. Who does the cooking, cleaning, and shopping in your present home?
5. Who do you think should be responsible for household tasks?
6. What do you think of a man who walks out of a door before a woman who is also trying to leave?
7. Do you ever use the expressions
    a. Woman driver
    b. Henpecked husband
    c. Female gossip
    d. Man-sized job
    e. Catty women
    f.   The girls

sociological experiences as well as sexual attractions or behaviors. The individual can be better understood if seen in relation to his or her environment and in relation to those who live within that environment. A term frequently used to describe the negative emotional reactions of heterosexual people toward gay men and lesbians is *homophobia*. This reaction is associated with a deep-rooted fear and accompanying hatred of homosexual lifestyles and individuals. Historically, homosexuality was described in the helping professions as a disturbance or illness. Today, it is referred to as a sexual orientation.

The problems or needs brought to the attention of social workers by gay or lesbian clients are not necessarily related to sexual variations in lifestyle. There are, however, a number of tensions, needs, and problems an individual may experience as a result of being gay or lesbian. A knowledgeable and sensitive social worker may assist the individual in these problematic areas. For example, as a person (at any age) begins to recognize an attraction to members of the same sex or to explore the possibility that he or she may be homosexual, he or she may experience strong feelings of fear, confusion, or guilt. For many, there is no one to turn to for an open, honest discussion about their questions and concerns. Some, particularly adolescents, find the internal conflict so overwhelming that they turn to drugs or suicide (McNaught, 1981). Social workers can be very helpful as individuals struggle over questions about their sexual identity or decision to choose or not choose a gay or lesbian lifestyle, or to "come out" (make their sexual orientation known). Help may be needed in planning when and how they will share their decisions with significant persons in their lives. Coming out can be extremely traumatic for a person unless there has been careful planning with supports available. What is at stake may include the loss of a job, marriage, children, or self-esteem.

Gay or lesbian persons also may seek help from social workers because of problems with interpersonal relationships. Individuals or couples may seek help to decide about improving, maintaining, or terminating a relationship or lifestyle. If two gay or lesbian people decide to make a lifelong commitment to each other, they may ask a social worker to help them find a way to legitimate their relationship. They may not know about relationship contracts or joint wills. Problems and needs may develop after one of the two dies. The remaining partner may need someone else to help him or her grieve over the loss of the other. Biological family members may have legal access to the remaining assets of the deceased. Even if there has been a joint will, the family may contest it.

As lesbian and gay individuals get older, a number of institutional, legal, emotional, and medical problems may emerge. Institutional problems may include housing or nursing home practices that do not permit two nonrelated members to dwell together. If one partner is in a nursing home or hospital, the other may not be allowed to visit or make medical decisions for the institutionalized person without legal documents, such as durable and medical powers of attorney, because there is no legal or blood relationship. Legal problems may include restrictive laws regarding property or wills as well as the absence of laws to prevent discriminatory practices by judges, police, or insurance companies. The emotional problems of elderly lesbians and gays may include feelings of rejection by the gay or lesbian community and feelings of abandonment or loss after the death of a partner. The medical problems of homosexuals at any age may include sexually transmitted diseases (pharyngeal or anal gonorrhea or AIDS, for example).

In addition to the help offered directly by the social worker, lesbian or gay persons may need support and services from a variety of professionals and other systems. As they interact with people in diverse settings, they need to be understood and accepted as unique individuals. Social workers can assist by locating available, appropriate resources for gay and lesbian clients. The resources needed may include knowledgeable and accepting physicians, lawyers, clergy, and insurance companies. Gay men and lesbians also may be enabled to deal with their tensions and problems through active participation in self-help groups, supportive networks, and related political action movements. Sometimes social workers provide services for members of families of gay and lesbian individuals. For example, counseling sessions or groups led by social workers for wives of gay and bisexual men may help them deal with such feelings and issues as anger, betrayal, homophobia, sexuality, care of children, and support.

Self-Assessment of Homophobia.   There is clearly a need for social workers to understand their attitudes and assumptions about gay and lesbian persons. The questions in Exercise 3.4 constitute a brief exercise for self-reflection and discussion about sexual orientation and homophobia.

E X E R C I S E **3.4**

Sensitivity to Sexual Orientation

1. If you learned that a person were gay or lesbian, would it influence your decision about sitting next to him or her?
2. Have you worked with gay or lesbian clients?
3. Do you think gay or lesbian individuals could benefit from being placed in a mixed group (heterosexuals and homosexuals)?
4. Would you protest if an antihomosexual joke were told?
5. Do you think gay or lesbian individuals have had disturbed relationships with one or both parents?
6. Do you have social contacts with gay or lesbian persons?
7. Would you ever discourage gay or lesbian clients from disclosing their sexual orientation to their family, friends, or co-workers? Why?
8. Do you think of homosexuality as a sickness or as a natural variant in human sexuality?
9. What would be your response if you learned that your sibling or child was gay or lesbian?
10. Do gay or lesbian persons have a right to be ministers, schoolteachers, social workers, or legislators?

Perceptions of Illness Behavior and Health.   All groups and societies view illness as a negative phenomenon. Illness behavior has always been defined through culturally derived perceptions of thoughts, feelings, and acts pertaining to symptoms, the meaning of illness and disabilities, and the consequences. Culture exerts a fundamental and far-reaching influence on the interpretation of health and illness. For example, in some groups, people are expected to be stoic in bearing pain. In others, they are expected to express pain vociferously and publicly. Illness reflects an adaptive social process in which participants are often actively striving to meet their social roles and responsibilities, to control their environment, and to make their everyday circumstances less uncertain and therefore more tolerable and predictable (Mechanic, 1978). Determining a client system's view of illness, physical aberrations, disabling conditions, and mental symptoms becomes an important part of social work assessment in the General Method. In modern Western society, most people continue to attribute illness to physical causes (i.e., associated with biological factors such as chemical or hormonal imbalances, genetic predispositions, degenerative processes, and hereditary malformations; environmental factors such as infections and toxins; and individual factors such as improper nutrition, lack of physical exercise, and difficulty coping with stress). Their beliefs are predominantly secular, rational, and future oriented. Because people tend to be receptive to diagnoses and treatments that match their expectations, mainstream Americans seek to eradicate the cause of illness with antibiotics, vitamins, hormones, medications, surgical procedures, radiation and chemotherapy, exercise, proper rest, and psychotherapy as preferred ways of treatment. They remain skeptical of alternative treatment approaches that do not immediately or easily fit into their cultural perceptions of illness. Thus, the U.S. health care system is, in large measure, an outgrowth of reverence for science and technology as well as a conviction that nature can be mastered.

By contrast, many ethnic minority clients espouse markedly different beliefs (frequently related to spirituality, magic, and family rules of behavior) about the causes of illness and other health afflictions. For example, Native Americans view good health as a balance of living in harmony with nature, a view that depends on adhering to a strict set of cosmic laws (Applewhite, 1995; Lake, 1983). Thus, healing means that the individual must be recreated, reconnected, and live in balance with nature. Hispanic groups believe that health is subject to God's judgment and that suffering is a consequence of having sinned and is a punishment *(castigo)* for disobeying God's laws. Thus, only a *curandero* (folk healer who has been chosen by God) can provide an appropriate cure (Applewhite, 1995; LeVine & Padilla, 1980). Puerto Ricans have *espiritistas,* who are believed to have supernatural inspiration for dealing with health and illness through exorcising harmful spiritual influences and strengthening benign spiritual influences (Guarnaccia, 1993). Asian/Pacific Islanders tie their views about health and illness to beliefs about magic, spirituality, and family ancestral rules of behavior. Many use a combination of healers ranging from traditional folk healers to homeopathic herbalists and acupuncturists (Pearl, Leo, & Tsang, 1995; Schultz, 1982).

Most non-Western societies represented by ethnic minorities in the United States, especially those who are poorly educated and from low socioeconomic levels, hold onto beliefs about health and sickness that are primarily rooted in traditional cultural folkways. These typically involve beliefs in supernatural forces, the use of home remedies, and the assistance of folk healers as ways to eliminate illness and restore good health. When major discrepancies exist between a client system's expectations and medical recommendations for treatment, client systems often reject both medical diagnosis and treatment. To the extent these types of belief systems intertwine with Western health care systems, experienced practitioners recommend that health care professionals, including social workers, learn to convey any discussion about health and treatment in ways that the individual may understand, using language, expressions, and services that are culturally salient. For example, the client's primary language may be used in conveying treatment recommendations. Cultural community brokers may be used to find appropriate alternative medicine treatments and community supports (Canda, 1983; Kumabe, Nishida, & Hepworth, 1985; Land & Hudson, 1997).

Challenges in Physical and Mental Ability. Deviations in human physical and mental abilities carry different meanings for different societies throughout the world. Values attached to disability vary both geographically and historically as well as based on various cultural beliefs associated with the meaning of individual responsibility. In ancient Greece, for example, malformed babies were thrown over a precipice. In other societies, persons with disabilities have been imbued with supernatural divine powers (on the primitive Truk Islands) and accorded positive societal attitudes (in modern-day Denmark) (Dybwad, 1970; Mackelprang & Salsgiver, 1996).

Today, more than two million people in the United States have serious and persistent mental illnesses such as schizophrenia, bipolar disorder, and major depression (Gerhart, 1990; Horwitz & Scheid, 1999). Nine to ten million are afflicted with alcoholism and other drug addictions; the highest percentage are those of ethnic minority descent who have low incomes (Native American Indians, African Americans, Hispanics, and Pacific Islanders) (Substance Abuse and Mental Health Services Administration, 1995). These neurobiological illnesses, addictions, and other disabilities have a devastating effect on individual functioning and ability to work and live independently. They also carry social stigma and result in much discrimination.

Congress's passage of the Americans with Disabilities Act of 1990 (P.L. 101-336) represents acknowledgment that the 43,000,000 Americans with disabilities have been subject to serious discrimination without legal recourse (Mackelprang & Salsgiver, 1996). Historically, these patterns of discrimination were based on (1) beliefs from the Middle Ages that people with physical and mental disabilities had experienced God's wrath, (2) stereotypes that people with disabilities and health problems were nonproductive, and (3) the sick role that Western culture expected persons with disabilities to fulfill. Such attitudes and resulting policies were shaped primarily by philosophies of utilitarianism, humanitarianism, and human rights (Newman, 1991). Fears about social disorder, for example, created a shift from home care to institutionalization in early to mid–nineteenth-century U.S. society. The creation of institutions paralleled the influx of large numbers of immigrants. As families became more transient and society encountered varying ethnic attitudes about sickness, health, and disability, institutional care began to be seen as a socially unifying force and began replacing certain welfare functions (Berkowitz, 1987; Lazerson, 1975). Concurrently, describing deviance from social norms, including disability, came to be defined as a social problem, and institutional services were deemed better than those available in individual communities. The subsequent shift from institutional care toward deinstitutionalization, which took place in the latter part of the twentieth century, has been credited with the following:

- Revealing the inhumanity and financial drain of large residential settings that abrogated individual and family needs and did not produce the promised rehabilitation of persons who deviated from societal norms
- Producing improvements in general knowledge about health, illness, and disability disorders as well as new medical treatments involving advanced technology, drugs, surgery, and various therapies to alter human behavior
- Recognizing the role of holistic protective factors, such as personal strength and resiliency, and the use of personal and community social supports in facilitating the goodness-of-fit between individuals and their environmental systems
- Stimulating the special education, mental health, independent living, and grass-roots self-help treatment movements that emphasized principles of normalization, least restrictive settings, and recovery in service delivery and human rehabilitation

These principles created a perspective of people with disabilities as active and responsible consumers of services and as persons entitled to control their own lives.

The *normalization* principle particularly humanized the health, education, and social service delivery systems by suggesting that all people, whether different or not, should be integrated to the maximum extent possible into the mainstream service delivery system and that services should promote those personal behaviors and characteristics that are culturally as normative as possible (DeJong, Batavia, & McKnew, 1992; Wolfensberger, 1972). The *least restrictive environment* principle supported normalization beliefs by shifting the focus from large impersonal institutional settings to community and family care as the primary environmental settings for delivery of services to people with exceptional physical and mental needs (Seligman & Darling, 1997). The *recovery* principle further underscored the deeply personal process that takes place in coping with health limitations (caused by mental illness, drug addictions, and deteriorating physical or emotional functioning) by documenting that people who are afflicted with such health problems are able to carry on a rich, satisfying, and productive life (Anthony, 1993).

Currently in the health care service delivery system, *rehabilitation* focuses on restoring human capacities that have been lost due to poor health, illness, or injury. *Habilitation* extends this focus into maximizing and promoting normal human potential in all health functioning and across all life situations. Social work helping strategies with client systems experiencing challenging conditions typically involve the following:

1. *Micro approaches* that focus on
   - Individual and family education about the conditions and options for (re)habilitation (Seligman & Darling, 1997), the process of recovery (Taylor, 1997), and the availability of community resources (Laborde & Seligman, 1991)
   - Change strategies for reframing the personal meaning of the affliction (Marshak & Seligman, 1993) and for coping with and adapting to the chronicity (Opirhory & Peters, 1982; Salsgiver, 1993)
   - Skills training and parent management (Marsh, 1992)
2. *Mezzo approaches* that use
   - Collective group education and mutual self-help to improve and empower specific groups of people (Brown, 1984)
   - Community outreach to mobilize specific group community services (Rivera & Erlich, 1998)
3. *Macro strategies* that focus on
   - Education and training to improve the quality of services and service delivery to specific groups of clients (Mackelprang & Santos, 1992)
   - Education and training to increase community awareness and understanding of various social problems and challenging conditions (Miley, O'Melia, & DuBois, 1998)
   - Social planning for the development and coordination of human services (Hardcastle, Wenocur, & Powers, 1997)
   - Community development (Rubin & Rubin, 1992), coalition building (Mizrahi & Rosenthal, 1993), and class advocacy to promote specific group and community empowerment while engaging political, economic, and legislative systems to facilitate equitable redistribution of resources and justice for disadvantaged or oppressed populations (Lewis, 1991)

A Holistic Framework for Sensitivity to Human Variability

All people have basic needs of food, clothing, and shelter and share similar desires and goals to improve the quality of their lives (Maslow, 1968). The way people seek to achieve these desires and goals, however, usually depends on their experience with multiculturalism, stratification influences of social pluralism, and personal socio-demographic variability in endowment, personality, age, gender, sexual orientation, health, and physical and mental abilities. Thus, although all persons have the same problems, concerns, and aspirations, the "isms" (such as racism, classism, sexism, and ageism, to name a few) block opportunities and compound the problems experienced by certain groups of people.

For example, besides poverty, racism continues to be one of the pervasive problems facing people of color and their communities. It is viewed as the root cause of generational poverty, diminished self-esteem that promotes community violence and self-medicating through drugs and alcohol, and disproportionate involvement in the criminal justice system. But despite the fact that wages and income, promotion rates, middle and top management, contractors, and manufacturing firms all document the same historical story of continued discrimination, there is a growing perception that white Americans, especially white males, are now experiencing reverse discrimination as an outcome of affirmative action policies and practices (Axinn & Levin, 1997). A survey by the National Opinion Research Center, however, found that, although 70 percent of the U.S. public believed that whites were being hurt by affirmative action policies, only 7 percent reported experience with reverse discrimination (Patterson, 1995). This backlash against people of color is further evident in several recent pieces of legislation that underpin the present climate of delivering services. For example, Propositions 187 and 209 in California respectively prohibited social services to all persons who could not document their legal status and prohibited preferences based on race and gender in public education, employment, and state contracting (Karger & Stoesz, 1990).

Although discrimination based on race is illegal, it is still prevalent and continues to be the basis for many macro issues that affect societal participation, relationships, and resource distribution for all people in general but people of color in particular. Social workers must guard against institutionalized practices that perpetuate unequal treatment of communities of color as well as unequal practices with individuals of color. Social workers must use practice approaches that are suited to work with particular multicultural groups. Such approaches acknowledge the existence of multicultural, socio-pluralistic, and socio-demographic differences while celebrating the resourcefulness and creativeness of human potential. They focus on human empowerment within the context of the client system's environment.

Such strengths-based social work practice helps client systems uncover and promote strengths from within (Saleebey, 1997). Cultural values and traditions, resources, coping strategies, family, friends, and community support networks represent potential individual strengths. Collective history and traditions, mutual support, and group resources represent collective community strengths. The client system is viewed as an expert in identifying past successes and in developing solutions based on past experiences. These past experiences are particularly emphasized in General Method problem solving. Methods that focus on concrete specific tasks and objectives (Reid, 1996; Reid & Epstein, 1972) may work better with people of color than more abstract methods (Freeman, 1990; See, 1998). Empowerment seeks to promote a power-shared relationship, competency-based assessment, collectivity for mutual aid, education for critical thinking, and knowledge and skills for finding resources and taking action within the context of the client system's environment (Parsons, Jorgensen, & Hernandez, 1994). It requires a holistic view (as found in Figure 3.2) about the interactive effect of people's concerns, perceptions, values and beliefs, unique persona, and cultural risks and resiliencies.

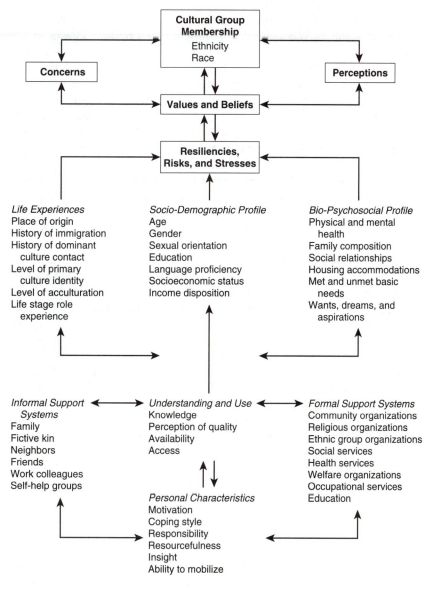

FIGURE 3.2   Holistic View of Human Diversity

To help client systems identify the micro-, mezzo-, or macro-level problem(s) for which social work intervention may be needed, client systems must be allowed to tell their stories in their own way and to construct their own versions of reality (Saleebey, 1994). In many cultures, storytelling or narration has long been used to record history. Since it allows for the incorporation of cultural references and perceptions, it is a natural way to develop the helping relationship across diverse client systems. However, the social worker needs to become an active listener and participant in this two-way interaction process by using professional skills to guide client systems through their narration and to uncover and construct the meaning of their personal or collective social reality. The social worker may also need to learn to use metaphor as a way of linking past history to present interpretation of perceived needs and problems and thereby facilitate client systems' recognition of strengths. In this narrative approach, client systems tell their story from the beginning to the present or from the end back to its origin. In the process, clients' conceptions of self, relationships, life, and communal experiences take shape and provide meaning and purpose (Goldstein, 1990). This ethnically sensitive approach does not require a long assessment period gathering scientific data but rather the ability to:

- Listen actively and nonjudgmentally to each client system.
- Recognize that client system perceptions are shaped by individual, personal, and collective experiences.
- Understand that cultural values affect all human individual, family, group, organization, and community interaction.
- Acknowledge that all people translate nonverbal communication (such as spatial observances, handshaking, and eye contact) in different ways.
- Recognize that within each culture there exists much human variability in how people think, feel, act, and express their physical and emotional characteristics.
- Recognize that the route for seeking services (or help seeking) is affected by cultural values underpinning the delivery of human services, personal resiliencies, social stratification of access to resources, historical client systems, life experiences, and the placement of societal values on personal and collective responsibilities for self-care, financial independence, social relationships, and the client system's past experiences with discrimination.
- Recognize that verbal communication patterns differ based on personal and collective community cultural interpretations and experiences, life-stage development, and language competency.
- Acknowledge that cultural values affect personal perceptions and behavior in all facets of human interaction across all levels of service delivery.

Conclusion

A sensitivity to human diversity from a holistic multivariant perspective is essential for effective generalist social work practice. This sensitivity becomes competency in diversity when the social worker's experiential awareness and knowledge of multiculturalism, social pluralism, and socio-demographic variability join with the social worker's skill in providing effective and sensitive services to meet the needs of diverse client systems. This is a process in which the social worker needs to integrate knowledge about multicultural, social stratification, and socio-demographic influences on human perceptions, beliefs, values, and actions with a reflection about self-awareness and insight as well as honed skills.

In micro-level service competency with diverse client systems, a primary social work task is to assist the client system at the point of interface between the client system and environment in empowering the client system to sort out needs, wants, and goals and in providing assistance with the client system's coping, strengths and competence, and resource utilization in achieving those goals. In mezzo-level service competency, a social worker's primary task is to facilitate family or group development, encourage mutual support, and empower toward mastery. In guiding the family or group through its normal developmental process, the social worker pays particular attention to how the "isms" and their issues of oppression, prejudice, bias, and perceptions of conflict affect family or group cohesion, developmental progress, and goal accomplishment.

In macro-level service competency, the social worker involves community and large client and action systems in addressing diversity issues in the delivery of services to all persons, promoting social equality and justice, and reducing social violence. The tasks of communities self-identified by commonalities of race, ethnicity, social stratification, sexual orientation, physical or mental challenges, or other diversity involve bringing together various community support networks (churches, indigenous service providers, and public and private human service organizations) and mobilizing their resources to provide a safe and just path for community development or community acculturation in the case of immigrant ethnic groups. Through social organization and planning for social action, the social worker helps community systems uncover common bonds around values and goals while creating community coalitions, mobilizing resources, advocating, negotiating, and brokering services.

Following through each stage of the General Method, the social worker embarks on a journey of knowledge and skill development and sensitivity to diversity. The integration of content on multiculturalism, social pluralism, and socio-demographic variability within each chapter is a deliberate attempt to highlight the importance of cultural sensitivity and competence throughout the use of the General Method. Besides gaining knowledge and skill development in the application of the method, each chapter focuses on human diversity issues with different client systems in a variety of fields of practice.

CHAPTER

4 Engagement

The first stage of the General Method is called *engagement*. Whether the generalist begins to work with a client, target, or action system, and whether the client system is an individual, family, group, organization, or community, the first thing the social worker tries to do is to open up the boundary between them (client system and social worker) for positive interaction. Frequently, there is some resistance by a client system to any possible change or intrusion from the outside. From the inception of contact with a client system, the generalist needs to use skill and knowledge along with professional values and principles for effective engagement.

In the first stage of the General Method, the social worker has three guiding landmarks that help in the initial movement of the procedure. As the generalist begins to interact with a client system, the three focal points of problems, feelings, and goals are kept in mind. All three are often in focus at the same time in the conversation and transactions between social worker and client system. The generalist makes sure that all three points have been addressed before proceeding to the next stage of the method.

In this chapter, each of the three central elements of the engagement stage will be studied. Techniques will be presented for working with diverse client systems on their problems, feelings, and goals. Case vignettes will demonstrate the first stage of the General Method with a variety of systems. Considerations will include the use of the social work foundation (Table 1.3 in Chapter 1) during the engagement stage of generalist practice.

Getting to the Problem

Before actually discussing the problem with a client system in any depth, it is necessary for the social worker to prepare for the contact. He or she tries to learn as much as possible about the culture, needs, and resources of the client system. The social worker tries not only to understand the system that he or she will interact with but also to understand his or her own culture, needs, and resources and how the two, social worker and system of contact, may form a "fit" for positive interactions. If it appears that there will be stress or difficulty in the match between social worker and client system, the practitioner seeks help from a supervisor.

At the point of initial contact, after brief introductions, the purpose for coming together needs to be expressed. Within the description of purpose, a problem may be mentioned. The social worker keeps this in mind for reference when the time is appropriate.

If the service setting is concerned about a problem and initiates the contact with the client system, the social worker states the purpose. If the client system or a referral system initiates the contact with the service system, the social worker encourages the initiating client system to say why the contact was made. For example:

Case 1: Concern Originates in Service Setting
SW: Good morning, Mrs. B. I am Mary Costello, the school social worker. I would like to talk with you about your son Johnnie and how he's doing at school.

Case 2: Concern Originates in Client System
SW: Good morning. I am Mary Costello, the school social worker. I understand you wanted to talk with me.
CLIENT: Yes, I'm Mrs. B, Johnnie's mother. His teacher said that maybe I could talk to you about the problems I've been having with my son lately.

The generalist asks himself or herself: What is the issue, problem, need, or question that appears to be the major concern for this client system? Is there really a problem (or problems) that the client system will identify and invest energy in for resolution? The social worker begins to clarify the problems he or she and the client system are going to work on together.

The General Method is permeated with the ecological-systems perspective. The generalist knows that when an environment gives an organism the inputs needed for thriving, there are certain outputs that the environment expects from the organism. The environment and the organism have role expectations for each other. Each is expected to behave and produce in a way that is conducive to the well-being of the other. In the General Method, the problem is defined initially in terms of what is taking place at the point of interface and interactions between organism and environment. The problem is seen at the boundary point where a system interlocks with some aspect of its surrounding environment or with some other system in that environment. The expected inputs and outputs for each problem situation are considered.

In time, the plan of intervention developed in the procedure may be directed toward a system or its environment rather than toward the boundary where the two come together. As brought out by Hearn (1969, p. 69): "In short, social work activity is focused inside, outside, and at the boundary between the system and its environment." The initial problem description, however, focuses on the boundary point where there is a need or desire to direct attention to the functioning of client system and environment in relation to each other.

For example, in Case 1, the problem as presented by the social worker is between Johnnie and the school. He is not behaving or performing academically at the level expected for him to "fit" into the system and be promoted by the school. The problem as introduced by Mrs. B in Case 2 is between Johnnie and his mother at home. He is not acting in the manner his mother expects and thus is not receiving her approval and affection. Every effort should be made to relate the problem as directly as possible to the system in contact with the social worker. The more distant the problem, the more difficult it is to involve the client system in a timely change effort. Usually it is not necessary to identify clearly the causes of the problem in the engagement stage. During data collection, stage 2, there is opportunity to obtain information on causes. Sometimes, however, facts relating to cause may need to be presented to promote greater incentive for cooperation. The social worker may need to present data in order to determine the validity of the apparent causes of a problem presented by the client system.

For example, if Mrs. B identifies the main problem as Johnnie's not getting along with his teacher, she may think there is little she has to work on to improve the situation. If, on the other hand, it is pointed out to Mrs. B that Johnnie's school problems are showing up in classes with different teachers, and if she is helped to see that his problems started around the time her husband was laid off from work and she began working, Mrs. B may begin to get more involved in looking at the problem.

The timing and techniques used in presenting facts to stimulate involvement are dependent on the sensitivity and skills of the social worker. Presenting facts too soon or too abruptly may cause the client to become distressed or inhibited. Mrs. B, for example, may find it difficult to talk about her husband or the financial constraints that necessitated her going to work. She may become distressed as she begins to see a correlation between her son's school problems and what is happening with herself and her husband.

In beginning to identify the problem with a client system, the skilled generalist is sensitive to delicate, feeling-filled areas. The social worker knows that feelings relevant to the problems must be recognized, understood, and expressed if there is to be real movement toward problem resolution. As feelings are disclosed, new problems or a clearer understanding of the problem may emerge. As stated, problems are not fixed, but evolving, and feelings and cognitions are forces that help move the problems into clearer focus.

Identifying Feelings

A basic practice principle, as described in Chapter 1, is *purposeful expression of feelings* (Biestek, 1957; National Association of Social Workers, 1996). The social worker does not encourage indiscriminate ventilation of feelings about any or every issue. The General method is a purposeful process that calls for the social worker to have expertise in the realm of feelings. The generalist strives to become aware of the feelings of the client system as they relate to the problem situation. The social worker recognizes when the client system is expressing unrelated feelings and uses skill in deciding whether these feelings indicate other problem areas in need of attention or whether their expression is an attempt to avoid facing the problem at hand. If the former, the social worker and client system may need to reconstruct or add to the identified problem; if the latter, the social worker may need to discuss the avoidance with the client system and redirect the conversation back to the identified problem.

There is also the basic principle called *controlled emotional involvement* (Biestek, 1957; National Association of Social Workers, 1996). It points to the need for the social worker to have self-awareness in terms of his or her own feelings surrounding the problem-client system-environment situation. Prior to and throughout the process of working with others, the generalist realizes the fact that he or she has feelings also. At times, these feelings may be very strong and in need of control while he or she works with particular client, target, or action systems or problems. If this is difficult for the social worker, he or she should seek help from a supervisor.

In the General Method, the identification of feelings, as well as problems, is done basically on a rational level. The knowledge foundation of social work practice looks at the whole of human nature and enables the social worker to be aware of unconscious as well as conscious factors that influence human behavior. In general practice, however, the feelings encouraged and expressed are mainly conscious and identifiable. The approach of the social worker may be described primarily as rational or cognitive. In the cognitive approach, conscious thought is considered the principal determinant of emotions, motives, and actions. Thus, the feelings, incentives, and action behaviors brought to the social worker's attention are problems in the client system's conscious awareness (Beck, 1979; Granvold, 1994; Robbins, Chatterjee, & Canda, 1998). The generalist does not discard the notion of the unconscious in human behavior, but recognizes that his or her competence is for working on the rational, conscious level. The feelings addressed in practice are conscious or able to be brought into consciousness with a little effort.

Carkhuff and Anthony (1979, p. 243) point out that each feeling has a rational reason that can be identified:

> The thing the helper must remember is this: Regardless of the apparent nature of the cause of a particular helpee's feelings, each of those feelings will always turn out to have a sufficient and rational reason! One of the most important goals of all helpee exploration is to identify—to the helper as well as to the helpee—the real reason for each of his or her real feelings.

Even though feelings may be conscious, the social worker knows that often they are difficult to share. It may be awkward for a person to engage in a discussion about private feelings with a professional person in the early stages of a working relationship. As stated earlier, in some cultures, words are seldom used to express feelings, particularly with someone outside of the family (Chao, 1992; Marsella, 1993). In many cultures, feelings of inadequacy are particularly difficult to express. Among others, these feelings may include feelings of being no good, unable to do things, unable to do something about a situation, or unable to handle affection from others. These feelings may also include feelings about being hurt or rejected, guilt, shame, passivity, helplessness, and dependency, or they may include feelings that come from a need to be punished or a need to punish someone else (Egan, 1998).

Poor families have often been described as unable to express concerns well enough to talk about them with a social agency, and so inarticulate that they literally do not have the words for their emotion. Hollis (1965) disagrees with this judgment and reports that most social workers do not have difficulty getting clients to express their feelings if the social workers themselves use appropriate language. She points out that social workers should not let simplicity of language be understood as incapacity. Often, simple words or expressions are the most valid and meaningful. "Exploration may sometimes proceed at a slower pace than the more verbal, better educated client. But once the low-income client's confidence has been established, he is likely to speak freely, particularly of feelings of anger and frustrations, sometimes directed against the worker himself" (Hollis, 1965, p. 469).

To be able to help a system discuss relevant feelings, the generalist needs to have a broad vocabulary to describe feelings. As brought out by Hallowitz (1979, p. 111):

> The worker also helps the client with feelings that impair his ability to deal with the problems at hand—e.g., anxiety, conflict, resistance. He encourages the client to do the problem-solving work to the fullest possible extent. When the limits of this are reached, he contributes his own thinking and suggestions.

The suggestions offered to help a client with describing feelings have to be carefully and appropriately selected. The word list in Figure 4.1 may be helpful to social workers as they search for ways to describe particular feelings most aptly. Each word may be modified for more accurate indications of degrees of intensity by using such descriptive words as *a little, somewhat, moderately,* and *very.*

Feelings are not described in one or two words. They may be expressed through phrases, behavioral descriptions, and stated desires (Egan, 1998). For example, to feel "happy" may be described as "I feel great," "I feel as free as a bird," "I feel I could jump for joy," or "I feel I would like to reach out and hug everyone

FIGURE 4.1   Words to Describe Feelings

Positive Feelings	Negative Feelings
Relaxed	Uptight, nervous
All together	Spacey, mixed up
Whole	Falling apart
Confident, adequate, potent	Confused, unsure, inept
Graceful	Awkward, clumsy
Well organized	Disorganized
Accepted	Rejected, abandoned
Appreciated	Unappreciated
A part of things	Out of step, left out
Loved	Unloved
Full of life	Burned out, exhausted
Strengthened, firm	Weakened, weak
Witty	Dull
Able to cope	Overwhelmed
Good	Bad
Warm	Cold
Delighted	Unhappy, frustrated
Great	Small
Glad	Sad
Pleased	Displeased, angry, outraged
Loving	Hateful, hostile, furious
Daring	Afraid
In control	Out of control, helpless
Hopeful	Hopeless
Full	Empty
Built up	Put down, crushed
Serene	Disturbed
Energetic	Exhausted
Healthy	Sick
Powerful	Powerless
Free	Trapped

here." The important point in the engagement stage is not so much *how* the feelings are expressed but that they *are* expressed in whatever manner has the most meaning to the client system. Central to the art of social work practice is the awareness of feelings in human systems and of the value in their purposeful expression.

As stated earlier, when feelings are expressed, the social worker needs to explore with the system of contact the rational reason for the feelings. A technique frequently used as the practitioner clarifies the feelings is to say, "I understand that you are feeling _____ because _____," or "Is it that you feel _____ because _____?" or "You seem to be feeling _____ because _____."

It is always necessary to receive feedback from the client system after a reason for feelings is suggested. This may be accomplished by adding a statement such as, "Is that correct?" "What do you think?" "Am I right?" or "Is that it?" In this way, the client system is encouraged by the social worker to participate in the process of finding reasons for feelings, and to accept, modify, or reject the suggested description of feelings offered by the social worker.

As the social worker moves with the client system from the identification of feelings to the reasons for the feelings, the social worker tries to utilize the ecological perspective. An effort is made to incorporate a view of the system in relation to the environment within the definition of the reason for feelings. The more the members of a client system see the part they play in the reason for the feelings, the more chance there is that they will begin to use their feelings in dealing with the problem. For example, the social worker in Case 1 may say:

> Mrs. B, I can see that you are troubled because you can't understand why your son is not getting along in school lately. Is that right?

or

> Mrs. B, you seem to be very upset right now. Is it because you don't want to hear that Johnnie is having school problems at a time when you and the family are having so many other difficulties?

In the second case, the social worker might say:

> You are feeling very frustrated because you can't seem to get along with your son lately. Is that it, Mrs. B?

or

> You are very angry with your son lately because he is not behaving the way you expect of him. Is that correct?

The reason for the feelings may be closely related to the problem as presented, or after further exploration, the social worker may find that the reason for the feelings as clarified becomes a means for uncovering issues that need more immediate attention. In the first case, for example, the social worker may begin to see that Mrs. B is currently feeling overwhelmed because of extensive family problems, and Johnnie's behavior at school is but an indicator of a very troubled family situation. In the second case, Mrs. B expressed feelings that relate directly to the presenting problem. The feelings she expressed were caused by a problem in parent-child interaction.

As the feelings are refined and the problem reformulated, it may become apparent through the exploration of feelings and their reasons that there is a problem needing to be addressed, but that it is outside the scope of the competence of the generalist or the agency's services. A referral to another service may be necessary. When several problems have emerged and at least one problem continues within the social worker's domain, a resource may need to be contacted for a collaborative effort. It is important for the social worker to keep in mind that every step in the process of the General Method may change the nature of the problem.

When needs or expectations are unmet, client system members begin to feel unfulfilled. Negative feelings, including anger and rage, may develop. Negative feelings drain energy from a client system. When the reason for these feelings is identified and if through some process or intervention the reason may be reversed, there is then new energy available for more effective social functioning. Positive feelings generate vitality and energy for growth-promoting transactions. The reasons for positive feelings are seen as something to be maintained or enhanced. As long as the reasons persist, the energy level continues to expand for effective social functioning.

The reasons for feelings may relate closely to the problems and also to the goals. The stating of reasons for negative or positive feelings helps to move the social worker and the client system into recognizing and discussing goals. The introduction of suggestions for preliminary goals should come only after the client system has confirmed the stated reasons for feelings. If the suggested goals are unrelated to the feelings of the client system, they may be a reflection of the social worker's hopes and expectations rather than the client system's actual goals.

Feelings in Macro Systems

The engagement stage initiates the General Method as used with client systems of any size or type. Even when working with a target or action system, the generalist tries to discern how the problem is perceived, what feelings exist about the situation, and what goals would be acceptable and feasible for involvement by the particular system.

As defined earlier, target systems need to change for goal accomplishment. They do not necessarily want to or agree to work with the social worker. Action systems cooperate with the social worker to achieve goals or influence target systems. And client systems request or agree to work with the social worker to receive benefits from the service.

A target, action, or client system may be an individual, family, group, organization, community, social institution, or society. These are the systems of contact in social work practice. As the generalist works with diverse systems, an important consideration is the distinguishing characteristics that are generally recognized among systems. As depicted in Figure 4.2, human systems have a basic set of characteristics that vary according to the type of system. The social worker prepares for contact with a client system by recalling or trying to find out as much as possible about the system. Working from foundation knowledge, the practitioner makes every effort to become aware of the client system's characteristics and the degree of intensity of feelings.

For the range of major systems of contact in social work, there are characteristic polarities with intervening degree scales that may be considered (Figure 4.2). The polarities include facts versus feelings, goal orientation versus process orientation, formality versus informality, explicit nature versus implicit nature, organization versus little organization, structure versus little structure, objectivity versus intimacy, social control versus human concern, and law and work versus circumstance and love.

In Figure 4.2, feelings and goals are associated with certain types of client, action, and target systems. As indicated in the diagram, there are basically greater expectation and awareness of feelings and process with smaller systems and greater expectation and awareness of facts and goals with larger systems. In beginning to work with a larger system, the generalist sees the need to come prepared to present facts and to work with structure and formality. Generally, feelings are not readily considered or expressed in larger systems.

To work with any client, action, or target system, the social worker deals with human beings who naturally have feelings. The social worker tries to identify feelings as they relate to the problem and to the social worker's efforts. Skill is used to distinguish between those feelings that are the personal feelings of individual representatives and those of the larger system. Whereas the social worker may be

FIGURE 4.2   Polarities in Systems

Individual . . . Family . . . Group . . . Organization . . . Community . . . Institution . . . Society

Feelings	Facts
Process orientation	Goal orientation
Informality	Formality
Implicit nature	Explicit nature
Little organization	Much organization
Little structure	Much structure
Intimacy	Objectivity
Human concern	Social control
Circumstance	Law
Love	Work

able to discuss feelings and relationships with individuals, it often takes longer to recognize and discuss them with individuals who represent a large system. There is a possibility that the expression of feelings will not be able to influence or change a situation in a larger system because of policy and structure. Carefully presented facts, however, could be most effective.

In terms of goals, larger systems enter very readily into a dialogue about their goals and expectations. They usually have explicitly stated goals that can be utilized as the social worker tries to engage the client, action, or target system in mutual goal setting. The smaller system, however, may take more time and need more help in understanding and expressing its goals.

As implied in Figure 4.2, while working with the three major components of the engagement stage (i.e., problems, feelings, and goals), the social worker usually finds a natural tendency to get into feelings and relationships with the smaller systems (i.e., individuals, families, groups, and some communities) and to get into facts and goals with larger systems (i.e., some communities, as well as organizations, institutions, and society). As stated, however, all three components—problems, feelings, and goals—must be considered by the social worker for successful movement in the engagement stage.

Goal Recognition

The social worker asks the question: What is it that this client system really wants? In the first case cited, the social worker is hearing that Mrs. B wants Johnnie to remain in school and get promoted, but she also wants some relief from heavy family burdens. In the second case, Mrs. B is clearly focusing on the goal of improving her relationship with her son. Such clarification of goals is imperative for the social worker to determine how to proceed with the client system. Goals have to be expressed, understood, and agreed on by both client system and social worker before they can move on to the second stage of the method.

What is a goal? Epstein (1985, p. 125) gives a very direct answer: "The idea of a goal is straightforward. It is the end toward which effort is directed. A goal is a point beyond which something does not or cannot go. . . . Therefore a goal is an attainable wish."

In the General Method, a goal is conceptualized as including objectives, tasks, motives, and attainable desires. Goals are the desired outcomes toward which intervention activity is directed. Although goals naturally flow out of the data collection and assessment phases, the establishment of the beginning goals needs to take place during engagement. It is during this time that the social worker and the client system not only explore the extent of problems but also begin considering the potential consequences of their possible resolution. Typically, client system goals may take many forms (Kirst-Ashman & Hull, 1999; Sheafor, Horejsi, & Horejsi, 1997):

- *Learning a skill or acquiring particular knowledge* for decision making or fulfilling a particular role

- *Making an important decision* about a course of action, such as deciding to change a lifestyle or marital status, relinquish custody of a child, or obtain mental health services
- *Obtaining information* in order to make a decision
- *Assessing problems or concerns* to decide whether attention or help may be needed
- *Making plans* to address a particular concern
- *Changing behavior* to increase a desired outcome
- *Altering feelings or attitudes* toward self or others
- *Gathering information about availability of services or programs*
- *Becoming connected or enrolled in a program*
- *Resolving a conflicted relationship*
- *Changing appraisal of life events or circumstances* to develop a new perspective

Goals are the end toward which the social worker and the client system(s) direct their efforts. Goals are explicated in the General Method when there is mutual agreement by social worker and client system. It is possible that the method may be arrested because no goals can be established by mutual agreement. To proceed without this mutuality would be futile.

Although initial goals may be expressed in broad, general terms, the practitioner and the client system work toward formulation of concrete goals. General and specific goals of the General Method are of a social-functioning nature, and they are conceptualized from an ecological-systems perspective. General goals relate to social situations in which the exchange at the interface between client system and environment is central. As the goals are stated, clarified, and refined, the social worker keeps in mind the need to have goals be measurable and attainable. They should be practical, limited in number, and obviously related to the identified problems.

As the General Method proceeds into data collection, assessment, and planning, goals may be reformulated and refined for greater specificity. Goal setting leads to the identification of specific tasks that need to be performed for goal accomplishment. The actions needed to obtain the stated goals will be clarified within an identifiable and realistic time span. When completed, the identified problems should have been addressed, alleviated, or resolved.

Moving from identifying preliminary general goals that are stated ecologically and that are related directly to the presenting problems, the generalist helps the client systems develop more specific measurable and practical goals and tasks. For example, a general goal stated by Mrs. B may be to improve interactions between herself and her son. As the social worker gets more involved with Mrs. B and her son later on in the course of the Method, they would be expected to agree on the general goal and to identify their specific goal objectives and tasks in terms of behaviors and conditions. These might include the following:

General Goal: To improve relations between Mrs. B and her son

Specific Goal Objective 1: Mrs. B and her son will spend more time together.

- Task 1: Mrs. B will spend half an hour after her son gets out of school listening and talking about his day.

- Task 2: Mrs. B will discuss with her husband the need for him to help their son with at least two homework assignments each week.
- Task 3: Mrs. B will take her son to a movie or other fun activity once a month.

Specific Goal Objective 2: Mrs. B will gain a better understanding of parenting teens.

- Task 1: Mrs. B will attend a parenting class once a week for eight weeks at the agency.
- Task 2: Mrs. B will go to the library and read at least one book on parenting boys.
- Task 3: Mrs. B will arrange a time for herself and her husband to discuss her concerns about parenting their son.
- Task 4: Mrs. B will leave the room when her feelings escalate in managing her son's discipline.

Specific Goal Objective 3: Johnnie will gain more self-control in managing conflict.

- Task 1: Mrs. B, her husband, and Johnnie will attend a follow-up session with the social worker to assess the extent of their conflicts.

Goals in the engagement stage of the General Method are beginning goals in a process of goal setting. The main purpose for goal identification in the initial stage is to let the client system know that the social worker is listening and that he or she hears what the client system is saying about wants, needs, or values. The social worker skillfully begins to engage the client system in thinking about goals, with the hope that this engagement will motivate the system for deeper involvement in a collaborative problem-solving effort. As the Method proceeds, the social worker and the client system gain a clearer understanding of problems, feelings, and goals.

Decision Making

Engagement sets the tone for the helping process. With client systems, but not necessarily action or target systems, the beginning professional relationship reflects empathy, warmth, and genuineness and offers energy, hopefulness, and confidence in creating a working climate in which the client system's fears, problems, needs, and goals are explored.

First, the stage of engagement is an interpersonal exchange process during which the client system and the social worker must reach an understanding about why the client system is seeking help and what the client system hopes to accomplish from the initial encounters. Second, the social worker and the client system engage in a mutual exchange around problem appraisal to get a sense of the number of problems and their severity, duration, and impact as well as any previous remedies sought and any success or lack thereof. Third, the social worker presents information about the agency's purpose, any eligibility requirements, policy about confidentiality, and available agency resources. Fourth, the client system and the social worker consider three possible outcomes of their actual engagement in the General Method of social work practice:

- *Role induction:* The client, action, or target system agrees to proceed with the outlined intervention process.
- *Referral:* Because the client, action, or target system cannot be adequately served by the present agency, and the social worker has an obligation to help client systems gain access to needed services, a linking/brokering service is offered.
- *Discontinuation of services:* The client system and social worker agree not to continue because (1) the problems and issues presented cannot be addressed by the agency services, (2) the client system and social worker agree that the initial contacts were sufficient to mobilize problem-solving processes and resources, or (3) the client system chooses not to invest further time, energy, or resources in pursuing help.

As the social worker engages the client system in the helping process, the social worker and the client system also begin to make decisions about problem clarification and prioritization so that client system goals can be pursued. For example, the numerous problems that occur on multiple levels of many client systems may be overwhelming and immobilizing: interpersonal conflicts, dissatisfaction with social relationships, difficulties in role performance, faulty cognitive appraisals, problems in role transitions, inadequate resources, problems in decision making, problems with organizations and communities, and cultural conflicts. In sorting out and prioritizing problems with client systems, social workers have long been guided by six practice principles:

1. *Start with the problem the client system identifies as important.* Although the social worker may not agree with the client system about where the problem stands in a prioritized list of all problems involved, the social worker begins where the client system is in identifying the problem of primary concern. In the course of their discussion, the problem list may be reframed and reprioritized for purposes of their work together. It is important to note that role induction and forward progression through the next five stages of the General Method cannot take place unless there is an agreement during the engagement phase about which problem merits mutual attention and work at this point in time.

Court-ordered and other nonvoluntary client systems, who have been brought to the social worker's attention by external authority sources, often pose particular challenges to the engagement process. Typically, these clients may resent being ordered to speak with a social worker and may deny the existence of a problem. With client systems who are reluctant to engage, social workers usually follow one of two approaches. They may recommend that a specific amount of time be spent searching for the existence of a problem or issue with which the agency can help. The client system is asked to withhold judgment about the need for service or the social worker's usefulness until the problem/situation has been examined in greater depth. In the event this approach is unsuccessful and when the client system understands the social worker's explanation of the possible consequences of discontinuing service, the social worker may terminate contact with the client system. In both approaches, the social worker may provide the client system with alternative resources.

2. *Redefine the problem in behavioral terms and cast the behaviors within a strengths/ needs orientation.* Each problem/situation is clarified as to what exactly it is, why it is a problem, whom the problem affects, how severe it is, how long it has been going on, what has been tried before to ameliorate it, what success was evident in the previous helping attempts, and what will resolve it.

3. *Prioritize the problems listed in order of their importance to the client.* The focus is on "what the client system wants" and not on what the social worker thinks the client system may need. The target problem is not necessarily limited to what the client system wants initially but rather to what is wanted after a mutual process of deliberation and thought—after data collection, after assessment, or even after beginning intervention. That is, the client system's initial expression of concerns and problems to which the social worker contributes his or her own knowledge and clarifying technique often evolves into a different facet of the problem or even a different, seemingly unrelated problem focus. It is also not uncommon for client systems to renegotiate their initial agreement about problems and goals at a later stage of the helping process.

4. *Assist the client in selecting two or at most three problems to which the client system attributes most priority.* The social worker helps the client system explore the identified problems in view of (a) the client system's feelings about the problem's consequences if left unaddressed; (b) which problems are of most interest to the client system; (c) which problems might be corrected with only a moderate investment of time, energy, cost, or other resources; and (d) which problems would require extraordinary investment, energy, and resources.

5. *Help the client system consider beliefs and goals relevant to the problems presented.* As they explore the nature of the problems and the surrounding feelings and behaviors, the social worker also helps the client system identify beliefs and goals about the problems presented and how these may influence possible outcomes.

6. *Establish initial agreement with the client system to engage in the helping process while continuing to identify problems that will be further addressed through data collection.* Written documentation of this initial agreement with the client system is important not only for the client system but also for assessment of goal accomplishment and for agency record keeping.

Working with Different Client Systems

The following complex case situation is offered to provide a better understanding of the application of the engagement stage of the General Method to different systems. The social worker for the family will begin to use the General Method to work with client, target, and action systems. The systems of contact range from an individual to a large business.

Case Examples

Mrs. Armez was sent to the Unity Social Service Department by her pastor. Her husband had to go into the hospital for an operation, and, after a few weeks, was told by the doctor he could return to work. When Mr. Armez tried to return, he was told they didn't need him any longer, and he was laid off. While he had been in the hospital, Mr. Armez's place of employment had been bought by another company, and Mr. Armez thinks the new management does not like Hispanic people. Mr. Armez continues to feel weak and doesn't know if he could work the way he used to. Mrs. Armez said that since Mr. Armez's unemployment benefits ran out and the family went on welfare, he hasn't been acting right. He drinks more, and he fought with her when she began to do some part-time work. The children are not doing well in school lately, and the school social worker is afraid that they are being overly disciplined by Mrs. Armez and her husband.

Micro Example 1: Generalist with Mrs. Armez (Client System)

SW: Good afternoon, Mrs. Armez. My name is Katherine Brown. I understand Rev. Growth suggested that you get in touch with us.

CLIENT: Yes, he thought you might be able to help me.

SW: I'd be glad to work with you, Mrs. Armez. Where would you like to begin?

CLIENT: I'm not sure. It's just that nothing seems to be working out right now, and I don't know how to explain it.

SW: I can imagine that it isn't easy for you to begin to talk with me. Was it difficult for you to come in today?

CLIENT: I came right after work. I know my husband would be mad if he knew I stopped off here. I just can't let things go on the way they've been going these last few months.

SW: It sounds like you are under a lot of pressure right now. Am I right?

CLIENT: I'm so upset with all that's happening at home. It's too much for me to take.

SW: You're feeling very upset because you just don't know how to handle the many problems at home right now.

CLIENT: Yes, please understand, I love my children and my husband. It's just that everything is going wrong. He's changed since he lost his job. He can't get work, and he's mad that I'm working. I can't let my children starve. I iron for some people in the morning, and that helps a little. The welfare money isn't enough. He just doesn't care—I don't know how to reach him. He's drinking so much lately.

SW: I can see that you love your children and your husband. You're feeling confused because you can't understand your husband any more, and he doesn't seem to understand what you are trying to do. Is that it?

CLIENT: Yes, but—he's just a man, and in his country, women don't work. He's feeling bad he can't get work. I don't blame him.

SW: You are trying very hard to understand him. I can see that.

CLIENT: Yes, and it's not just him. The kids are sick a lot lately, and the school is saying they are not behaving themselves. I try to get after them, but they're getting so fresh. And that place where we live—it's getting worse. The landlord doesn't care. I try to clean it, but with my husband home all day—I'm tired of fighting with them.

SW: Mrs. Armez, I hear you mentioning many problems that you are facing right now—your husband can't find a job and you're worried about his drinking, your children are often sick and having troubles in school lately, you are not pleased with where you are living, and you and your husband and children are not getting along. I can understand that you are feeling overwhelmed because you can't handle all of these problems by yourself.

CLIENT: (Shakes head and begins to sob.) I can't deal with it. It's just too much. I need some help.

SW: I can see that you are feeling very helpless because you can't change the situation, and you want some help with trying to deal with it all. What is it that you are hoping for, Mrs. Armez?

CLIENT: If only things could be different. I wish Hector could go back to work. He liked where he was, and we were getting along fine. And I wish the kids weren't so sickly and that they would mind in school. I guess I just want things the way they were. Maybe we should move away but how? It's just so bad right now. If only something could be done.

SW: I'll be glad to begin to work on it with you, Mrs. Armez. We can't tackle all of these problems at once, but we can take one at a time to see what can be done. But first, would you please talk a little more about the situation with me so that I can understand it better?

In this case vignette, the generalist began with introduction and reviewed the purpose for Mrs. Armez's coming. She gave the client time and encouragement to express her feelings about coming and moved on to clarify problems, feelings, and goals. With the identification of so many problems, the feelings and goals remain at a very broad level until further information can be obtained and until problems are prioritized.

The social worker will need to offer Mrs. Armez much support as the procedure moves into data collection. The social worker will need to know information to answer such questions as: Why was the husband laid off? How does he perceive the family problems at this time? What are the children's health problems and behavioral problems? How involved is the school or any other agency with the family? When did each problem begin? How motivated are family members to work for change? These questions all fall within an ecological-systems perspective for data collection, which will be presented in the next chapter.

The generalist working with the family would use the General Method for working with several interlocking systems. The target and action systems to be contacted could include employment agencies, hospital and health services, the school, the city's Income Maintenance Department, the landlord, housing authorities, programs for alcoholics, shelters for battered wives, protective services, and other agencies or social institutions.

> ### Mezzo Example 2: Generalist with the Manager (Bill Jones), the Personnel Director (Tom Wilson), and the Foreman (Joe Casey) of the Factory Where Mr. Armez Had Been Employed (Target System)
>
> (This interview takes place after the social worker had met with Mr. Armez in his home and received from him permission to talk with his employer.)
>
> SW: Good morning. I'm Katherine Brown, a social worker from Unity Social Service Department. I've asked to meet with you to discuss Mr. Armez, one of your past employees. I understand Mr. Armez was not accepted back to work after he recovered from his hospitalization. Is that correct?
>
> PERSONNEL DIRECTOR: Yes, Mr. Armez was only with us about a year before he took off, and we had to hire someone else.
>
> SW: I see. Mr. Armez wasn't with you very long before he took a sick leave. Let's see. I believe Mr. Armez said he began to work here in October of last year, making it 14 months of employment before he requested a sick leave. Is that correct?
>
> MANAGER: I'll tell you, Miss Brown, quite honestly, the company had some concerns about taking him back. We didn't think he was able to work at the level we expect of our employees.
>
> SW: I appreciate your honesty, Mr. Jones. You're saying that Mr. Armez wasn't accepted back because the company feared he wouldn't be able to do the work expected. May I ask why you thought that?

MANAGER: Well, let's see—do you remember, Tom?

PERSONNEL DIRECTOR: Yes, I believe we even had questions about his performance before he took off. Let's check with Joe about that. Joe Casey was the foreman over Mr. Armez. Could we get him up here, Bill?

MANAGER: (calls on phone)

SW: Thank you for trying to trace this back for me.

MANAGER: What's the matter, Miss Brown? Hasn't he found work anywhere else?

SW: No, he hasn't. I understand he liked his work here and thought he was doing a good job.

MANAGER: Here's Joe. Let's find out how he was doing. Joe, this is a local social worker asking about Hector Armez. Do you remember who he is?

FOREMAN: Oh yeah, the Spanish guy. He had to leave for some kind of operation, I think.

SW: He had trouble with his arm and needed to be hospitalized for an operation.

PERSONNEL DIRECTOR: Joe, his performance on the job wasn't that great, was it? We thought it wouldn't be wise to take him back at the time. Do you remember?

FOREMAN: I don't know. He was with us about a year or so and was coming along OK. He was still learning. After he left, we needed someone on the machine. We couldn't wait forever. He had been out a lot, and I had given him a warning.

SW: I believe I hear three reasons for not taking Mr. Armez back: (1) He was out a lot, (2) you needed a replacement, and (3) there were questions about his performance level. Is that right?

FOREMAN: Well, he was doing OK, but we just couldn't wait that long.

MANAGER: And, you know, after being in the hospital and all, maybe he wouldn't be able to man that machine. It's heavy work we do here.

SW: There was some risk involved in taking him back?

MANAGER: Well, we take risks, but not if we can avoid it. We needed to keep the machines going, and we couldn't count on him.

SW: I see. You needed to keep the machines going. May I ask how your personnel policy addresses the need for sick leave?

PERSONNEL DIRECTOR: Our employees can take a sick leave when they need it, but we get concerned when it's a new man and he's out a lot.

MANAGER: We often get new people, like Armez, who just want to take off a few weeks—or even a summer—and we can't be bothered with them.

SW: It sounds as if you really doubted that Mr. Armez had to leave for medical reasons because he's a member of a certain group of people.

MANAGER: Listen, Miss Brown, I don't have anything against Spanish people or any other group of people. We just didn't want to take him back. You heard the foreman say we gave him a warning for his absenteeism, and he continued to take off.

SW: I understand that you didn't want to take him back at the time, and I can see that it's not easy to talk about this. I really don't want to cause any difficulty, but I would like to try to see if there is any way that Mr. Armez could come back to work here. I can understand your limitations in keeping someone who misses a lot of work. Could you tell me how many days did he miss while he was working here?

PERSONNEL DIRECTOR: I'll have to review his file to find out the exact number of days he wasn't here.

MANAGER: Why are you so concerned about him, anyway? Is he asking for welfare? What do you want from us?

SW: I am working with the family while Mr. Armez is trying to find employment. Mr. Casey, the foreman, says that Mr. Armez was doing OK on the job, but he was out a lot. I know Mr. Armez had a health problem that needed medical attention. Apparently, Mr. Armez did not have the opportunity to show that he was better after his hospitalization. I hear that your personnel policy does have sick leave written in it, yet Mr. Armez was not given the chance to come back. What I'm hoping is that there will be some way that we can work together toward giving Mr. Armez the opportunity to return to work here.

MANAGER: What is he able to do now? Can he take on a heavy job?

SW: The doctor said he could return to work two weeks after the operation.

MANAGER: We never saw any doctor's statement. I don't know. We'll have to talk more about it here at our next administrative meeting. I'll meet with you again early next week. No promises.

SW: All right. I hope we will be able to work together on this.

MANAGER: We'll see what we can do. I'll need that doctor's statement. Why don't you set up another appointment with my secretary for early next week.

In this vignette, it is obvious that the social worker needed to have some basic facts (e.g., date employment began, reason for hospitalization, doctor's statement) to break through efforts at avoidance. She was sensitive to feelings and skillfully recognized them. Confrontation, with mention of legal action, was not needed at this time. Initial identification of problems, feelings, and goals took place. The social worker would want to move on to clarify why Mr. Armez was absent, what the company expects of its employees, and what the stated benefits are that Mr. Armez could have expected from the company.

It is possible that a social worker will not be able to get beyond the engagement stage with a target system. A social worker, either alone or with other systems (client or action), may work toward bringing about change in a target system, even if the system refuses to engage in the process. Strategies may be implemented outside of the target to cause the change necessary for goal accomplishment. The social worker may use the General Method to join with other resources and services to form an action system.

Mezzo Example 3: Generalist with Doctor at Hospital Clinic (Action System)

(This interview takes place after the social worker has received and delivered release-of-information forms signed by Mr. Armez.)

SW: Good afternoon, Dr. Jackson, I'm Kathy Brown from Unity Social Services. Thank you for agreeing to meet with me to discuss Mr. Armez, one of your patients.

DOCTOR: Yes, Miss Brown, I hope I may be of some help to you.

SW: Dr. Jackson, I am working with Mr. Armez and his family. Mr. Armez has not gone back to work yet. I am wondering about Mr. Armez's condition and his ability to take on a physically taxing job at J. B. Barnes Tractor Factory. I spoke with his employer, and there is hesitancy to take Mr. Armez back. One of the reasons given is their fear he will not be able to do the job because of his operation. Mr. Armez himself says he still feels some weakness in his arm, even though you said he could resume work a few weeks after the operation. I understand that the work Mr. Armez would do calls for heavy lifting and pulling on an assembly line that make tractors. I am wondering if Mr. Armez is able to take on this kind of work, and I would appreciate your professional assistance.

DOCTOR: Yes, I'm sorry to hear that Mr. Armez hasn't gone back to work yet. There was a growth on the arm that had to be removed. It was not malignant, and when the wound healed, he was discharged from the clinic. I was not aware that Mr. Armez was continuing to feel weakness in the arm. It could be simply because it hasn't been used for a while and it needs exercise.

SW: I see. The employer has requested a written medical statement about Mr. Armez's ability to work.

DOCTOR: I am concerned that Mr. Armez continues to feel weakness in his arm. I would be glad to take another look at it, Miss Brown, and let you know what I find.

SW: I can see that you are concerned about the situation, Dr. Jackson, and I am glad you are interested in working with me to help Mr. Armez get back to work.

DOCTOR: Yes. If I find that he should be able to do the work, I'll be happy to write up a statement to that effect.

SW: I'll suggest to Mr. Armez that he contact you for an appointment and I'll call you after you have seen him. Is that all right with you?

Here too, the social worker tries to engage a system in joint action as they work on the identification of problem, feelings, and goals. The social worker senses the concern and willingness of the doctor to get involved in the situation. Without becoming defensive, the doctor agrees to reconsider his assessment. The social worker recognizes this openness and moves quickly to initial goal setting. The doctor agrees to become engaged in the process and will proceed with Miss Brown in collecting data. This stage of the method would not have proceeded so smoothly if the doctor had to bring up policy constraints or rules and regulations of the clinic about taking back discharged patients. In this case example, the doctor as a staff member of the clinic apparently did not find any conflict in being able to cooperate with the social worker for goal accomplishment.

As the social worker continues to work with the Armez family and their multiple problems, additional client and action systems might emerge. It is possible she would begin macro practice and engage with a community or a group that would include members of the Armez family. For example, it could become apparent that poor housing conditions are felt by many people in the apartment complex of the Armez family. A community effort by all of the tenants might be the most effective means to improve the macro social situation.

It could be that the company would not take Mr. Armez back, and that Mr. Armez would tell the social worker he knew of six other Hispanic men who were laid off since the company went under new management. The social worker could meet with all six as a group, who might collectively agree to involve the Human Rights Commission.

With all of these examples, the generalist begins by engaging the client system in the identification and expression of presenting problems, purposeful feelings, and desirable goals. As stated, the General Method is applicable to client, action, or target systems of any size.

Using Social Work Foundation Knowledge in Engagement

As the generalist begins to have contact with a system, and throughout the process of the General Method, the foundation knowledge, values, and skills (see Table 1.3 in Chapter 1) are called into action. The perspective of the social worker is pervasively ecological as he or she observes the matching and interacting of systems and carefully applies theories and skills to practice.

As pointed out in this chapter, the generalist demonstrates in words and actions an unfolding of the principles of acceptance, individualization, nonjudgmental attitude, purposeful expression of feelings, controlled emotional involvement, self-determination, and confidentiality (Biestek, 1957; National Association of Social Workers, 1996). In the engagement stage, relationship and problem-solving skills are readily applied. The social worker uses skills in listening, responding, guiding, paraphrasing, and clarifying, along with skills for identifying problems, feelings, and goals. It is also possible, as in the target-system example, that some political skills may be needed. In trying to engage a target system in the initial stage of the General Method, the generalist may need to provide evidence, enter into bargaining, or propose legal action.

Knowledge about people, families, organizations, and communities as well as concepts from role theory and stress theory are very helpful to a social worker in exploring problems, feelings, and goals during engagement. In the case vignettes just presented, the problems included the stresses associated with the major life events of Mr. Armez's illness, surgery, and job loss and how these stressors altered performance of his role within the community and spousal roles within the family. No longer able to fulfill his valued roles of worker and family breadwinner, Mr. Armez experienced family role strain, personal distress, and decreased self-esteem. In formulating descriptions of the problems, feelings, and goals of the situation, the social worker used knowledge of people, their environments, and the interdependence of both. Problems were seen as taking place at the interface between a client system and other systems in the environment. Feelings and their reasons were related to a need or failure in matching expectations between client systems and environmental systems. Goals were generally described in terms of developing or enhancing the fit and transactions among client systems.

The use of foundation knowledge, values, and skills from an ecological systems perspective and with an open selection of theories and concepts continues as a generalist moves into the second stage of the General Method. As data are collected, the social worker knows that in the evolving procedure of the method, a refinement takes place in identifying and expressing problems, feelings, and goals—the three guiding landmarks of the engagement stage. Although each of the six stages of the General Method has its own particular landmarks to guide the social worker and client system, the elements of foundation and the landmarks of earlier stages remain present and are called on throughout the procedure.

Human Diversity in Engagement

As stated earlier, sensitivity to human variability is needed within each stage of the General Method of social work practice. During engagement, for example, as a social worker and a client system begin to identify purpose, problems, feelings, and goals, an awareness of the culture of the client system can help the social worker create an atmosphere of understanding and responsiveness. Care can be demonstrated even in the selection of place for the initial contact. To foster a sense

of security and trust, it may be more appropriate to meet with members of a particular cultural system outside of the office or agency. For example, outreach in
the neighborhood and home visits have proven to be effective especially within the
Hispanic community (Castex, 1994; Marin, 1993; Ordaz & DeAnda, 1996).

Members of ethnic groups incorporate knowledge of their ethnic history and
personal experiences with people of diverse cultures as they relate cross-culturally.
(*Cross-culturally* refers to systems of different cultures.) Consumers of services
may view service providers and agencies from different perspectives, particularly if there are no apparent members of the consumer's culture in the service-
providing system. Guardedness, hostility, fear, and defensiveness are often
present when a client system begins to have contact with a social worker from a
different culture. Defenses vary according to ethnic backgrounds. Chinese culturally derived defenses, for example, include politeness, quietness, and friendliness
when the individual is confronted with potential threatening situations (Ching,
McDermott, Fukunaga, Yamagida, Mann, & Waldron, 1995; Lie, 1999).

In approaching a client, action, or target system and beginning to identify
the purpose of contact, a social worker needs to be sensitive to basic communication patterns, according to the culture of the system. To give and to expect eye-to-
eye contact with Native Americans or Asians, for example, would be insensitive,
because eye contact is generally considered to mean lack of respect in these cultures (Devore & Schlessinger, 1999; Williams & Ellison, 1996). Although a social
worker may feel more comfortable with informality toward client systems (i.e., using
first names, casual dress, attitude of friendliness), members of certain cultures, such
as Asian American and African American, may need and expect a formal approach
from a professional social worker, at least initially. Asian Americans are particularly uncomfortable with functioning in ambiguity. During first contacts,
they need to have the purpose and function of a service clearly stated (Brown &
Broderick, 1994; Chung, 1992; Pinderhughes, 1989).

In proceeding, the social worker keeps in mind the time orientation of a culture. Urban African Americans and Japanese Americans may need time to build
up a sense of trust and openness; by contrast, Mexican Americans move quickly
into relationships and decision making, relying heavily on inferential abilities.
Repetition and calculations are often unwelcomed by Mexican Americans as they
proceed with problem solving (Lum, 1999; McAdoo, 1993; Pedersen, 1997).

Diversity is also found among cultures when it comes to identifying and
expressing feelings. People from Eastern European ethnic groups, such as Poles,
Hungarians, Czechs, and Slovaks, have strong feelings of shame over having to
seek professional help (McGoldrick, Giordano, & Pearce, 1996). Members of some
ethnic groups are very reluctant to talk about personal feelings and problems
with outsiders. This is particularly true of Asians and Native Americans. On the
other hand, members of Jewish and Italian cultures are often openly expressive
of their feelings, needs, and problems (Blount, Thyer, & Frye, 1992; Huang, 1991;
McGoldrick, Giordano, & Pearce, 1996).

Problems or needs may be perceived and described from various perspectives,
according to culture. For example, Chinese Americans and Mexican Americans
basically see problems collectively rather than individually. The deviant behavior of

one is seen as a direct assault on the pride of the community (Green, 1999). Also, problems may need to be described in material rather than emotional terms. Huang (1991) found, for example, that many Chinese clients would work on emotional problems only if they were receiving concrete assistance at the time.

Although a problem may come to the attention of a social worker as a personal problem of an individual or group, a culturally sensitive social worker is cognizant of the fact that environments themselves, with their institutional pressures and prejudices, may really be the problem that needs to be addressed. In the engagement stage, a social worker fosters a sense of openness when the person or people that make up a client system can begin to see that the social worker understands both the real problem and how they perceive and experience it.

Goals may be more clearly understood and articulated if a social worker is aware of a culture's value orientation. The aspirations and goals of individuals, families, groups, and communities usually reflect the values that have been transmitted through their culture.

The values of *person, family, tribe,* and *community* are commonly upheld by several cultures. There may be, however, discrete meaning for such values in particular groups. For example, although individualism is valued by Puerto Rican Americans, there is a distinction that should be noted by social workers as they begin to work with Puerto Rican Americans. The Puerto Rican culture centers attention on those personal inner qualities that constitute individual uniqueness and personal worth in and of themselves, in contrast to the prevalent individualism in the United States that values individual aspiration and ability to compete for higher social and economic status (Garcia-Preto, 1996).

An astute understanding of values helps a social worker locate what motivates members of the client system and give direction on expressing relevant goals. Members of the Puerto Rican American culture, for example, would be motivated to work on goals that appeal to personal responsibility and leadership, rather than those that appeal to platforms or programs.

Throughout each stage of the General Method, a social worker should demonstrate sensitivity not only to multiculturalism but also to social pluralism and socio-demographic differences. During engagement—for example, as purpose and problems are identified—the social worker shows respect and acceptance by beginning where the client system is. He or she should focus on only those problems and needs that the client system wishes to address. When a social worker knows that an individual is of a lower socio-economic class, of a homosexual orientation, physically challenged, or mentally challenged, there must not be a hidden agenda on the social worker's part, in which he or she expects to discuss (or to change) the lifestyle of the individual. If the client system is having difficulties that relate to human diversity, a social worker may begin to be helpful by making known that he or she is aware of the pressures and problems persons often have to face in U.S. society. As generally found in helping relationships, a client is usually more comfortable by beginning with external problems (related to societal institutions, policies, and practices). Eventually, problems that are more interpersonal (primary relationships, for example) and then more intrapersonal (dual identities, self-esteem, fears) may be shared.

During engagement, a social worker encourages and accepts a client's expression of feelings. For client systems who experience themselves as being apart from the mainstream, these feelings may include loneliness, alienation, isolation, hurt, and anger and outrage toward a rejecting, condemning family or society. A social worker who becomes defensive or judgmental will be indicating a lack of self-awareness and sensitivity to the needs of the client system.

As initial goals are stated during engagement, the social worker carefully listens and articulates the aspirations and expectations of a client system. If the social worker cannot support the goals of a client system in any way, this circumstance should be recognized and resolved before proceeding into the second stage of the General Method. Often problems associated with multiculturalism, social pluralism, and socio-demographic diversity are caused by discriminatory practices of large institutions. Goals, therefore, are often long-range, social-change goals as well as personal, immediate-need goals. The social worker takes time throughout the General Method to engage the client system in the process of realistically stating, understanding, and refining long- and short-range goals, which may be personal, interpersonal, institutional, or societal in nature.

Engagement in Micro, Mezzo, and Macro Practice in Diverse Field Areas

Each chapter of this text that describes one of the six stages of the General Method (Chapters 4 through 9) contains a section that has case examples of micro, mezzo, and macro practice from diverse areas of the field of social work. Examples are selected from the areas of child welfare, gerontology, public social welfare, community services, education, corrections, and homeless shelters. The examples demonstrate the apparent applicability of the General Method, with its six stages and major focal points for each stage, in all areas of the field of practice. Although the persons, problems, and needs addressed in each example relate directly to a specific field area, the General Method is used by all of the social workers.

In the following section, the application of knowledge and skills during the *engagement stage* of the General Method will be demonstrated by entry-level generalists in seven diverse field areas.

I. Field Area: Child Welfare

A. Agency: State Department of Children's Services
B. Client System

K is a 15-year-old female of French American ethnicity. The police referred her to Children's Services two and a half years ago because she was physically abused by her mother. K had also been sexually abused by her stepfather on two occasions. She was committed to the state and placed in a group home, where she lived for over two years. She then requested and was placed in foster care. After two months in a foster home, K ran away. The police picked her up and placed her in an emergency shelter. She was at the shelter when the case was assigned to a new social worker from the State Department of Children's Services.

C. Engagement

Problem: During engagement, K said she knew she had two problems: (1) she had no place to go to live and (2) she was missing school. She said she did not want to return to her foster home, but would not say why she ran away. She shared that she had run away with a boyfriend, who left her after a few days. K spoke about hating herself and knowing that no place or school would want her. She described herself as "dumb" and "ugly." During engagement, the worker identified additional problems. These included the personal problems of (1) poor self-esteem, (2) identity confusion, (3) problems concerning her sexuality and how to relate to males, and (4) depression.

Feelings: K expressed feelings of nervousness and loneliness. She said she knew she was "jittery" and just couldn't settle down to anything. She also said that she "hated" her mother and stepfather and never wanted to see them again. She wished she could live with her "real father."

At one point, K began to cry and left the room. When she returned, the social worker identified feelings of pain and depression. K admitted that she was "really down" and believed that no one really cared if she lived or died. She said that her "rotten boyfriend" got tired of her, even though she "gave him everything," and she knew her parents couldn't stand her either.

Goals: K's stated goals were (1) to obtain and maintain a permanent placement (permanent placement *means a place to live until adulthood*) and (2) to get back into school as soon as possible. K said she wanted to leave the shelter but didn't know where to go. She thought she would like to go back to the group home where she had lived before she had been placed in the foster home. The social worker hoped that K would eventually see the need for help with her more personal problems, although K was not ready to discuss this need at the time of engagement.

D. Charted Progress

By the end of the engagement period, the social worker recorded the items in Table 4.1 to begin to chart a formal plan of action (explained in detail in this chapter).

TABLE 4.1 Initial Recording

Date Identified	Problem/Need	Client System Feelings	Goal
1/12	No permanent home	Loneliness Restlessness Hatred of self and others	a. To obtain a permanent placement b. To maintain a permanent placement
1/12	Out of school	Depression	c. To reenter school
1/12	Personal problems a. Poor self-esteem b. Identity confusion c. Sexuality (relationships, behavior) d. Depression		

The date of contract, the problems identified at the time by the worker or the client, and the goals mutually agreed on by both K and the social worker were listed as in Table 4.1.

II. Field Area: Gerontology

A. Agency: Seaside Nursing Home

B. Client System

Mrs. J is an 80-year-old Portuguese American woman who was admitted to the skilled-nursing facility at Seaside Nursing Home two weeks ago. She was released from the hospital with a diagnosis of "organic brain syndrome." The summary from the hospital social worker indicated that Mrs. J was a housewife with no formal education. Her family refused to be involved with her and left no name or address for contact. Mrs. J cannot remember where members of her family live. At the nursing home, she remained seclusive and appeared to be afraid to leave her room. An entry-level generalist was assigned to work with Mrs. J to help her adjust to the nursing home.

C. Engagement

Problem: During the first interview, Mrs. J expressed displeasure with her placement in the institution. She said she did not like it at the nursing home and wished she could go somewhere else. She did not respond when asked where she would like to go. Mrs. J could not speak English fluently, and wished there was someone who could speak Portuguese with her. She said she was afraid that if she left her room, her things would be stolen. She would only leave her room if someone came to take her to the dining room for meals.

Feelings: Mrs. J began to express feelings of distrust, anger, and abandonment. She did not feel comfortable in a cross-cultural environment. Whenever the social worker began to talk about where Mrs. J came from or where she would like to go, Mrs. J became quiet and looked very sad and hurt. She would shake her head and look out the window. During the second interview, she said she had three children but they all had gone away and left her. She would not talk about her husband.

Goals: Mrs. J said that she wished she were able to go out on her own. She realized that she first had to be able to leave her room before she could go anywhere else. She did not think she liked the people at the nursing home, but was willing to meet twice a week with the social worker to talk about how she was getting along. She said she hoped that someone who spoke Portuguese would come to see her.

The goals for Mrs. J that were agreed on by herself and the worker during engagement were (1) to be able to leave her room on her own, (2) to have someone who speaks Portuguese visit with her, and (3) to get to know the staff and resources of the nursing home.

D. Charted Progress

The social worker charted progress at the end of the engagement stage, identifying dates, problems, and goals, as shown in Table 4.2. At this time, it was also possible to record the initial contract for biweekly meetings of the social worker and Mrs. J.

TABLE 4.2 Initial Recording

Date Identified	Problem/Need	Client System Feelings	Goal	Task	Contract	Date Anticipated
9/25	Poor adjustment: seclusiveness— not leaving room alone	Distrust Fear Anger Abandonment	To be able to leave room alone			
9/25	Cultural isolation: need to communi- cate in native language		To be visited by someone who speaks Portuguese			
9/27	Unfamiliar with staff and resources of the nursing home		To get to know the staff and resources of the nursing home	Meet twice a week with social worker	Social worker and Mrs. J	10/4 and every Tuesday and Thursday thereafter

III. Field Area: Public Social Welfare

A. Agency: State Social Services

B. Client System

Mr. and Mrs. P and their two children, ages 2 and 4, arrived at the agency with their suitcase. Mrs. P's father had called the agency a week earlier, saying that his daughter and her two children had come to live with him, but he didn't have any room. He wanted "the state" to find housing for his daughter and grand-children. He also said that his daughter and her husband were separated, but that her husband was waiting at their old apartment to take their AFDC (Aid to Families with Dependent Children) check. Mrs. P's father wanted the check held for his daughter, who would come in to pick it up. When the P family arrived at the Social Services unit, the case was assigned to an entry-level generalist.

C. Engagement

During the initial interview, because of the urgent nature of the situation, the problem, feelings, and goals of engagement were explored and specific data were collected. Preliminary assessment, planning, and intervention also took place during the first day of contact with the family.

Problem: In this situation, housing was the obvious immediate problem. Because of repeated tardiness in paying their rent, the P family had been evicted from their apartment. Mrs. P thought that she and her children could find temporary shelter with her father. After two weeks, however, he said they would have to leave. Mr. P expected to take the money from their welfare check and return to Maine, where his mother lived. He said he had planned to send for his family once he got settled. At this time, however, Mr. and Mrs. P said that they decided they would prefer to find another apartment locally.

TABLE 4.3   Initial Recording

Date Identified	Problem/Need	Client System Feelings	Goal
9/28	Housing for P family	Helplessness Anger Rejection Confusion	a. To find emergency shelter for the P family b. To locate an apartment for long-term residence by the family

Feelings: Mrs. P was feeling rejected by her father and blamed him for their current problem. Mr. P was angry at the state for not sending their check and food stamps. (After the initial call from Mrs. P's father, the check and food stamps had been held by the post office and were later returned to the central welfare office.) Both felt that no one really wanted them or cared. They appeared to be confused and said that they were feeling helpless and did not know what to do.

Goals: When asked what they hoped the social worker could do for them, the P's said that they wanted him to find them a place to stay. The social worker clarified his own role and said that he could assist them by locating temporary shelter, but that they would have to become active in searching for and in documenting their search for more permanent housing. The immediate goals agreed on by the social worker and Mr. and Mrs. P were (1) to find emergency shelter for the family (short-range goal) and (2) to locate an apartment in the local or neighboring geographic area for extended residence by the family (long-range goal).

D. **Charted Progress**

As the social worker began recording for a formal plan of action, the basic information obtained through engagement was charted as in Table 4.3.

IV. **Field Area: Community Services**

A. **Agency: Clayton Neighborhood House**

B. **Client System**

Mrs. T lives with her husband and three children in a one-room apartment at 33 L Street. She came to Clayton House to request clothing for her children and to complain about the lack of heating in their room. She informed the social worker that there were three other Hispanic families in their building who also were without heat. None of the adults in the four families spoke English. A Spanish-speaking entry-level generalist visited all four families. They met to organize and work together to obtain heating in their homes.

C. **Engagement**

Mrs. T was encouraged to express her problems, feelings, and goals when she met with the social worker. Her initial request for clothing was granted on the same *day at the first interview. She was directed to the clothing room at Clayton House and told to take whatever she needed.*

After the social worker and Mrs. T talked together about the heating prob-lem, the client system in this case expanded to include members from the other three families who shared the problem. Before trying to resolve the issue with Mrs. T, the social worker wanted to meet with the others who were experiencing the problem and to find out more about the situation. After visiting each family individually in their apartments, the social worker met with members of all four families in Mr. and Mrs. T's room. Together, they began to identify problems, feelings, and goals.

Problem: *The basic problem identified during the engagement period was the lack of heat on the second floor of the L Street apartment building. All of the resi-dents who met with the social worker lived on the second floor. They said that they had had very little, if any, heat over the past month. There were some nights when the temperature dropped below freezing, and the only means of keeping warm was to turn on all of the burners and the ovens of their stoves.*

When the social worker inquired about the residents on the first floor, she was told that they do not have a heating problem. They were described as "English speaking," and it was felt that they received better treatment from the landlord.

Feelings: *The community of residents who met with the social worker shared feel-ings of frustration and victimization. They felt helpless and angry. They did not think that their landlord listened to them or cared about what happened to them. They were afraid that if they put pressure on the landlord, he would evict them and they would not be able to find another place to live.*

Goal: *All present agreed that something had to be done. They asked the social worker to help them. A mutually agreed-on goal was to get their apartments heated. They wanted assurance that heating would be provided consistently throughout the winter.*

D. Charted Progress

The social worker recorded the basic information obtained during engagement as outlined in Table 4.4. She saw a possible problem of discrimination by the land-lord, but decided to wait until further data were collected before recording the problem in the record.

TABLE 4.4   Initial Recording

Date Identified	Problem/Need	Client System Feelings	Goal
12/3	Lack of heat on second floor	Frustration Helplessness Fear Anger	To obtain consistent, adequate heating for second-floor residents of L Street apartment house

V. Field Area: Education

A. Agency: Keeney Elementary School
B. Client System

Jim G is an 8-year-old African American child in third grade. His teacher referred him to school social services because he began to miss school or to come late each morning. His behavior was becoming increasingly inappropriate. He often kept his head down on his desk and remained silent when his teacher called on him. He no longer raised his hand in class or showed any interest in learning. His grades were beginning to drop, and his teacher feared he would get so far behind in his work that he might have to be moved to a different classroom. The teacher also noted that Jim was not eating his lunch. These behaviors were not apparent until the second month of the school year. An entry-level generalist was assigned to talk with Jim and to make a home visit.

C. Engagement

Problem: *When Jim entered the social worker's office, he sat at the table and kept his head down. The social worker asked if he knew why she wanted to see him, and he shook his head negatively. She reviewed his teacher's concerns and assured Jim that the people at school wanted to try to help him so that he would not get behind in his schoolwork. The social worker wondered if Jim could talk about what was bothering him lately. Jim didn't answer, but got up and walked over to the book-case containing toys and games. He asked who the toys were for, and the social worker explained that any of the children who came to the office could use them. Jim took out the game "Chutes and Ladders" and asked if the social worker wanted to play it with him. As they were setting up the game, the social worker said that she could see that it wasn't easy for Jim to talk about what was troubling him, but she hoped that he would eventually. With his mother's permission, the social worker began to see Jim twice a week in her office.*

After the first meeting with Jim, the social worker visited his mother at home. Jim lived with his mother and father in a middle-class neighborhood. Mrs. G expressed concern over her son's regressive school behavior and said that she noticed that lately he was acting somewhat strange at home also. He wouldn't go to sleep at night unless his mother stayed in his room and kept a light on. She could not identify anything different or painful that Jim might have experienced since school began. She said that her son had done excellent schoolwork when he was in first and second grades, and she could not understand what was happening to him to bring about the changes he was going through. She offered to work with the school in whatever way possible. She stated that she would see that Jim got to school on time each day even if she or her husband had to drive him. Mrs. G agreed to come to school to talk with the social worker again in two weeks.

The problems identified during the initial interviews with Jim and his mother were (1) school tardiness and absenteeism, (2) declining academic functioning (interest, participation, grades) and (3) refusal to sleep without his mother and a light in his room.

TABLE 4.5   Initial Recording

Date Identified	Problem/Need	Client System Feelings	Goal	Task	Contract	Date Anticipated
11/1	Jim's school tardiness and absenteeism	Depressed Sad	To improve Jim's regular school attendance (on time each day)	1. See that Jim gets to school on time each day.	1. Mrs. G	11/5 and each school day thereafter
11/1	Jim's declining academic performance		To improve academic functioning (interest, participation, grades)	1. Talk with Jim about school problems.	1a. Social worker and Jim b. Mrs. G and Jim	11/6 and twice a week thereafter
11/2	Jim's getting to sleep at night					

Feelings: In early sessions with Jim and with his mother, very little feeling was expressed by either of them. Jim avoided talking about anything personal. Mrs. G only expressed concern over her son's school performance.

Goal: Mrs. G and the social worker agreed to work together to help Jim improve his attendance at school and his academic performance. Both agreed to talk with Jim to try to motivate him to want the same goals.

D. Charted Progress

As the social worker extended the engagement period with Jim and his mother, she recorded the initially identified problems as found in Table 4.5. She also recorded the goals and tasks that she and Mrs. G developed.

VI. Field Area: Corrections

A. Agency: Juvenile Court

B. Client System

A group was formed for seven male adolescents, all age 14, who were on probation for burglary, theft of automobiles, or minor larceny (shoplifting). The usual probationary period was six months. If a youth attended and participated regularly in group meetings and met all of the other requirements of probation, the time of probation could be reduced to four months. All of the group participants knew that they were expected to attend weekly group meetings from four to six months, depending on when their probationary period would be over. A new B.S.W. female social worker was assigned to co-lead the group with an M.S.W. male social worker who had worked in corrections for six years and who had specialized in social group work while in graduate school.

C. Engagement

Problem: The presenting problem shared by all of the youths was being on probation for illegal actions. Discussion centered on clarifying the problem. Was it being on probation or was it committing illegal acts? At this time, most of the group members saw the problem more in terms of having gotten caught rather than having broken the law. One member said that their basic problem was "law-breaking leading to probation." All agreed that this was a good way to describe it.

As group participants began to talk more about themselves, several other common problems began to surface. The youths were surprised to learn that all of them were in special classes in school because of learning disabilities. They all said that they had "bad tempers" and made some reference to problems at home. Two of the youths mentioned their drug habits.

Feelings: In early group sessions, members expressed strong feelings of mistrust, particularly toward the group leaders. Some members complained about having to come to the group but eventually admitted that they were angry really because they had gotten caught by the police and put on probation. They said that it was "dumb" of them to get caught. Members repeatedly indicated a sense of little self-worth.

TABLE 4.6 Initial Recording

Date Identified	Problem/Need	Client System Feelings	Goal	Task	Contract	Date Anticipated
10/1	Law breaking leading to probation	Anger	To get off probation in four months	Attend weekly group meetings.	Seven members, two social workers	10/1 and each Monday at 4:00 P.M. for at least four months
10/1	Bad tempers		To learn to control temper in school, home, neighborhood			
10/1	Need to understand "changes" of teenagers		To learn about "changes" youths go through			
10/1	Parent-son conflicts					
10/1	Low self-worth					

Goals: The goal most clearly expressed by all of the participants was to get off probation as soon as possible. They also admitted that they wished they could stay out of trouble, but that it was not easy. They said, too, that they would like to be able to handle their tempers better. They expressed interest also in being able to understand more about "the changes" they were going through.

Although reference had been made to problems they were having with parents, there was not a general agreement that group members wanted to work on getting along better with their parents. They also did not like to talk about the fact that they did not think they were worth very much.

D. Charted Progress

The social worker recorded the problems and goals that were identified by the group during the engagement period, as found in Table 4.6. She did not list the problems of learning disabilities and drug habits, because the youths were receiving help with these problems from other services. The preliminary agreement of group attendance and participation in order to get off probation was recorded in the columns called "task," "contract," and "date anticipated."

VII. Field Area: Homeless Shelter

A. Agency: West End Community Shelter

B. Client System

José Romano, a 37-year-old Hispanic male, came to the emergency shelter on May 7. He had gone to the County Department of Social Services for assistance and they referred him to the shelter. During his intake interview with the shelter social worker, an experienced B.S.W., Mr. R said that he had been recently evicted from his apartment and that he was HIV positive. He had come to the mainland United States from Puerto Rico 20 years ago. He was divorced with no children.

C. Engagement

Problem: Mr. R told the social worker that he had completed a drug detox program six years ago and thought he had put his life in order. He was working as a chef in a nursing home when he found out that he was HIV positive. He quit his job because he did not think he would be allowed to work in a kitchen. He did not realize that he could not be fired because he was HIV positive. He could not find another job. After his money ran out, he lost his apartment, and his friends seemed no longer to be interested in him. His immediate needs were identified by Mr. R and the social worker as shelter, food, and health care.

Feelings: Mr. R was feeling abandoned and depressed. He said that he had no place to turn and did not know what was going to happen to him. He knew he was not feeling well physically and was afraid that he was getting worse.

Goals: Mr. R said that he would like to get medical help for his condition. He also said he needed a place to stay. He understood that the shelter had a 60-day limit and he would need some place to go after that. He wondered whether the shelter would keep him even for 60 days if his sickness got worse. He said he wished he could be working. He wanted to be able to pay for his food and lodging.

TABLE 4.7   **Initial Recording**

Date Identified	Problem/Need	Client System Feelings	Goal
5/8	HIV positive, lack of knowledge	Fear Abandonment	To obtain ongoing medical care and information
5/8	Homeless/hungry		To obtain immediate housing/food
			To obtain long-term housing
5/8	Unemployed (no financial support)		To obtain employment—part/full time
			To obtain public assistance/social security (long range)

Goals were identified as (1) to get medical care, (2) to locate housing (short- and long-term), and (3) to locate employment (part or full time).

D. Charted Progress

The identified needs and goals agreed upon by Mr. R and the social worker were recorded (see Table 4.7). The worker knew that Mr. R eventually would not be able to work and would need some other source of financial support. At the present time, however, Mr. R was highly motivated and appeared able to engage in some type of employment.

Conclusion

In this chapter, focus was on the engagement stage of the General Method. The three focal points of problems, feelings, and goals were highlighted. Skills for working in these three major areas were identified. The use of the ecological-systems perspective throughout the stage was emphasized. The traditional purpose of social work, to enhance social functioning, was evident as the engagement process was described within a strengths/needs orientation.

Case vignettes offered a demonstration of the use of skills, the ecological-systems perspective, and the three guiding landmarks of the engagement stage. Examples described the work of a generalist as she began to engage a family, a business employer, and a health care service in the General Method. The use of foundation knowledge, values, and skills during engagement was discussed. Additional examples included cases from diverse field areas. Several ways in which a social worker demonstrates sensitivity to human diversity during engagement were also described.

The expected timing of the engagement stage was not stated in this chapter because actual timing of any stage in the General Method is not clearly predictable. Sometimes a social worker and client system may move through engagement or any other stage in one interview. Sometimes it takes months, or as discussed, it may never be completed. The method and each of its stages have an evolving, dynamic, and relative nature.

In the next chapter, the generalist will be seen in movement to the second stage of the method: data collection. The overlap and natural flow from the first to the second stage will be shown. In the second stage of the systematic procedure, the social worker and system of contact take a deeper and sharper look at the issue, need, question, or difficulty brought forth for study and action.

5 Data Collection

As the social worker engages the client system in problem and goal prioritization by gathering more information, the social worker and the client system move into the second stage of the General Method. Usually, the social worker collects information first from the client system (unless referring information has been forwarded before the initial meeting) and second from other relevant sources deemed necessary for verification and comprehensiveness. When the information that the social worker collects can be verified as fact, it becomes data. Demonstrating the scientific aspect of professional social work, the generalist uses research skills to distinguish fact from impression, assumption, or conclusion. Inasmuch as possible, the social worker strives to acquire information that is factual in the data-collection stage of the General Method.

Using an ecological-systems perspective, the generalist directs inquiry to find out about the problems presented, the persons involved in the problems, and the potential or actual resources and barriers in the environment that may affect the person-problem-environment situation. Specifically, the social worker collects information about the problem, the person, and the environment.

Gathering Data

Although the social worker's unit of attention typically centers on the individual client, it can also encompass the family, small groups of unrelated persons, organizations, or communities. Usually, most of the data are gathered through the identified client about the client system. However, it may be equally important to gather information through a client's relative(s) (spouse, child, or other related member), a significant friend(s) who has an immediate impact on the client's day-to-day living, and/or an outside person(s) in the client's immediate environment. The outside person(s) may include human service personnel, health personnel, treatment professionals, teachers, and employers, to name a few. To gain an understanding of the micro system or the client's internal frame of reference about a particular problem or situation, it is helpful to collect information in the following four major areas:

1. Explore the scope, or breadth and depth, of the client's presenting problem
   - Who has the problem: the client, the significant other in the client's life domain, or a person outside of the client system?
   - How is the problem manifested? Can specific behaviors, actions, or events be observed?
   - Is it a new problem or an ongoing one? Why is the client seeking help now?
   - Where does the problem occur in the client's environment?
   - How often does the problem happen? Can a beginning frequency of problem manifestation (i.e., a baseline) be obtained?
   - What is the severity, intensity, and duration of the problem manifestation?
2. Determine the client's degree of functioning in several major dimensions of life.
   - What is the client's age and developmental life stage? Are they congruent?
   - What role does the client need to fulfill?
   - What dimensions of the whole person (cognitive, behavioral, biological, emotional, spiritual) does the problem affect?
   - Is the problem creating a crisis for the client's functioning and/or role fulfillment?
   - How successful is the client in role fulfillment with and without the problem?
   - What other significant persons in the client's life domain are affected by the presenting problem? How are they affected? What has been their response?
3. Explore the historical and idiosyncratic ways in which the client has attempted to cope with the problem.
   - What meaning does the client attribute to the problem presented?
   - What cultural, ethnic, and spiritual beliefs and values are important to the

client and relevant to the current problem situation? Which values and beliefs may pose barriers to problem solving?

- How difficult does the client view the problem?
- How satisfied is the client with his or her own role functioning in view of the problem?
- How interested or motivated is the client in seeking resolution for the problem?
- What outside aversive or discomfort factors impinge on the client's present degree of action or inaction?
- How resilient is the client in coping with stress in general and with the presenting problem in particular?

4. Identify the resources available to address the presenting situation.
   - What personal strengths does the client possess (educational level, problem-solving approach, mood disposition, relationship with others, and health disposition)?
   - What economic and environmental resources does the client possess for meeting the basic needs of income, child rearing and child care, housing, food, clothing, household items, personal care and recreation, health care, and access to phone and transportation?
   - What familial or informal resources does the client possess? Which people are significant in the client's life? Does the client have significant persons who might be enlisted for support?
   - What external or formal resources are available in the client's life domain?

To understand the problems, needs, and goals of the mezzo systems, such as a family or small group, the challenge is to collect enough information about each individual member while collecting information about the whole group:

1. Find out the purpose of the group as articulated by the mission of a particular organization and by as many members as possible.
   - What is the written purpose of the group system or the purpose as articulated by the leader of the group? By the members?
   - What is the purpose of members' participation? What do members hope to gain by being in the group?
   - What are the explicit and implicit tasks of the group?
2. Determine the function of this group.
   - Is this a family group? What is its composition: nuclear or blended; traditional or nontraditional? Who are its members?
   - Is it a therapeutic group? What therapeutic mode of treatment does it use?
   - Is it a civic group? What civic action purpose does the group seek?
   - Is it an educational group? What knowledge does it seek to impart?
   - Is it a skills training group? What particular skills are being sought?
3. Identify the cultural, ethnic, and spiritual beliefs and values that are important to the group's functioning, purpose, or mission.
   - Do individual members' beliefs and values pose a barrier to the group's cohesion?

- Do the overall beliefs and values of the group pose a barrier to some other system?
- What are the strengths of the group's beliefs and value system?

4. Identify the operating processes of the group.
   - How often does the group meet? Where?
   - Is there a fee for joining or participating in the group?
   - Are there any specific responsibilities required of the participants? Are these responsibilities or tasks clearly stated or written out for participants at the time of joining?

5. Identify the point of the group interface affected by the problem presented.
   - Does the problem reflect intragroup relationships and communication?
   - Does the problem reflect intergroup relations and operation?
   - What other external systems are involved in the problem presented?

To understand the problems of large macro systems, the data collection focus expands to include gathering information about the cultural, political, and economic contexts of the social structures and people involved. Societal attitudes and expectations about social problems and social institutions vary. By sanctioning or developing means of problem control, amelioration, or prevention, these attitudes and expectations influence the tasks of large macro systems. Three areas form the central organizing principles underlying data collection with macro systems: understanding the social problem, the social task or goal, and the means of social service system delivery. For example, it is often useful to collect information about the following:

1. Identify the social problem by locality of the affected macro system.
   - Is the problem found in a local community? Does it show lack of relationships? Lack of problem-solving capacities? Lack of something else?
   - Is the problem found in the community at large? Does it affect larger social systems of education, health, employment, and the general welfare of citizens?
   - Is the problem apparent in the community at large or in predominantly disadvantaged populations? Does the problem involve social injustice, deprivation, or resource inequity?

2. Identify the social goals of the affected system.
   - Are the social goals related to the self-help capacity and integration processes of the local community?
   - Are the social goals related to community social planning or problem solving in relation to substantial community problems and specific task goals?
   - Are the social goals related to social action or a shifting of power relationships and resources? Do they seek basic institutional change? Do they require both process and task goals?

3. Identify the historical and idiosyncratic strategies that the macro system uses for facilitating change.
   - Is the typical approach to involve a broad cross-section of people in determining and solving their own problems through consensus?

- Is the strategy to gather facts about problems and decide on the most rational course of action through seeking consensus or through conflict?
- Is the strategy to shift the power structure and/or crystallize issues and concerns in order to take a stand through seeking conflict, competition, confrontation, direct action, or negotiation?

4. Identify the medium of change that would use the identified strategy for seeking change.
   - Does the change process involve creating a new or an existing small process and task goal-oriented community group (or several groups)?
   - Does the change process involve manipulation of formal organizations and data analysis?
   - Does the change process involve manipulation of mass organizations and political process?

5. Identify the boundaries of the client or target system needing the change.
   - Is it a local community? What are the geographic referents or endpoints? Is it one community or several?
   - Is it a subsystem or a local or large community? Is it a functional subpart of a community social system?
   - Is it a subpart or a segment of society?

6. Identify the most salient role of the social worker that will be needed to accomplish the change.
   - Does the generalist need to be primarily an enabler/catalyst, coordinator, teacher of problem-solving skills and ethical values, and/or a supporter in emphasizing common group objectives?
   - Does the generalist need to be an expert diagnostician, fact gatherer, and/or analyst in building a social plan, implementing a program, or interpreting research for practice application?
   - Does the generalist need to be an advocate, community organizer, or a social activist in organizing client or action groups to act in their own behalf in redressing injustice and promoting fairness?

Information may be gained directly through personal interviews, questioning, listening, and observing or indirectly through secondary sources such as records, documents, written materials, and verbal or written communication with outside systems. Collecting information through a personal interview may be characterized as having a conversation with a purpose. In a sense, the interview is a natural measuring instrument in which the respondent's answers to structured and unstructured questions may be translated into measures and used as data for monitoring client progress or evaluating outcomes (Kerlinger & Lee, 2000; Rubin & Babbie, 1997). Having begun to identify what information is needed for accurate assessment, the social worker begins to plan how to formulate questions for gathering the needed data.

Besides using the direct approach in questioning, social workers also find answers through listening and observation. Whereas direct structured questioning may sometimes elicit fear or defensiveness, skilled listening with minimal prompts or unstructured questioning and observing may disclose the needed information without provoking discomfort. If a social worker has any doubt about interpreting what is being seen or observed, the social worker has the responsibility to seek validation through multiple sources. Sometimes, this situation leads to a request for formal testing using standardized psychometric instruments. For example, the social worker may observe that the client's mood appears depressed and seems to interfere with problem solving. At the same time, the client overtly expresses anger and denies any feelings of sadness. To get a better handle on the client's affective state and to help the client recognize the effect of feelings on actions, the social worker requests that the client fill out a preliminary mood screening inventory. Subsequently, the social worker and the client discuss the results and plan for appropriate intervention. Pending the severity of the client's mood scores, observed affective expression, and psychosocial functioning and the purpose of the social worker's agency, the social worker's initial process of listening, observing, and data collecting may lead to a formal request for a full mental health evaluation by a clinical social worker, psychologist, or psychiatrist. When rapid assessment instruments are used as part of data collection, the social worker bears the responsibility of appraising the client if further testing or professional evaluation is needed.

Data may also be collected through secondary sources, such as evaluations from other agencies or professionals, public records, and other verbal or written communication with outside systems. Before any information is requested, or released, a written release-of-information form must be signed by the client system, with a copy placed in the agency records and the original sent to the source from which the information is sought. The release of information must reflect the client system's informed consent to release information to the social worker and agency and must explain how the information is to be used. An example of a release-of-information form may be found in Figure 5.1. What type of information is being requested and why the information is needed should be clearly explained to clients before a social worker asks for information or a signature on a release form. If data are being obtained through a study of public documents (i.e., state records of births, marriages, deaths, etc.), no permission is needed. Only information that is relevant and necessary for an accurate assessment should be sought by the social worker. It is possible that the system of contact will not allow the social worker to collect information on some problems; therefore, the social worker will have to limit the focus of attention to those problem areas accepted by the client system for study and intervention. If a client system will not give permission to release information that must be obtained in order to proceed with a case, the social worker may have to point out that services will be terminated unless the information is made available.

Fact versus Assumption

As a social worker collects data, skill is needed to distinguish between fact and assumption. Interpretation of what is heard or seen may be influenced by the social worker's frame of reference, past experiences, values, needs, and impressions.

FIGURE 5.1   Release-of-Information Consent Form

I _____ give permission
          (person giving consent)

for _____ to release to
          (system with information)

_____ the following
          (system to receive information)

information:

_____

_____

_____

_____

_____

_____

I understand that _____
                          (system receiving information)

will use this information for the following purpose:

_____

_____

_____

_____

_____

_____

This consent is to expire on   _____
                                        (date)

Signed _____   _____
                                                   (date)

Witness _____   _____
                                                   (date)

Agency representative _____   _____
                                                   (date)

Through personal experience, a social worker may quickly assume that one word, description, or event is similar to another, and a label may be given that is actually incorrect. When a social worker believes data have been found, he or she should ask: How is this documented? Did I really see this—hear this—find this?

Facts answer the question: Is this true or false? Assumptions, because they are not based on facts, may be either true or false. With assumptions, missing information is taken for granted. An activity to help refine one's skill for data collection is given in Exercise 5.1.

EXERCISE **5.1**
Information

A woman was leaving the office when a man appeared at the door and demanded money. The secretary opened a drawer. The contents of the drawer were scooped up, and the man sped away.

If the following statement is true, circle *T*. If it is false, circle *F*. If the statement is an assumption, circle *?*

1. A man appeared as a client was leaving the office.	T	F	?
2. The intruder was a man.	T	F	?
3. No one demanded money.	T	F	?
4. The secretary was the woman who opened the drawer.	T	F	?
5. The man took the contents of the drawer.	T	F	?
6. Someone opened a drawer.	T	F	?
7. Money was in the drawer.	T	F	?
8. The man ran away.	T	F	?
9. The man demanded money from the woman.	T	F	?
10. There are three people in this story.	T	F	?

In this exercise, all statements contain assumptions except for number 3, which is false, and number 6, which is true. The assumptions that cannot be substantiated by the words of the story are the following:

1. It is assumed that the woman is a client.
2. It is assumed that the man is an intruder.
3. False
4. It is assumed that the secretary is a woman.
5. It is assumed that the contents were taken (not just "scooped up") and that this was done by the man.
6. (True)
7. It is assumed that the contents were money.
8. It is assumed that "sped away" means "ran away."
9. It is assumed that the money was demanded from the woman and not from the secretary.
10. It is assumed that the woman was not the secretary.

These assumptions could be correct, but they could be incorrect also. In this exercise, the question mark should have been circled for 8 out of 10 answers.

A social worker tries to tap all possible resources for reliable data before beginning to make an assessment. The validity of each piece of information is considered before an effort is made to categorize and to integrate information. If the social worker recognizes that he or she is drawn toward making an assumption, the question should be asked: Why am I assuming this? It is possible that the assumption comes from one's "sixth sense," which may be a useful guide to tracking down the facts for a valid assessment.

The Problems/Needs

As stated earlier, when data are gathered, they are clustered under the three headings of "problem," "person," and "environment." The *problem* is the need, concern, issue, or difficulty that has been identified for study and action by both the social worker and the system of contact. Before deciding what needs to be done, or even which problem or need should be considered first, the social worker and the client system need to have a clear understanding of the scope, duration, and severity of each problem or need.

What is the scope of the problem or need? How many people are involved in the cause or the effect of the problem? What other systems are feeling this problem? Where can the boundary be drawn between those who have the problem or need and those who are outside of it?

The social worker also studies the duration of the problem or need. When did it begin? How long has it been going on? Has it been continuous or intermittent? The longer a problem exists, very likely, the longer it will take to break the pattern and bring about whatever change is needed. The shorter the duration, the greater the chance of quick and effective intervention.

And finally, the social worker asks: How serious is this problem or need? A guide for understanding the severity of a problem is to consider it in terms of a life-or-death scale. If, for example, the problem is physical, the social worker asks: Is the illness terminal? What is the potential for cure? If the problem is more interpersonal or social, the social worker considers the possibility of its leading to the breakdown or destruction of the family, the person, the group, the community, or the relationship.

The Persons

Another major category for data collection is the *person or persons* who are experiencing the problem or needs. A central concern is the coping capacity of the persons who have the problem. To what extent are the persons experiencing this problem capable of maintaining or improving their level of functioning? How have the persons been able to cope with this or similar problems before? Do the persons have physical, psychological, intellectual, economic, and spiritual strengths for dealing with the problem or need?

In addition to coping capacity, the social worker seeks indicators of the extent of motivation the persons have to work on the problem. Do they express a desire to change the situation or to overcome the problem? Do they have hope that things can change? Is any person feeling distress, enthusiasm, fear, or pressure that is directly related to the problem, and can this serve as impetus for change? Where do the persons want to begin? Why there? If any person does not seem to have hope that a particular situation can change, why not? What could be a source for motivating this person? What does this person value or want?

The Environment

The third basic category for data collection is that of the *environment* that surrounds the persons and problems under study. What is there in the environment that could be relating to this person-problem-environment situation? An ecological-systems perspective emphasizes the need and potential for transactions between organisms and their environments. Environmental factors, qualities, or systems may be present that could serve as resources. Currently, the persons may not be utilizing these resources, owing either to a lack of awareness or understanding or to a fear of rejection. To identify formal and informal resources, the social worker gathers information from systems in the environment as well as from client systems. The person is asked: What have you tried before? Did you go anywhere or to anyone to receive help with this problem before? Explorations move from a consideration of the person's immediate environment—with informal resources of family, friends, and local community services—to a study of more formal resources, public or private, in the extended societal environment. The social worker asks: What resources are available and appropriate to meet this need with these persons at this time?

In addition to gathering data on environmental resources, the social worker looks for information about systems or circumstances in the environment that may have a negative influence on the persons or that may be a contributing factor to the problem. These, too, may be informal sources—family, friends, community—or formal systems, such as schools, hospitals, and organizations. Is the problem caused or compounded by the person's interaction or interdependence with the environment? More specifically, what systems of the environment relate to the person-problem-environment situation, and how do they promote or prevent the growth or functioning of the persons involved?

In summary, the social worker asks: What is the scope, duration, and severity of the problem or need? Do the persons have the capacity and motivation to work on the problem? What resources or influences are there in the environment that could or do have an impact on the problem? After data are gathered in all three categories for each identified problem or need, the social worker proceeds in the General Method to a collective, comprehensive study for preliminary assessments and problem prioritization.

Throughout all the stages of the General Method, the skilled social worker is recognizing and processing data. As with the identified problem and goals of other stages, the information collected is dynamic and changing. Newly acquired data may lead to a reformulation of the problem, goals, assessment, or planned intervention. It is in the second stage of the General Method that particular emphasis is given to procuring and documenting any information that is missing and believed essential for effective assessment and planning.

Maintaining Confidentiality

Throughout the process of collecting data, the social worker demonstrates belief in the dignity of persons by respecting a client's right to privacy. The social worker understands and upholds the principle of confidentiality when information about a client system is requested, released, and utilized. Prior to receiving any information about a client system, the social worker must be sure of having the informed consent of the client. When requesting information, the social worker has the responsibility to clarify why the information is needed, how it will be used, and who will have access to the data collected.

In interacting with client systems, the social worker helps the client understand the implications of sharing information. A client who comes to an agency for help is asking for service from the agency. Occasionally, a client may ask a social worker not to tell "anyone," including other agency employees, what is being disclosed. In this case, the social worker will need to point out to the client that information is shared with those in the agency whose roles relate directly to service delivery, such as supervisors, secretaries, or other service providers who are working on the case. This type of sharing is not a breach of confidentiality. It is in accordance with the Federal Privacy Act of 1974 (Section 552a; b, 1), which recognizes the need for information exchange among those employees of an agency "who have a need for the record in the performance of their duties."

The client system should be assured that information shared with a social worker will not go outside of the agency without the client's permission. Exceptions to this (e.g., if the person threatens to harm another person or the social worker, or if the record is subpoenaed by the court) should be stated also. Unless a state has privileged-communication statutes for social workers, a social worker will be expected to comply if issued a subpoena requesting disclosure of information about a client to the court. A social worker who receives a subpoena should consult with an attorney to discuss how information is to be disclosed or retained.

As stated earlier, before requesting or releasing information about a client from or to a third party, a social worker needs to have the expressed consent of a client. According to Wilson (1978, p. 57), 10 conditions must be met if a client system is to give his or her informed consent:

1. The consumer must be told that there is a desire or a request to release certain data.
2. The consumer must understand exactly what information is to be disclosed. He cannot intelligently decide if he wants it revealed unless he knows exactly what material is in question.
3. In order for the consumer to know what is to be released, he should actually see the material and/or have it read to him and explained in terms he can understand.
4. The consumer must be told exactly to whom the information is being released—name, position, and affiliation.
5. The client must be told why the information is being requested and exactly how it will be used by the receiving party.
6. There must be a way for the consumer to correct or amend the information to ensure its accuracy and completeness before it is released.
7. The consumer must understand whether or not the receiving party has the right to pass the information on to a third party. The consumer must have the right to specify that this not be done without his knowledge and consent.
8. The consumer should be fully informed of any repercussions that might occur should he (a) grant permission for the disclosure or (b) not give permission.
9. The consumer should be advised that his consent for release of information is time-limited and revocable. He should be advised how he can withdraw his consent and be given periodic opportunities for doing so.
10. The consumer's consent for release of information must be in writing on a "Release-of-Information Consent Form."

Generally, social workers are cautious in disseminating confidential information to outside agencies. There are times, however, when social workers are somewhat careless in discussing the lives and problems of their clients. Occasionally, social workers feel a need to let go of the heavy input received during interviews, and to find outlets during informal situations with family, friends, or colleagues. This is not only a serious failure in confidentiality, but also a failure to use supervision or other appropriate channels for ventilation and support.

As data are received, skill is needed in selecting and documenting information for the record. Clients have the right to verify personally the accuracy of information recorded in the permanent files of the agency. When a social worker explains what will be done with the information collected, the client should be told about the kind of record kept by the agency and the policy regarding access to records. Discussion about records and confidentiality does not have to be prolonged enough to cause alarm or suspicion. A social worker uses skill in determining when and how to talk about different aspects of confidentiality with a client system.

Case Examples
Example 1: Agency Boundary

CLIENT: Miss Brown, there's a problem I'm having right now at home that I'd like to talk with you about, but I don't want Mr. Johnson, my husband's social worker, to know about it. He would tell my husband, and there would be trouble.

SW: I'd be happy to talk with you about any problem you may be having, Mrs. Armez, but I'm afraid I can't agree to withholding information from Mr. Johnson. Mr. Johnson and I are working as a team with your family, and we do share information. Is it that you are afraid that Mr. Johnson will discuss the problem with your husband?

CLIENT: Yes, I don't trust Mr. Johnson. He sees my husband every week, and I know they talk about me. He would end up telling my husband what I said.

SW: You are afraid of what would happen if your husband found out about the problem, is that it?

CLIENT: Yes, I couldn't deal with it if he found out. It would be awful. Do you think Mr. Johnson would tell my husband?

SW: Mr. Johnson and I talk together to help each other gain a more total understanding of the family situation. We respect what each of you shares with us, and we do not report back on what was said by one to the other.

CLIENT: I don't think I could risk it.

SW: I can see that you are troubled, Mrs. Armez, and I hope that you will grow in trusting us here at the clinic. I would like to see you get help with whatever is bothering you.

Example 2: Release of Information

SW: Mr. Armez, when I spoke with your employer, he said he needed a doctor's statement indicating that you are ready to go back to work. I understand that you had a doctor's examination last week. Is that right?

CLIENT: Yes, I saw the doctor last Tuesday. He said I could go back to work by Thursday.

SW: Fine. In order for me to get a statement from the doctor for your employer, I need to have your consent in writing. I will indicate on this release-of-information form that the doctor's statement will be sent to your employer with a copy to be kept in our file. Is this agreeable with you, Mr. Armez?

CLIENT: Yes, sure. That's OK.

SW: All right. Let's go over what is stated here on this consent form before you sign it.

In the first example, the social worker encourages the client to speak about her problems but makes it clear that what she says will be shared with the co-worker for the case. It is better to have the client hold back from sharing at this time than to have co-workers holding back information from each other. The honesty and concern expressed by the social worker in this case help strengthen the client's trust in the social workers and in the agency. In the second case, the social worker points out what information is needed, from whom, and for what purpose. The content of the consent form is carefully described and reviewed before the form is signed.

Recording Data

Because of the possibility of a client's misunderstanding or misusing information found in his or her record, one might ask: Why bother to keep records? A social worker needs to record data for several reasons, including:

1. To enhance service delivery through monitoring progress or regression
2. To account for services and to document need
3. To allow for easy transferability if a social worker leaves an agency
4. To contribute to research leading to improved services

Each service agency has its own identified methods for keeping records. Three commonly known ways of recording in social work are (1) process recordings, (2) summary recordings, and (3) problem-oriented recordings.

Process Recordings

Most agencies do not use process recordings for their permanent records. This type of recording is a lengthy narrative that describes in detail the interactions and communications that took place during a single interview. This recording may be subdivided into four basic parts: (1) presenting situation, (2) narrative (interview), (3) social worker's impressions, and (4) future plans. An example of a process recording may be found in Figure 5.2. After stating the basic information of who, when, where, and why in the section called "presenting situation," the social worker narrates what actually took place in the interview. This narrative should include not only what the client said but also what exactly was said by the social worker in the sequence as it happened.

The third section of a process recording is for the social worker's initial impressions of the person-problem-environment situation and of the social worker and client system relationship, based on what was said and felt during the interview. This is not a formal assessment of the case, but rather a current indication of the social worker's thoughts about the case and the interview. The social worker tries to clarify what he or she thinks now about the persons, problems, and environment and the social worker–client system interaction that just took place. Impressions may include a consideration of how the social worker thinks he or she conducted the interview.

In the fourth section of a process recording, the social worker describes future plans for the case. He or she asks the question: What next? This section includes what the social worker and the client system have agreed on as the next step in the process, and any other actions the social worker expects to take concerning the case.

FIGURE 5.2   **Process Recording**

Case of Mr. D

I. Presenting Situation

Mr. D is a 40-year-old African American male who was seen by Social Services on 10/7 at his own request. He was presently hospitalized for surgery on his ankle, which did not heal properly. The initial injury occurred about a year ago, at which time, according to the patient, he fell off a ladder.

II. Narrative (Interview)

Mr. D was dozing when I entered the room but stirred and said he was willing to talk for a few minutes. I asked him how he was feeling following his surgery 10 days ago. He stated that his ankle was better but his hip was sore from being in bed so much. It is still painful if he moves too much.

He then asked me what I had been able to find out about financial help, since he no longer had any health insurance and the money he received for Social Security Disability could not possibly take care of the hospital bills. I said that I had been in contact with our business office, which informed me that the necessary forms had been sent to the Department of Social Services informing them of Mr. D's need for assistance. I explained that DSS would contact him following his release to try to reach an agreement regarding his bills.

At this, Mr. D expressed his impatience over his hospitalization. He said he was anxious to be released from the hospital, feeling that he can sit in bed at home as well as he could here. When I suggested that perhaps he was still in need of special services that could best be delivered in the hospital, he replied that he was not receiving any special services that would keep him from going home. Mr. D stated further that he "doesn't trust" the staff. I asked him why he felt this way. He said the doctors did not tell him the truth when he was seen in the clinic prior to his hospital admission. He said he was left with the impression that they were going to break and reset his ankle. He felt that they knew at the time that more extensive surgery was possible, and that he should have been told about this. He was not informed of their decision to do a bone graft until the day he was admitted to the hospital before his surgery. I suggested that perhaps they had not made a definite decision until they had made a more careful examination of his X-rays following his visit to the outpatient clinic. I agreed that they could have informed him that this type of surgery was a possibility. Mr. D seemed to accept what I said and made no further comments on the subject.

I then asked Mr. D how things were going at home. He said that his mother, who lived in the apartment below, continued to take care of his two boys and that the boys came to see him almost every afternoon. Mr. D. seemed a bit reluctant at this point to discuss his home situation in much depth. When asked about his divorce, he said that this did not become final until last April. Neither he nor the boys ever see his ex-wife. He stated that he had to fight to get custody of the boys but felt his wife didn't want them very much, since she makes no attempt to see them. Mr. D mentioned that during his past hospitalization, his sister, rather than his ex-wife, had taken care of his daughter. I asked where his daughter was now, and he said

FIGURE 5.2 Continued

that she had fallen through the ice at Carney park and drowned last winter while he was recuperating at Rocky Neck Veterans' Home. I asked him how he felt about this incident. He said, while looking out the window toward the park, that his feelings did not matter. His concern was for his sons at present, particularly the older boy, age 11, who was with his sister at the time. When asked how he felt the boys were doing, he said he thought they had recovered all right, and things were pretty much back to normal. Mr. D seemed particularly uneasy during this part of our conversation, during which time he began fidgeting with his covers and gazing out the window. Since I did not feel that he trusted me enough at this point to explore his feelings any further, I closed this part of the discussion by saying that perhaps in time it would be easier for him to talk about it. He agreed by saying "yes."

I asked Mr. D if he would like me to come back again next week, if I could stop in for a few minutes to see how he was doing. I mentioned that perhaps by then he would be allowed to get up and around a bit. He added that he had hoped he would be home by next week but if he was still here, he wouldn't mind if I came to see him.

III. Social Worker's Impressions
My impressions of this client, and this interview in particular, were that there was a great deal to be discussed here, but that at the present time, Mr. D was reluctant to discuss many of his feelings with me. He was satisfied insofar as Social Services had met his financial needs. He did not seem to want the help that could be provided in a social work relationship, helping him to work on his feelings in many areas, including his hospitalization, his divorce, and his daughter's death.

IV. Future Plans
While the patient refuses to discuss his feelings and concerns regarding areas such as his daughter's death and his divorce at this time, he may open up after a few more interviews. I plan to see him again next week.

Process recording is primarily a tool for supervision. It is submitted to a supervisor for review prior to a supervisory session. The supervisor reviews the record with the social worker and indicates strengths and weaknesses in interviewing skills. The social worker is helped to consider possible options or directions for proceeding with the case. Usually, process recordings are kept in a separate folder for the social worker and do not become a part of the permanent record.

Summary Recordings

Many agencies use a type of summary recording for their permanent records. Here, contacts for a period of time, generally not longer than three months, are summarized. In a summary recording, a social worker follows a four-part outline similar to that of process recording. The topical headings used are (1) basic information, (2) content summary, (3) social worker's impressions, and (4) future plans. The basic information given in a summary recording states the dates and places of contact, the persons interviewed, and the purpose for coming together. The content section highlights the topics and themes addressed during sessions, along with any major decisions reached during the period of time covered in the summary. The last two sections give the social worker's impressions of what has happened over the period of time covered and the future plans for continued work by social worker and client system.

Problem-Oriented Recordings

A problem-oriented recording (POR) is a clearly identified system of recording that originated with Dr. Lawrence Weed (1971) in health care systems. Several modified versions of this method are presently in use by many human service agencies (Martens & Holmstrum, 1974). Using a problem focus, recording usually begins with a list of all the problems identified to date, with an indication of when the problem was first recognized. For each problem listed, a brief assessment is given according to a "SOAP" format. The **S**ubjective data (according to client's perception of the problem), the **O**bjective data (as documented by testing, observation, and written and oral verification), the **A**ssessment (social worker's judgment) and the **P**lan (immediate) for each problem on the list are stated in a concise manner.

For example, a problem listed for Jerry (15 years old, oldest of five children, both parents at home) was "below-average school performance—potential school dropout." The SOAP assessment for this problem was recorded as follows:

S   7/10: Jerry says he finds school boring, and he plans to quit when he is 16. 7/12 and 7/14: His teachers say he doesn't seem to be able to grasp the material, although he tries very hard.

O   Jerry's full-scale IQ is 80 (Performance 90, Verbal 70, WISC-R, 5/21/99). He repeated eighth grade. With current grades, he may have to repeat ninth grade. There is only one ninth grade at Brown Junior High, and it is geared toward students of average or above-average intelligence.

A   Jerry is finding school work difficult, owing to his limited intellectual abilities and his being placed in a class for students with average or above-average intelligence. He has a growing sense of inferiority and will probably drop out if he does not receive help.

P   1. Discuss Jerry's learning needs with Jerry, his parents, the school principal, and Jerry's teachers.
2. Explore resources for tutoring and supportive services for Jerry.
3. Explore other schools for Jerry.
4. Work with all people in item 1 to provide Jerry with the learning opportunities he needs.

Prior to closing a case with POR, a "closing summary" for each problem is stated that includes (1) status of the problem, (2) prognosis, and (3) recommendations.

The problem-oriented recording method emphasizes the importance of organization and preciseness in recording. Information is recorded in a manner that is very available for research, documentation, and evaluation. The method offers a framework for immediate recall and immediate information provision. The social worker is challenged to clarify problems and to progress in a skillful, accountable way. This recording method is particularly appropriate for general practice in which a problem-solving approach is used throughout the process of service.

Other Record Forms

In addition to the three types of recording cited, information collected on a case may also be recorded on fact sheets and in social histories or referral summaries. In most agency files, a basic fact sheet is found inside the cover of each record (see the example in Figure 5.3). Names of the family members and related resources, dates, addresses, and other factual information are often listed on fact sheets.

In social histories, a brief narrative is given for a variety of general headings. These include family composition, family background, developmental history, education, work, health, religion, economic history, other agencies involved, problem assessment, goals, and future plans. In a referral summary, the social worker may add or delete any of these headings, depending on the nature and needs of the setting receiving the referral.

In any recording for permanent records or referrals, the information presented should be as factual as possible. Social workers need to be able to document their statements and to substantiate their conclusions. If a social worker is making a statement that is an assumption or an opinion, it should begin with such phrases as "It appears to me at this time that . . . because . . ." or "Based on. . . , my impressions at this time are. . . ." Accurate, effective recording calls for skill and sensitivity. As a social worker collects data in the second stage of the General Method, it is essential that he or she have skill in recognizing and recording relevant, accurate data in a systematic and professional manner.

Working with Different Client Systems

Is there a difference in data collection when it is done with client systems of different sizes? Are there variations in the techniques or processes used when a social worker is gathering information about a group or community rather than an individual? How is information about a group or community kept confidential when it is frequently disclosed in the presence of several people who are not agency personnel? Is there a different method for recording information when working with a family, group, or community?

FIGURE 5.3   Identification and Summary Sheet

Admission no. _____ Date of admission _____ Room no. _____
Patient's name _____ Sex _____ Phone _____
Home address _____
　　　　　　　　street　　　　　　　　　　town　　　　state　　　　zip
Admission date _____ Discharge date _____
Prior admission _____ Admission date _____ Discharge date _____
Admitting diagnosis _____
_____

Financially responsible party _____ Relationship _____
Address _____ Phone _____
　　　　　　　　　　　　　　　　　　　　　home　　　work

Power of attorney　　　　　Yes _____ No _____
Notify in case of emergency _____ Relationship _____
Address _____ Phone _____
　　　　　　　　　　　　　　　　　　　　　home　　　work

Date of birth _____ Age _____ Place of birth _____
U.S. citizen _____ Religion _____ Church _____
Marital status: S M W D _____ Medicare no. _____
Social security no. _____ Insurance no. _____
Welfare: Title XIX no. _____ Others _____
Attending physician: Name _____ Phone _____
Address _____
Previous physician: Name _____ Phone _____
Address _____
Pharmacist: Name _____ Phone _____
Dentist: Name _____ Phone _____
Podiatrist: Name _____ Phone _____
Funeral director: Name _____ Phone _____
Hospital preference _____ Phone _____
Discharged diagnosis _____
_____

Discharge date _____ to _____

The size of a client system does not alter the framework for organizing data under the three basic headings of "problem," "person," and "environment." The process and techniques used in collecting data, however, may differ when one is working with a larger system, such as a group or a community. Keeping in mind that the system of contact is made up of distinctive parts, the social worker is sensitive to the needs and perceptions of individual members. Focus, however, is directed toward identifying the felt needs of the client system as a whole. The social worker's focus is the client system in its entirety, while helping its members to grow in an awareness of their common identity and concerns.

Techniques are needed to locate information of a common nature and to sift out uncommon information of a personal nature. To determine the problems, motivation, and capacity of a larger system, and not just of a few outspoken members of the larger system, is a major challenge for a social worker. In the data-collection stage of the General Method, the social worker tries to become aware of the problems, persons, and environmental resources and influences of the entire client system. An effort is made to collaborate with the members of the client system in collecting information. They are encouraged to distinguish fact from assumption, to be open to diverse perceptions and feelings, and to focus on common problems and needs.

Even prior to bringing the members of a client system together to engage in a working relationship, social workers frequently begin the process with a preliminary period of data collection by individual contact. Before convening the entire client system, the social worker needs to find out what constitutes the boundary of the client system and to develop an initial awareness of its members and their felt needs. A social worker will often speak with individual members of a family, group, or community to give them the opportunity to share freely and in confidence their perceptions of the client system and its problems. This enables the social worker to locate motivating issues and potential leaders for the system. Once the client system and the social worker start to work together for identified goals, they jointly collect data on particular problems, related influences, and resources.

Although the categories for data collection within the ecological-systems perspective of problems, persons, and environment are basically the same for all client systems, the nature of the content addressed may differ. When working with a larger client system—such as a community, for example—the resources for and influences on the environment are generally of a formal nature. These may include foundations, federal and local policy makers, and organizations or their representatives. Information collected has to be clearly factual with documentation. Although skill for recognizing feelings is strongly needed when collecting information with smaller client systems, skill in acquiring and presenting facts is paramount in working with larger systems. Social workers need to be aware of the general feeling tones of larger client systems and their individual members, but change in larger client systems is strongly dependent on documented facts. Members of an organization may be very sympathetic toward a cause, but they may not be able to change their larger structure unless there is documented evidence of the need for and value in changing the policies or procedures of the organization. With larger complex systems, the information collected is mainly of a formal, factual nature.

As mentioned, a person may be hesitant to speak out about issues or concerns in a large client system. This hesitance may be due to a fear of reprisal later by other members of the system or by outsiders who have been informed of what the person said. Before they can develop confidence in sharing openly, members of a large system need clarification of what will happen when information is disclosed within the system. Although a social worker may state how he or she and the agency will handle information obtained, the social worker is not able to guarantee that other members of the client system will keep in confidence what will be shared. Prior to encouraging the disclosure of information within a client system, a social worker makes an effort to get the members of the client system to mutually agree on a code for themselves regarding how they will treat what is said at their meetings. This code should be restated or reconsidered whenever new members are added or there is some question whether it will continue being enacted.

Case Example
Group

SW: Before we go on, I would like to talk with all of you about the confidential nature of what goes on in this group. As far as the agency is concerned, anything shared within the group is kept within the agency unless we all give our consent to have certain information shared outside. A summary of each meeting is recorded in the agency record, and any group member may request to review these recordings. The only exception for allowing information to go outside the agency would be if you revealed that you planned to injure someone or if I or our records were subpoenaed to court. Any questions about this?

MARY (GROUP MEMBER):   Yeah, but what about everyone else here? How do I know that what I say won't be talked about out on the street by someone here?

SW: Well, let's talk about that. What do we think about a group member sharing what is said here with someone outside of the group? How do you want to handle what is said during our meetings?

MICHAEL (GROUP MEMBER):   I don't think it's right to go and tell other people. We came here because we wanted help, but I don't want everyone in the world to know my business.

SW: I hear you saying that you don't think members should talk about what we share here with others. I wonder what the rest of the members think about this.

OTHERS: (Five others speak in support of Michael's position.)

SW: Are we saying as a group that we will keep in confidence whatever is said within this group? Are there any exceptions to this?

In terms of record keeping, all of the three methods described earlier for recording data collected during an interview (process, summary, problem oriented) may be used to record contacts with client, action, and target systems of any size. Whether working with an individual, family, group, organization, or community, the social worker records fundamental facts about the presenting situation (who, when, where, why), the essential content addressed during the contact (problems, needs, feelings, decisions), and the goals and plans that were established. In recording each contact or contacts over a period of time, a social worker may also include his or her impressions of the person-problem-environment situation.

When recording about a large system, a social worker needs to distinguish between what is recognized as a problem or need of one or some members of the system and what is seen as a common problem or need of the entire system. For example, when compiling the problem list for a problem oriented recording for a family system, the social worker indicates when a problem belongs to one or some members rather than to the whole family.

Case Example
Problem List

Active	Date
Father's unemployment	10/2
Inadequate housing	10/2
Father's drinking	11/3
Mother-father communication	11/3
Ryan's sore throat	11/3

In this example, whereas the housing need is common to all, it is apparent that there are individuals within the family who have particular problems that influence the functioning of the entire family: the unemployment and drinking problems are the father's; mother and father have a problem with communication; and Ryan has the sore throat.

In using summary recording to record an activity group session, a format may be followed such as that illustrated in Figure 5.4. Here again, the social worker basically indicates the presenting situation, central content (activity, process, problem), the leader's impressions, and future plans. The recording format provides opportunity for the social worker not only to describe the problems and behaviors of the group, but also to identify the problems and behaviors of individuals that influence the functioning of the group.

Making a process record of a community meeting may be extremely lengthy and time consuming. The framework found in Figure 5.5 provides guidance for highlighting important aspects of a meeting. Basically, the content addressed includes facts about the presenting situation, content discussed, and future plans and goals. The topics that are covered include how the social worker perceived his or her role, before, during, and after the meeting, as well as the social worker's impressions. This recording, as with all process recordings, may be used in supervision as a teaching tool. It lends itself to pointing out a social worker's skill and sensitivity for working with communities.

FIGURE 5.4   Weekly Group Record

Date _____

Group _____   Leader _____

Attendance: Total members present: Male _____   Female _____

      Visitors _____

Brief description of meeting: Please record briefly important discussions, decisions, and problems. *Give your own evaluation of the meeting.*

What was the main activity of the group at this meeting? Who initiated the main activity, and how did the group as a whole respond to the suggested activities? What program suggestions did you mention or bring up in the meeting?

Situations requiring individual attention: Please record problems, group or individual conflicts, and other incidents that you may want some help with from your supervisor.

Leader's interpretation regarding behavior of individuals: If there was any unusual behavior, why do you think the individuals and the group as a whole behaved as they did?

Plans for the next meeting:

FIGURE 5.5   **Process Recording for a Community Meeting**

I.   *Presenting Situation*
     Social worker's name
     Name of community
     Place of meeting
     Date of meeting
     Who called the meeting?
     For what purpose
     Number of people attending
     Who were the people at the meeting? (Whom did they represent?)

II. *Meeting*
     What took place? Topics, decisions, actions (including worker's), in sequence.

III. *Social Worker's Impressions*
     How do the community members see themselves? See you?
     Do they see themselves as a community?
     What are your impressions of the roles and behaviors of participants?
     What do they want to accomplish individually? As a community?
     What do they want from you?
     Did they and you come away with something as a result of the meeting?
     How did you use yourself during the meeting?
     How did you feel about the meeting—before, during, and after?

IV. *Future Plans*
     What do they do now?
     What do you do now?

Using Social Work Foundation Knowledge in Data Collection

In the second stage of the General Method, the social worker uses values, knowledge, and skills from the social work foundation identified in Table 1.3 in Chapter 1. The practice principles of confidentiality, self-determination, and nonjudgmental attitude are strongly apparent in the actions and transactions of the social worker during data collection. As pointed out, the client system has the right to choose what personal information will be disclosed, as well as to choose how this information will be used. The social worker strives to gather factual information for a documented assessment that is free from assumption or personal value judgments.

In proceeding in the helping process with collecting data about persons and environments, the social worker uses assorted theoretical and conceptual knowledge to comprehend the nature and functioning of client, target, and resource systems. Through observing and inquiring directly or indirectly, he or she obtains information in a manner that reflects the use of theories from the holistic foundation. Seeing the data collected in the light of basic theory, the social worker is able to identify such characteristics as coping capacities, developmental levels, communication patterns, and role expectations. Theory also helps the social worker recognize whether certain factors are the cause or the effect of problem situations. For example, in inquiring about the time when 8-year-old Alex started to insist that the light be kept on in his room at night, the social worker learned that it was around this same time that Alex started to have learning problems at school, to become increasingly possessive of his mother, and to act fearful toward his father. Knowledge of such theories as psychosexual and psychosocial development, as well as role and stress theory, helped the social worker pursue inquiry for understanding the regressive behavior.

The skills of the social work foundation that are used in the data-collection stage of the General Method include relationship skills, problem-solving skills, and professional skills. In sifting out facts of importance for understanding and planning, the social worker listens, questions, and clarifies. He or she may work with various systems to identify problems and needs or to collaborate in exchanging information for effective teamwork. Recording and research skills are used to test out and to register the findings collected.

Human Diversity in Data Collection

From an identification of problems, feelings, and goals in the engagement stage, the social worker and client system move on to gathering information for problem assessment. As a social worker begins to collect information about problem, person, and environment, some cultural systems may be hesitant to give information about personal or family problems, particularly to someone from a different ethnic group. The social worker must therefore be explicit in making known what information is needed and how it will be used. Whereas some client systems may wish to move quickly through this stage, with reliance on intuition (Mexican Americans, for example), others may need to move cautiously, with reliance on fact and reason (Japanese Americans, for example).

To collect data on the actual participants in a problem-person-environment situation, it is important for a social worker to understand the roles and structures in the culture of the system. For example, there is a fourfold structural typology found among Puerto Rican American families: (1) extended family systems—a wide range of natural or ritual kin; (2) the nuclear family—father, mother, and children; (3) father, mother, their children, and children of other unions of the husband or wife; and (4) the mother-based family with children of one or more men, but no permanent male figure in the home (Garcia-Preto, 1996).

In locating resources or influences in the environment, a social worker needs to know who or what resource would be appropriate to contact for certain problems. In the Puerto Rican culture, for example, there may be ready acceptance to have *compadres* and *comadres* (godparents) become foster parents if a child needs to be placed. To mediate in matters such as property disputes, however, it may be more appropriate in this culture to use distant relatives, in order to avoid the risk of losing friendships with closer relatives if they became involved (Garcia-Preto, 1996; Marin & Marin, 1991).

During data collection in the General Method, as the three focal points of problem, person, and environment are explored, a social worker looks to see if an individual has a nurturing system as well as a sustaining system in his or her environment. The social worker also considers the values and expectations of all three (individual, nurturing system, and sustaining system), realizing that the more they share in common, the greater their congruence, goodness of fit, (Germaine & Gitterman, 1979, 1996) and mutual health and growth. Even if an individual is found to be different or nonacceptable by a sustaining system, he or she can grow and thrive, provided there is a strong, supportive nurturing system. Unfortunately, many individuals who are perceived as having different lifestyles or as being physically or mentally challenged have no nurturing system where they are understood and supported, and they live in a very rejecting, condemning sustaining system.

In collecting data, a social worker inquires about a client system's current and potential environment. When working on problems related to human diversity, a social worker gathers information not only about existing resources in the client system's life space but also about possible formal and informal resources that could offer support for persons in their environments.

A social worker also needs to be sensitive to cultural and social role expectations when information about problem, person, and environment is gathered. For example, men who believe they should be strong and successful might resist exposure of their personal, family, or social problems. Their environments might be limited in nurturing networks. They might withdraw from talking about themselves at any length, perhaps feeling comfortable only when talking objectively about their work or society at large with its organizations and institutions. Women might express feelings of helplessness and even fear of succeeding in resolving their problems. Perhaps they will struggle over a sense of being disloyal or ungrateful if they criticize or talk about their husbands or family problems.

In collecting data, a social worker is also sensitive to the socio-demographic variables of age and stages, endowment and personality, value systems, social class, and geographic location. The social worker's skill in inquiry, use of informative resources, and ability to recognize facts, custom, and feelings will reflect the extent of sensitivity the social worker has to various dimensions of human diversity.

Data Collection in Micro, Mezzo, and Macro Practice in Diverse Field Areas

In the following section, the application of knowledge and skills during the *data-collection stage* of the General Method will be demonstrated by entry-level generalists in seven diverse field areas.

I. Field Area: Child Welfare

A. Agency: State Department of Children's Services
B. Client System

K, a 15-year-old female is in an emergency shelter. (For more background information, see Chapter 4, Engagement in Micro, Mezzo, and Macro Practice in Diverse Field Areas, I. Child Welfare.)

C. Engagement Summary

The feelings expressed during engagement included loneliness, restlessness, hatred of self and others, and depression. The problems and goals identified during this stage are listed in Table 4.1 in Chapter 4.

D. Data Collection

<u>Problem:</u> *During data collection, the social worker learned that K was well liked by those who lived in the group home where she was first placed. The group parents described K as quiet and fearful. She seemed to get lost in the group; therefore, they thought a foster home was a good plan for her at the time. The foster-home parents described K as stubborn and pouty. She never seemed to get enough attention and didn't want to do her share of the work. They said they tried to tell K to stay away from the boy she ran away with, but she would not listen to them.*

In school, K had been performing at an average level while she lived in the group home. During her stay in the foster home, she remained in the same school she had attended while in the group home. Her grades started to drop before she ran away. Her teachers said that K daydreamed a lot, but they thought she did have the potential for at least average achievement. As her marks started to drop, the school personnel had a pupil-appraisal team meeting. The Children's Services social worker who had the case prior to the current social worker attended the meeting. It was agreed at this meeting that K would be referred to the local mental health center for counseling. K refused to go to the center, saying she was not "crazy."

<u>Person:</u> *During data collection, the social worker discovered that K was extremely motivated to work on her two stated goals. She said she missed school and even missed her teachers. She wished she could go back to the group home, where they were "nice" to her. K began to say that she knew that she was "messed up" and that she probably needed to go for counseling. She hoped someone could help her so she wouldn't feel "so awful inside." She thought that a boy at the shelter was starting to like her, but she was "afraid of getting too close." The social worker at the shelter described K as "shy" and "noninvolved with the activities or residents of the shelter."*

<u>Environment:</u> *The emergency shelter had a residence time limit of four weeks. In exploring possible resources for K, the social worker learned that K's biological father had moved out of state and left no forwarding address. K's stepfather had been taken to court for child sexual assault, and her mother blamed K for reporting it. K's mother did not want K to be returned home, "ever." There were no relatives interested in caring for K. K's foster parents did not want her to return either. Although there was no opening in K's previous group-home placement,*

TABLE 5.1   Ongoing Recording

Date Identified	Problem/Need	Goal
1/12	No permanent home	a. To obtain a permanent placement b. To maintain a permanent placement
1/12	Out of school	c. To reenter school
1/12	Personal problems	Personal goals (1/19)
	a. Poor self-esteem	a. To feel better about self
	b. Identity confusion	b. To clarify identity
	c. Sexuality (relationships, behavior)	c. To be able to have good friendships with males
	d. Depression	d. To stop "feeling down"

the social worker located another group home with an opening in a neighboring city. Services available for residents in this home included ongoing casework by an M.S.W. and weekly peer-group meetings, where discussions focused on such topics as "sex," "parents," and "growing up confused."

E. **Charted Progress**

During the process of data collection, goals were expanded to include K's expressed desire to get help with her personal feelings and problems. These new, mutually agreed-upon goals were added to the two goals identified during engagement and were recorded as shown in Table 5.1. Since the date when these goals were agreed on was different from the date of problem identification, the later date was recorded in the "goal" column.

Note: The paperwork required throughout the process of working with K included the following:

Summary recordings of all contacts with K and related resources
Referral summary for the group home
Case summary for the court in preparation for a petition to seek continuance of commitment
Transfer summary at termination

II. Field Area: Gerontology

A. Agency: Seaside Nursing Home
B. Client System

Mrs. J is an 80-year-old Portuguese woman in a skilled nursing facility. (For additional background information, see Chapter 4, Engagement in Micro, Mezzo, and Macro Practice in Diverse Field Areas, II. Gerontology.)

C. **Engagement Summary**

The feelings expressed during engagement included distrust, fear, anger, and abandonment. The problems and goals identified during this stage are listed in Table 4.2 in Chapter 4.

D. **Data Collection**

<u>*Problem:*</u> *The social worker attended a patient-care conference on Mrs. J with the staff of the nursing home. She learned at this time that Mrs. J was causing a disruption on her floor. She was fighting with the nurses when they came to give her a bath. She sometimes stood at the door of her room and called the other residents names. On occasion, she would refuse to go to meals or to leave her room. She was often found talking to herself in Portuguese. Also reported were minor incidents of confusion and irrational mood swings.*

<u>*Person:*</u> *As data were being collected, Mrs. J began to talk more freely with the social worker about herself and her background. She said she came to America when she was 20 years old. She married shortly after arriving and had three children by the time she was 25. Her husband left the family when the youngest child was 13 years old. Mrs. J used to clean houses and take in washing to earn money. All of her children had to leave school and get jobs. She said she was "hard" on her children and wished she had been nicer to them. Mrs. J said she wished she could go back to Portugal, where she believes her husband is living. She could not recall the marriage names of her children or the name of her husband's village.*

Mrs. J began to express an interest in knowing more about the other residents. She said she yelled at them because they would not look at her. She was angry at the nurses because they tried to undress her for a bath late in the morning after she was up and dressed. She wished the nurses and the people would like her and agreed that she was willing to try to get along better with them.

<u>*Environment:*</u> *During data collection, the social worker learned from the hospital social worker who made the referral to the nursing home that one of Mrs. J's daughters had admitted her to the hospital. During admission, the daughter stated that her father left the family several years ago and could not be located, and that Mrs. J had been living alone until she no longer could go out by herself. The daughter said that she was moving out of state and would send a forwarding address (which never arrived). She said that her sister and brother also lived out of state.*

The social worker also learned that there was no one in the nursing facility who spoke Portuguese. The director of volunteers offered to try to locate someone who spoke the language and who would be willing to visit with Mrs. J. The social worker learned from Mrs. J that she used to attend a church where the pastor and several members of the congregation were Portuguese. The social worker located the church, and the pastor said he would go see Mrs. J. Other resources available to Mrs. J in the nursing home included program planning, recreational therapy, choir, and church services. There were also weekly resident meetings that Mrs. J could attend.

E. Charted Progress

During the data-collection stage, the problem list was extended to include Mrs. J's disruptive behavior on her floor. The additional problems were recorded as indicated in Table 5.2. Mrs. J's organic brain syndrome was not listed as a problem in the social service record because she was receiving treatment for this from the medical staff.

Note: *The recording required throughout the process of working with Mrs. J included the following:*

Intake summary
Weekly summaries of contacts with Mrs. J
Patient-care conference reports
Social service tasks, entered in the problem-oriented recordings of the nursing home
Record of outside contacts made and information obtained as data were collected
Ongoing contracted plan
Termination summary

TABLE 5.2 Ongoing Recording

Date Identified	Problem/ Need	Goal	Task	Contract	Date Anticipated	Date Accomplished
9/25	Poor adjustment; seclusiveness—not leaving room alone	To be able to leave room alone				
9/25	Cultural isolation; need to communicate in native language	To be visited by someone who speaks Portuguese				
9/27	Unfamiliar with staff and resources of the nursing home	To get to know the staff and resources of the nursing home	Meet twice a week with social worker.	Social worker and Mrs. J	10/4 and every Tuesday and Thursday thereafter	10/4, 10/9, 10/11, 10/16
10/2	Fighting with nurses over bath	To work out bath schedule with nurses				
10/2	Calling residents names	To stop calling residents names				

III. Field Area: Public Social Welfare

A. Agency: State Social Services

B. Client System

Mr. and Mrs. P and their two children, ages 2 and 4, are in need of emergency shelter and more permanent housing. (For more background information, see Chapter 4, Engagement in Micro, Mezzo, and Macro Practice in Diverse Field Areas, III. Public Social Welfare.)

C. Engagement Summary

The feelings expressed during engagement included helplessness, anger, rejection, and confusion. The problems and goals identified during engagement are listed in Table 4.3 in Chapter 4.

D. Data Collection

Problem: Shelter is a basic human need. There is a lack of available housing for low-income families in the local city and surrounding areas. Housing is a crucial need for the P family at this time. The Ps have had several moves since their marriage five years ago. They have been evicted from apartments at least three times in the past because they failed to keep up with rent payments. The Ps said that they had to use the money they received from AFDC to buy food. The social worker also learned that they currently had no money left for food. The family receives AFDC because Mr. P's psychological problems prevent him from maintaining employment (confirmed by Income Maintenance Department's eligibility technician, who has letters from psychiatrists on file). The AFDC check and food stamps for the month are being held at central office until the status and address of the family are clarified.

Persons: Although Mr. P said he bought a newspaper to see if there are any available apartments in the area, he and his wife do not appear to be motivated to get involved in apartment hunting. They are anxious to be relocated, but they expect that others (the state or Mrs. P's father) will find a place for them. They are blaming others (the state, Mrs. P's father, landlords, friends) for their problem of being homeless. They express a strong dependency on others to meet their needs. They do not seem to have the ability or the desire to become actively involved in problem solving or in changing their perspective or behavior. With Mr. P's written permission, the social worker contacted his psychiatrist at the mental health center, Saint John's Hospital (where he had been treated), and also got in touch with the Vocational Rehabilitation Department (where he had been tested). Mr. P's mental illness and continued inability to work were verified. The psychiatrist said that Mr. P is faithful in keeping his weekly appointments at the center. The children appear to be in good health. Mrs. P said that it was about time for the children to go for a checkup at the health clinic, but that she had lost their medical card. She said the income-maintenance worker was sending her another one.

Environment: Mr. and Mrs. P said that they have no family or friends who are willing to take them in, even for the night. Mrs. P said she knew that her father was trying to find a place where she and the children could live.

Three possible temporary shelters were located: (1) Salvation Army, (2) City Hotel, and (3) Center City Motor Inn. For more permanent housing, the

*social worker contacted five social service agencies in the surrounding area. None
was able to provide any information on possible housing. The process of making
a Section-8 (rent subsidy) application to the Housing Department was reviewed.*

*During the initial period of data collection, the social worker also explored
possible resources for emergency food donations. The following sources were identified: (1) Community Renewal Center, (2) Salvation Army, (3) Saint Michael's
Church, (4) Center City Churches Food Bank, and (5) Good News Soup Kitchen.*

*Throughout the entire process of working with the P family, information
continued to be collected as additional needs and possible resources emerged.
Data collection extended to information about the following (including referral
procedures):*

> *Protective services (possible placement of children)*
> *Social security*
> *Appeal process when placement extension was refused (fair hearing)*
> *Housing resources*
> *Emergency fuel banks*
> *Moving coverage*
> *Medical transportation service*
> *Appliance repair*
> *Resources for Thanksgiving basket and children's Christmas presents*
> *Community health services*

E. Charted Progress

*Adding to the recorded problem and goals, the social worker listed the immediate
need for food and the identified problem of poor money management (Table 5.3).
The family agreed with the goal of securing food, but they were resistant to admitting that help was needed with managing their money (no goal recorded).
Although the social worker became aware of the additional problems of Mr. P's
unemployment and mental incapacity, these problems were not added to the*

TABLE 5.3 Ongoing Recording

Date Identified	Problem/Need	Goal
9/28	Housing for P family	a. To find emergency shelter for the P family
		b. To locate an apartment for long-term residence by the family
9/28	Emergency food	a. To obtain emergency food supply
		b. To find resource to supply food until AFDC check is received
9/28	Poor money management	

problem list for service from the social worker, because they were already being addressed by the Income Maintenance Department and the mental health center.

Note: *Information about Mr. P's unemployment and mental illness was recorded as part of data collection in the record. Additional paperwork during the total time the generalist worked with the P family included the completion of the following:*

> *Authorization forms for placement of family*
> *Section-8 housing application*
> *Emergency food applications*
> *Documentation that the Ps were searching for housing*
> *Letter to authorize medical care*
> *Request for medical transportation*
> *Release-of-information forms*
> *Request for extension of emergency placement*
> *Request for fair hearing*
> *Application for social security benefits*
> *Application for energy assistance*

IV. Field Area: Community Service

A. Agency: Clayton Neighborhood House

B. Client System

Four Hispanic families are without heating in their apartments on the second floor of 33 L Street. (For more background information, see Chapter 4, Engagement in Micro, Mezzo, and Macro Practice in Diverse Field Areas, IV. Community Services.)

C. Engagement Summary

As the social worker engaged the families in the problem-solving process, they expressed feelings of frustration and helplessness. There were also feelings of fear and anger expressed toward the landlord. The problem of inadequate heating was identified, and all agreed on the recorded goal, "To obtain consistent and adequate heating for second-floor residences of the L Street apartment house."

D. Data Collection

<u>Problem:</u> *As the social worker explored the problem further, she learned that residents were paying a monthly rent of $250 for one-room apartments. The families were told that heating was included in the rent. Although one person in each of the families was employed, they said that they could not afford any increase in rent or to pay for heating themselves.*

The social worker had brought a thermometer with her on the visit. She checked the temperature in each of the apartments, and all of them registered about 50°F.

Since none of the residents at the meeting had lived in the building the previous winter, they did not know if a similar problem had existed last year. They shared how difficult it was for them to find a place to live. No one was requesting help with relocation at this time.

Persons: *The social worker learned that there were 15 children (ages 6 months to 16 years) and seven adults (no one over age 50) living in the four apartments. Although the residents were motivated to come together to discuss their heating problem, everyone was afraid to have a direct confrontation with the landlord. Mrs. T said that she and he husband had tried to call the landlord, but he was not available and never returned their call. Some members said he is hard to talk with, because he doesn't understand Spanish and they don't speak English. The residents were motivated to work on the heating problem with the social worker, but they asked her to contact the landlord in their behalf.*

Environment: *The social worker learned from those attending the meeting that an individual who lived downstairs worked as a janitor in the building. They said that they had complained to him about a lack of heat upstairs, but he told them they would have to tell the landlord. The social worker stopped at the janitor's apartment on the way out, but he was not home. The name and phone number of the landlord were obtained from the residents.*

With further inquiry, the social worker learned that the landlord lived in a neighboring town, and that he had owned two other buildings in the same area where the L Street apartment was located. The two buildings were recently sold to the city.

When the social worker called Mr. X, the landlord, he said that he was not aware of a problem with heating for the second floor. The social worker informed him that each of the apartments on the floor was registering a temperature of 50°F or below. Mr. X said that he had asked the janitor of the building to help keep heating costs to a minimum, but he didn't realize this was being done through an uneven distribution of heat in the building. He said he would contact the janitor and have the problem taken care of right away.

The social worker inquired if Mr. X knew that his residents had tried to reach him to tell him about the heating problem. Mr. X said he was very busy and often found it hard to return all of his calls. He said also that his secretary finds it difficult to understand what the Spanish-speaking tenants are trying to say over the phone.

E. Charted Progress

The social worker entered a summary report of her visit to L Street in the record. She recorded pertinent information collected from speaking with the landlord and the residents. Paperwork completed while working with the community of residents included a planned contract that was developed with the residents (see Chapter 6).

V. Field Area: Education

A. Agency: Keeney Elementary School
B. Client System

Jim G is an 8-year-old African American third-grader with regressive behavior in school and at home. (For more background information, see Chapter 4, Engagement in Micro, Mezzo, and Macro Practice in Diverse Field Areas, V. Education.)

C. Engagement Summary

Although presenting problems and goals were discussed with Jim and his mother (as outlined in Table 4.5 in Chapter 4), feelings were not expressed, and there was not a clear understanding of the cause of Jim's problems throughout the first three weeks of contact. The social worker proceeded with data collection, realizing that the engagement period needed to be extended.

D. Data Collection

Problem: *The social worker reviewed Jim's school record and the nurse's report. Jim was in good health and he had performed at an above-average academic level during his first two years of school. His teacher said that in September, when school first started, Jim seemed happy and interested in school. She wondered if he should be placed in a special needs classroom because he was getting so far behind in his work. Jim's previous testing and academic performance showed that he did not have a learning disability.*

Persons: *Although Jim seemed to like meeting with the social worker, he did not care if he did not do well in school. He hoped he wouldn't have to repeat a grade. He said his father had told him that school wasn't really that important and that Jim could come to work with him in the car lot when he got older. Whenever Jim or the social worker began to talk about home or his parents, Jim became restless and looked a little frightened.*

In one session, after meeting for three weeks, Jim began to play with the black man and woman puppets. He had them begin to dance together and then they started to hit each other. He took the frog puppet and had him yell out, "Hey, stop that!" The social worker commented, "It sounds like froggie wants them to stop." Jim continued with the frog shouting, "Stop that fighting, do you hear?" The social worker said it looked like froggie was getting upset, and she wondered what froggie was feeling. Jim said, "He's scared. He hates it." The social worker said, "I wonder what froggie's afraid of." Jim took the woman doll and put her back on the shelf. He then became quiet and sat down. The social worker asked if that was it. "Was froggie afraid that she would go away?" Jim didn't answer. The social worker softly said that she knew that sometimes children are afraid that their parents will go away if they fight with each other. Jim looked away. The social worker asked if Jim was ever afraid that his mother might go away. Jim whispered, "Sometimes." The social worker then asked if Jim ever told his mother what he was afraid of, and Jim shook his head negatively. The social worker wondered if Jim would mind if she told his mother what he was afraid of, and as he got up to leave the room he said, "I don't care."

Environment: *The social worker learned from the school record that Jim's mother was a nurse and that his father managed a car lot. During the second interview with Mrs. G, the social worker asked if she could meet with Jim's father, but Mrs. G said that he was always very busy and worked long hours running the car lot. At the third meeting with Mrs. G, the social worker shared with her what had happened in play with Jim. Mrs. G's eyes filled with tears. She then told the social worker that in October, she learned that her husband had gone out with another woman. She said that she didn't think Jim noticed that she and her husband were quarreling. She recalled that at one point she did tell her husband that she might take off and leave him and the children. She said she wouldn't really do it but just wanted to scare him. She said her husband assures her that he will never see the woman again, but she finds it hard to trust him and to forgive him.*

TABLE 5.4 Ongoing Recording

Date Identified	Problem/ Need	Goal	Tasks	Contract	Date Anticipated	Date Accomplished
11/1	Jim's school tardiness and absenteeism	To improve Jim's regular school attendance (on time each day)	1. See that Jim gets to school on time each day.	1. Mrs. G	11/5 and each school day thereafter	11/5–ongoing
11/1	Jim's declining academic performance	To improve academic functioning (interest, participation, grades)	1. Talk with Jim about school problems.	1a. Social worker and Jim	11/6 and twice a week thereafter	11/6, 11/8, 11/13, 11/15, 11/20, 11/27
				b. Mrs. G and Jim	11/2	11/2
			2. Follow up.	2. Social worker and Jim	11/5	11/5, 11/21
			3. Talk with Jim about home tensions and assure him she will not leave.	3. Mrs. G and Jim	11/21	
			4. Meet to discuss Jim's problems in relation to parents' problems.	4. Social worker, Mr. and Mrs. G	11/27	
11/2	Jim's getting to sleep at night					
11/21	Strain in Mr. and Mrs. G's marital relationship					

The social worker encouraged Mrs. G to talk with Jim about his fear and to assure him that she doesn't plan to leave home. The social worker also asked if Mrs. G could talk with her husband about what was happening with Jim. Mrs. G said that she would try to get her husband to take time off to come in to see the social worker with her next week.

E. Charted Progress

During the process of data collection and the extended engagement period, the social worker added the newly identified problem of Mr. and Mrs. G's strained relationship to the problem list, as shown in Table 5.4. The plan to have Mrs. G talk with Jim and to have Mr. G come in to meet the social worker with Mrs. G was also recorded.

Note: *The recording of the social worker included an ongoing contracted plan developed by the social worker, Mr. and Mrs. G, and Jim (presented throughout Chapters 4 through 9), which was kept in the social service file. The social worker also recorded basic factual information in Jim's school record. In addition, a summary of each contact was included in the social service file, and a closing summary was added at the time of termination.*

VI. Field Area: Corrections

A. Agency: Juvenile Court

B. Client System

A group of seven male adolescents (all 14 years old) are on probation. (For additional background information, see Chapter 4, Engagement in Micro, Mezzo, and Macro Practice in Diverse Field Areas, VI. Corrections.)

C. Engagement Summary

During engagement, the primary goal of getting off probation as soon as possible was clearly stated by all members of the group. The youths also wanted help both with controlling their tempers and with understanding better the "changes" they were all going through (as outlined in Table 4.6 in Chapter 4). Although they recognized problems they were having in communicating with their parents, they did not want to work on trying to improve their relationships with them. They did not want to talk about their low self-esteem. They expressed anger at having been picked up by the police and put on probation.

D. Data Collection

After an initial period of testing and attempted manipulation of the leaders, group members began to talk more openly about their family backgrounds and life experiences. In addition to collecting data from the youths themselves, the two social workers visited the homes of each group member and talked with parents. The social workers also talked with the youths' teachers and social workers at the schools they attended. The files of the court for each of the youths were also reviewed carefully.

Problem: The social workers learned that each member of the group had committed more than once the offense that led to his being put on probation. All seven of the youths were seen in their schools as "problem students" who had difficulties in learning and in getting along with teachers and classmates. They were de-

scribed by teachers as "trouble-makers" or "attention seekers." Two of the youths were believed to be junior members of the Savage Nomads or the Ghetto Brothers street gangs.

The group members said that they got into trouble usually when they were mad about something or dared to do it by friends. In one case, breaking and entering was required for initiation into a gang.

<u>Persons:</u> Three of the group members were highly motivated to get the most out of the group and to get off probation (MK, ML, and B). Two others laughed a lot and seemed to take the group "as a joke" (J and T). The remaining two were quiet and less easy to understand (A and C). C appeared very upset over being on probation.

The school reported that test scores indicated that two of the boys had borderline intelligence (A and MK). The others had average or above-average intelligence, even though they had problems with learning.

The racial/ethnic backgrounds of the group participants were as follows: one Italian American, one Irish American, two white with mixed ethnic backgrounds, two African American, and one Hispanic.

<u>Environment:</u> All of the youths came from single-parent families. Five lived with their mothers, one lived with his father, and one lived with his grandmother. All came from lower-class or lower-middle-class neighborhoods. The youths had not been active in local recreational centers or programs. Three said they used to attend some church activities for teenagers, but they only went to church when their parents made them go.

The parents and grandmother of the youths expressed interest and concern for their children. Three mothers and T's grandmother said they were afraid that they had no control over their sons (grandson). They all hoped the youths had learned their lesson and would now stay out of trouble. C's father spoke only Spanish. He appeared to be totally overwhelmed, and said he might have to send C back home to Puerto Rico. J's mother had an apparent drinking problem. She said she was thinking seriously of "putting J away" because he was getting too hard to manage. She did not say where she thought she might put him. She had heard that J's father was in jail. Three other group members had older brothers who were in jail or correctional centers (A, T, and ML).

E. Charted Progress

Summary recordings were written that briefly described contacts with the group members' parents, teachers, and school social workers. Brief entries were made each week in the records to indicate attendance and participation in the group. Later, detailed studies of each youth were written when he became eligible to be removed from probation.

VII. Field Area: Homeless Shelter

A. Agency: West End Community Shelter

B. Client System

José Romano, a 37-year-old Hispanic male, is homeless and HIV positive. (For additional background information, see Chapter 4, Engagement in Micro, Mezzo, and Macro Practice in Diverse Field Areas, VII, Homeless Shelter.)

C. Engagement Summary

Mr. R had worked hard to lead an independent lifestyle. After testing HIV positive, he left his job and lost his apartment. During engagement, he shared with the social worker strong feelings of fear and abandonment. The goals they identified focused on locating health care, housing, and employment.

D. Data Collection

<u>*Problem:*</u> *Mr. R believed his illness was caused by his use of unsanitary needles during his drug addiction more than six years ago. He experienced frequent colds and fatigue. He had not been to a doctor in four months because he couldn't afford it and no longer had health insurance.*

<u>*Person:*</u> *Mr. R was hesitant to take drugs for his illness because he had previously been a drug addict. He knew he needed to talk with a doctor about this and to find out more about his illness. Mr. G said that he was willing to take any kind of job at this point because he needed money. His work history over the last five years was strong in terms of dependability and performance. Mr. R's work experience and skills were limited to cooking and farming.*

<u>*Environment:*</u> *Mr. R was not aware of any relatives in the state. His ex-wife had moved back to Puerto Rico. He said that he regretted that he had fallen away from his church and wished that he could "get back in God's graces."*

In the building next to the shelter, there was a free health clinic for people in the neighborhood. The staffing of the clinic was provided through voluntary service from the doctors and interns of the city hospital. A grant provided funding for supplies and equipment. Mr. R would be able to receive medical care and information from the clinic.

With Mr. R's permission, the social worker contacted the Social Security Administration and the Department of Social Services. She learned that after Mr. R became "significantly impaired" and became active with AIDS, he would qualify for (1) Social Security and Supplemental Security Income and (2) general emergency assistance until he received his first SS check.

An organization called "Harmony" offered a variety of services for people with AIDS or HIV. Services included legal advocacy, a buddy system, a support group, transportation, and limited assistance with paying bills. Also, in the surrounding area, the social worker located two residences (Hope Home and Christian House) for persons with AIDS. Currently, all of their nine beds were full (nine beds total).

Following up on Mr. R's interest in returning to his church, the social worker was informed of the names and locations of the two Catholic churches in the area. She learned also that there was one church with a weekly service for a large Hispanic population.

Mr. R approved of the social worker's contacting his past employer. His employer said that Mr. R was never a problem and that they missed him at the nursing home. He had heard about Mr. R's illness from another employee. He did not have any job openings for Mr. R at the Hope Home. The state employment office was contacted for a listing of possible job openings, and Mr. R was encouraged to look in the employment section of the shelter's newspaper each day.

TABLE 5.5   **Ongoing Recording**

Date Identified	Problem/Need	Goal
5/8	HIV positive, lack of knowledge	To obtain ongoing medical care and information
5/8	Homeless/hungry	To obtain immediate housing/food To obtain long-term housing
5/8	Unemployed (no financial support)	To obtain employment—part/full To obtain public assistance/social security (long term)
5/10	Spiritual void	To return to church

E. **Charted Progress**
    During data collection, the social worker became aware of Mr. R's desire to return to God and the Catholic church. The need for religious enrichment was added to Mr. R's progress chart. Also added was Mr. R's desire for more information about his illness (see Table 5.5). Basic information was recorded on the face sheet of his record. In summary recordings, additional information obtained during data collection was included.

Conclusion

Although the process of data collection, which includes recording and documenting facts, may be seen as somewhat arduous and unsatisfying, it is an essential component of professional practice. In this chapter, central focus was given to identifying and organizing relevant data, distinguishing fact from assumption, understanding the meaning of informed consent, and using appropriate recording formats to document information in writing. These dimensions of data collection are basic to the process, and they prepare the social worker to move on to the next stage, assessment. As with all of the stages of helping, circumstances change in human situations, and the art of identifying facts about current realities goes on throughout the dynamic process. A social worker must remain open to reformulating or supplementing the information collected, even after it has been organized and used in developing an assessment and planned intervention.

6 Assessment

Throughout the helping process, a social worker is listening, evaluating, and acting. There is, however, a certain period of time in the process that is specifically designated as the assessment stage. Assessment is a time for appraising the *person-in-environment* configuration, for planning interventions, and for setting the structure for evaluation of outcomes. Assessment is inherently linked to data collection in that while data collection gathers information (both subjective and objective) used for making inferences, assessment is the intellectual activity of interpreting and drawing inferences derived from the collected data. It is basically an activity that is focused on gaining understanding of clients' problems(s) or situation(s) and then formulating a plan of action (prioritizing problems, setting goals, planning interventions, and anticipating evaluation and termination) through framing solutions to identified problems. Collaborative judgment and collaborative decision making are central characteristics of this stage of the General Method.

In a joint effort, the client system and social worker try to make sense out of available facts, observations, and other information and then use that understanding as a basis for deciding what can be done about the client system's concerns or problems. Both the client system and the social worker actively invest in the planning process, but each brings a different expertise and takes on a different role. Client systems bring significant expertise to the assessment process. They usually know what they want, they can describe what they are willing to do, and they can demonstrate their own capabilities. Clients have the ultimate power over the direction of the assessment plan. Social workers contribute technical knowledge and skills for constructing plans and knowledge of the resources available for implementing them. Client systems have the right and responsibility to say what they can and will do, whereas social workers offer suggestions and provide feedback about possible consequences of chosen action or inaction.

A primary consideration in good planning is the concept of building on strengths while addressing client system limitations. Sometimes, limitations constitute barriers that need to be circumvented or overcome. However, assessment begins with and incorporates the strengths/needs orientation. That is, the social worker identifies the capacities and the potential of the agency, the community, the situation involving the problem and needs, the social worker, the client system, and the client system's immediate environment as well as any factors in human diversity that might come into play. The social worker needs to be aware and sensitive to his or her own perceptions as well as those of the other systems of contact involved in the context of the situation presented. In a problem-focused approach, there is danger of perceiving the situation only in terms of what is wrong. Such an approach can easily lead to blaming, loss of hope, and seeing the situation only from the perspective of client system weakness. The strengths/needs orientation, on the other hand, supports the cardinal value of social work—namely, belief in the value and worth of every individual and belief in client self-determination. Thus, valuing people inherently as human beings, the strengths/needs orientation directs the social worker and the client system toward exploring and uncovering client system abilities and micro-, mezzo-, and macro-level resources and toward valuing the contribution client systems can make toward bringing about change in themselves and/or their surrounding environment.

The three major components of the assessment stage are (1) an assessment statement, (2) problem prioritization, and (3) the contracted plan. All three dimensions need to be addressed prior to intervening. The social worker who moves directly into implementing change, without taking time for assessment and planning, frequently has to undo or add to the actions taken as he or she comes to realize that such interventions were precipitous or inappropriate.

It is possible that in certain situations a social worker will have to act before a full assessment has been completed. A client system may have immediate, urgent needs that must be met before the necessary data can be collected for a formal assessment. There may not be time to plan and contract with a client system before intervening in a crisis situation. Action may have to be taken immediately in order to stabilize a life-at-risk situation. Once this is accomplished, however, every effort is made by the social worker to involve the client system in a mutual process of assessment.

Assessment Statement

After much listening and gathering of information, the social worker is expected to write an *assessment statement* for each problem identified. In the past, an assessment statement was referred to as a *diagnosis* in social work. In 1917, Mary Richmond modified the concept for greater relevance to the profession by calling it a *social diagnosis*. Problems frequently brought to the attention of generalist social workers are of a material, interpersonal, institutional, or interdependent nature. Using the term *assessment* rather than *diagnosis* helps avoid the possible inference that an identified problem is seen as a client's illness.

In the assessment statement, the social worker begins by clearly indicating who has the problem, what the problem is, and why the problem exists at this time. By the third stage of the General Method, the social worker should have sufficient data to describe the actual scope and cause of each problem. A simple formula to keep in mind for initiating an assessment statement is:

_____ has _____ because _____
$\quad$ (who) $\qquad$ (what problem) $\qquad\qquad$ (why)

The "why," or cause of the problem, may be seen in many layers. Often, an immediate causal factor has touched off the problematic situation. In addition, several sequential factors may have led to the immediate cause. For example, Mr. L may be unemployed because he does not have marketable skills in this state, but he lacks such skills because he came from a country where he was socialized into a work world of a very different nature. Or, a client system may be unemployed because he was laid off from his job, and maybe this was the result of fiscal cutbacks by the national administration.

In looking for the cause of a problem, the social worker realizes that there is a wide range of possible causes, from personal to interpersonal to structural or societal. The cause cited in an assessment statement should be the one most directly related to the problem. If, in the social worker's judgment, it is necessary to go back further to preceding causes in order to understand the problem for planning and intervention, these causes should also be cited, with a clear explanation of how they are connected to the problem.

In addition to the opening causal statement, an appraisal of the change potential of the problem should be presented in a full assessment statement. A problem's change potential is dependent on the three variables of problem, person, and environment. All three factors are interdependent, with direct impact on the maintenance or resolution of the problem.

First, the social worker and the system of contact consider the nature of the problem itself, asking how serious the problem is and what its change potential is.

Is this a problem that can be resolved? Is the problem of such a nature that it is irreversible (e.g., suicide, terminal illness, bankruptcy)? More specifically, how wide or deep is the problem? Are many people involved, and to what extent? How long has it been going on?

Second, the strengths and needs of the client system with the problem are assessed. What is his or her or their motivation and capacity to make whatever changes may be necessary? Are they able to cope with it alone or to accept help from others? What is their change potential? In order to document a clinical assessment of the strengths, needs, and limitations of a person or a relationship, *rapid-assessment instruments* are available for use during interviews. A social worker's appraisal of client systems in such areas as anxiety level, social interaction, marital adjustment, assertiveness, and alcohol or drug use may be supported by scores obtained on the assessment instruments. Of course, there are limitations in the use of scores from questionnaires. A social worker would want to cite additional evidence, such as documentation from other professionals and direct observation, to support the assessment.

The third area to be considered before an integrated assessment of the problem's change potential can be made involves the environment in which the problem is located. What is available in the environment in terms of formal or informal resources to promote the necessary changes? Are there restraining forces in the environment that are stronger than supportive resources? With optimum use of available resources, what is the expected outcome? What is the change potential of the environment for dealing with the problem?

After the three variables of problem, person, and environment are assessed individually, a cumulative assessment of the potential for change may be made for the particular problem within its person-environment context. Basically, the social worker's statement may be framed as follows:

The change potential for _____ problem/need of _____
                                       (whose)   (what problem)

is assessed as _____ because _____
                        (high, somewhat   (reasons: nature of problem,
                         high, medium,   person's motivation or capac-
                        somewhat low, or   ity, resources and restraints
                              low)   in the environment)

In addition to a causal statement and a change-potential statement, the assessment statement should include a judgment about the seriousness or urgency of the problem. The question to be asked here is: To what extent is this a life-or-death matter for these people (or this person) at this time? Even if the change potential for a problem is judged to be very low, immediate attention has to be given to a life-endangering situation. Action must be taken in whatever way possible to protect the lives of those involved. In critical situations, the social worker may have to make an immediate referral or serve as an advocate, even though there is little support from the persons or environment involved with the problem. Further considerations of types of interventions will be presented in the next chapter. The point being highlighted here is that an assessment statement should include a professional judgment on the urgency and seriousness of the problem, with supportive data.

Case Examples

*Micro Example 1: Mr. L, 37 Years Old, French-Canadian, Unmarried,
      No Family*
Problem: Unemployment
Assessment Statement

Mr. L has the problem of unemployment because he is unskilled and unmotivated to seek employment. The nature of the problem is such that the potential for change is very low. Mr. L has been out of work since he moved to this state three years ago. His capacity for work is limited because he does not have the skills sought by employers in this area. He has low motivation to seek work because he experienced a series of rejections in his early efforts to find employment. He is feeling hopeless and depressed. Resources for training or hiring unskilled laborers are extremely difficult to locate in this state. For these reasons, the overall change potential for Mr. L's problem of unemployment is assessed as very low. This is a very serious problem for Mr. L, because he does not qualify for public assistance in this state, and the savings he brought with him from Canada are depleted.

*Macro Example 2: North Central City Community (Approximately
      600 Families, Six-Block Area, Low-Income Housing)*
Problem: No Public Transportation
Assessment Statement

The North Central City Community has a need for public transportation because the local bus company recently cut off its route into the neighborhood. The problem is somewhat serious, as most people in the neighborhood do not have cars and they now have to walk eight blocks to get a bus. The people of the community are highly motivated for active involvement in resolving the problem, and they have an organized leadership. The bus company has expressed an openness to reconsider its action and to meet with community representatives. In this situation, the change potential is assessed as high, since resources are available inside and outside of the community.

In assessing data according to the triplex of problem, person, and environment, a social worker needs to maintain a holistic perspective of the dynamic interrelationships of social, cultural, and psychological factors. Tools and instruments have been developed to help the professional see the relationship of a client's psychological and social needs with institutional and environmental resources. In juxtaposing one's professional assessment of the problem, person, and environment triplex, a social worker may see more clearly how to partialize and prioritize multiple problems in complex situations.

Problem Prioritization

Before entering into the goal setting and contracting of this stage of the method, the social worker and the client or action system need to prioritize the problems identified and assessed. The questions asked are: What problem do we work on first? Where do we begin? On what basis should a problem be selected as the primary focus for intervention?

As the social worker compiles, categorizes, and reviews data, it often becomes apparent that several problems are in need of attention. In response to the question of where to begin, the social worker and the client or action system enter into a process for prioritizing the problems identified. To select the most appropriate starting point, the social worker must reconsider the initial assessment of the information that was gathered according to the problem-person-environment triplex for each identified problem.

In studying each problem or triplex, the social worker keeps in mind the fact that a client system needs to build up a sense of trust in the social worker's and agency's ability to be helpful. To foster client involvement in a growing, working relationship with the social worker, there has to be an experience of success or satisfaction of need as soon as possible. The social worker therefore tries to select *first* a problem that has a high change potential for resolution or need satisfaction.

As stated earlier, in writing an assessment statement for a problem, the social worker asks: What is the change potential of the problem itself, of the persons involved, and of the related environment? Only after assessing all three dimensions for a problem will the social worker be able to arrive at a comprehensive and accurate prognosis that can be used for problem prioritization. For some problems, the persons may have high motivation and capabilities, but the environment may provide little opportunity to actualize the persons' potential. An unemployed person, for example, may have skills and high motivation to find a job, but there may be no job openings in the environment. A person may have a problem or need that does not appear to be serious in nature, such as an absence of a support system. If, however, the person has little motivation, or if there are no available support groups or resources in the environment, the prognosis for change in this problem area is low. After considering the total change potential for problems such as those just cited, the social worker would continue to try to find a problem with high potential for change in all three areas before beginning to intervene with the system.

At times, it may be impossible to find a starting problem with high change potential in all three areas. From a list of problems, it may be very difficult to distinguish and select the one that should be given priority. A tool has been developed to assist a social worker in conceptualizing and analyzing a number of problems. It serves as a framework to compare change expectations for different problems and, through juxtaposition, to visualize which problems have the greatest change potential.

According to the tool depicted in Table 6.1, each problem is studied and scaled according to an assessment of the change potential of the problem-person-environment triplex. On the basis of data collected previously, the social worker estimates the potential for change, using a scale of 0 to 10. Scoring criteria are as follows: 0 = no potential, 1 = very low, 2 = low, 3 = somewhat low, 4 = somewhat high, 8 = high, 9 = very high, and 10 = maximum potential for change. For example, in looking at the problem identified as "child's illness" in Table 6.1, the social worker first asks about the nature and duration of the illness. If information has been gathered that indicates the child has just developed a strep throat, and the social worker knows that there is a high incidence of cure for this illness, the change potential for "problem" may be scored as high (8). If there are accessible health care resources and the parents and child will take or administer the prescribed medication, the change potential in "person" and "environment" is also high (scored 8 and 9). Because the total change-potential score for the problem of "child's illness" is very high (25), this problem may be seen as the highest priority on the list of problems for initial intervention.

The change potential scores for the problem identified as "father's drinking" are not as hopeful. On the basis of data observed and obtained, the social worker has assessed all three categories with extremely low scores. In looking at the nature and duration of the problem itself, the social worker knows that the problem has

TABLE 6.1 Problem Prioritization

Problem List	Change-Potential Scores (0–10)			Total Change Potential	Problem Prioritization	Severity
	Problem	Person(s)	Environment			
Child's illness	8	8	9	25	1	
Father's drinking	2	1	4	7	8	*
Father's unemployment	5	8	5	18	3	
Mother's depression	6	4	6	16	5	
Wife abuse	3	2	4	9	7	*
Housing conditions	6	5	3	14	6	
School truancy	8	7	8	23	2	
Husband-wife communication	6	5	6	17	4	

*Life-at-risk situation.

gone on for years and that alcoholism is a serious physical and socially pathological illness (scored 2). In terms of the father's motivation and capacity to change at
this time, the social worker assesses the "person" category also as very low (1),
because the father denies he has a drinking problem and refuses to go for help. The
social worker studied the formal and informal resources of the father's environment and averaged out a score of 4. Although formal resources are available in the
environment to help the father with his drinking problem (Alcoholics Anonymous
and local hospital and clinic), his wife and family deny that the father has a drinking problem, saying that he and most of his buddies are just heavy drinkers.
Apparently, the total change potential for the "father's drinking" is very low (7).
The social worker recognizes that it is a very serious problem, but one that will not
be resolved in the near future.

In selecting the problem with the highest change potential for beginning
intervention, the social worker is aware of the fact that there are problems of
greater severity in need of ongoing attention. It is expected that these problems
will probably take a long time before any marked change will occur. Because of the
serious nature of these problems, the social worker continues to direct efforts
toward overcoming them while at the same time working on those problems or
needs for which progress and success may be expected.

For example, in Table 6.1, there are two problems with low change-potential
scores (father's drinking; wife abuse). These problems are asterisked in the "severity" column because they are assessed as life-at-risk situations. The social worker
will continue ongoing efforts to study and intervene in these areas while working
with the family on problems that have high potential for change.

Contracting

Contract planning becomes the bridge between assessment and intervention and is
the activity focused on change. After a problem has been selected for action, the
social worker and the client and action system begin to plan what needs to be
done, by whom, and when. It is possible that they will choose to work on more
than one problem at a time. It is important that they clearly understand, however,
which problems are being addressed and which ones are not, and the reasons for
the selection.

Contract planning is a skill. As pointed out earlier, in the problem-solving
approach of the General Method, every effort is made to conceptualize and to verbalize the identified problems and corresponding goals. During the third stage of
the method, social worker, and client system also conceptualize and verbalize the
specific tasks that need to be performed in order to accomplish the goals. Not only
are the tasks identified but they are also placed in sequence. Dialogue between
social worker and client system includes a consideration of which tasks need to
precede others. The discussion about each task extends to a consideration of possible consequences that may result from its enactment.

A contract plan specifies the reason for each component and action in the plan. Accountability is an important aspect of any contractual relationship. A well-developed plan that specifies what is to be done and why it is to be done demonstrates a means of fulfilling the responsibility for accountability to client systems, agencies, and the supporting public.

In developing a contract, a client-centered perspective and process need to be maintained. This is a phase during which it is easy to leave clients out of the process. As the social worker collects information or data, he or she might be tempted to take over and write the contract without any client input. Sometimes this may happen because social workers feel pressured to complete the paperwork. Sometimes they are eager to start the change process. Other times, inexperienced social workers may feel uncomfortable with client systems being in control of the helping process. However, when clients do not fully participate or at the least have their input considered, the chances of contract failure increase because client systems are deprived of an opportunity to become empowered and to improve their problem-solving skills.

Therefore, careful planning is needed in determining who should be expected to perform what task. A basic guiding principle is: *Inasmuch as possible, a person should do for himself or herself.* A social worker would agree to carry out a task for a client system only when it is apparent that the individual, family, group, organization, or community is unable to perform the needed task and that no other resources are available to call on. Social workers do not foster dependency. Nevertheless, they do recognize that there are certain actions that some individuals are unable to perform, owing to internal or external circumstances. When such actions are necessary for goal accomplishment, a social worker using the general method would try first to mobilize other resources of the client system, such as family, friends, church, or community support systems. If no internal or informal resources are available, the social worker may initiate or execute a needed task. As quickly as possible, however, the social worker would try to enable the person to perform such tasks for himself or herself.

Case Examples
Micro Example 1
A client has been trying to contact his landlord for days to register a complaint. Although the landlord has been avoiding contact with the client, he may be more readily available when an agency social worker contacts him. The social worker would try to arrange for the landlord to meet with the client to discuss the complaint. If necessary, the social worker may have to go with the client. If neither of these two options is feasible, the social worker may have to go in behalf of the client.

Macro Example 2
A woman recuperating from an operation is unable to drive her son to the clinic. The social worker would try to see if another family member or neighbor could bring him. There may be a volunteer service within

or outside of the clinic that could be tapped to provide the needed transportation. Only after options such as these are explored would the social worker offer to go out and pick up the child.

During the contracting period, when social worker and system of contact clarify who will do what, it is important for both to identify the date when each task is expected to be carried out. Little progress can be made and time may be wasted unless timing is discussed and there is a sense of expectation for task and goal accomplishment.

As each goal is considered and contacted through mutual agreement on task assignments, an anticipated date is stated for the performance of each task, even though the date may have to be altered due to unexpected circumstances. The projection of dates for task execution serves as a guide for general planning and review. If a task is not completed on the expected date, social worker and client or action system can grow in understanding the dynamics of problem, person, and environment by asking why it was not accomplished as anticipated. More realistic comprehension and planning could result from this inquiry.

A tool for use in generalist practice has been developed that integrates the essential components of a contracted plan (see Table 6.2). As a social worker proceeds in the process of problem solving with a client or action system, this tool may be used to state in writing what is agreed on as (1) the problems or needs to be addressed, (2) the goals to be accomplished, (3) the tasks to be performed, (4) the persons to execute each task, (5) the dates anticipated to enact each task, and (6) the actual dates of task accomplishment. Once the tool is filled out by social worker and client or action system, they may refer to it each time they need to assess progress or impediments to progress. Skill is needed for precise identification of the problems and needs and the goals and tasks. The goals and tasks should focus on behaviors that can be measured or observed.

As each problem or need is selected for action, the name of the problem is entered on the instrument, along with the date when the social worker and the system of contact agree that it is a problem for intervention. The list of problems and needs should be prioritized according to the criteria and process stated earlier.

TABLE 6.2 Contracted Plan

Date Identified	Problem/ Need	Goal	Task	Contract	Date Anticipated	Date Accomplished

Goals are conceptualized as the expected outcomes of the endeavor. Because overall client goals may be too broad, they are often partialized into intermediate goals or specific goal objectives. Goals are written to satisfy the principle of

Who . . .
Will do what . . .
To what extent . . .
Under what conditions . . .
By when?

Therefore, the tasks to be accomplished for each goal or goal objective need to be written in sequence. The person or system indicated as contracting to perform each task should be identified in accordance with the principle of "doing for self as much as possible." The dates anticipated are written down after realistic consideration of what is feasible. As each task is accomplished, the final column should be filled in with the accurate date of completion.

The instrument, as shown in Table 6.2, can be placed in the front of any record for immediate identification of plan and progress. It becomes obvious, on first glance at the "date accomplished" column, whether there are tasks that were contracted but not completed. Rather than having to review all of the recordings of various contacts contained within a record to find out what has been happening with a case, the social worker (or supervisor), by reviewing the instrument, can receive a synthesis of the essence of the work being done to date.

The instrument in Table 6.2 fits well with problem-oriented recording (POR) described in Chapter 5. The contracted plan (Table 6.2) may be seen as a direct follow-up and complement to the steps taken for the POR. The problems and dates identified on the problem list of the POR are readily available for problem prioritization and listing in the first and second column of the contracted plan. Also, the "assessment" and "plan" stated in the "SOAP" for each problem with the POR will help in the identification of goals, tasks, contracts, and dates anticipated to be listed on the contracted plan. As each task of the contract is performed, its date of accomplishment is indicated on the contracted plan. This information will facilitate the writing of summary statements, as expected for each problem in a POR.

The contracted plan (Table 6.2) is a tool for ongoing use. Problems and needs, goals, tasks, and contracted enactor may change in the course of service. Once begun, there is a need for continued updating and review of the plan. As brought out in a later chapter, this tool may also serve as a major instrument for evaluation through goal analysis.

Mezzo Example 3
An example of a contracted plan for the problems prioritized in Table 6.1 may be found in Table 6.3. For the first problem, child's illness, it is clear in the "contract" column that the social worker planned to take Mrs. C and her child to the clinic. She (social worker) did this because Mrs. C had a history of missing clinic appointments. Also, Mrs. C had no way of get-

TABLE 6.3 Contracted Plan: The C Family

Date Identified	Problem/Need	Goal	Task	Contract	Date Anticipated	Date Accomplished
2/8	1. Child's illness	1. To improve child's health—treat strep throat	1. Call health clinic for appointment. 2. Take child to clinic.	1. Mrs. C 2. Mrs. C and social worker	2/9 2/12	2/9 2/15
2/8	2. School truancy	2. To attend school daily	1. Speak with mother. 2. Speak with child. 3. Speak with teacher. 4. Wake child on time. 5. Put child on bus.	1. Social worker 2. Mrs. C and social worker 3. Mrs. C and social worker 4. Mrs. C 5. Mrs. C	2/9 2/9 2/12 3/1 3/1	2/9 2/12 2/12 3/1 3/1
2/8	3. Father's unemployment	3. To obtain steady employment (father)	1. Discuss with Mr. C. 2. Contact employment agencies. 3. Checkout training programs. 4. Locate job or training (J/T) for Mr. C. 5. Apply for J/T.	1. Social worker 2. Mr. C 3. Social worker 4. Mr. C, employment agencies, or social worker 5. Mr. C	2/15 2/16 2/16 2/25 3/16	2/18 2/19 2/17 3/15 3/16
2/8	4. Lack of communication between husband and wife	4. To improve husband-wife communication (talking out instead of fighting out)	1. Speak with Mr. C. 2. Speak with Mr. and Mrs. C. 3. Refer Mr. and Mrs. C to marital counseling center. 4. Contact marital counseling center. 5. Attend sessions at marital counseling center. 6. Support their attendance.	1. Social worker 2. Social worker 3. Social worker 4. Mrs. C 5. Mr. and Mrs. C 6. Social worker	3/22 3/25 3/25 3/26 4/5 4/5	3/22 3/25 3/25 3/29 4/5 4/5
2/8	5. Overcrowded housing	5. To obtain larger living quarters	1. Discuss with Mr. and Mrs. C. 2. Explore housing options and contact possible resources. 3. Apply for housing. 4. Move family.	1. Social worker 2. Mr. and Mrs. C and social worker 3. Mr. and Mrs. C 4. The C family and movers	4/7 4/8 5/10	4/7 4/8

ting to the clinic except by bus. The social worker was unable to locate any available informal resources to provide transportation.

As the social worker proceeded in problem solving with the family, she found that some of the problems identified during the first interview had decreased, owing to relief in other problem areas. For example, once Mr. C returned to work, Mrs. C was not so depressed and there was less physical abuse by her husband. Both Mr. and Mrs. C recognized their need to better understand and communicate with each other, and they agreed to go for marital counseling. They were also ready to begin to work in finding better housing. Mr. C was not ready, however, to talk about his heavy drinking. He and his wife denied that this was a problem, especially now that Mr. C was back at work. The social worker planned to continue to be involved with the family as they worked on finding better housing, but she was not able to go any further with Mr. C's drinking problem at this time.

Working with Different Client Systems

As stated earlier, the General Method of social work practice is applicable to working with a variety of client, action, and target systems. A social worker may be working with a family, an individual, a group, or a community, but in any case, the social worker and the client system go through an assessment stage. A question to be considered is: Are there any differences in writing an assessment statement, prioritizing problems, or drawing up a contracted plan when working with different-size client systems? Various writers in the field of social work have focused on the art of assessment with particular systems, such as group, family, organization, and community. The approach and tools presented in this chapter, however, are used in working with any type of client system.

In applying and adopting assessment tools to particular client systems, a social worker is sensitive to the knowledge that exists about each. In working with a community, for example, the social worker knows that a community consists of a complex body of persons with a common characteristic of place, problem, heritage, values, or commitment. There are often very distinctive subsystems within a community that may contract, contest, and conflict with one another. The social worker calls on the knowledge and skills identified in the profession by those who have expertise in community work and supplements their work with the newly developed tools for generalist practice.

Ross (1955) identified the process of organizing a community according to the following six stages:

1. Identify the community's needs and objectives.
2. Order or rank the needs or objectives.
3. Develop the confidence and will to work on the needs and objectives.
4. Find resources (internal and/or external) to deal with the needs or objectives.

5. Take action in respect to the needs or objectives.
6. Extend and develop cooperative and collaborative attitudes and practices in the community.

The stages for community organization as described half a century ago and more recently (Hardcastle, Wenocur, & Powers, 1997; Kretzmann & McKnight, 1993; Tropman, Ehrlich, & Rothman, 1995) are basically consistent with the stages of the General Method. In both processes, social worker and community go through phases where problems and objectives are identified, data are collected, and action is taken. It is implicit that prior to taking action, needs assessments are conducted, problems are prioritized with an appraisal of resources, and then actions are planned. Before moving into the action stage, the social worker and community now have tools available to help them with prioritizing problems and planning interventions.

For example, in the South End Community, the stated problems and needs were listed as follows:

High prices at local grocery stores
Rat- and roach-infested housing
No local control or input in neighborhood schools
Gang wars among community youths
No traffic light at the corner of Fifth Street and Silver Street

After drawing on assessment statements for each of these problems, the tool for prioritization of problems was completed, as found in Table 6.4.

Apparently, the community was motivated to begin to work on the need for a traffic light and the problem of high prices in local stores. In addition to motivation, the social worker assessed the nature and scope of each problem, as well as the extent of related resources. After all factors were considered, it became clear that the problem with the highest change potential was the need for a traffic light. This was a serious (life-at-risk) problem with a good chance of resolution. The

TABLE 6.4 Problem Prioritization: The South End Community

Problem List	Change-Potential Scores (0–10)			Total Change Potential	Problem Prioritization	Severity
	Problem	Person(s)	Environment			
High prices	3	8	3	14	2	
Infested housing	3	5	3	11	3	
No school control	2	3	2	7	5	
Youth fights	3	4	2	9	4	*
Traffic light	8	7	8	23	1	*

*Life-at-risk situation.

problem of gang wars was seen as serious (a youth having been stabbed last month), but community members did not indicate high motivation to work on this. They said gang wars had been going on for years because people from certain blocks just didn't get along. Also, few resources were available for youth in the area. The social worker, while not losing sight of this problem, would begin with an issue with high success potential in order to build up a sense of trust and accomplishment within the community.

After prioritizing problems and needs, the social worker and community would move to planning specific tasks and responsibilities for goal accomplishment. The tool for contracted planning could aptly be used at this point. An example of how a contract could be developed with this community is found in Table 6.5. In this case, as community members begin to witness success from their efforts, a sense of pride and power develops. They begin to hope for greater accomplishments and to demonstrate motivation to work on complex tasks, such as finding funding sources and writing grant proposals. In time, the community begins to focus on what could be as well as what was, on prevention as well as problem resolution. Residents begin to talk about the need for them to overcome their interpersonal conflicts because they could gain so much more by working together. Some people identify past feelings of helplessness or isolation. According to Table 6.5, once the community finds out that there is funding for building a youth recreational center, they begin to think about other projects for enriching the community. The social worker's role as leader and activator decreases as members feel more confident and assume more leadership themselves.

Although the complexity of community work may be somewhat frightening to entry-level social workers, the general tools for assessment, as demonstrated, enable a social worker to partialize and to coordinate the complex dimensions of needs and actions within community practice. As stated earlier, these assessment tools may be applied similarly when working with groups, families, or individuals.

There may be a major shift in the size of the system of contact during the helping process, as tasks become identified and implemented. Client systems may expand or decrease in number. Although a social worker may begin contact with an individual, in the course of planning it may become apparent that the social worker will need to intervene with the family or a larger system to achieve goals. Fortunately, a social worker using the General Method employs knowledge and skills that are applicable to systems of any size. General practice does not have the limitation of size as found in the traditional methods of casework, group work, or community organization.

Using Social Work Foundation Knowledge in Assessment

The skills and approach a social worker uses in the assessment stage should reflect the foundation value of *belief in the dignity and worth of every person* (see Table 1.3 in Chapter 1). As the social worker and system of contact collaborate in assessing

TABLE 6.5 Contracted Plan: South End Community

Date Identified	Problem/ Need	Goal	Task	Contract	Date Anticipated	Date Accomplished
3/15	1. Need for traffic light	1. To have a traffic light installed at Fifth and Silver Streets	1. Inquire about meeting with traffic commissioner (in three weeks).	1. Mr. G and social worker	3/19	3/24
			2. Draw up a petition.	2. Petition committee (Mr. and Mrs. K, Mr. F, Ms Q, Mrs. R) and social worker	3/20	3/26
			3. Get 500 signatures.	3. Petition committee and six others (Rev. J, Mrs B, Capt. P, Mr. S, Mr. and Mrs. B)	4/3	4/5
			4. Collect information on accidents at Fifth and Silver Streets.	4. Mrs. A	3/20	3/22
			5. Draw up a traffic-flow chart.	5. Traffic committee (Mr. and Mrs. M, Mr. McN, Ms. W, Mr. T) and social worker	4/3	3/31
			6. Meeting of community.	6. Whole community	4/4	4/4
			7. See commissioner with petition and information.	7. Petition committee, Mr. G, and social worker	4/9	
			8. Discuss cancellation by commissioner at committee meeting.	8. Community and social worker	4/13	4/13
			9. Arrange to meet with mayor.	9. Mr. G	4/15	

(continued)

TABLE 6.5   Continued

Date Identified	Problem/ Need	Goal	Task	Contract	Date Anticipated	Date Accomplished
			10. Meet with mayor.	10. Same as for contract 7	4/30	
			11. If task 9 is not possible, meet to plan a demonstration.	11. Community and social worker	4/20	4/20
			12. Make signs.	12. Traffic committee	4/22	4/22
			13. Notify communications media.	13. Mr. G and Mrs. P	4/26	4/26
			14. Demonstration at Fifth and Silver Streets.	14. Community and social worker	4/27	4/27
			15. Get traffic light.	15. Town officials	5/3	5/4
			16. Community meeting.	16. Community and social worker	5/7	5/7
3/15	2. High prices	2. To lower prices in local grocery stores	1. Compare prices and prepare report.	1. Comparative price committee (Mrs. B, Mr. G, Mr. and Mrs. N, Ms. W, Mr. T)	5/12	5/12
			2. Meet with store owners and present data.	2. Teams a. Mr. B, Mrs. Q, Mrs. J b. Mr. and Mrs. K, Mr. F	5/20	5/27
			3. Community meeting.	3. Community and social worker	5/27	5/27
			4. Meet with consumer-protection worker.	4. Mr. G, Mr. F, Mrs. J	6/3	6/3
			5. Meet with store owners and consumer-protection worker.	5. Comparative price committee, Mr. F, Mrs. J, social worker, store owners, and consumer-protection worker	6/20	6/22
			6. Monitor prices.	6. Teams as in contract 2	6/30 and ongoing	

Problem		Goal	Tasks	Persons responsible		
3. Infested housing	3/15	3. To exterminate rats and roaches in community housing	1. Community meeting.	1. Community and social worker	6/24	6/24
			2. Identify locations and extend of infestation—bring in housing inspector.	2. Data collection committee (Mr. and Mrs. M, Mrs. B, Mr. F, Ms. R, Mr. McW)	7/9	7/8
			3. Draw up petition and get signatures.	3. Petition committee	7/17	7/17
			4. See landlords with data and petition.	4. Teams a. Mr. F, Mrs. Q, Mr and Mrs. M b. Mr. B, Ms. J, Mrs. R	7/30	7/31
			5. Speak with Housing Authority and Housing Court.	5. Mr. G, Mr. F, Mrs. J	8/6	8/10
			6. Community meeting.	6. Community and social worker	8/10	8/12
			7. Withhold rents.	7. Tenants of infested housing	8/31	8/31
			8. Get publicity.	8. Mrs. P and Mrs. Q	8/30	8/29
			9. Hire sanitation specialist.	9. Landlords	9/2	9/10
4. Gang wars	3/15	4. To end gang wars	1. Community meeting.	1. Community and social worker	9/7	9/7
			2. Identify scope and cause—talk with youth and with police.	2. Data collection committee (Mr. F, Mrs. Q, Ms. R, Rev. J, Mr. McN)	9/20	9/22
			3. Locate funding to build recreation hall for community youth—talk with local officials.	3. Mr. G, Mrs. R, and social worker	9/20	9/24
			4. Draw up funding proposal.	4. Funding committee (Mr. and Mrs. S, Ms. N, Mr. T)	9/30	10/8

(continued)

TABLE 6.5 Continued

Date Identified	Problem/Need	Goal	Task	Contract	Date Anticipated	Date Accomplished
			5. Build recreational center (on church grounds).	5. Contractors and community	8/30	11/30
			6. Hire recreation director.	6. Recreation center committee (Rev. J, Mrs. R, Mr. and Mrs. M, Ms. Q, Mr. G)	10/30	11/20
			7. Monitor center.	7. Recreation center committee	11/1	
6/15	5. No school input or control	5. To have direct input into local school	1. Community meeting.	1. Community and social worker	8/24	8/24
			2. Study structure of school and compare with other schools.	2. School committee (Mr. and Mrs. K, Mr. F, Mrs. W)	8/30	9/4
			3. Meet with principal.	3. Mr. G, Mr. and Mrs. M	8/26	8/29
			4. Meet with Board of Education.	4. Mr. G, Mrs. Q, Rev. J, Mr. W	9/14	9/15
			5. Locate funding sources.	5. Mrs. R, Mrs. P, Mr. F	9/11	9/20
			6. Get other community people involved—elderly, singles, etc.	6. Rev. J, Capt. P, Mrs. R, social worker		
			7. Draw up proposal for community programs of school.	7. Mrs. R, Mr. W	9/30	

and planning, the basic practice principles—particularly individualization, self-determination, and acceptance—are demonstrated.

A client or action system needs to have an individualized assessment. No two people or client systems are exactly alike. Each one has a unique combination of problems, needs, resources, and circumstances. Thus, the principle of *individualization* is highlighted in the assessment stage of the General Method.

In prioritizing problems, the social worker knows that an essential factor to consider prior to problem selection is the extent of motivation in a client or action system to work on a particular problem or need. Unless there is client *self-determination* in problem prioritization, a social worker will undoubtedly meet with resistance and failure. The social worker who forges ahead for problem resolution will be unsuccessful without the agreement and support of the client system.

Although it is easy to wish that a client or action system have greater strengths or motivation, the social worker must convey an attitude of acceptance toward the client system as it is. If several problems are assessed as having low potential for change, the social worker may feel a sense of frustration or helplessness. He or she must begin with accepting the client system "as a given." Through discussion, support, and assessment, within an atmosphere of acceptance, the social worker enables the client system to view itself more realistically and to consider possible and desirable goals.

In addition to foundation values and principles, a social worker in the assessment stage uses knowledge and skills from the holistic foundation for general social work practice (Table 1.3 in Chapter 1). When writing a statement of cause for a problem, the social worker may be using concepts from theories to explain how a client system has been influenced by others. Knowledge of cultures, policies, and formal and informal resources is used in developing priorities for planning and intervention. The social worker utilizes various theories to understand persons, problems, and environments and their interactions as an appraisal of their change potential is being made.

The foundation skills that are used during assessment include goal setting, planning, contracting, and recording. As the social worker involves the client system in contracting, interviewing skills such as clarifying, bargaining, and confronting may be needed. The supportive skills of listening, guiding, and feeling and sensing are prevalent throughout the assessment process. With the individualization of each person-problem-environment triplex during assessment, the social worker applies foundation skills and theories as deemed appropriate to the situation.

Human Diversity in Assessment

During the assessment stage, as problems and needs are prioritized and contracts are formulated, a social worker and client system may find it difficult to determine where to begin, particularly when the work is with minorities. Often, the problems identified are both personal and societal in nature. Although it may be necessary to invest major energy first in providing for immediate material needs, a social worker should also plan to deal with the larger social-change issues that need to be addressed. A social worker's involvement in the larger issues helps demonstrate his or her understanding and acceptance to the client system. As interventions are contracted, the social worker strives to promote empowerment by strongly encouraging and supporting minority members to speak and act for themselves to meet immediate needs and to bring about institutional change.

In working out a contract with a client system, the social worker may find different degrees of participation and active involvement by systems, depending on cultural orientations. When a social worker is seen as an authority person in a lineal relationship (as with Asian Americans), members of the client system may show passivity and dependence. The speed with which a contract is drawn up may also be influenced by the culture of a particular client system.

The planning and selection of tasks on a contract should reflect a sensitivity to cultural values and beliefs. For example, to suggest institutional care of the elderly as a plan for many African Americans, Puerto Ricans, or Asians would be inappropriate. Similarly, placing a child with a relative in the tribe would be a much more acceptable plan for a Native American family than a foster-home placement would be.

As noted in Chapter 3, the core issues related to institutional racism, cultural diversity, gender-role expectations, sexual orientation, and socio-economic status need to be incorporated into the assessment process. This applies to assessing unmet needs and resource availability of client systems at the personal micro level, the family or group mezzo level, and the broader macro level.

Many personal problems may be assessed as stemming from tensions and rejections the individual has experienced when trying to participate in societal systems. The social worker and the client system study all of the identified problems, but priority is given to those with high potential for change. The broad, general goals that were stated during engagement are refined during assessment into more specific, attainable, measurable goals for contract formulation. In every possible way, the social worker tries to empower the client system to implement independently the tasks identified in the contract or to implement them with an action system or community of others who face similar pressures or injustices.

Information gathered about potential supportive resources is discussed during assessment, and the plan drawn up by social worker and client system may include initial contact with outside resources. If no local resources are available, the plan may be developed to organize a support group in or outside of the social worker's agency.

Using an ecological-systems perspective in planning, a social worker realizes that an individual with a goal of changing his or her behavior and image may experience pressure and negative reactions from the environment. For example, in any work on redefining gender roles—whether with men or women, individually or in groups—attention needs to be given to the possible consequences that may result from any change. The reality is that change is usually a painful process for both the individual and the environment. Although a person may become self-sufficient and independent, it is true that no person can be an island, totally independent from others, for very long. Human beings by nature are interdependent. To move into a truly collaborative, balanced interdependence, however, may be impossible for some individuals in their existing environments. Women who have been greatly dependent, for example, may have to go to the other polarity of total independence before they and others can see them as equal, complementary counterparts. The implications of these and other possible actions and reactions need to be given serious consideration before choices and changes are made. Various support systems and reinforcements need to be located and ensured if such change is to be positive and stabilized. Thus, in writing assessment statements, prioritizing problems, and contracting with different systems, social workers use their knowledge of and sensitivity to multiculturalism, social pluralism, and socio-demographic diversity.

Assessment in Micro, Mezzo, and Macro Practice in Diverse Field Areas

I. **Field Area: Child Welfare**

   A. **Agency: State Department of Children's Services**
   B. **Client System**
   K, a 15-year-old female, is in an emergency shelter. (For more background information see Chapter 4, Engagement in Micro, Mezzo, and Macro Practice in Diverse Field Areas, I. Child Welfare.)
   C. **Summary of Preceding Stages**
   The problem and goals identified during engagement and data collection are listed in Table 5.1. During engagement, K expressed feelings of loneliness, hatred, nervousness, and depression. In collecting data, the social worker learned that K had experienced some difficulty adjusting in both the group home and the foster-home placements that she had before she ran away, particularly in the foster home. Her schoolwork had also deteriorated prior to her running away and being placed in the emergency shelter. After exploring informal and formal resources in the environment, the social worker located a group home for young women (ages 14 to 19) in Jenett City that had an opening. K expressed a strong desire to move into a group home, to return to school, and to get help with her personal problems.
   D. **Assessment**
   Assessment statement: K has no permanent residence because she cannot live at home with her abusive parents (mother and stepfather), and she ran away from her foster home. She has personal needs (problem 3 in Table 5.1) that interfere with her functioning. The etiology of K's personal problems go back to her traumatic home environment, where she was physically and sexually abused. K is out of school because she is living in a temporary shelter awaiting placement. Her

school performance had dropped to below average while she was living in the foster home because she became involved with a boyfriend and was having an increasing number of arguments with her foster parents.

The change potential for K's problem of homelessness is assessed as somewhat high because K is motivated to accept a group-home placement and a resource is available. The change potential for K's need to reenter school is assessed as somewhat high because there is a school near the group home. The change potential for K's problems with adjustment to placement and school is assessed as somewhat high because K is now motivated to accept ongoing help with her personal problems and because there will be opportunity for K to receive help individually and in group while living in the group home.

Problem prioritization: The problem-prioritization tool was used by the social worker, as recorded in Table 6.6

The need for a placement is given top priority because it has the highest change potential (24) and also because of the urgency (severity) of the situation (living in temporary shelter). Finding a school placement is not a difficult problem to resolve. It received the second-highest score and became second in priority.

The personal problems have lower change scores because it is expected that these problems will take more time for resolution. K is particularly motivated to try to get over "feeling down." She is ready to talk about how hurt and angry she is. She also wants to feel better about herself and to understand what has happened to her. She hesitates to talk about her sexuality, even though problems related to her sexual identity, behavior, and relationships are assessed as serious (severity). K ran away form home when she became involved with a boyfriend, and she fears new heterosexual friendships. Since the social worker has been able to locate environmental resources for all the problems listed, the change potential scores in the "environment" column are high (9s). Even though the problem relating to K's sexuality is prioritized last, the social worker sees the seriousness

TABLE 6.6 Problem Prioritization: State Department of Children's Services

Problem List	Change-Potential Scores (0–10)			Total Change Potential	Problem Prioritization	Severity
	Problem	*Person(s)*	*Environment*			
No permanent home	7	8	9	24	1	*
Out of school	7	7	9	23	2	
Personal problems						
Poor self-esteem	5	6	9	20	4	
Identity confusion	5	6	9	20	4	
Sexuality	5	5	9	19	6	*
Depression	5	7	9	21	3	

*Life-at-risk situation.

TABLE 6.7 Contracted Plan: State Department of Children's Services

Date Identified	Problem/Need	Goal	Task	Contract	Date Anticipated	Date Accomplished
1/12	1. No permanent home	1a. To obtain a permanent placement b. To maintain a permanent placement	1. Make referral. 2. Visit group home. 3. Move to group home. 4. Follow up.	1. Social worker 2. K and social worker 3. K, with social worker's help 4. Social worker, K, and group-home staff	1/19 1/22 1/24 1/30 and every second week	
1/12	2. Out of school	2. To reenter school	1. Enroll in local school. 2. Follow up.	1. K and group-home staff worker 2. Social worker, school personnel, group-home staff	1/28 1/30 and other school conferences	
1/12	3. Personal problems a. Depression b. Poor self-esteem c. Identity confusion d. Sexuality	3. Personal goals (1/19) a. To stop "feeling down" so much b. To feel better about self c. To clarify identity d. To be able to have good friendships with males	1. Have weekly individual sessions with social worker at the group home. 2. Participate in weekly peer-group meetings. 3. Follow up.	1. K and group-home social worker 2. K 3. Social worker, K, and social worker at group home	1/25 and once a week thereafter 1/25 and once a week thereafter 1/30 and every second week	

*of this problem and will bring it to the attention of the person who will be work-
ing with K individually in the group home.*

*Contracting: Building on the list of problems and goals identified during engage-
ment and data collection, the social worker and K then began to plan the tasks
that needed to be performed to achieve the stated goals. They also identified who
would be responsible for carrying out each task, and they set the dates when task
completion could be anticipated. Their contracted plan is given in Table 6.7.*

II. Field Area: Gerontology

A. Agency: Seaside Nursing Home
B. Client System

*Mrs. J is an 80-year-old Portuguese woman in a skilled-nursing facility. (For
more background information, see Chapter 4, Engagement in Micro, Mezzo, and
Macro Practice in Diverse Field Areas, II. Gerontology.)*

C. Summary of Preceding Stages

*The problems and goals identified during engagement and data collection may be
found in Table 5.2. During engagement, Mrs. J expressed feelings of distrust,
fear, anger, and abandonment. In collecting data, the social worker learned that
Mrs. J's failure to adjust included disruptive behavior in the unit. She was agi-
tating the nurses and the residents. More information was obtained about Mrs.
J's history and her family, who could not be located. Portuguese-speaking
resource people in the nursing home (a new volunteer) and in the community (the
church pastor) were being located to visit with Mrs. J. The client herself was
becoming more open and motivated to adjust to the nursing home.*

D. Assessment

*Assessment statement: Mrs. J is seclusive, uncooperative, and agitated because
she is culturally isolated in the nursing home and because she has been abandoned
by her family. She will not leave her room alone because she is afraid that the little she has left will be stolen. She finds it difficult to go out and meet with others
because she can't speak English fluently, and she feels uncomfortable with people
of a different culture. Mrs. J fights with the nurses when they come to give her a
bath because it distresses her to have to get undressed at 10 o'clock in the morning. Mrs. J has been yelling at the residents and calling them names because she
wants to get their attention and to make them communicate with her. She displays anger and confusion at times, as a result of her organic brain syndrome.*

*The change potential for Mrs. J to overcome her seclusiveness is assessed as
medium high because Mrs. J is somewhat motivated to be able to leave her room
on her own and because she is physically able to do so at this time. The potential
to overcome her cultural isolation is assessed as medium because she can speak
some English, a volunteer has been located who is Portuguese, and the pastor of
Mrs. J's former church will also come to see her. The change potential for Mrs. J
to get to know the staff and the resources of the nursing home is assessed as high,
because Mrs. J has agreed to meet twice a week with the social worker, and she has
expressed interest in meeting other staff members and hearing about available*

resources. Her involvement in activities at the nursing home will depend on how comfortable she feels with the activities and with those who participate in them.

The change potential for overcoming the bath-schedule problem is assessed as high because the nurses are open to reconsidering the time Mrs. J is scheduled for her bath. Mrs. J and the head nurse are willing to meet to discuss the problem. The change potential for overcoming Mrs. J's yelling at the residents is also assessed as high, because Mrs. J is motivated to work for better communication with others. She says she will stop the name-calling.

Mrs. J's overall functioning and adjustment are dependent also on the rate of deterioration due to organic brain syndrome.

<u>*Problem prioritization:*</u> *The social worker prioritized the identified problems, using the prioritization tool as shown in Table 6.8.*

The problem of seclusiveness has a high change-potential score (9), because in considering the nature of the problem itself, residents who are physically able to leave their rooms may do so. The change potential for "person" is assessed as somewhat high (7). Although Mrs. J has the physical capacity to leave her room and expresses a desire to get out more, she still feels afraid and strange in the nursing home. "Environment" is also assessed at a 7 for this problem. Resources (persons and programs) in the nursing-home environment are available to help Mrs. J leave her room. They do not, however, reflect her culture, except for one possible volunteer. Mrs. J's problem of seclusiveness is asterisked in the "severity" column, because it can be seen as potentially a life-or-death issue. If Mrs. J regresses to the point of refusing to leave her room even for meals, she could become seriously ill and have to be moved into the chronic-care unit.

In assessing the problem of cultural isolation, the change potential is seen as medium, and scored as a 6. People of different cultures do not have to feel or be

TABLE 6.8   Problem Prioritization: Seaside Nursing Home

Problem List	Change-Potential Scores (0–10)			Total Change Potential	Problem Prioritization	Severity
	Problem	*Person(s)*	*Environment*			
Seclusiveness: not leaving room	9	7	7	23	3	*
Cultural isolation	6	8	7	21	5	
Unfamiliarity with staff and resources	9	8	9	26	1	
Fighting with nurses over bath	7	8	9	24	2	
Calling residents names	7	9	6	22	4	

*Life-at-risk situation.

isolated. Even though Mrs. J does not speak English fluently, she can carry on a conversation in English ("person" score of 8). She could help others in the environment to understand and respond to her cultural needs. Although there are no Portuguese residents or staff members in the nursing home at the time, this may change, because the number of Portuguese moving into the local geographic area is increasing. Mrs. J has also expressed some desire to get to understand others at the nursing home, and the staff of the home, particularly those who speak Spanish, have indicated an interest in helping Mrs. J feel welcome. They talked about serving Portuguese food and playing music from Portugal at the next resident-and-staff party. The "environment" assessment at this time is scored a 7. If a Portuguese volunteer or Mrs. J's pastor becomes actively involved with her, the environment score may be raised.

The lack of familiarity with the staff and resources of the home was seen as a problem easily remedied (9). Mrs. J is capable of understanding the staff and resources, and she is somewhat motivated to learn about them (8). The program planner, recreational director, head nurse, chaplain, and others on the staff of the nursing home are very willing to talk with Mrs. J and to develop an individualized program for her. The planned program for Mrs. J could include recreational, social, and spiritual activities. "Environment," therefore, is given a high change-potential score (9) for the problem of "unfamiliarity with staff and resources of the nursing home.

The potential for changing the problem of fighting with the nurses over the bath is assessed at 7. Even though the problem is not a life-or-death issue, changing the schedule for Mrs. J's bath time would affect the schedule for many others. It is possible, however, for the schedule to be changed and thus prevent further fighting by Mrs. J over the bath. The change potential for "person" is 8 because Mrs. J is capable of being cooperative and has said she would like to get along better with the nurses. The nurses are open to rescheduling Mrs. J's bath time, and the head nurse has agreed to meet with Mrs. J about it ("environment" score of 9).

In considering the problem of calling other residents names, the social worker assessed the change potential for the problem itself as 7. The act of holding back from name-calling is possible for Mrs. J. She realizes that it isn't right and wants to stop this behavior (9). The residents ("environment") are not interested in going near Mrs. J at this time (change potential of 6), but some will probably respond if they are encouraged by the staff to try to reach out to her.

In totaling the change potential scores, the problems become prioritized as follows: (1) unfamiliarity with staff and resources, (2) fighting with nurses over bath, (3) seclusiveness: not leaving room, (4) calling residents names, and (5) cultural isolation.

<u>Contracting</u>: Building on the prioritized problem list, the social worker and Mrs. J began to plan and to contract for what needed to be accomplished in order to achieve their mutually agreed on goals. The contracted plan they developed is shown in Table 6.9.

TABLE 6.9 Contracted Plan: Seaside Nursing Home

Date Identified	Problem/Need	Goal	Task	Contract	Date Anticipated	Date Accomplished
9/27	1. Unfamiliarity with staff and resources of nursing home	1. To get to know the staff and resources of the nursing home	1. Meet twice a week with social worker.	1. Social worker and Mrs. J	10/4 and every Tuesday and Thursday thereafter	10/4, 10/9, 10/11
			2. Meet with program planner.	2. Social worker, Mrs. J and program planner	10/16	
			3. Meet with a person from recreation staff.	3. Social worker, Mrs. J and recreation staff person	10/23	
10/2	2. Fighting with nurses over bath	2. To work out bath schedule with nurses	1. Meet with head nurse to discuss bath schedule.	1. Mrs. J and head nurse	10/16	
9/25	3. Seclusiveness: not leaving room alone	3a. To leave room alone (at least once a day)	1. Walk down to nursing station alone at least once a day.	1. Mrs. J	10/25 and each day thereafter	
		b. To attend a house activity, program, or meeting (at least once a week)	1. Go to a house activity, program, or meeting (at least once a week).	1. Social worker or staff member and Mrs. J first two times	Starting week of 10/22	
				2. Mrs. J with residents each week thereafter	Starting week of 11/5	
10/2	4. Calling residents names	4. To stop calling residents names	1. Stop name calling.	1. Mrs. J	10/16 and thereafter	
			2. Say "hello" to residents.	2. Mrs. J	10/16 and thereafter	
9/25	5. Cultural isolation	5. To share culture with others	1. Meet director of volunteers.	1. Mrs. J, social worker, and director of volunteers	10/25	
			2. Visit with Portuguese volunteer.	2. Mrs. J and volunteer	?	
			3. Visit with pastor of church.	3. Mrs. J and pastor	?	

III. Field Area: Public Social Welfare

A. Agency: State Social Services

B. Client System

Mr. and Mrs. P and their two children, ages 2 and 4, are in need of emergency and permanent housing. (For additional background information, see Chapter 4, Engagement in Micro, Mezzo, and Macro Practice in Diverse Field Areas, III. Public Social Welfare.)

C. Summary of Preceding Stages

The problems and goals identified during engagement and data collection are listed in Table 5.3. During engagement, Mr. and Mrs. P expressed feelings of helplessness, anger, confusion, and rejection. As data were collected, the social worker learned that the P family had a history of frequent moves, often caused by evictions due to their failure to pay the rent. The Ps were receiving AFDC but had difficulty in planning and budgeting their money. Mr. P was unable to maintain employment because of his psychological incapacity. He was receiving weekly outpatient treatment at the local mental health center. At the time of initial assessment, the Ps were asking for help only in locating housing and food.

D. Assessment

Assessment statement: The P family does not have a place to stay because they were evicted from their apartment two weeks ago for not paying their rent on time. They do not plan and budget the money they receive from AFDC to last throughout the month. The Ps are in need of emergency food because they do not have any money left from last month, and the check and food stamps for this month are being held at central office until the family is relocated.

The change potential for the P family's housing problem is assessed as low because of the Ps limited motivation to become actively involved in searching for an apartment. Although there are possible resources for emergency shelter, the authorized payment for temporary placement is only for a maximum of 14 days.

The potential for meeting the need for food is assessed as high because several resources are available. Finding a way to transport a food supply to the Ps should not be a problem unless the social worker is unable to get an agency car.

Problem prioritization: During initial assessment, the social worker used the problem-prioritization tool for conceptualization. It was clear and urgent that the first two areas in need of immediate attention were food and temporary shelter for the family. In prioritizing, the housing problem was divided into the two parts of (1) emergency shelter and (2) long-term residence. The food need was also subdivided. Considering these two housing needs along with the two food-supply needs, the social worker drew up the prioritization shown in Table 6.10.

The problem/need with the highest change potential is obviously finding immediate food for the family. The second-prioritized area is emergency shelter. The social worker and the family will then need to plan for receiving a food supply to last until Mr. and Mrs. P receive AFDC income and food stamps. The fourth problem area, the last prioritized because of its low change potential, is the need for a long-term residence for the family. There is a pressing need to work on

TABLE 6.10   Problem Prioritization: State Social Services

Problem List	Change-Potential Scores (0–10)			Total Change Potential	Problem Prioritization	Severity
	Problem	Person(s)	Environment			
1. Housing						
a. Emergency shelter	8	8	8	24	2	*
b. Long-term	2	1	2	5	4	*
2. Food						
a. Emergency food	9	9	8	26	1	*
b. Until check and food stamps	8	8	7	23	3	*

*Life-at-risk situation.

this fourth problem, because the temporary shelter can only be for two weeks. The social worker knows also that the only way the temporary placement will be supported financially by the agency is if the Ps make ongoing efforts to secure more permanent housing. An extension in temporary placement is granted only if there is evidence that every effort is being made by the family to locate a residence. Through problem assessment and prioritization, it became clear to the social worker that pressure needed to be exerted on Mr. and Mrs. P to have them become more actively involved in the search for housing.

Contracting: The social worker and Mr. and Mrs. P developed the contract identified in Table 6.11. Permission was given by Mr. and Mrs. P to have the social worker discuss their plan and progress with Mr. P's doctor and the income-maintenance technician. The social worker asked Mr. P's doctor and the family's income-maintenance technician to help with motivating the Ps to become more involved.

IV. Field Area: Community Services

A. Agency: Clayton Neighborhood House

B. Client System

Four Hispanic families are without heat in their apartments on the second floor of the 33 L Street apartment building. (For more background information, see Chapter 4, Engagement in Micro, Mezzo, and Macro Practice in Diverse Field Areas, IV. Community Services.)

C. Summary of Preceding Stages

The problem and goal identified during engagement and data collection are stated in Table 4.4. During engagement, residents from four apartments met with the

TABLE 6.11 Contracted Plan: State Social Services

Date Identified	Problem/ Need	Goal	Task	Contract	Date Anticipated	Date Accomplished
9/28	1. Food—emergency food	1. To obtain emergency food supply	1. Discuss resources.	1. Social worker and Ps	9/28	
			2. Contact resource.	2. Social worker and Ps	9/28	
			3. Obtain food.	3. The Ps	9/28	
9/28	2. Housing—emergency shelter	2. To move into emergency shelter	1. Locate resource.	1. Social worker	9/28	
			2. Discuss resources.	2. Social worker and Ps	9/28	
			3. Contact resource.	3. Social worker and Ps	9/28	
			4. Move to resource.	4. Ps with social worker's help	9/28	
9/28	3. Food until AFDC check and food stamps arrive	3. To receive a food supply until AFDC check and food stamps arrive	1. Locate resource.	1. Social worker	9/29	
			2. Discuss resource.	2. Social worker and Ps	9/29	
			3. Contact resource.	3. Social worker and Ps	9/29	
			4. Receive food.	4. Ps and resource	9/29 until check and food stamps arrive	
9/28	4. Housing—long-term	4. To move into an apartment for long-term residence	1. Explore resources.	1. Mr. and Mrs. P and social worker	9/29	
			2. Contact resources.	2. Mr. and Mrs. P	9/29	
			3. Move.	3. The Ps	10/12	
			4. Update.	4. Social worker, Mr. P's doctor, income-maintenance technician	9/29 and weekly	

social worker and expressed feelings of anger, frustration, fear, helplessness, and victimization. In gathering information, the social worker learned that residents were paying $250 for one-room apartments, heat included. The name and address of the landlord was obtained and he was contacted. Because of the urgent nature of the problem, the social worker and the residents moved quickly through engagement, data collection, and assessment.

D. Assessment

Assessment statement: The four families who live on the second floor of the 33 L Street apartment building do not have adequate heating because the heating for the building has not been regulated for adequate, even distribution. There also is a problem with direct communication between residents and the landlord. The residents and the landlord do not speak the same language, and the landlord does not return calls made to him by tenants. (The social worker added the communication problem to the problem list in the record; see Table 6.12.)

The change potential for the problem of inadequate heating is assessed as somewhat high at this time because Mr. X, the landlord, is now aware of the problem and has stated that he will see that it gets resolved. As long as the problem of poor communication between residents and landlord remains, however, there is a possibility that a heating loss could recur and that the families would continue to have difficulty in notifying Mr. X.

The problem of poor communication has a low potential for change at this time, because neither the families nor the landlord appear motivated to work on improving their communication. The families are afraid that if they meet with Mr. X, he may think that they are complaining too much and raise their rent. Mr. X indicated that he is very busy, with no time to contact residents.

TABLE 6.12   Contracted Plan: Clayton Neighborhood House

Date Identified	Problem/ Need	Goal	Task	Contract	Date Anticipated	Date Accomplished
12/3	1. Lack of heat on second floor	1. To obtain consistent, adequate heating for second-floor residents of L street apartment house	1. Contact janitor. 2. Contact landlord. 3. Meet for follow-up.	1. Social worker 2. Social worker 3. Residents and social worker	12/3 12/4 12/5	12/4 12/5
12/5	2. Communication problem with landlord					

Problem prioritization: Because there was only one problem that the client system was presenting at this time, the social worker did not use the problem-prioritization tool. The need for heating was primary and urgent.

Contracting: The social worker and the residents developed the contracted plan shown in Table 6.12 during their first meeting. The communication problem was added after the social worker had contacted the landlord.

V. Field Area: Education

A. Agency: Keeney Elementary School
B. Client System

Jim G is an 8-year-old African American third-grader with regressive behavior in school and at home. (For additional background information, see Chapter 4, Engagement in Micro, Mezzo, and Macro Practice in Diverse Field Areas, V. Education.)

C. Summary of Preceding Stages

The problems, goals, and tasks identified prior to a formal assessment are indicated in Table 5.4. Through play, Jim began to express his fear that his mother might leave him. Mrs. G shared feelings of anger and hurt regarding her husband and their relationship. She was finding it difficult to forgive him and to trust him. A meeting was arranged for the social worker to meet with Mr. and Mrs. G to discuss Jim's problems and how they were being affected by the problem between Mr. and Mrs. G.

D. Assessment

When the social worker met with Mr. and Mrs. G, they moved into the assessment stage of the General Method. Problems and goals were clarified, and a contracted plan was articulated by the social worker, Jim, and both of his parents.

Assessment statement: Jim has a problem being present at school physically, emotionally, and cognitively, owing to his upset feelings and his fears, which are caused by tension and quarreling at home between his parents. Jim has refused to fall asleep at night unless his mother is with him and a light is on in the room, because he is afraid that she will leave him, as he overheard her saying to his father. He was overly tired in school because he was trying to keep awake during the night. He did not want to go to school because he feared his mother would leave for good while he was gone. Mr. and Mrs. G have been quarreling because Mrs. G recently learned that her husband had gone out with another woman.

The change potential for Jim's school and home problems is assessed as high. The problems have had a short duration. Jim is reacting to external circumstances, and Mr. and Mrs. G are eager to improve the situation. Mrs. G is reassuring Jim that she will not leave him, and she and her husband are willing to go for professional help with their relationship.

Problem prioritization: The social worker used the problem-prioritization tool as shown in Table 6.13.

The change potential for the school tardiness and absenteeism problem was assessed as very high (9), because Jim did not have a history of missing school and

TABLE 6.13   Problem Prioritization: Keeney Elementary School

Problem List	Change-Potential Scores (0–10)			Total Change Potential	Problem Prioritization	Severity
	Problem	*Person(s)*	*Environment*			
School tardiness and absenteeism	9	5	9	23	1	
Declining academic performance	6	5	9	20	3	
Sleeping problem	5	3	5	13	4	*
Strain in marital relationship	6	8	9	23	1	

*Life-at-risk situation.

the problem merely involved physical presence. The "person" change-potential score was assessed as medium (5). Even though Jim has the capacity to go to school, he did not appear to have the necessary motivation. The potential of the "environment" to change for problem resolution was assessed at a 9, very high, because Mr. and Mrs. G were being very cooperative and gave assurance that they would see that Jim came to school on time each day.

The change potential for the problem of declining academic performance was assessed as a 6 (medium—leaning toward high) because the nature of the problem was reactive (related directly to external circumstances) rather than internalized (present regardless of external circumstances) and because the problems had only become observable over the past month. It could become a serious problem if it persisted and Jim had to be removed from his classroom (asterisk in "severity" column).

The change-potential score for "person" as related to the school-performance problem was assessed as 5 (medium), because here, too, although Jim has the capacity to do the work, he is not motivated for school achievement at this time. The "environment" score was appraised as a 9 (high), because Jim was beginning to be helped by his parents and the school. His parents were committed to try to reduce the causes for Jim's decline in his school work.

The change potential for Jim's problem with falling asleep was given a 5 (medium), because of the somewhat serious nature of the problem, even though it had only recently developed. If Jim continued to get little sleep, he could become physically ill. The "person" potential was assessed as a 3 (somewhat low) because Jim was too upset to sleep and he continued to want a night-light even after his mother assured him she would not leave. The "environment" score was a 5 for this problem, because Jim's parents were unable to make Jim fall asleep and they did not want to give him sleeping pills.

The change potential for the problem of a strained marital relationship was assessed as high (8) because Mr. and Mrs. G said that this was the first time they had had such a problem. Mr. G said that it was the first time he had gone out with someone else and that it would not happen again. The "person" potential was seen as high (8) because both Mr. and Mrs. G were motivated to work on their problem and to seek outside help. The "environment" potential was seen as very high (9) because several resources for marital counseling were available in the area.

Through problem prioritization, it became clear that the first two areas to be addressed were (1) Jim's school attendance and (2) Mr. and Mrs. G's marital relationship. With improvement in these two areas, it was hoped that Jim's school performance and sleeping at night would improve. Efforts for problem resolution and sleeping at night would improve. Efforts for problem resolution would be primarily directed, therefore, according to the following sequence: (1) Jim's school tardiness and absenteeism, (2) the strain in Mr. and Mrs. G's relationship, (3) Jim's declining school performance, and (4) Jim's sleeping problem.

Contracting: When the social worker met with Mr. and Mrs. G, they reviewed the problems, goals, and tasks that were identified earlier, and they agreed on the contracted plan outlined in Table 6.14. As highlighted in the "contract" column, Mr. and Mrs. G planned to become actively involved in going for help with their marital relationship and in working with Jim and the school on Jim's school problems.

VI. Field Area: Corrections

A. Agency: Juvenile Court

B. Client System

Seven male youths, age 14, are on probation and attending weekly group meetings led by co-workers at Juvenile Court. (For further background information, see Chapter 4, Engagement in Micro, Mezzo, and Macro Practice in Diverse Field Areas, VI. Corrections.)

C. Summary of Preceding Stages

The problems and goals identified by the group during engagement and data collection are outlined in Table 4.6. The youths in the group had low self-esteem and frequently referred to themselves as "stupid." All of the youths were in special classes at school for learning disabilities. The social workers also learned that all of the group participants were from single-parent homes and had trouble communicating with their parents. In visiting the homes and schools, the co-leaders learned that all seven youths were seen as "problems" by parents and teachers. The group members agreed to come to weekly group meetings in order to get off probation sooner (possibly a two-month reduction from a six-month probationary period).

D. Assessment

Assessment statement: The youths in the group are on probation because they committed the following crimes: three members—breaking, entering, and stealing from homes; two members—theft of automobiles; two members—shoplifting. The problem of law breaking is assessed as very serious for at least five of the youths

TABLE 6.14 Contracted Plan: Keeney Elementary School

Date Identified	Problem/Need	Goal	Task	Contract	Date Anticipated	Date Accomplished
11/1	1. Jim's school tardiness and absenteeism	1. Jim's regular school attendance (on time every day)	1. Get J to school on time each day.	1. Mr. and Mrs. G	11/5 and each school day thereafter	11/5–ongoing
11/21	2. Strain in Mr. and Mrs. G's marital relationship	2. Improved marital relationship (less quarreling, growing trust)	1. Explore counseling resources. 2. Select resource. 3. Contact resource for appointment. 4. Attend counseling sessions.	1. Social worker and Mr. and Mrs. G 2. Mr. and Mrs. G 3. Mr. G 4. Mr. and Mrs. G	11/27 11/27 11/28 Beginning week of 12/3	11/27 11/27
11/1	3. Jim's declining school performance	3. Improved school performance (interest, participation, grades)	1. Talk with Jim about school problems in relation to home problem. 2. Check on Jim's performance. 3. Update Mr. and Mrs. G on Jim's school performance. 4. Continue to meet with Jim. 5. Home meeting to evaluate progress.	1. Mr. and Mrs. G, Jim and social worker 2. Social worker with Jim's teacher 3. Social worker 4. Social worker 5. Social worker, Mr. and Mrs. G, and Jim	11/27 11/28 and weekly 12/4 and 12/11 telephone contacts 11/29 12/17	11/27
11/2	4. Jim's problem getting to sleep at night	4. Jim's going to sleep at night without mother in room	1. Continue to assure Jim that Mrs. G is not going to leave him.	1. Mrs. G	11/27 and each night thereafter	

(J, T, ML, B, and A). There is a history of law breaking in their families (by fathers or brothers), and little discipline or support is offered in their homes. All of these five express a desire to get off probation and to make sure they "don't get caught again." They do not have a strong motivation to keep within the law. Although C appears to be sincerely sorry that he got into trouble and upset his father, the problem could become serious if he continues with the street gang he has joined. MK's offense was shoplifting for the third time. His mother said she never has enough money to provide for the children, and she thinks MK was trying to bring home things for her and his sisters and brother. Although Mrs. K was finding it difficult to discipline MK, she said she had started attending a "parenting" class at church that was helping her to work better with him. She was trying to get her son to promise that he would not steal any more.

The youths in the group are having a problem generally with their development and their feelings because they are entering adolescence with low self-concepts and limited support systems at home and in school. Low self-esteem is reinforced by placement in special classes at school. All of the members have said that they don't like being told what to do, and that they get angry when someone puts pressure on them. They wish they could be independent, but they are afraid to try to make it on their own. They don't understand "the changes," physical and emotional, that they are going through, and they said there isn't someone they can talk to about them.

The lack of understanding about their "changes" has a high change potential because issues and topics related to the boys' development can be addressed and discussed in group meetings. Efforts can also be made through the group to help them with gaining temper control. The youths' motivation to work on both of these problem areas ("changes" and "temper") also contributes to an affirmative assessment of change potential.

Problem prioritization: In prioritizing problems, the social workers considered mainly those problems that the group members said they wanted to work on. Although parent-son conflicts and low self-worth were seen by the social workers as two problem areas, the group proceeded with identifying goals and tasks only for the following: (1) law breaking leading to probation, (2) bad tempers, and (3) lack of understanding of the changes they were experiencing.

All of the youths knew that probation requirements included abiding by the rules of society and school, attending school, and obeying at home. They were also expected to attend weekly group meetings and to actively participate in them. If the youths had not agreed to the group, they would have been required to have weekly contact individually with a probation officer.

In discussing the prioritization of problems and goals with the group, everyone said top priority was to be given to getting off probation in four months (shortest possible time period). They knew that to achieve this goal, they had to meet all of the requirements of probation. In order to get along and abide by the rules at school and at home, the youths knew that they needed to work on controlling their tempers. They listed this as the second most important problem to be addressed. Finally, they agreed that basically they really didn't understand *themselves and what was happening to them. They wanted to talk about the changes they had to learn to deal with.*

Without having to use the prioritization tool, therefore, the group prioritized and clarified their goals as follows: (1) to get off probation in four months, (2) to control their tempers at home and at school, and (3) to learn more about some of the changes they were facing (including becoming independent, understanding sex and family planning, and getting training and jobs).

There was a lengthy discussion over goal 1. Some wanted to add "and to stay off." What it would take "to stay off" was debated. Some said it meant they couldn't break the law any more. Others said they would just have to be more careful. The social workers said that, hopefully, as participants grew in understanding and respecting themselves and others, they wouldn't need to be involved in law breaking, and this would ensure their not getting caught again.

Contracting: Using the prioritized problems and goals, a contracted plan was initiated with the group, as shown in Table 6.15. As indicated in the diagram, no goals or tasks were specifically planned at this time for problems 4 and 5, because the group didn't want to work on these problems. Since the group gave first priority to the goal of getting off probation, the planned contract centered on this problem. Later, additional tasks were added to the contract for accomplishment of goals 2 and 3 (described in Chapter 7).

E. **Ongoing Evaluation**

During the assessment period, as the plan was made to chart progress weekly in the areas required for probation, evaluation graphs (explained in detail in Chapter 8) were designed to show the following: (1) group attendance, (2) group participation, (3) behavior in school (i.e., compliance with rules and expectations) and (4) behavior at home (i.e., compliance with rules and expectations). (See Figures 6.1, 6.2, 6.3, and 6.4.) Assessments of group attendance and participation were first scored by the co-leaders, and eventually by the youths themselves. The home assessments were made by the parents and given weekly over the phone to the social workers. The school evaluation was made weekly by the youths' teachers and given to the school social worker, who had weekly contact with the court workers.

In addition to these weekly assessments, the social workers checked each week to see if any of the group members had been reported to or picked up by police. Any incident was recorded in the youth's record and discussed with the youth individually.

As indicated in Figure 6.1, group attendance was charted by a graph point that indicated the number of the meeting (1, 2, 3, etc.) and an attendance score of 0, 1, or 2. A score of 0 meant "no attendance." A score of 1 was used if a youth came late or left early. A score of 2 meant he was on time and stayed for the full meeting. The youths knew that to get a two-month reduction in probation, they needed to maintain a score of 2 every week unless they were excused by a social worker.

In Figure 6.2, group participation was assessed on a 0–4 vertical scale in terms of 0 = none, 1 = little, 2 = some, 3 = much, and 4 = full. The points were plotted to indicate (X) the number of the weekly meeting and (Y) the score for

TABLE 6.15 Contracted Plan: Juvenile Court

Date Identified	Problem/ Need	Goal	Task	Contract	Date Anticipated	Date Accomplished
10/1	1. Law breaking leading to probation	1. To get off probation in four months	1. Attend and partici- pate in weekly group meetings.	1. Seven members, two social workers	10/1 and each Monday at 4:00 P.M. for at least four months	10/1–8/15
			2. Participate in group meetings.	2. Seven members	10/1 and each Monday at 4:00 P.M. for at least four months	
			3. Obey rules of school, home, and community.	3. Seven members	10/1	
			4. Receive weekly reports on behavior from home and school.	4. Social workers, parents, school social workers	Week of 10/1 and once a week for four months	
			5. Chart progress at meetings.	5. Social workers and members	10/22 and at each meeting thereafter	
10/1	2. Bad tempers	2. To control tempers in school, home, and neighborhood	1. Discuss the problem dealing with anger.	1. Social workers and members	10/22	
10/1	3. Need to understand "changes" of teenagers	3. To learn more about "changes" (including becom- ing independent, sex and family planning, and job training)	1. Select first topic.	1. Social workers and members	10/22	
10/1	4. Parent-son conflicts					
10/1	5. Low self-worth					

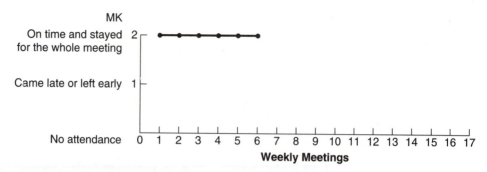

FIGURE 6.1   Group Attendance

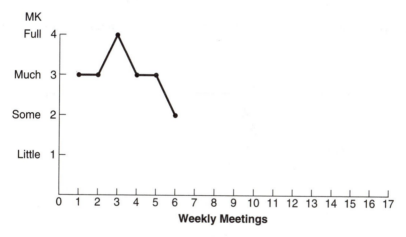

FIGURE 6.2   Group Participation

participation. An attempt was made to give more specific criteria for participation scores by the leaders. If a youth came and did not seem interested and never said anything at the meetings, he was given a 0. If he spoke at least once or twice at the meeting, he was given a 1. Speaking up about three or four times and being somewhat interested earned a 2. Sharing or responding five or six times and showing much effort at a meeting to participate was a 3, and being fully involved and fully sharing at a meeting was a 4. Group members were informed that they would need to average 3 points in group participation if they were to have a reduced probationary period.

The graphs for charting home and school reports on behavior had scale points ranging from 0 to 4 (0 = total noncompliance, 1 = poor, 2 = fair, 3 = good, 4 = excellent). The social workers requested descriptions of behaviors and incidents if a youth was assessed by his parent or teacher as showing "poor" or "fair" behavior (Figures 6.3 and 6.4).

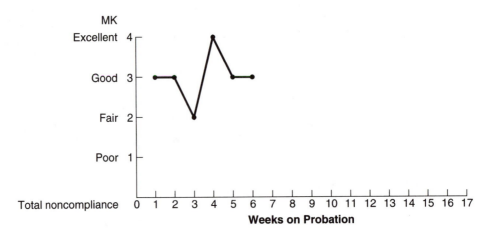

FIGURE 6.3   School Behavior (Compliance with Rules and Expectations at School)

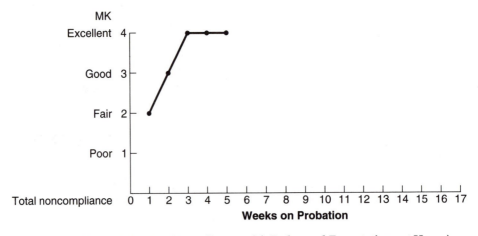

FIGURE 6.4   Home Behavior (Compliance with Rules and Expectations at Home)

VII. Field Area: Homeless Shelter

A. Agency: West End Community Shelter

B. Client System

José Romano, a 37-year-old Hispanic male, is homeless and HIV positive. (For additional background information, see Chapter 4, Engagement in Micro, Mezzo, and Macro Practice in Diverse Field Areas, VII, Homeless Shelter.)

C. Summary of Preceding Stages

During engagement and data collection, the social worker learned that Mr. R completed a drug detoxification program over six years ago. Since that time, he had been living a productive, independent life until he learned that he was HIV positive. At the time of intake, Mr. R was homeless and without any medical care. He had strong feelings of depression and loneliness. In addition to a recognized need for food, shelter, and health care, Mr. R expressed a need for more information about his illness and a desire to return to his Church (see Table 5.5). During data collection, the social worker and Mr. R had some success in locating possible resources. These included a local free health clinic, a support system of HIV/AIDS victims, a Catholic church with a large Hispanic Outreach Program, and two residences for individuals with AIDS. They were also exploring possible full- or part-time job opportunities.

D. Assessment

Assessment statement: Mr. R is not receiving any health care because he has no money or health insurance and because he is afraid of taking medications due to his past history of drug addiction. His physical condition (HIV positive) is expected to become increasingly worse because he has a progressive terminal illness (currently). Mr. R is homeless and without food because he does not have a job and his financial resources have been depleted. He does not have a job because he left his employment as chef in a nursing home when he learned he was HIV positive, and he has limited occupational skills (cooking and farming). Mr. R is recognizing a spiritual void in his life because he has been thinking about the terminal nature of his illness. He dropped away from church ("and God") as he became involved with drugs.

Although the change potential for Mr. R's illness is low because he has a progressive terminal illness, the social worker assessed a moderate to high change potential in other problem areas because of Mr. R's strong motivation and the number of available resources. Both the social worker and Mr. R recognized that progress in achieving goals was greatly dependent on the extent to which his illness progressed.

Problem prioritization: The problems identified in Table 5.5 were prioritized using the problem-prioritization tool as shown in Table 6.16.

The illness received a score of 2 on the problem prioritization scale. Although there currently is no cure for AIDS or HIV, research continues and medications are available to provide some relief from pain and some delay in disease growth. "Person" (Mr. R) received a 4 due to Mr. R's high motivation, and "environment" received a 4 because of the availability of the health clinic. The change potential for "lack of knowledge" received a high score (8) because of the increasing amount of information available about the disease, particularly at the free clinic. The shelter could provide immediate shelter and food (total of 27), but, after 60 days, Mr. R would need to go to one of the residences for AIDS patients or find another location (15). Finding a job for Mr. R was seen as possible, since he was highly motivated with a good work history, and currently his illness was not too severe to prevent at least part-time employment. It was also possible that if Mr. R's health did become worse, he could start to receive public assistance and social security (rated a total of 18). Having Mr. R return to church was highly rated, since he was very anxious to go to the church in town where he could be with people of his native culture (25).

TABLE 6.16   Problem Prioritization: West End Community Shelter

Problem List	Change-Potential Scores (0–10)			Total Change Potential	Problem Prioritization	Severity
	Problem	Person(s)	Environment			
HIV+	2	4	4	10	6	*
Lack of knowledge re: HIV	8	8	8	24	3	
Homeless/Hungry						
a. Emergency	9	9	9	27	1	
b. After 60 days	5	5	5	15	5	
Unemployment	6	6	6	18	4	
Spiritual Void	8	8	9	25	2	

*Life-at-risk situation.

Contracting: After prioritizing the problems, Mr. R and the social worker developed a contracted plan of action (see Table 6.17).

E. **Charted Progress**

Mr. R's progress in the problem-solving process was summarized in ongoing summary recordings. The problem-prioritization tool and the contracted plan developed during assessment were placed in his record for additional information and ongoing indication of progress. A copy of the planned contract was given to Mr. R to remind him of the goals, tasks, and dates he and the worker decided on.

Conclusion

In this chapter, the assessment stage of the General Method was described as consisting of the three major dimensions of (1) assessment statement, (2) problem prioritization, and (3) contracted plan. Tools were presented to assist the general practitioner in this stage of the Method.

A point emphasized in this chapter is the need for documented assessments and plans for each case before a social worker takes action. Even when working with a crisis, the social worker needs to demonstrate skill in planning where, when, and how to intervene. Through practice and supervised experience, the generalist learns to apply the tools in the process of assessment very quickly and accurately.

The Generalist Method and each of its stages is a dynamic process. As circumstances change, the social worker needs to be open to the possibility of having to reassess a situation or to reformulate a contract. There has been an indication that some social workers resist finding out new information that would necessitate a reformulation of goals and plans. A major challenge of general practice is to be

TABLE 6.17 Contracted Plan: West End Community Shelter

Date Identified	Problem/Need	Goal	Task	Contract	Date Anticipated	Date Accomplished
5/7	1. Homeless a. Short term	1. To obtain emergency shelter	1. Enroll in shelter.	1. Mr. R and social worker	5/8	
5/8	2. Spiritual void	2. To reunite with church	1. Go to service.	1. Mr. R	5/10	
5/8	3. Lack of knowledge re: HIV	3. To gain information	1. Review information at shelter. 2. Go to free clinic and ask for help.	1. Social worker and Mr. R 2. Mr. R	5/9	
5/8	4. No income/job	4. To get income	1. Search for job. 2. Apply for job. 3. Start job. 4. Seek SS/public assistance.	1. Mr. R. and social worker 2. Mr. R 3. Mr. R 4. Mr. R	5/9– 5/15 5/20 Depends on illness	
5/7	5. No housing after 60 days	5. To locate residence	1. Look for apartment or home for AIDS victims. 2. Get on waiting list of home for persons with AIDS.	1. Social worker and Mr R 2. Mr. R	5/8 5/11	
5/8	6. HIV positive	6. To receive medical care	1. Make appointment. 2. Go to free clinic. 3. Continue treatment.	1. Social worker and Mr R 2. Mr. R 3. Mr. R	5/8* 5/9 Next appointments	

*Because of the asterisk at problem 6 (life-threatening problem), the worker continued to keep this problem in focus even though the problem has the lowest change potential.

able to stand on a diversified but solid foundation where one is expected to demonstrate flexibility and adaptation to emerging tensions, growth, and change.

Although the range of tasks and interventions by a generalist appears to be limitless, some parameters and guidelines need to be identified. An entry-level social worker does have limitations in knowledge and skills. A skillful assessment may lead to a plan for referral to a specialized service. In the next chapter, an effort will be made to clarify and to categorize the interventions of a general practitioner during the fourth stage of the Generalist Method. In the intervention stage, the social worker collaborates with other resources and service systems in carrying out the plan that was contracted during assessment.

CHAPTER

7

Intervention

The goal of social work intervention is to facilitate empowerment transactions between client systems and their environments, or, more specifically, to enable people to overcome those conditions that keep them from participating in the benefits of society and to find ways of meeting their needs so that they may develop and function within their environment to the best of their potential. Facilitating a client system's ability to engage in empowerment transactions with their environment involves strengthening the client system's attitudes and beliefs about their efficacy in taking action, developing their ability to think critically about their world, facilitating acquisition of the knowledge and skills needed to take action, facilitating development and availability of support and mutual aid systems, and developing their ability to take action that leads to change in the face of impinging problems (Saleebey, 1997).

To achieve the goal of client system empowerment, the generalist social worker stands at the interface of client systems and their environments and carefully tries to collaborate with both in a planned change process that enhances their fit and interaction with each other. Thus, the role of the social worker during the intervention stage of the General Method evolves according to the principles of empowerment through the goals and tasks identified in the contracted plan described in the previous chapter. Each professional role is taken in order to create a particular kind of change. With client micro systems, such a role typically encompasses teaching, training, educating, linking to resources, and advocating on the individual client system's behalf. With client mezzo systems, the generalist's role involves activities ranging from teaching, training, and educating through creation of or linkage to mutual aid support systems such as self-help groups, therapeutic support groups, educational groups, and social action groups. With large macro systems, the role includes consultation, skill building, social planning, policy development, community organization, social development, and legislative campaigning.

Before assuming any particular role, however, the generalist needs to clarify the nature of the problem to be addressed, the goals to be accomplished, the resources to be utilized, and the plan to be followed. Only after a period of engagement, data collection, and assessment will the social worker be ready to assume the role necessary for appropriate intervention at any particular time. A generalist may move from one role to another or may assume multiple roles while using interventions during the process of helping. Often, a social worker may move from working with one to working with many, from the individual to the large bureaucracy. In general, the various change-oriented activities of the entry-level generalist may be classified under the four major headings of (1) direct intervention, (2) information and referral, (3) case management and teamwork, and (4) indirect intervention. With each of these four major interventions, particular techniques and skills are used to work with different problems, age groups, or types of systems. In this chapter, the four broad types of intervention will be presented as they are found in generalist practice.

Change Roles and Strategies

Social workers are change agents (Parsons, Jorgensen, & Hernandez, 1994). Through a variety of strategies and tactics based on factors such as professional style as a change agent, approaches to managing conflict, and agency sanctions and goals, generalist social workers pursue various forms of change in a planned systematic way. In pursuing client system change, the social worker may enter interventive roles of conferee (or interviewer), enabler, broker, advocate, reformer, mediator, counselor, educator, and guardian (Wood & Middleman, 1989). Although these roles are presented as distinct, it is not uncommon for social workers to find themselves in more than one role simultaneously. For example, when the social worker engages in problem solving, the initial interviewing role of the social worker, or the conferee role, calls for social worker–client system collaboration in exploring and assessing problems, formulating goals and objectives, identifying tasks, and planning for mutual work in problem solving. If the plan calls for the social worker to continue as the sole source of problem solving (i.e., as a therapist or counselor), the specialized role would require the clinical expertise of a graduate-level social worker.

When the social worker moves into other interventive roles, the conferee role serves as the data-gathering springboard to other practice demands based on the client system contract. As an enabler, the social worker structures and arranges events, interactions, and other environmental factors in order to facilitate and enhance client system functioning. Such activities might involve facilitating education, skill training, health aid, and self-help as well as conducting family or group therapy. As a broker, the social worker links the client system with existing goods and services through case management, networking, and inter- and intra-organizational linking. As an advocate, the social worker secures services or resources on behalf of client systems in the face of identified resistance by those who control resources, or when resources are unavailable and must be created. Such activities might involve case and cause advocacy, grant writing, and social planning. As a mediator, the social worker engages in righting social injustices and finding new ways of problem solving. Such activities may encompass all of the previous role tasks as well as demand the use of new innovative change strategies and technologies. Finally, as a guardian, the social worker performs a social control function and acts on behalf of a client system when client system competency falls below minimal standards. Such activities include, for example, gaining court control of abused or neglected children, initiating a mental health holding in circumstances of danger to self or other, and returning probationers to court and parolees to prison.

To bring about planned change in a client system, social workers rely on three types of interventive strategies: rational empirical, normative reeducative, and power coercive (Chin & Benne, 1969). *Rational-empirical change strategy* is based on the assumption that people follow their rational, logical self-interests and will want to change if they have something to gain. For example, if a social worker is trying to influence a local community system to create a coalition of family support programs, he or she would gather facts and figures about the needs of the community as well as the anticipated costs and perceived benefits of operating such programs.

Normative-reeducative strategy does not deny people's rationality and intelligence but rather focuses on the complexity of human motivation. That is, people's patterns of actions and behaviors are reflected in socio-cultural norms and will change only when all of their motives—ideas, feelings, and conventions—are affected. For example, to change a parent's way of disciplining a child, the social worker would not only need to educate and train the parent about childhood development and appropriate behavior discipline but also help the parent gain understanding and attitudinal change that is culturally normative and empower the parent to the point that he or she is willing to give up old patterns of behavior and develop commitments to new ones.

Power-coercive strategy is based on the application of power in some form. People's motivation to change is based on their position of power; they will act in ways that either gain greater power or at least maintain existing power. Change strategies involve uncovering the client system's underlying sources of power and motives, convincing client systems with power to back the proposed change, or minimizing power differentials between client systems affected by the change.

Human systems are complex and operate under a mixture of assumptions about effecting change. Each, however, tends to hold a predominant orientation. Thus, any successful change effort needs to assess accurately the client system's orientation toward change and to develop appropriate intervention strategies to respond to that orientation (Parsons, Jorgensen, & Hernandez, 1994).

Power and Change

Because power is a critical component in any client system functioning, empowerment is the key process in planning any interventive strategy (Maluccio, 1981). As noted earlier, social work intervention takes place in the transactions between individual client systems and their environments. The power differential between individual client systems and environmental systems is often so great that individual client systems sometimes cannot perceive themselves as competent to take action on their own behalf. This marginalized status may increase from being perceived and labeled by others as simply different to being perceived and labeled as deviant and devalued by society.

When planning an intervention, six interrelated practice components must be present for the intervention to contribute to the empowerment of client systems (Parsons, Jorgensen, & Hernandez, 1994): power-shared relationship, competency-based assessment, normalization, collectivity for mutual aid, critical thinking and problem solving, knowledge and skills for finding resources, and skills for taking action. In a *power-shared relationship*, client systems are viewed as having equal and legitimate expertise in relation to their own problems and solutions. Being able to accept clients' definitions of their own problems is a critical part of empowerment practice (Gutierrez, 1990). Although the generalist social worker brings expertise about social problems, problem definitions, assessment, goal setting, planning, and intervening to the collaborative process, client systems generally know what they need and, with heightened self-awareness and support, are able to choose a good alternative for action on their own behalf. They are competent to identify and understand their problems and to choose adequate solutions.

To understand client systems' strengths and coping skills rather than their weaknesses and deficits in coping, the social worker needs to uncover their motivation, capacity, and opportunities for change (Maluccio, 1981). To plan an intervention that will empower the client system, the social worker and the client system engage in a *competency-based assessment*, or power analysis, which examines the conditions of powerlessness affecting the presenting situation, the power resources, and the effects of the social-structural context (Gutierrez, 1990). Specifically, the generalist looks for the client system's desire, perceived hope, belief that change can come about, knowledge and skills for making change, and environmental impingements that may facilitate or hinder change.

The development in clients from powerlessness to personal autonomy and from alienation to interdependent mutual aid and personal or political power requires a blending of action, reflection, and consideration of environment. The screen of *normalization* implies viewing the client systems' problems in terms of the environmental context, cultural conventions and values, and purposefulness of behavior. The idea of building *collectivity for mutual aid* is inherent in this helping process. Collectivity offers clients an opportunity to interact with other people who have similar problems and concerns and to receive validation from others in their situation. Through mutual collective aid, for example, parents gain the support to act on their own behalf as well as learn to solve parenting problems and develop new ways of coping with child-rearing issues.

Dialogue, interaction, and education with others in similar circumstances help client systems develop critical consciousness regarding their own subjective conditions and problems. Acquisition of knowledge and skills for common problem solving most often occurs through the group process (Gutierrez, 1990). Gaining specific information regarding the problem at hand as well as the *skills for taking action* are important parts of empowerment. For example, when working with client systems struggling with chronic illness, dialogue around the illness condition and health needs can provide an opportunity for individuals to tell their stories to people who understand their plight, listen to others, find out about resources, discuss ways of coping with the condition and general life stress, or share skills and understanding. Specifically and most importantly, chronically ill persons and their support systems receive a critical education by expanding their understanding of their own personal and collective problems from an inward context to a broader collective socio-environmental context and back to a focus on self and how to cope. Acquisition of critical thinking skills, knowledge regarding resources, and skills for taking action are necessary components of successful living.

Direct Intervention

When a social worker, in agreement with a client system, intervenes directly with the client system, that social worker is engaging in *direct intervention*. The goal of direct intervention is to promote client empowerment through the objectives of

1. Providing support to a system as it carries out contracted tasks
2. Assisting the system to bring about planned change
3. Creating opportunities for the client system to gain mutual collective aid
4. Educating the client system about resources, critical problem solving, and skills for taking action

Planned intervention that directly involves a client system and a social work generalist may be brief or extended, depending on the identified need or problem and the capacities of the client system and the social worker. The extent of direction or leadership offered by the social worker in direct intervention is influenced also by the seriousness or crisis level of the situation and by the strengths and coping capacities of the client system. The nature of the interaction promotes growth and encourages the client system in self-direction as much as possible without creating harm to the well-being of the client system.

The generalist uses a broad range of relationship and problem-solving skills in the course of intervening with members of a client system. The relationship itself is central to the entire process. Particularly in the intervention stage, a strong working relationship is necessary. During the course of direct intervention, the social worker may use the relationship skills of listening, responding, guiding, paraphrasing, clarifying feelings, sensing, and, possibly, confronting. In addition, the problem-solving skills of problem and need identification, data collection, assessment, problem prioritization, goal setting, planning, contracting, and evaluating may be repeated as problems are added or changed.

A client system may begin with identifying immediate material needs or problems with institutions. As a working relationship develops and the social worker is able to help with the presenting problems, client systems frequently begin to discuss more interpersonal or personal problems. Information is gathered and assessments are made regarding each of these problems. Social worker and client system may agree to tasks on the contracted plan that entail direct, ongoing contact between social worker and client system. This contact may be seen as a means for the client system to achieve greater understanding of self and others or to bring about a change in self. If the goal identified is to bring about a change in someone outside of the client system, the intervention will need to include the outsider directly (becoming a part of the client system) or indirectly (becoming a target system). For example, if Mrs. N wants her husband to overcome his drinking problem, there is little chance of accomplishing this goal by direct intervention only with Mrs. N.

In addition to the foundation skills identified in Table 1.3 in Chapter 1, contemporary techniques are being used, primarily by graduate-level workers, in direct practice with particular systems. Entry-level generalists are not expected to use these techniques unless they have studied and practiced them under supervision. For example, eco-maps (Hartman & Laird, 1983; Nichols & Schwartz, 1995), sculpting (Bardill, 1997; Duhl, Kantor, & Duhl, 1973), and genograms (McGoldrick & Gerson, 1985; McGoldrick, Giordano, & Pearce, 1996) are valuable tools to use when working with a family. They provide a technical and vivid means for helping clients understand diverse perceptions of the family. (These techniques may also be adapted for use in working with individuals, groups, and communities.)

For working with groups, techniques and concepts have been identified to enable a social worker to handle disruptive behavior (Brown, 1992) and scapegoating (Worden, 1999). The use of force-field analysis (Braeger & Holloway, 1978; Brueggeman, 1996; Homan, 1999; Lewin, 1951) helps a social worker pinpoint the supportive and the constraining forces that have impact on the life and growth of an organization. The technique of force-field analysis and techniques to handle disruptive behavior and prevent scapegoating may also be adapted for use with individuals and families as well as groups, organizations, and communities.

For working with adolescents, an effective technique to promote greater self-awareness is the use of the adolescent grid (Anderson & Brown, 1980). By recalling major events within a visible framework, the adolescent can avoid the discomfort often felt in face-to-face interviewing. The grid identifies crisis points chronologically, according to place, family, school, health, activities, and other areas. Adults or children, individuals, groups, or families may also find that this structured instrument is a helpful device for overcoming their fears of interacting with a social worker.

The use of play is a valuable communication technique for working with children. Basically, a child is limited in communicating only with words. Play is a natural means for children to express fears, wishes, hurtful experiences, and unmet needs. Repetitive play helps a child master difficult experiences. Children usually expect adults to speak to them in order to teach, direct, or correct them. A child may feel great fear and discomfort on being led into a room where there is nothing to indicate that it is a place for children. To expect a child to be able to talk freely in such a place with an adult stranger about his or her problems or painful experiences is unrealistic and insensitive. Social workers can learn how to select appropriate toys and to engage in play that is supportive and helpful to children. This technique is useful during every stage of the General Method when working with children. If it becomes apparent that the child's behavior patterns are inappropriate for the current reality, and that the supportive intervention of the generalist is insufficient to bring about the necessary change, a referral should be made to a child specialist. Through play therapy, a child may be helped to grow in understanding, learning to cope, and gaining the emotional freedom to find appropriate responses to life situations (Timberlake & Cutler, 2001).

As a social worker intervenes directly with any person, family, group, or community, it may become clear that giving support or understanding is insufficient to achieve certain goals. If it is necessary for a change to take place in a client system, the social worker may use some techniques from behavioral modification, as well as problem-solving skills. In addition to helping a client system develop a rational, systematic way to solve problems, a social worker may use specific behavioral techniques for more immediate control of undesirable behaviors, thoughts, or feelings. Although behavior modification in its entirety is a specialized treatment approach, individual techniques such as behavior reinforcement, cognitive restructuring, relaxation exercises, and thought stopping can be selected for use in generalist practice (Doyle, 1998).

All of the contemporary techniques that have been cited are supplementary to the basic skills found in the foundation of generalist practice (Table 1.3 in Chapter 1). Eco-maps, sculpting, genograms, techniques for handling disruptive behavior and scapegoating, force-field analysis, the adolescent grid, communicating through play, behavior reinforcement, cognitive restructuring, relaxation exercises, and thought stopping are tools that enable a client system to grow in understanding. They facilitate change in a client system by helping to clarify, objectify, and promote greater control of self or a situation.

There are times when it becomes clear that a client system needs to change through gaining understanding. If a pattern of behavior emerges that continues to cause problems, the generalist will try to confront the client system about it in a cognitive, supportive, and problem-solving type of intervention. Some of the preceding techniques may be utilized. If this is insufficient to bring about the change necessary for goal achievement, the generalist has to be able to realize that a client system may need more intensive help to overcome its problematic behavior. For the individual, family, group, organization, or community, this could involve delving into buried feelings or past experiences over a prolonged period of time. In time, the client system can be helped to connect current behaviors with feelings that are triggered by certain situations that relate to past experiences. Barriers and dynamics that cause conflict and broken relationships can be exposed. Through this intensive work, the client system may be freed to choose more acceptable behaviors in the future.

However, this intensive direct work is not within the parameters of entry-level generalist practice. Occasionally, a client system may come with enough strengths or past experiences to be able to grow in such insight with support from the generalist. Usually, however, the generalist brings the client system with this type of need to the point of realizing that more specialized help is needed, and they enter into the process of referral. Whether the client system is an individual, family, group, organization, or community, there are times when the generalist is unable to help the client system bring about the change needed through direct intervention, and a referral is made. A social worker, for example, may find that major factions within a community are preventing goal accomplishment. The power and political struggles may be so intense that the generalist is unable to break through these dynamics. A referral would be made to a community organizer with advanced skills and experience.

Information and Referral

At times, it becomes apparent that a client system does not have the information needed for problem resolution. Often, clients have received misinformation or they have misconceptions about environmental resources. They may contact a social worker to receive assistance that the social worker or agency may not be able to provide. In these cases, the social worker's intervention is primarily that of information and referral.

The process in which a social worker directs a system to another resource for help with an identified problem or need is called *referral*. In referring client systems, the social worker should be guided by the principles of least restrictive environment and normalization. These principles suggest that the more informal network systems of help, including mutual-aid and self-help groups, be explored before seeking help from formal helping organizations. Referral and linkage of client systems with informal and formal helping systems is done under the assumption that client systems may seek out additional resources or help on their own. Often, social workers are surprised to learn that a resource has not picked up on a case as expected. Several factors can lead to an unsuccessful referral. There is, in fact, an art to knowing where, when, and how to make a referral. Time, planning, and processing are needed for an appropriate match between the client system in need and an available resource. The act of referral may be described as a six-stage process. If any one of the stages is overlooked, the referral may fail. The experience of an unsuccessful referral may build up in the client system feelings of negativism and fear, as well as resistance to reaching out and trying again with another resource.

The referral process consists of the following essential stages to be enacted by the social worker and the client system in need:

1. Clarifying and stating the problem or need for which help is sought and the goals to be accomplished
2. Researching appropriate and available resources and informing the client system about them
3. Discussing options and selecting resources with the client system in need
4. Planning and contracting the means of contact with the selected resource (initial contact, sending information, providing transportation, client-resource meeting)
5. Meeting of the client system in need with the resource
6. Following up by the social worker to see if the goal is being or has been accomplished

The basic principle of having the client system do for itself is paramount throughout the referral process. Only when it is clear that the client system does not have the knowledge or ability to carry out a task in the process should the social worker intervene and take action.

In stage 1, the generalist helps the client system clarify what the problem or need is that cannot be taken care of by the generalist. The feelings and goals that relate directly with the identified problem or need are also expressed. The feelings both client system and social worker may have about sending the client to a different resource need to be expressed. Either one might see a referral as a personal failure and feel somewhat guilty. The limitations of the social worker and/or the agency should be presented as factually as possible. The client system may need to be reassured that the referral is not a rejection by the social worker. The social worker needs to convey to the client system a sincere desire to see the client system achieve its goals and a strong belief in the ability of a resource to make this possible.

In stage 2 of the process, social worker and, if possible, client system work on locating resources to meet the identified needs. Both formal and informal resources are explored. If a need or problem can be resolved through utilizing informal resources (family, friends, community), this may be more desirable to the client system. Some clients may prefer not to have these local networks know about their problem, and formal resources (agencies, programs, institutions) will need to be considered.

It is imperative to find resources that are appropriate and available. A resource is appropriate not only because it provides services that address the identified problem or need but also because it suits the persons and environment of the particular system in need. For example, a person who speaks only Spanish would need to receive help from a social worker who understands and works with Hispanic people. Further, if the resource is not accessible to people from the neighborhood or environment of the client system, it is usually not an appropriate resource. If contact with the resource is expected to be brief and transportation can be assured, it is possible to use a resource that is not located near the environment of the client system. Sometimes, social workers incorrectly assume that client systems are able to find bus fare or transportation on their own.

Agency resources may not be available for certain clients, owing to the hours when services are provided. Although a resource may be appropriate, it may have a long waiting list because of an insufficient number of staff members available to deliver the services. Moreover, the cost for the service may be outside the price range of some clients and therefore the resource is not available to them.

In stage 3 of the referral process, the social worker and the client system share their findings about possible resources, but the client system is the one to choose the resource to be contacted. The social worker helps the client system consider alternatives, with probable outcomes or consequences for each option. If there is some question or doubt about a resource, this should be explored. No false hope or reassurance should be given. Even when it appears that an appropriate and available resource has been located and selected, it may prove beneficial to help the client system at this time to identify a second choice in case the first does not work out.

In stage 4 of the referral process, time is given for planning and contracting to decide who will (1) make the initial contact with the resource (usually by phone), (2) give whatever information is necessary for the referral to be accepted, (3) arrange for transportation or provide it, and (4) meet with the resource to initiate the services. A whole range of possible ways exist to achieve each of these four tasks. The two extremes on a scale to indicate the range of options would be (1) the client system carrying out the task and (2) the social worker carrying it out. In between are different social worker–client system combinations for which the task may be subdivided. For example, in the first task of initial contact, the social worker could (1) dial the number and have the client speak; (2) dial and speak first and then put the client on the phone; (3) have the client dial, but the social worker speaks; (4) have a three-way conference call in which social worker, client system, and resource person all speak together. The initial contact might also involve writing a letter or going to the agency to set up an appointment. These tasks also could be done by the social worker, by the client system, or by some combination. The same range of options exists for deciding about giving information, arranging transportation, and having the first client system-resource meeting. The guiding principle of having the members of the client system do for themselves whenever possible should be used as the contract is formulated and tasks are planned.

In stage 5, the new helping process begins as the client system meets directly with the resource. Here, too, the art of referral operates, in the social worker's careful assessment of whether the client system can or should have the first session alone with the resource. The social worker considers not only the motivation and capacity of the client system to have this be a fruitful encounter but also the motivation and capacity of the resource itself to truly be of help to the system in need. In some individual situations, it may be better to have the social worker present in the first contact to offer support, information, or advocacy if needed. As soon as possible, however, the social worker should back out and let the client system become involved with the resource on its own.

Every referral should have some type of follow-up by the social worker. When a person, family, group, organization, or community come to a professional person or agency for help, they share—sometimes painfully—their problems, needs, and aspirations. The professional person and human service agency show a sense of respect and commitment to people in need by working diligently at getting the necessary help for them. People asking for help are often vulnerable and dependent on the expertise and sensitivity of those sanctioned to give service. Social workers are expected to know what resources are available and how to help people utilize them. It is true that many times circumstances outside of the control of a social worker or agency prevent a service from being carried out. However, the social worker must find out if the person who asked for help did receive it. If the person did not receive help, the social worker needs to find out why help was not given and to consider whether anything else could have been done.

The social worker finds out if help was provided by checking directly with the resource, with the client system, or with both. It is important that both resource and client system know that the social worker will be calling back, and when to expect the follow-up. This should be clarified prior to the social worker's last contact with each. In planning, the social worker will skillfully discern what a follow-up contact with the client system might do to the beginning working relationship of the client system and the new resource. The social worker will also need to consider what effect it might have on the client system to hear that the social worker called the resource to see how things were going. Negative repercussions will be avoided as long as all three parties (social worker, client system, and resource system) know in advance that the social worker will be doing a follow-up and it is clear who will be contacted and when.

When it appears that the goals for the referral are being accomplished, the social worker is able to close the case. If there are other problems or needs that are not being addressed by the resource, and the client system continues to ask for the services of the social worker, a collaborative arrangement must be worked out between the resource and the social worker. Using a holistic perspective, the generalist knows that problems and needs of a client system are interdependent, and that when service provision is carried out by more than one resource, collaboration and teamwork among the resources are needed. Thus, a third type of intervention frequently found in general practice may be identified as teamwork.

Case Management and Teamwork

Because of the nature of the work of the generalist, an entry-level social worker frequently needs to call on other resources for collaboration in providing service. On a contracted plan (Chapter 6), the identification of who will complete the task often includes a social worker with one or more other helping persons. The individuals, groups, families, organizations, or communities that seek help from a generalist usually have many problems and therefore need assistance from several service providers. The generalist has skills to form action systems with these other resource persons in a cooperative effort to achieve their common purpose of providing human services.

Case management is a contemporary term that is used to refer to the actions taken by a social worker to mobilize and to bring together the various services needed in a case for efficient, effective service delivery. A case manager aims to ensure a continuum of care to client systems with complex, multiple problems and disabilities; attempts to intervene clinically to ameliorate the emotional problems accompanying illness or loss of function; and utilizes social work skills of collaborating, promoting teamwork, brokering, negotiating, mediating, and advocating as a boundary approach to service delivery (Vourlekis & Greene, 1992). A case manager aims to provide services in the context of the client system's least restrictive setting while promoting client system self-determination and normalization. Although case management is viewed as a process of service coordination, accountability, and a method of ensuring a client system's right to service, its hallmark feature is to hold the social worker in the case management role responsible for overcoming fragmentation in the service delivery system. When identified as the case manager, the generalist must use skill to work with the various resources for a case to develop an atmosphere of shared leadership and openness. When diverse resources work together in common planning, decision making, and consolidated action, the efforts of this organized group may be called *teamwork*. Unless the service providers who are working with one client system move to become a team, the generalist may carry the heavy burden not only of managing the case but also of being seen as primarily responsible for its outcome. When resources truly become a team, there is a strong sense of sharing and commitment and of a group responsibility for final outcome.

Within case management, the aim of *multidisciplinary collaboration* is coordinated and integrated service delivery across education, health, and social services. Achieving this aim requires participating professionals from multiple disciplines to take an active role in blending not only the organizational purpose, policies, and procedures of their agencies but also their own diverse professional values, knowledge base, perspectives, and intervention approaches in the interest of client service. The case management function of bridging organizational and professional boundaries and building well-functioning multidisciplinary teams is a complex effort that is well guided by the principles and practices of collaboration (Sabatino, 1999) and negotiation.

To understand case management collaboration, the social worker must first understand the multiple forms coordination assumes depending on the intended purpose (Mulroy, 1997). For example, from the perspective of organizational planning, collaboration is used as an intervention method for coordinating activities across administrative hierarchies. From the perspective of a generalist practitioner in a case management role, collaboration usually means a sense of cooperation among individuals working on a common task within a service system or across service systems (i.e., interprofessional collaboration and team building) (Sabatino, 1999).

In addition, one must understand the underlying assumptions in collaboration. Successful collaboration is assumed to contribute to the professional growth of team members by enhancing their professional capabilities. Multidisciplinary teams have more opportunity to deal with the whole picture in data collection, assessment, and intervention planning. Thus, in developing and implementing a service delivery system for a client system, a multidisciplinary team addresses more of the nuances and complexities associated with specific problems and needs and this particular person-in-environment configuration. As team members become familiar with their teammates' understanding, their own knowledge base expands. As mutual understanding increases, team sharing in planning and delivering services builds interest, partnership, and consensus and thereby breaks through categorical approaches to health, education, and social services (Sabatino, 1999).

To begin to grow in the art of teamwork, it is important to realize that there is no *one* model of teamwork that should be used at all times. Some teams have a designated leader, and some have a rotating leadership. A leader needs to have an understanding of group process, as well as goal-directed abilities and skill in bringing forth contributions and leadership from other members of the group.

There are nine basic principles for effective teamwork. When a team is not achieving its goals, a review of the principles could reveal possible causes for difficulties incurred. The principles are summarized as follows:

1. *Obtain sanction:* Team members must be free to communicate openly in collaborative service planning and provision. The client system in need must sanction the team with the understanding that there will be open communication among members.

2. *Build supporting structure:* Each team member brings the professional knowledge, values, and skills of his or her own discipline and the concern (whether conscious or not) that blending interprofessional strategies will erase their discipline. In some instances, collaboration necessitates a shift in work culture and attitude about cooperation and acting together. In other instances, collaboration necessitates revisions in policy, job descriptions, and accountability requirements (Gallesich, 1982; Sabatino, 1999).

3. *Know yourself:* All members of the team must clearly know their own professional identities and the distinctive contribution they and their agencies can make to the team.

4. *Maximize resources:* Inclusion of professionals from multiple disciplines in joint planning and shared decision making creates the opportunity for maximizing resources by generating new paradigms for data collection, assessment, planning, intervention, and evaluation (Gallesich, 1982; Sabatino, 1999).

5. *Respect one another:* Members of the team must respect each discipline, recognizing similarities and differences without being threatened or "turf protective." They must understand the service orientation, recognize the competencies, trust the communications, and rely on the work of each team member (Sabatino, 1999).

6. *Meet regularly:* The team must meet on a regular basis for shared communication, planning, and evaluation.

7. *Define task assignments:* The team must define clearly each person's tasks and role in providing service. Roles and assignments must be explicit and agreed upon. Goals and methods must be clarified (Sabatino, 1999).

8. *Examine team process and achievement:* The team as a whole must systematically review its own process in working toward goal achievement. To ensure accountability in service delivery, the team must explore both its successful accomplishments and failures to understand what processes lead to effective teamwork (Gallesich, 1982; Sabatino, 1999).

9. *Share responsibility:* The team must assume collective responsibility for service outcome.

A team proceeds through stages that are similar to the six stages of the General Method. Collectively, members of the team clarify the problem and purpose for organizing, share data, agree on goals and a plan for intervention, assign tasks, evaluate, and terminate contact. The struggle for power or status, the emergence of conflict, and the development of group norms and expectations are important dimensions of a growing team, as they are for any human system.

At times, however, in order to achieve unified teamwork, or collaboration, the social worker has to negotiate, mediate, or even arbitrate between client systems and their impinging environments, between service systems on behalf of client systems, and between client groups. *Negotiation* involves direct communication between two parties. If conflicting parties cannot negotiate a solution, a third party is needed to mediate and promote communication and conciliation. If a third party is unable to promote negotiation between the parties, an arbitrator may be needed. The arbitrator does not attempt to promote communication and negotiation. Instead, like a judge, he or she hears both sides of the conflict situation and decides the resolution. Finally, if the arbitration is not successful, the social worker would refer client systems for litigation, in which each party is represented by an attorney (Parsons, Jorgensen, & Hernandez, 1994).

Negotiation and mediation involve a process of facilitating communication between opposing positions around mutual interests. Mediating is appropriate only when there is perceived definable mutual interest; whereas when conflict of interest is perceived, advocating is more appropriate (Compton & Galaway, 1999). In negotiating and mediating, the effort is to secure resolution benefits through give-and-take on both sides. In advocacy, on the other hand, the effort is to win for the client or help the client win for himself or herself. In practice, both of these approaches tend to mesh and overlap.

Negotiating and mediating focus on behaviorally oriented change. The tactics or strategies do not focus on personality change, attitude change, or therapeutic process of the participants. Attitudinal change, however, may very well follow behavioral change. The goal is to create choices so that reconciliation, settlement, compromise, or understanding can take place between party systems. The process assumes that the involved parties are able to isolate issues, interests, positions, alternatives, and resources to find agreed-upon solutions. The desired outcome is a behavioral agreement mutually agreed on by the parties.

The framework for negotiating and mediating is based on integrative problem solving, which typically involves four steps (Fisher, Ury, & Patton, 1991):

1. Separate persons from problems.
2. Focus on interests instead of positions.
3. Create options for mutual gain.
4. Select criteria for choosing alternatives.

Although conflicts usually begin around some substantive issue, they often quickly progress into an emotional arena of the participants while the substantive issue itself is lost. The first step in negotiation and mediation is to ask each participant to describe the problem and state his or her feelings about the problem. The social worker's skills are to help clarify perceptions, reframe the problems presented in the interests of the participants present, and validate each participant by using reflective listening techniques. Each participant needs to be heard. The social worker often asks participants to repeat in their own words what they heard the other party saying and encourages each party to use "I" statements instead of "you" statements. By sharing with each other, the participants are able to begin to define the problem as separate from the person. Once the problems are out on the table, the social worker and the participants can begin to build an agenda for work.

As the problems are presented, the social worker enters the second stage by listening for the interests behind the positions, or the wants as opposed to needs of the participants. For example, a position of "My father does not want to go to a nursing home" may actually reflect an underlying interest of "I need to feel that my father is getting the best care available" or "I need to feel not guilty about the proposed plan of care for my elderly father." The key to interest-based problem solving is to find the common interest of the participants or at least some compatible individual interests. When participants hear and see that their needs may not be so very different, they often are able to negotiate a solution out of those interests instead of remaining entrenched in their previous positions. Sometimes the social worker has to point out the areas of common interests because they are hidden behind emotions.

To pursue a client system's mutual interests, the social worker creates opportunities for generating options during the third step of integrative problem solving. The social worker encourages the participants to brainstorm and discuss various options that others may have used for solving the presenting situation. The social worker should refrain from premature feedback on potential solutions; rather, he or she should encourage the participants to critically explore and examine the path and consequences of presented options. Using humor and even exploring frivolous alternatives tends to help alleviate the emotional stress that parties sometimes feel in their pursuit of solutions.

Finally, when a number of alternatives have been generated, selection can take place. The social worker assists the participants in deciding how alternatives will be selected. As part of the final step in integrative problem solving, the social worker helps participants identify and select what objective criteria will be used for choosing a particular option. When participants can agree to select alternative solutions using an acceptable set of criteria, the resolution is practically complete. Criteria are often based on developmental, economic, and growth-promoting interests of the participants. For example, in elder care decision making, the objective criteria are likely to be based on economic feasibility, quality of care, and access to companionship. Once the criteria are chosen, alternatives are selected, spelled out procedurally, written down, and distributed to all relevant participants. Plans are then made to carry them out. This is also a time to decide about follow-ups or any check-in procedures. Fisher, Ury, and Patton (1991) note that a collaborative, integrative negotiation or mediation produces a wise agreement or an agreement that meets the main interests of all the participants.

Throughout the negotiation, the social worker is expected to assume neutrality subject to professional values and agency policies. Participants must be judged to be competent to negotiate. People who are chemically dependent or mentally incompetent are not considered appropriate participants, for they may not be able to follow through with a behavioral contract to resolve problems. Obviously, life-threatening situations are not amenable to negotiation. Instead, they often must be handled in a more direct, expedient manner.

Common questions about this process include: How does one get to the task or problems for resolution when emotions are running high? Don't people's feelings have to be considered before addressing their tasks? Integrative problem solving does not discount emotions but they are not the focus of the process. Emotions must be heard, listened to, and reflected on. They must be dealt with to the extent that they get in the way of problem resolution. The goal is always to create workable solutions that promote mutual gain, decrease conflict, and empower the participants.

Although both the relationship of participants and the outcome of negotiation are important in the problem-solving process, the *outcome is the goal* and the *relationship is a by-product*. The emphasis may vary based on the anticipated future contact of the participants (Fisher, Ury, & Patton, 1991). That is, if participants are to maintain a close contact in the future, the relational component of negotiation becomes important and must be one of the options and selection criteria for alternatives sought. For example, if participants are family members, significant persons, or individuals who have to co-exist in close proximity, emotions must be addressed as part of the solutions sought. On the other hand, if participants are parties who will not be expected to maintain future close contact, as in the case of group members who come together for a specific task solution, the outcome or the mutual gain takes precedence over the relationship.

Although negotiation and teamwork may be emotionally draining and time-consuming components of case management, they avoid excessive demands on limited resources and prevent fragmentation and overlap of service delivery. Through a case management approach, client systems are not left with the burden of trying to integrate services on their own, and a sense of mutual aid, shared unity, and community is fostered.

Indirect Intervention

The concept of *indirect practice* is defined in different ways within the profession of social work. On the one hand, it refers to practice in such areas as administration, supervision, management, or class advocacy. From this perspective, the practitioner is not having direct client system contact. On the other hand, the term refers to work with target systems or outside agencies in order to achieve goals for a social worker's client or client system. Because of possible confusion in the use of the concept, a distinction is made in this book between *indirect practice* and *indirect intervention*. *Indirect practice* means advanced professional activities, such as administration and management. *Indirect intervention* refers to interactions with systems that affect clients during the intervention stage of the General Method. The social worker intervenes with these systems in order to bring about changes needed for client systems to achieve their identified goals.

Getting a client system involved and responsive frequently requires a social worker's political skills. The generalist may find a potential resource that is resistant to the requests of a client system or the social worker. Such skills as providing evidence, publicizing, bargaining, organizing, demonstrating, taking legal action, and influencing policy development may have to be utilized. For example, a hospital social worker with refugee patients has been unsuccessful in obtaining services from a refugee program. The social worker knows that the program is being funded to offer the services requested. The generalist may need to present to her supervisor and to the administrator of the refugee program evidence that several requests were made without results. If this intervention is unsuccessful and efforts at bargaining are also unproductive, a form of publicizing may need to take place.

Often, a social worker will need to use a combination of political skills to bring about change in a target system. For example, legislators may have to be contacted for funding to be allocated to expand needed programs. Evidence of need will have to be presented, and bargaining or demonstration may take place. The generalist may have to give testimony or to speak at open hearings. Interested groups may have to be organized for their participation in the change process. As indirect interventions are planned, the social worker keeps in mind the need to involve the client systems—those that are suffering from the problems—as much as possible in all of the planned activities.

Indirect interventions may be enacted with any size or type of system. A social worker and client system may be unable to achieve identified goals because of a refusal or resistance on the part of an individual, family, group, organization, or community. Frequently, a social worker serves a client system through indirect interventions with target systems that are represented by members of various professions. Although every effort is made to develop a cooperative working relationship with these representatives, the generalist may have to move into an adversary process on behalf of the client system.

As a client advocate in an adversary process, a social worker tries to persuade a target system to decide in favor of the client system. The role of adversary is often difficult for a social worker with a basic practice principle of self-determination. The competition or drive for victory in an adversary process can become very strong. It may not be easy for a social worker to remain calm and emotionally controlled if the opponent is presenting half-truths or attacking what the social worker has presented as valid.

To interact effectively with members of different professions or within their work environments, a social worker needs to understand each profession and environmental system. For example, if social workers are to form alliances or adversary systems with lawyers, they need to have a working knowledge of the vocabulary, methods, and motivations of lawyers; the requirements of law; and the functioning of the legal system. Unfortunately, research shows that there is often a tense, untrusting relationship between social workers and lawyers (Mueller & Murphy, 1965; Swenson, 1993). The frustration that exists as these two professions interface may be due to a basic lack of understanding of each other. The use of words and the approach to problem solving found in each discipline are different. The professionals may use the same words, but not mean the same thing. For example, the use of the words *contract* and *fact* may cause confusion in communication between lawyers and social workers. A contract used in the process of assessment by a social worker is not the same as the legal contract used in a legal process. Social workers collect data on feelings and attitudes as well as such facts as names, dates, and circumstances. They are concerned with *why* something happened in order to arrive at a plan for problem resolution. A lawyer is concerned with evidence and *what* happened to see if legal action can be taken. Although a social worker may know that something is true, it is not useful information in the court unless it can be documented and admitted into evidence. Whereas the law of the lawyer is technical and specific, the theory of the social worker is dynamic and evolving (Swenson, 1993; Wilson-Coker, 1982).

Prior to any indirect intervention, the generalist needs to prepare for interaction with a client, action, or target system by studying the system and its representatives. It may be helpful to consult with someone from a similar system or discipline to identify the most effective way to contact, communicate, and intervene with the particular system.

Indirect interventions are usually the most challenging and difficult type of interventions for entry-level generalists. Social work education programs seldom provide students with a working knowledge of other professional disciplines. Beginning generalists are primarily prepared for direct work with client systems. The entry-level social worker therefore needs strong educational and emotional support through supervision and consultation to persevere and accomplish indirect interventions.

Social Development

A social worker who perceives needs on the broader societal level may wonder where to start and how to carry through with efforts to bring about social change or development. Time and energy limitations of the social worker should be realistically recognized, with activities carefully planned to avoid wasted effort. For social change or social development, the General Method is somewhat modified, because the system of contact usually does not have the identified need, nor does that system see any reason to respond to the need, even though it has the power to do so. Although the method has been described repeatedly as a collaborative process between a social worker and a client system, in this type of work the social worker often executes the process alone. Sometimes the work involves advocacy for particular client systems. In these cases, every effort is made to involve and empower the client systems in each step of the process. At times, however, a social worker is advocating for a class of people or for a policy change that affects people in society at large. Although a social worker may try to join with others in coalitions, teams, or action systems to bring about the desired change, it is possible that the process will have to be initiated and perhaps completed by the social worker alone. Whether alone or with others, the procedure for work in the extended environment can be guided by the six stages of the General Method.

An outline of the General Method as designed in this text is repeated in Figure 7.1. Having first identified both a need in society and the client systems primarily responsible for meeting the need, a social worker can follow the outline as a guide for action. The questions raised during each stage of the method may be modified or expanded for greater relevance. For example, the three main components of the first stage are shown as problems, feelings, and goals. In beginning to engage in the process, the social worker first studies the problem, need, or issue in the extended environment by asking the following questions:

1. **What is the problem or need as perceived by**
   a. **Me (social worker), my agency, my profession?**
   b. **The systems with the power to respond to the problem or need?**
   c. **Others**
      i. **The group of people feeling the problem or need?**
      ii. **People in society at large?**

FIGURE 7.1   The General Method

I. Engagement
   a.   Problems
   b.   Feelings
   c.   Goals

II. Data Collection
   a.   Problems
   b.   Persons
   c.   Environment

III. Assessment
   a.   Assessment statements
   b.   Problem prioritization
   c.   Contracting (plan)

IV. Intervention
   a.   Direct
   b.   Indirect
   c.   Teamwork
   d.   Referral

V. Evaluation
   a.   Goal analysis
   b.   Contract review
   c.   Contract reformulation

VI. Termination
   a.   Decision: transfer, refer, terminate
   b.   Plan: timing, follow-up
   c.   Termination: feelings, life-cycle approach

The social worker then proceeds to an inquiry about feelings and goals as the following questions are asked:

2. **What feelings surround the problem or need as felt by**
   a. **Me, my agency, my profession?**
   b. **The power systems?**
   c. **Others: those with the problem or need, society at large?**
3. **What goals related to the problem or need can be identified by**
   a. **Me, my agency, my profession?**
   b. **The power systems?**
   c. **Others: those with the problem or need, society at large?**

Moving into data collection (stage II), the social worker gathers information about problems, persons, and environment. Questions to be answered in this stage are as follows:

4. **What is the scope (number of people), the duration (length of time), and the severity (degree to which it is a life-or-death issue) of the problem or need?**
5. **Who are the persons suffering from the problem or unmet need? What is their motivation and capacity to work on the problem or need?**
6. **Who are the people in the power systems (titles, roles, personal characteristics)? What is their motivation and capacity to work on the problem or need?**
7. **What are the power systems—structure, channels, lines of authority, processes, rules of procedure? How are decisions made?**

Question 7 is extremely important if a social worker is to intervene effectively in a power system. If, for example, a social worker enters the legislative arena with the intent to have a bill introduced or passed, it is imperative that he or she have knowledge of the legislative process, as well as of the legislators themselves. If the social development is occurring in a nondemocratic society, the social worker needs to understand the overt and covert governing and decision-making processes used by the society's formal and hidden power structures.

Supplementing information about the identified power systems, the social worker needs to know the following:

8. **Are there any other systems with the potential for meeting the identified need or for resolving the problem?**
9. **Are there other systems that could influence or put pressure on the power systems?**
10. **Are there other resources to support, or to collaborate with, the social worker in his or her efforts?**

On the basis of the data collected, the social worker is then in a position to make a clearer assessment of the problem or need and to plan interventions. The questions raised in the assessment (stage III) include these:

11. *Who* has *what* **(problem or need) and** *why?*
12. **If more than one problem or need has been identified, how should they be prioritized?**
13. **What is the most effective plan to work on the problems or needs as prioritized?**

As a plan is developed, the social worker would recall and may plan to use the political skills, program analysis, tactics, and testimony guide suggested earlier. As tasks are listed sequentially on a contracted-plan sheet, a social worker might include efforts to mobilize other individuals, groups, or organizations to work with him or her on mutual goals stated on the contract. If others become involved in the action, the tasks may be distributed and contracted among the participants. As pointed out, however, it is possible that all of the tasks will have to be carried out by the social worker alone.

In intervention (stage IV) during indirect work, a social worker may have face-to-face contact with the power systems and use various political skills and tactics. (Because a power system is not a client system, such intervention is not considered direct intervention.) The social worker may act as a team member in a coalition or may refer the issue to another resource for action. Throughout the intervention stage, the social worker (team) asks these questions:

14. **Am I (are we) completing the tasks as planned?**
15. **Am I (are we) ready to move on to the next planned task?**

As the social worker moves into evaluation, the questions asked are the following:

16. **To what extent has (have) the goal(s) been accomplished?**
17. **If there has been goal accomplishment, was this the result of my (our) efforts? If there has not been goal accomplishment, why not?**

Here, too, the contracted plan developed during assessment is carefully reviewed if goals have not been accomplished. Timing anticipated, resources contracted, and tasks sequenced along with stated goals and problems on the plan are reconsidered.

The social worker (team) then asks the following question:

18. **Is there a need to reformulate goals or any other dimension of the plan? Are more overt political behaviors needed?**

In the final stage, the social worker (team) makes the decision regarding termination of his or her involvement in the issue with the identified power systems. Questions raised in this stage include these:

19. **Is it time for me (us) to refer, transfer, or terminate my (our) efforts to bring about change in the extended environment in relation to the identified problem or needs?**
20. **How do I (we) plan to terminate?**
    a. **When?**
    b. **Will there be a follow-up?**
    c. **In terminating, are there feelings that need to be expressed? by me? the power systems? others?**
21. **Using the life-cycle approach, what is the past, present, and future of my (our) involvement in working on these problems or needs in the extended environment?**

If the social worker is an entry-level generalist, the time may come in the process when a referral or transfer needs to be made to a social worker with advanced expertise in political strategies or policy formation. Systems with greater legal access and authority may need to step in and take over the role of advocate.

Social problems in society at large are seldom resolved fully. Even when legislation is passed and programs are initiated, ongoing monitoring of change is usually needed. Social workers may therefore build in a role of monitoring as part of their follow-up plan for the future.

Although entry-level generalists may not possess advanced, sophisticated political skills to work in complex political structures, they are the ones most likely to be aware of the pulse and the pain of the disadvantaged in society. Their first-hand experience and documentation, with a strong sense of commitment and perseverance, may be the most valuable forces to bring about change in the extended environment. Generalist practitioners are prepared primarily for direct practice with client systems, but they do not forget that efforts for social change in society at large are also essential to their holistic approach to social work practice.

Designs for General Interventions

The four major types of intervention by a generalist may be depicted in designs composed of circle clusters. In Figure 7.2, the social worker (SW) is seen in inter-action with a client system (C) through overlapping circles. This simple design is used to demonstrate *direct intervention.*

A case example for Figure 7.2 is a generalist working with a family (father, mother, and son) as they grow in understanding the changing behaviors of their adolescent son (age 15).

In Figure 7.3, a *referral* is pictured by a social worker (SW) interacting with a client system (C) as the client begins to interact with a resource (R). If contact with

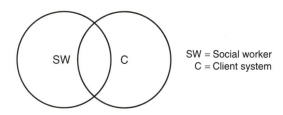

FIGURE 7.2   **Direct Intervention**

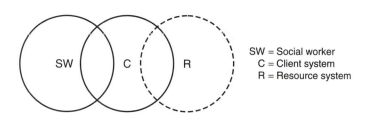

FIGURE 7.3   **Referral**

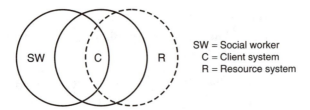

FIGURE 7.4   Social Worker and Client Contact

a particular resource system has not yet been actualized, but is the intent of the intervention, the resource system (R) may be depicted by a broken line. If both a social worker and a client system have direct contact with a resource, the SW circle would extend to the right and intersect the R circle also (Figure 7.4).

An example for Figures 7.3 and 7.4 would be a social worker whose client system is a depressed woman who is talking about suicide. As indicated in the design, the social worker is trying to help the client face the seriousness of her problem and admit herself to the local mental health center.

In the design found in Figure 7.5, the social worker and other resources (A, B) join together in a team effort. Collectively, the social worker (SW) and other resources (A, B) interact with a client system (C). The overlapping circles reflect the *teamwork* in human service provision. For example, in working with a community that has experienced a number of unexplained fires lately, a generalist may be working with representatives from the fire department and the local police force to help the community members express their concerns and to find ways to combat fires and to report suspected arsonists. In Figure 7.5, all three resources (social worker, fire department, and police) are shown as coming together to form a team for ongoing service to the community. In Figure 7.6, the social worker remains in the role of case manager because teamwork has not been established with all three resources to work together. The local police and the fire department are called on by the social worker to meet separately with the community on different occasions.

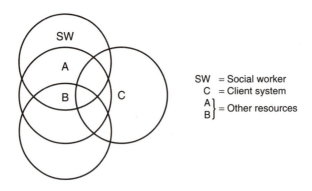

FIGURE 7.5   Teamwork

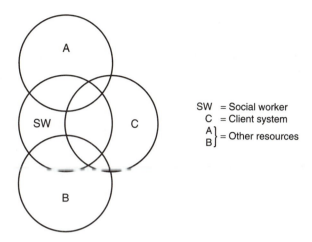

FIGURE 7.6   Case Management

The absence of an ongoing team effort is depicted in Figure 7.6 boundaries that do not overlap (A and B), except with the social worker (SW), who contacts and coordinates the services for the community.

Figure 7.7 is a diagram of *indirect intervention*. In this design, the generalist (SW) is interacting with a target system (T) to mobilize it to meet the needs of a client system (C).

A case example of indirect intervention as shown in Figure 7.7 could involve a group of youngsters who need tutoring. The generalist (SW) can be seen as putting pressure on the school system (T) to provide the services needed for the group (C).

Additional designs in intervention may be drawn up to reflect combined intervention types. Sometimes, as shown in Figure 7.8, a generalist (SW) may be involved with a number of community resources (A, B) in a team effort to influence a target system (T) for client service (C).

For example, a generalist (SW) working in behalf of an elderly community (C) plagued by vandalism may join with town officials (A) and the local newspaper (B) to advocate better police protection (T) of the elderly community.

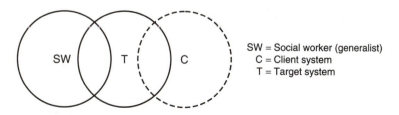

FIGURE 7.7   Indirect Intervention

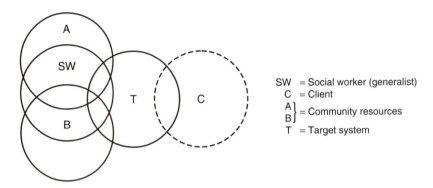

FIGURE 7.8   Combined Interventions

In the course of working with a system, a generalist may change the design of intervention as problems or needs emerge or are resolved. At any given time, a social worker should be able to identify the design (or designs) currently being used.

Working with Different Client Systems

As stated in the section on direct interventions, a generalist has skills and techniques for work with client, action, or target systems of any size. In addition to the relationship skills, problem-solving skills, and political skills, as categorized in the foundation framework (Table 1.3 in Chapter 1), there is a range of techniques that can be called on as needed with particular client, action, and target systems. Techniques may be appropriately identified as generalist-practice techniques if they can be used with more than one type of system or problem. Specialized techniques are specifically designed for and used in a particular area of specialization, according to problem, population, institution, traditional or specialized method, or theoretical approach. Some techniques that originate in a specialized area may later be extended for use with a variety of social systems by the generalist with additional knowledge, skills, and experience under supervision.

For example, although the technique known as *sculpting* has been used primarily in family work, as stated earlier, it could be used with a group or community. Basically, sculpting is a technique in which a person creates a live "sculpture" to portray the way he or she views the members of a client, action, or target system in relation to one another. The social worker asks a volunteer to create a space and action configuration. This means that the volunteer bodily places all members of the system, as he or she sees them, according to distance and body position in relation to one another and to the volunteer. When placed in the position, each person stays as still as a sculpture. The sculptor is encouraged to discuss how and why each person has his or her position, and every member of the configuration is asked to describe what it feels like to be in that position. Each individual in the system is given the opportunity to sculpt out his or her perception of the system. The technique enables all present to grow in understanding the perceptions and feelings of one another. It also helps break down any personal barriers against verbalization and lessens anxieties. Through this type of play activity, the less powerful or less verbal individuals in the system are freed to express their views and to receive the attention of everyone present (Perez, 1979).

Often, there is a need within a group or a community, as well as within a family, for greater understanding and sharing among members. Individual members of a group can be encouraged by a social worker to sculpt out how they see the interactions and relationships among group members through a sculpted tableau of the group.

In a meeting of a community, a generalist can ask for representatives of the subsystems that constitute the community to portray through space and action positioning how they perceive the relationships among the subsystems of the community. Other members of the subsystem may be allowed to help their representative find the best way to depict relationships within the community from the collective eyes of the subsystem. Again, the technique of sculpting can expand the sensitivity of the parts to the perceptions of the whole. Communications within a community can be enriched as fears and feelings of insignificance are exposed.

The sculpting technique may be used also by a group of professionals for team building. If the process of teamwork is not moving along, the technique may be introduced to help members of the team become more aware of how each of them sees the emerging relationships and lines of communication within the team.

Actually, the sculpting technique may be used with different client, action, or target systems during any of the stages of the General Method. In addition to intervention, sculpting may facilitate progress during engagement, data collection, assessment, evaluation, and termination. The technique may be helpful in identifying goals as well as problems and feelings. Not only could the generalist ask the volunteer to sculpt out how he or she perceives the particular system at present (identifying problems and feelings) but also how he or she would hope to see the system of contact in the future (goals). Through a discussion about each member's views for the future, a consensus may be reached on goals for the client, action, or target system.

Another example of the generic nature of techniques used by a generalist can be found in the behavioral technique of relaxation. The technique of relaxation exercises is done usually on a one-to-one basis. However, just as the individual becomes tense during times of stress, there are obvious periods in the meetings of families, groups, organizations, and communities when tensions rise and stress is heightened. As stress builds up within any one of these client systems, energy to think and act rationally can become blocked. The generalist can help reduce the mounting anxiety through a relaxation exercise.

Members of the client, action, or target system are first encouraged to become aware of the reality that tension is building, and they are asked to stop the process and the conversation for a few minutes to relax. One relaxation technique is to have members alternate in tensing and relaxing various muscles and to focus on the different feelings that result. They begin to sense the power within themselves to control the mounting or releasing of tension within their bodies. In addition, members are asked to take deep breaths and to be sensitive to the way deep breathing helps relax muscles. As the system of contact becomes peaceful and progressively relaxed, some cue words—such as *calm, still,* and *serene*—may be said. Later, if tension begins to build again, these words may be used to help the system of contact recall the relaxed state. With anxiety reduced, the particular system may be helped to talk about what was triggering the mounting stress. Usually, something has been said that caused members of the client, action, or target system to feel threatened, angered, or afraid.

Force-field analysis is a third example of a technique that may be used by a generalist during intervention with systems of different sizes. This technique, based on Kurt Lewin's (1951) field theory has been developed primarily as a tool to assist in data collection and assessment of organizations (Braeger & Holloway, 1978; Brill, 1995; Brueggeman, 1996). With a little creative thinking and modification, the technique can readily be used in generalist practice with individuals, families, groups, organizations, and communities. Whenever any client system is not able to change or to accomplish tasks that were identified in a contracted plan (Chapter 6), there are usually restraining forces operating that are stronger than the driving forces. The generalist may try to offer the client system support and understanding of the situation by using a force-field analysis.

Basically, the technique is a procedure that uses a framework to organize information as it relates to the accomplishment of a goal. The forces that influence those individuals responsible for enacting tasks necessary for goal accomplishment are organized and classified as either driving or restraining forces. The process begins with a clarification of a specific goal. Then, those who are the primary actors or persons needed to achieve the goal are identified. Next, each of the forces impinging on these persons is categorized as either driving or restraining. The forces are then evaluated in terms of their openness to and potential for change. The consistency and stability of each force during a period of change is also questioned. Finally, a judgment is made regarding the strengths of the driving forces as compared with restraining forces in the light of the desirable goal. If there is no imbalance in which the change-producing forces have greater weight, the failure in goal accomplishment can be understood and predicted. The technique can help any individual, group, family, community, or organization see more clearly why certain tasks are not being performed and goals are not being accomplished. It also provides direction for planned intervention to counteract the restraining forces and to build up those that are change producing.

The technique of force-field analysis has characteristics similar to those of the tool used for problem prioritization, as found in Chapter 6, and of the procedure used for evaluation through goal analysis to be presented in the next chapter (Chapter 8). In addition to using the technique during direct intervention, the generalist and other resources of a team may find it helpful as they collectively plan strategies for intervention with target systems.

There are several other techniques that a generalist may use in the General Method when working with more than one type of client, action, or target system and problem. The four basic interventions (direct, information and referral, case management and teamwork, and indirect) are selectively applied with a range of techniques as the generalist interacts with different client systems.

Using Social Work Foundation Knowledge in Intervention

Basic values, theories, and skills used by the generalist during the intervention stage of the General Method are identified in the holistic conceptualization of the foundation for social work practice (Chapter 1). The practice principles that reflect the basic values of social work are very evident in the judgments and actions of the social worker as interventions are planned and implemented. Interventions by a social worker are dependent on the willingness of a system to accept and cooperate with the social worker. As much as possible, the system of contact is given the opportunity to determine for itself the types of involvement the social worker will provide. Each problem-person-environment situation is individualized as the social worker accepts or suggests certain rules or task responsibilities.

Throughout the four major types of interventions, different practice principles are highlighted. For example, *controlled emotional involvement* is a principle that is strongly needed during indirect intervention, especially when the social worker is in an adversary process. *Individualization* and *purposeful expression of feelings* are central to direct intervention. *Acceptance* is crucial for effective teamwork, and *confidentiality* and *self-determination* are highlighted during referral (Biestek, 1957).

Knowledge used during intervention varies according to the task at hand. During direct intervention, theories about the type of client system (individual, family, group, organization, community) the social worker is interacting with are used. With indirect intervention, knowledge of policies, procedures, institutions, and social-change theory is particularly relevant. In referral, the social worker uses knowledge about resources. For teamwork to be successful, individual members know about their own profession and other professions, as well as group dynamics and processes.

In addition to the various techniques used by the generalist as described earlier in this chapter, the skills listed in the holistic foundation (Chapter 1) are demonstrated during the intervention stage. Relationship skills and problem-solving skills are pervasive during direct intervention. Political skills are used primarily with direct interventions. In the referral process and during teamwork, a social worker may find it necessary to use all three major types of skills: relationship, problem solving, and political.

The heart of the General Method may be seen as intervention; the appropriate use of skills and techniques at this time is crucial to the fulfillment of the process. As emphasized, the selection of skills and techniques is guided by a social worker's application of basic values and knowledge. The holistic conceptualization of the foundation for practice is a helpful reference for the generalist who must artfully apply foundation knowledge, values, and skills when intervening in each unique situation.

Human Diversity in Intervention

The core human diversity issues related to social work intervention at the micro-, mezzo-, and macro-level systems include institutional racism, cultural diversity, gender-role expectations, sexual orientation, and socio-economic status. As brought out in this chapter, the interventions of the generalist may be identified as direct service, indirect service, referral, and teamwork. When a social worker is intervening directly with a client system of another culture, an interpreter may be needed to overcome language differences. In one sense, direct intervention becomes a type of teamwork when an interpreter is used. Although interpreters repeat what has been said verbatim as they translate, they also need the ability and sensitivity to convey the feelings and attitudes that are being communicated. Ideally, interpreters for social workers need to have some understanding of the basic principles and practices of the social worker. They need to realize the difference between relating to a friend and to a client, and to be able to convey the personal style of the social worker. Open communication with a strong sense of trust and mutual commitment should exist between the social worker and the interpreter. The social worker needs to make every effort to communicate directly and respectfully with a client system, even when an interpreter is being used. At no time should any member of the client system be made to feel like an object to supply information or to be talked about. Children should not be used as interpreters for their parents; such action puts them in a position that generally contradicts their role and place in their culture. It may also prevent a parent from dealing with content he or she does not wish to discuss in front of the children.

In addition to direct provision of services, a social worker may serve vulnerable populations through various types of indirect involvements with target systems. The nature of such involvements may be primarily educational, with presentations of research findings to document need. A social worker may be intervening through applying political pressures on institutions, legislators, or agencies. For example, a social worker may become actively involved in promoting legislation to ensure an adequate income for all children and families, or to change policies or structures of traditional agencies that have to be modified if members of vulnerable groups are to receive adequate services. Agencies may need to be encouraged to join up with representatives of diverse groups to develop more sensitive and relevant service provision. As brought out by Chestang and others (Chestang, 1982; Everett, Chipungu, & Leashore, 1991), the three essential criteria for programs serving minorities are proximity, relevance, and community participation.

When an agency cannot supply the needed type of intervention, a referral must be made. The social worker looks for resources that appear to be sensitive to the culture, social stratification characteristics, and socio-demographic characteristics of the client system. This may become apparent by considering (1) the cultural and social background and languages of those administering and providing the service, (2) the location of the service, (3) the involvement or input by the particular cultural and social group in the resource, and (4) the extent to which members of the cultural and social community have received satisfactory services from the resource in the past. Before contacting a formal resource, a social worker and client system should explore thoroughly the possibility of locating available informal resources. In meeting emotional, social, and personal needs, particularly for minority members, familial and community resources are often far more effective than formal agencies or programs. Also, informal resources usually provide greater stability through ongoing availability. It is in the black community, for example, that members of the African American culture receive their emotional support and positive identity. As Chestang (1982, p. 30) writes:

> The black person finds emotional solace within the black community. Here are the comforts of family, the protections of supportive institutions such as churches, fraternal organizations and civil rights groups. Here the black person has an opportunity to build self-esteem through the exercise of talents and skills, to develop a sense of personal identity through enduring relationships with family, friends and significant others, and to struggle in the company of others who face common barriers to the pursuit of a better life.

When a social worker intervenes through teamwork with other professionals, it is important to see that team members are sensitive to the culture of the client system receiving service. Ideally, the service team should seek periodic consultation from someone with knowledge, experience, and demonstrated competence in working with people of the particular culture, social background, and socio-demographic characteristics.

Especially for those individuals who do not have a nurturing, accepting family or community network, a group of people who share common values, problems, pressures, concerns, and lifestyle can be very supportive and strengthening. In working with vulnerable populations, a generalist will be promoting self-esteem and self-sufficiency by using the General Method because it is a collaborative, problem-solving approach that encourages assertiveness and empowerment. As presented throughout this text, a guiding principle is to have members of a client system do whatever there is to be done for themselves whenever possible.

Intervention in Micro, Mezzo, and Macro Practice in Diverse Field Areas

In the following section, the application of knowledge and skills during the *intervention stage* of the General Method will be demonstrated by entry-level generalists in seven diverse field areas.

I. Field Area: Child Welfare

A. Agency: State Department of Children's Services

B. Client System

K, a 15-year-old female, is moving from an emergency shelter into a group home. (For more background information, see Chapter 4, Engagement in Micro, Mezzo, and Macro Practice in Diverse Field Areas, I. Child Welfare.)

C. Summary of Preceding Stages

The problems, goals, and contracted tasks identified during engagement, data collection, and assessment are listed in Table 6.7 of Chapter 6. The three major problems were assessed in terms of change-potential scores and prioritized as follows: (1) permanent placement, 24; (2) school placement, 23; (3) personal problems— (a) depression, 21; (b) poor self-esteem, 20; (c) identity confusion, 20; and (d) sexuality, 19.

D. Intervention

The types of interventions by the social worker were (1) direct work, (2) referral, and (3) teamwork. In addition to working directly with K and making a referral to the group home, the child-welfare worker continued as K's state social worker (the state maintained custody) and formed an action system (teamwork) with the administrator and other members of the staff of the group home. The social worker also participated in school conferences on K, thus forming an alliance with the teacher and social worker of the school. Prior to K's placement in her present group home, the social worker had also worked collaboratively with the staff at the shelter. The design that primarily depicts the interventions of the child-welfare worker is found in Figure 7.9.

The direct work with K was primarily to give her support as she carried out the tasks identified in the contracted plan (Table 6.7 in Chapter 6) and to discuss her adjustment in the group home and in school. Contracts with personnel from the group home and school were mainly for the purpose of monitoring K's adjustment and personal growth and to see if any additional services were needed.

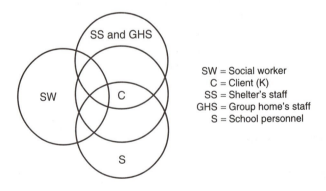

SW = Social worker
C = Client (K)
SS = Shelter's staff
GHS = Group home's staff
S = School personnel

FIGURE 7.9   Social Worker's Combined Interventions: Child Welfare

TABLE 7.1 Contracted Plan: State Department of Children's Services (Continued from Table 6.7)

Date Identified	Problem/ Need	Goal	Task	Contract	Date Antici- pated	Date Accom- plished
2/24	4. Need to remain in custody of state (abusive parents)	4. To obtain continuance of custody	1. Discuss.	1. Social worker and K	2/24	
			2. Prepare case summary.	2. Social worker	2/24	
			3. Petition court for continuance.	3. Social worker	3/1	
			4. Attend court hearing.	4. Social worker	3/30	

A month after K's placement in the group home, K and the social worker reviewed the reasons for K's commitment to the state. K understood the need for the social worker to petition the court for a continuance of her commitment. This need and its related goals and tasks were added to the planned contract, as recorded in Table 7.1. After K was in the group home for three months, the social worker and K evaluated the progress that had been made.

II. Field Area: Gerontology

A. Agency: Seaside Nursing Home
B. Client System

Mrs. J, an 80-year-old Portuguese woman, is in a skilled-nursing facility. (For additional background information, see Chapter 4, Engagement in Micro, Mezzo, and Macro Practice in Diverse Field Areas, II. Gerontology.)

C. Summary of Preceding Stages

The problems, goals, and tasks identified during engagement, data collection, and assessment are indicated in the contracted plan found in Table 6.9 in Chapter 6. During assessment, problems were prioritized as follows: (1) unfamiliarity with staff and resources of the home, (2) fighting with nurses over bath, (3) seclusiveness (not leaving room), (4) calling residents names, and (5) cultural isolation.

D. Intervention

Interventions by the social worker in this case were (1) direct work with the client through twice a week sessions and (2) teamwork with the nursing-home staff (nurses, program planner, recreational staff, volunteer director, and a volunteer) as well as with the pastor of the church Mrs. J attended before hospitalization. The designs that demonstrate these primary interventions of the social worker are found in Figures 7.10 and 7.11.

Through working with the church pastor, members of his congregation who knew Mrs. J began to visit her and to take her out to special church celebrations (a

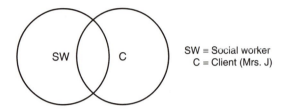

FIGURE 7.10   Direct Intervention: Gerontology

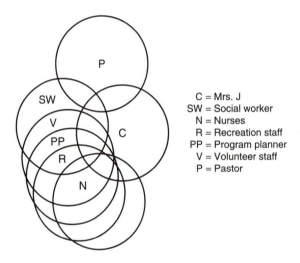

FIGURE 7.11   Teamwork: Gerontology

concert and the Christmas prayer service). Mrs. J was extremely happy to have them visit her and take her out to church activities. She also began to attend Bible services held in the nursing home. At first, she went with the social worker; later, she would go with other residents. Mrs. J began to carry on conversations with other residents at her dining-room table and on her corridor. She became friendly with her roommate, and they would go together to entertainments put on by the recreation department at the home.

Eventually, a Portuguese-speaking volunteer began to visit Mrs. J. This young woman came only three times before she dropped out of the volunteer program. The worker continued to try to locate Mrs. J's family members but was unsuccessful. If family members had been reached, they would probably have been target systems, and the social worker's indirect intervention would be depicted as shown in Figure 7.12. If Mrs. J's children had been responsive to the social worker's efforts and asked for the social worker's help, they would have become an extended part of the client system (Figure 7.10). If they joined with the

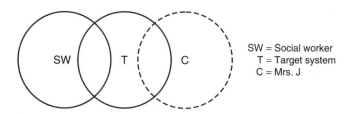

FIGURE 7.12   Indirect Intervention: Gerontology

social worker and the home in providing support for their mother, they would be seen as constituent members of the action system and perceived by the social worker and the staff as team members in collaborative effort for goal attainment (Figure 7.11).

  E. **Charted Progress**

  As the tasks of the contract were executed, the social worker recorded their completion by indicating the dates of accomplishment on the contracted plan. Visits by members of her former church were also recorded in the task column (see Table 7.2).

III. **Field Area: Public Social Welfare**

  A. **Agency: State Social Services**
  B. **Client System**

  Mr. and Mrs. P and their two children (2 and 4 years old) are in need of housing (emergency and long-term) and food (emergency and supply until AFDC payment). (For additional background information, see Chapter 4, Engagement in Micro, Mezzo, and Macro Practice in Diverse Field Areas, III. Public Social Welfare.)

  C. **Summary of Preceding Stages**

  The problems, goals, and tasks contracted as the social worker and Mr. and Mrs. P moved quickly (crisis situation) through the stages of engagement, data collection, and assessment are indicated in Table 6.11 in Chapter 6. The problems and needs of the family were prioritized as follows: (1) food—emergency food, (2) housing—temporary shelter, (3) food supply until AFDC payment, and (4) long-term housing.

  D. **Intervention**

  The types of intervention by the social worker were (1) referral, (2) direct interventions, and (3) teamwork. The social worker placed the family at Center City Motor Inn on the same day that they arrived at the agency. The family rejected the options of Salvation Army (mother and father would have been placed in separate facilities) and the City Hotel (disliked the location). Before going to the Motor Inn, the social worker took the family to the Good News Soup Kitchen for a meal and picked up a bag of groceries at the Center Churches Food Bank.

TABLE 7.2 Contracted Plan: Seaside Nursing Home (Continued from Table 6.9)

Date Identified	Problem/ Need	Goal	Task	Contract	Date Anticipated	Date Accomplished
9/27	1. Unfamiliarity with staff and resources of nursing home	1. To get to know the staff and resources of the nursing home	1. Meet twice a week with social worker.	1. Social worker and Mrs. J	10/4 and every Tuesday and Thursday	10/4, 10/9, 10/11, 10/16, 10/18, 10/23, 10/25, 10/30
			2. Meet with program planner.	2. Social worker, Mrs. J, and program planner	10/16	11/1, 11/6, 11/8, 11/13, 11/15, 11/20, 11/22, 10/27; 12/6, 12/11, 12/13
			3. Meet with a person from recreation staff.	3. Social worker, Mrs. J, and recreation-staff person	10/23	10/23
10/2	2. Fighting with nurses over bath	2. To work out bath schedule with nurses	1. Meet with head nurse to discuss bath schedule.	1. Mrs. J and head nurse	10/16	10/16
9/25	3. Seclusiveness: not leaving room alone	3a. To leave room alone (at least once a day)	1. Walk down to nursing station alone at least once a day.	1. Mrs. J	10/25 and each day thereafter	10/26; 11/6, 11/14, 11/20; 12/3 12/5, 12/12, 12/15

	Problem	Goal	Objectives	Persons responsible	Date started	Dates
		b. To attend a house activity (at least once a week)	1. Go to a house activity, program, or meeting (at least once a week).	1. Social worker or staff member and Mrs. J first two times	Starting week of 10/22	10/24, 12/30
				2. Mrs. J with residents each week thereafter	Starting week of 11/5	11/5, 11/12, 11/21, 11/28; 12/3 12/7, 12/12, 12/17
10/2	Calling residents names	4. To stop calling residents names	1. Stop name calling.	1. Mrs. J	10/16 and thereafter	10/16 until 10/20 (argument 10/21) and thereafter
			2. Say "hello" to residents.	2. Mrs. J	10/16 and thereafter	
9/25	Cultural isolation	5. To share culture with others	1. Meet director of volunteers.	1. Mrs. J, social worker, and director of volunteers	10/25	10/25
			2. Visit with Portuguese volunteer.	2. Mrs. J and volunteer	?	11/13, 11/20, 11/30
			3. Visit with pastor of church.	3. Mrs. J and pastor	?	11/14, 11/20, 11/30
			4. Visit with member of church.	4. Mrs. J, pastor, and congregation	11/20	11/30
			5. Go off grounds to attend church activity.	5. Mrs. J and congregation (Mr. and Mrs. T)	12/4, 12/17	12/4, 12/17

While at the motel, Mrs. P asked the social worker to try to get a medical card for her to take the children to the health center for a checkup. The social worker learned that the medical card was being processed at the central office and that it would take another eight days to arrive. The social worker wrote a letter to the health center, verifying the status of the P family. The letter was cosigned by the family's income-maintenance technician. Medical transportation was requested and provided for Mr. and Mrs. P and the children to go to the health center.

Mr. and Mrs. P did not actively search for permanent living quarters. They said that they didn't think they liked the locations of the apartments listed in the paper. The social worker offered to drive them to look at places, but they only went to two places with him. By the end of 10 days, the social worker stressed that their time was running out, and the Ps requested an extension of time. The application for an extension was denied, and the Ps asked for a fair hearing. They were again denied at the hearing and told that they would have to leave the motel by the following Monday. When Monday came, the Ps informed the social worker that they had located an apartment and requested help with moving their furniture from Mrs. P's father's house to the new apartment. After the family got the three required moving estimates, their moving expenses were covered through the Income Maintenance Department.

In their new apartment, the family requested help with obtaining fuel assistance. The social worker informed them that they needed to keep their fuel bills and showed them how to apply for assistance. Their AFDC check was detained because of the address change, and the social worker hand-delivered the check and food stamps.

The family had a problem with the refrigerator and asked the social worker to help them obtain funding to have it repaired. The social worker suggested that they try the Salvation Army, which might pay for new parts. The social worker learned later that the Ps received a new refrigerator and that this was handled through the income-maintenance technician. Mr. P asked if the social worker thought he should reapply to social security for Supplemental Security Income benefits. The social worker inquired about the procedure for reapplication and encouraged Mr. P to begin the process.

Mrs. P asked if the social worker knew of any place where the family could go to receive a Thanksgiving basket. Mr. P also wondered if there was any place where he could get Christmas presents for the children. The social worker inquired and informed Mr. P that baskets were being given by several local churches and that the Salvation Army had children's gifts.

At one point earlier, when it seemed that the Ps were not going to find housing, the social worker had explored the process for referring the family to the Protective Services Department. It appeared that placement of the children might be needed until housing for the family was located. Fortunately, this was not necessary.

In the case of the P family, a number of resources were mobilized by the B.S.W. worker. The social worker went with the Ps to obtain food and shelter. Ini-

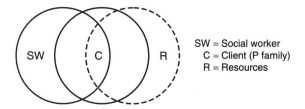

FIGURE 7.13   **Referral: Public Social Welfare**

tial contacts were made by the social worker for the Ps with the fuel-assistance program, social security office, medical transportation services, and Salvation Army (Figure 7.13).

In addition to referral, the social worker maintained ongoing direct intervention with the family for three months (Figure 7.14). Throughout this period, the social worker engaged in teamwork with the income-maintenance technician and with Mr. P's psychiatrist. Contact with the income-maintenance technician averaged once a week. The social worker spoke with the psychiatrist on five different occasions. These team efforts (Figure 7.15) provided the family with

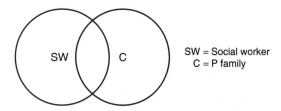

FIGURE 7.14   **Direct Intervention: Public Social Welfare**

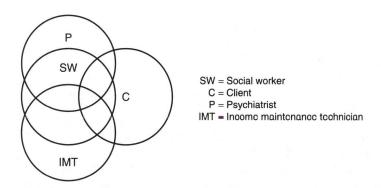

FIGURE 7.15   **Teamwork: Public Social Welfare**

coordinated services and offered the service providers an opportunity for shared service delivery.

E. Charted Progress

As various interventions were identified and enacted, the social worker recorded them, along with the dates of task accomplishment, on the contracted plan. After the Ps were placed in temporary shelter, the goal of locating a long-term residence took longer to accomplish than anticipated. The efforts to obtain a time extension for temporary placement were also recorded, as were additional problems and needs that surfaced. Goals and contracts for each new problem were developed with the Ps and charted on the contracted plan (see Table 7.3).

As indicated in the table, task 3 (move to new apartment) for problem 4 (housing—long-term) was not accomplished until 11/7, even though the anticipated date was "not later than 10/12." The additional needs of a medical exam for the children (including transportation), fuel assistance, AFDC check delivery, refrigerator repair, Thanksgiving baskets, and Christmas presents for the children were also listed and contracted.

IV. Field Area: Community Services

A. Agency: Clayton Neighborhood House

B. Client System

Four Hispanic families are without heating in their apartments on the second floor of 33 L Street. (For more background information, see Chapter 4, Engagement in Micro, Mezzo, and Macro Practice in Diverse Field Areas, IV. Community Services.)

C. Summary of Preceding Stages

The problem, goal, and contracted tasks developed by the social worker and the community of residents in earlier stages are outlined in Table 6.12 in Chapter 6. In addition to the need for heating in their apartments, the families recognized that they had a communication problem with their landlord. They were not, however, interested in trying to find ways to improve communication with him at this time.

D. Intervention

The interventions of the social worker were both direct and indirect. The social worker met with the residents directly to plan and monitor change. She also served as their advocate through indirect work with Mr. X, the landlord. Designs depicting the social worker's intervention are found in Figures 7.16 and 7.17.

When the social worker returned to meet with the residents on the day after she contacted the landlord, she found that their apartments were heated. She had brought thermometers with her for each apartment. They registered 68°. The residents expressed gratitude and hoped that the heating would continue throughout the winter. The social worker told the group about her conversation with the landlord. They admitted that they didn't really know the man but continued to be afraid to have contact with him. They agreed to monitor the heating in their apartments by checking their thermometers each day. They would meet with the social worker in one week to report on their findings.

TABLE 7.3 Contracted Plan: State Social Services (Continued from Table 6.11)

Date Identified	Problem/ Need	Goal	Task	Contract	Date Anticipated	Date Accomplished
9/28	4. Housing—long term	4. To move into an apartment for long-term residence	1. Explore resources.	1. Mr. and Mrs. P and social worker	9/29	9/30
			2. Contact resources.	2. Mr. and Mrs. P	9/29	9/30, 10/10
			3. Move.	3. The Ps	10/12	11/7
			4. Update.	4. Social worker, Mr. P's doctor, income-maintenance technician	9/29 and weekly	9/29; 10/6, 13, 20, 27; 11/3, 10, 17
			5. Request extension for temporary placement.	5. Social worker	10/11	10/11
			6. Fair hearing.	6. Mr. and Mrs. P, social worker, and department board	10/31	10/31
			7. Request moving assistance.	7. Social worker	11/5	11/5
9/28	5. Poor money management					
10/1	6. Medical exam for children	6. To have children examined at health center	1. Find out about medical care.	1. Social worker	10/2	10/2
10/1			2. See if health center will accept letter of authorization.	2. Social worker	10/2	10/2
			3. Write letter.	3. Social worker and income-maintenance technician	10/5	10/5
			4. Make appointment.	4. Mrs. P	10/5	10/8
			5. Make arrangements for medical transport.	5. Social worker and income-maintenance technician	10/8	10/8
			6. Take children to health center.	6. Mr. and Mrs. P and medical transport service	10/12	10/12

(continued)

241

TABLE 7.3 Continued

Date Identified	Problem/ Need	Goal	Task	Contract	Date Anticipated	Date Accomplished
11/14	7. Need for fuel assistance	7. To obtain fuel assistance	1. Explore resources. 2. Discuss. 3. Fill out application. 4. Follow up if necessary.	1. Social worker 2. Social worker and Ps 3. Ps with social worker's help 4. Mr. P	11/15 11/16 11/20 11/26	11/15 11/16 11/20
11/14	8. Check and food stamps	8. To receive AFDC check and food stamps	1. To find out about delay in delivery. 2. Get check at central office. 3. Deliver check to Ps.	1. Social worker 2. Social worker 3. Social worker	11/14 11/15 11/16	11/14 11/15 11/16
11/20	9. Malfunctioning refrigerator	9. To fix refrigerator	1. Get estimates on repairs needed. 2. Explore funding resources. 3. Contact Salvation Army. 4. Have refrigerator repaired. 5. Send bill to Salvation Army.	1. Mr. P 2. Social worker 3. Mr. P 4. Mr. P 5. Mr. P	11/20 11/20 11/22 11/23 11/26	11/20 (Problem withdrawn 12/4—new refrigerator)
11/20	10. Supplemental Security Income	10. To receive Supplemental Security Income	1. Contact social security office. 2. Discuss. 3. Complete application. 4. Follow-up call. 5. Go for interview.	1. Social worker 2. Social worker and Ps 3. Mr. P 4. Mr. P 5. Mr. P	11/21 11/22 11/22 11/26 11/27	11/21 11/22
11/20	11. Thanksgiving food basket	11. To receive a food basket	1. Explore resources. 2. Contact churches. 3. Got for basket.	1. Social worker 2. Mr. P 3. Mr. P	11/21 11/22 11/24	11/21
11/27	12. Gifts for children	12. To obtain Christmas gifts for children	1. Explore resources. 2. Contact resources. 3. Pick up gifts.	1. Social worker 2. Mr. P 3. Mr. P	11/28 11/29 12/5	11/28

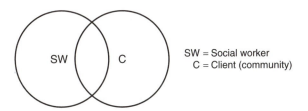

FIGURE 7.16   Direct Intervention: Community Services

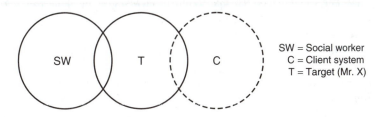

FIGURE 7.17   Indirect Intervention: Community Services

TABLE 7.4   Contracted Plan: Clayton Neighborhood House (Continued from Table 6.12)

Date Identified	Problem/ Need	Goal	Task	Contract	Date Anticipated	Date Accomplished
			4. Monitor heat daily in each apartment.	4. One person from each family (Mr. T, Mrs. V, Mr. A, and CR)	12/5 to 12/12	
			5. Meet to review findings.	5. Social worker and residents	12/12	

E. Charted Progress

As the social worker and the residents planned additional tasks, the social worker recorded the extended plan by adding items to the "task," "contract," and "date anticipated" columns of the contracted plan (see Table 7.4).

V. Field Area: Education

A. Agency: Keeney Elementary School
B. Client System

Jim G is an 8-year-old third-grader with problems at school and at home directly related to his parents' problem with their marital relationship. (For further background information, see Chapter 4, Engagement in Micro, Mezzo, and Macro Practice in Diverse Field Areas, V. Education.)

C. **Summary of Preceding Stages**

The problems, goals, and contracted tasks identified during preceding stages are outlined in Table 6.14 of Chapter 6. The two primary tasks prioritized and contracted for Mr. and Mrs. G were (1) getting Jim to school on time each day and (2) going together for marital counseling. Jim's poor school performance and his sleeping problem were seen as reactions to Mr. and Mrs. G's quarreling and, especially, to Mrs. G's threat that she was going to leave her husband and children. The social worker's primary contracted tasks included meeting with Jim, his teacher, and his parents regarding Jim's school performance and general progress.

D. **Intervention**

The interventions of the social worker may be identified as (1) direct (Jim; Mr. and Mrs. G; Jim and his parents) (see Figure 7.18); (2) referral (marital counseling for Mr. and Mrs. G) (see Figure 7.19); and (3) teamwork (social worker and Jim's teacher, working with Mr. and Mrs. G to help Jim) (see Figure 7.20). The social worker also attended a student study team conference on Jim with several members of the school faculty (principal, nurse, classroom teacher, learning-disabilities teacher, social service supervisor, social worker). Jim's parents had been invited to this conference but they said that they couldn't attend because they were working.

During their meeting with the social worker at school, Mr. and Mrs. G invited Jim to join them before the end of the meeting. At this time, Mr. and Mrs. G informed Jim that they knew that he had been worried about them because he

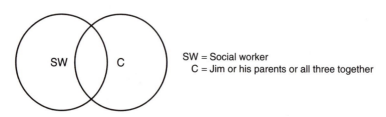

SW = Social worker
C = Jim or his parents or all three together

FIGURE 7.18   Direct Intervention: Education

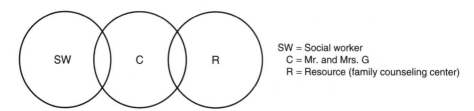

SW = Social worker
C = Mr. and Mrs. G
R = Resource (family counseling center)

FIGURE 7.19   Referral: Education

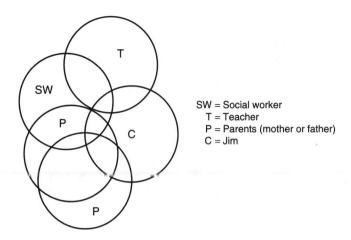

SW = Social worker
T = Teacher
P = Parents (mother or father)
C = Jim

FIGURE 7.20   Teamwork: Education

had heard them arguing. They admitted to Jim that they had been having some problems but assured him that they were going to get help themselves so they could learn to get along better with each other. They stressed that it was not Jim's problem and that he really didn't have to worry about them. They also assured Jim that neither one of them was thinking of giving up or leaving home. Jim was encouraged to try to do better in school. They said they knew it must have been hard for Jim. Mr. G said he knew it was hard enough for Jim to be "a little man in a big world," and that Jim didn't have to take onto this shoulders the problem of his mother and father. As he hugged his parents, Jim said he would try to work harder in school.

Before leaving this interview, it was agreed by all that the social worker would continue to see Jim twice a week and that the follow-up contacts between the social worker and Mr. and Mrs. G would be by telephone for two weeks. These would be followed by a home visit by the social worker, at which time they all would consider termination of planned contacts if progress was apparent.

In talking with Mrs. G on the telephone the following week, the social worker learned that Mr. G had made the appointment and that Mr. and Mrs. G had begun counseling sessions at the family counseling center. Mrs. G said that Jim still wanted a light left in his room at night but he didn't need to have his mother with him. He settled for a small night-light.

Jim's teacher reported that Jim was beginning to look happier and to show more interest in his schoolwork. The social worker continued to meet with Jim in her office twice a week, and Jim was interested in playing age-appropriate games. They drew up ongoing evaluation graphs to chart Jim's progress in school (to be presented in the next chapter).

E. Charted Progress

As tasks contracted in the plan developed by Mr. and Mrs. G, Jim, and the social worker (Table 6.14 in Chapter 6) were carried out, the social worker recorded the date they were completed in the "date accomplished" column of the contracted plan. At the last meeting of the social worker with Mr. and Mrs. G in their home, the social worker shared the updated plan with them as they reviewed and evaluated progress.

VI. Field Area: Corrections

A. Agency: Juvenile Court
B. Client System

Seven male adolescents, age 14, are on probation for burglary, theft of automobiles, or minor larceny (shoplifting) and are attending weekly group sessions led by co-workers from Juvenile Court. (For further background information, see Chapter 4, Engagement in Micro, Mezzo, and Macro Practice in Diverse Field Areas, VI. Corrections.)

C. Summary of Preceding Stages

The problems, goals, and contracted tasks identified in earlier stages are outlined in Table 6.15 in Chapter 6. The youths prioritized their problems as (1) law breaking leading to probation, (2) bad tempers, and (3) lack of understanding of the changes they were experiencing. Group members admitted that they didn't think much of themselves (low self-worth) and that they had problems with their parents (parent-son conflicts), but they didn't appear interested in working directly on these problems. In developing the contracted plan in the group, the need for ongoing evaluation instruments was recognized, and graphs were developed to monitor group attendance, group participation by members, and members' behavior at school and at home.

D. Intervention

The interventions of the B.S.W. worker were mainly varied types of teamwork. The social worker and her co-leader met with the seven youths in weekly group meetings, and the social workers engaged in ongoing communication with each other as team members. They met at least twice a week to discuss the process, problems, and progress of the group and any developments that were taking place with individual members. The social workers went together to visit every home of the group participants. They divided the task of visiting the schools (the B.S.W. went to four schools, the M.S.W. to three) and the tasks of receiving weekly reports from parents and school social workers. The approach used with teachers and parents also highlighted a team effort as they worked together to help the youths accomplish their goals.

The primary teamwork designs to depict the interventions of the B.S.W. worker are found in Figures 7.21 and 7.22.

After charting progress in group attendance, group participation, and school and home behavior, the group began to focus on their problem with their tempers. All saw a relationship between this problem and the problems they were having at home and at school. They agreed to take home an index card each week, and every time they lost their tempers, they would put a check on it. If they for-

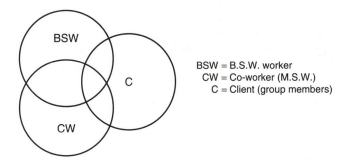

FIGURE 7.21   **Social Worker and Co-Worker Teamwork: Corrections**

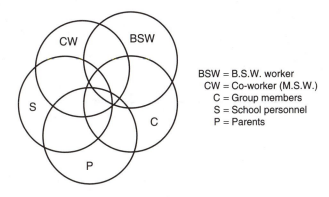

FIGURE 7.22   **Extended Teamwork: Corrections**

got during the day to check the card, they would try to remember the incidents and to mark the card each night before going to bed. They would bring the card back each week and report the total number of checks they had for the week to the group. At the meeting, members entered their total number of checks for the week on a weekly chart (Figure 7.23). The group members said that they also wanted to check on the other side of the card every time they felt like losing their tempers but didn't. The cards were labeled on each side "temper loss" or "temper control." A matching weekly chart was designed to indicate temper control (Figure 7.24). During meetings, the group also discussed ways to let out anger that are acceptable and not seen as a loss of temper. For example, some said they find it helpful when they start to feel angry if they can get out and play ball. Others suggested turning on the radio and singing, going for walks, or finding a friend to talk with. One youth said he learned that taking deep breaths and thinking about something that makes him happy help. They joked about what he might be thinking.

After six group meetings, A was picked up by the police and charged with breaking into a store (fifth time). He was found guilty and sent to a correctional

Weeks

Names	1	2	3	4	5	6	7	8	9	10	11	12	13	14	15	16
J																
MK																
T																
ML																
B																
A																
C																

FIGURE 7.23   Temper Loss

Weeks

Names	1	2	3	4	5	6	7	8	9	10	11	12	13	14	15	16
J																
MK																
T																
ML																
B																
A																
C																

FIGURE 7.24   Temper Control

institution for six months. J and T often came late to the meetings and continued to say they came only because they had to.

As the group began to work on goal 3 (to learn about "changes"), a topic or issue of interest was selected each week by the members, and a plan was developed to study the issue the following week. Topics studied included living in prison, human sexuality and birth control, vocational training and jobs, managing money, and cooking. Films and guest speakers were used to provide information for discussion. The group also went on a trip to visit a vocational-training school.

E. Charted Progress

Each week, as additional tasks were planned by the group, the social worker would record them on the contracted plan. For example, the additional tasks that were developed for goal 2 (to control tempers) and for goal 3 (to learn about "changes") were added, as outlined in Table 7.5.

TABLE 7.5 Contracted Plan: Juvenile Court (Continued from Table 6.15)

Date Identified	Problem/ Need	Goal	Task	Contract	Date Anticipated	Date Accomplished
10/1	2. Bad tempers	2. To control tempers in school, home, and neighborhood	1. Discuss the problem of dealing with anger.	1. Social workers and members	10/22	10/22
			2. Notice when angry.	2. Individual members	10/22 and each day	10/22-ongoing
			3. Find acceptable outlet.	3. Individual members	10/22 and each day	
			4. Keep track of successes and slip-ups on card.	4. Individual members	10/22 and each day	
			5. Report to group and chart number.	5. Individual members	10/29 and each Monday at group	
10/1	3. Need to understand "changes" of teenagers	3. To learn about some of the "changes" (including becoming independent, sex and birth control, and job training)	1. Select first topic—life in prison.	1. Group and members	10/22	10/22
			2. Plan program.	2. Group members	10/23	
			3. Call Prison Association for speaker.	3. Social worker	10/23	
			4. Have a talk and discussion.	4. Guest and group	10/29	

VII. Field Area: Homeless Shelter

A. Agency: West End Community Shelter

B. Client System

José Romano, a 37-year-old Hispanic male, is homeless and HIV positive. He has no family or close friends. He was referred to the shelter by the Department of Social Services. (For additional information, see Chapter 4, Engagement in Micro, Mezzo, and Macro Practice in Diverse Field Areas: VII. Homeless Shelter.)

C. Summary of Preceding Stages

During engagement, Mr. R shared his history of past drug addiction and divorce. He worked out a plan with the worker that involved his going to the free health clinic located near the shelter. He also planned to attend a local church service. Data collection continued as the social worker and Mr. R began to implement the contracted plan. Mr. R's illness was diagnosed as slowly moving into the second stage of the virus. He was having night sweats and shortness of breath.

D. Intervention

Mr. R and the social worker carried out the "tasks" of the contracted plan. The social worker used direct intervention and referral throughout the process (see Figures 7.25 and 7.26). After the first week, both Mr. R and the social worker recognized his need for additional social supports. Mr. R did not have a car or any money for public transportation. The void in social supports was added to the list of "problems/needs" in the contracted plan (see Table 7.6). Mr. R agreed to contact Harmony, Inc., a service that offered a buddy system and transportation for persons with HIV or AIDS. Mr. R was assigned a buddy who would visit him at the shelter occasionally and take him to the Harmony support group once a week.

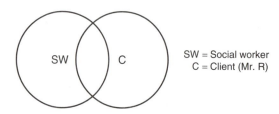

FIGURE 7.25   Direct Intervention: Homeless Shelter

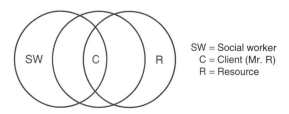

FIGURE 7.26   Direct Intervention: Homeless Shelter

TABLE 7.6 Contracted Plan: West End Community Shelter (Added to from Table 6.17)

Date Identified	Problem/ Need	Goal	Task	Contract	Date Anticipated	Date Accomplished
5/7	1. Homeless— short term	1. To find emer- gency shelter	1. Enroll in shelter.	1. Mr. R & social worker	5/8	5/8
5/8	2. Spiritual void	2. To reunite with church	1. Go to service.	1. Mr. R	5/10	5/10
5/8	3. Lack of knowledge, re: HIV	3. To gain information	1. Review information at shelter. 2. Go to free clinic, ask for help.	1. Social worker & Mr. R 2. Mr. R	5/9	5/9
5/8	4. No income/ job	4. To earn income	1. Search for job. 2. Apply for job. 3. Start job. 4. Seek SS/public assistance.	1. Mr. R & social worker 2. Mr. R 3. Mr. R 4. Mr. R	5/9 5/15 5/20 Depends on illness	5/17 5/19 5/21
5/7	5. No housing after 60 days	5. To locate residence	1. Look for apartment or home for persons with AIDS. 2. Get on waiting list for home for persons with AIDS.	1. Social worker & Mr. R 2. Mr. R	5/8 5/11	 6/24
5/8	6. HIV positive	6. To obtain medical care	1. Make appointment. 2. Go to free clinic. 3. Continue treatment.	1. Social worker & Mr. R 2. Mr. R 3. Mr. R	5/8 5/9 Next appoint- ments	5/8 5/9 5/19
5/12	7. Social void	7. To obtain social support	1. Contact Harmony, Inc. 2. Meet with staff person. 3. Meet "buddy."	1. Mr. R 2. Mr. R 3. Mr. R	5/12 5/13 5/20	5/12 5/13 5/20

> *On the days when Mr. R wanted a ride to church because he didn't feel well enough to walk, he was able to call his buddy for transportation. While attending a church service, Mr. R met a man from his hometown in Puerto Rico. The man told Mr. R that they were looking for additional help at the chicken farm where he worked. He agreed to pick up Mr. R and take him to see the farm supervisor. Mr. R was hired and worked for four weeks before he had to stop because of his illness. He then began working part time. On days when he felt able, he would call the supervisor to see if he could work. Mr. R applied for residence at Hope Home.*

E. **Charted Progress**

> *As planned tasks were operationalized, the social worker would indicate on the contract the dates of accomplishment. She shared the process of charting progress with Mr. R to promote his sense of control over what was happening in his life.*

Conclusion

In this chapter, the four major types of general interventions were presented. Designs to depict each type of intervention, along with case examples, were given. A number of techniques were identified, and their application to systems of different sizes was demonstrated. The use of these techniques throughout the General Method was also considered.

As the generalist interacts with a system for goal accomplishment, tasks are identified and implemented. The tasks of the social worker may be categorized individually or collectively as direct interventions, indirect interventions, information and referral, and case management and teamwork. While working in a helping capacity with one system over a period of time, a social worker may use more than one intervention. In addition to direct work, for example, the generalist may need to refer a system to an outside resource and collaborate with the resource in a team effort for integrated service delivery. Any individual task may in itself reflect a combination of interventions. For example, a social worker may meet with collaborating resources (teamwork), a client system (direct intervention), and a target system (indirect intervention) at the same time.

In each intervention, a social worker utilizes knowledge, values, and skills from the foundation for generalist practice. The art of generalist practice is highlighted in the careful selection and application of interventions and techniques at the appropriate time and in a manner that is sensitive to human diversity.

Throughout the General Method, social worker and system of contact are charting progress and monitoring change. As each task is carried out during intervention, an appraisal is made of its effectiveness. When all the contracted tasks have been accomplished, a formal period of evaluation takes place. In the next chapter, focus will be on the fifth stage of the General Method: evaluation.

CHAPTER

8   Evaluation

Measure, evaluate, estimate, and appraise your results, in some form, in any terms that rest on something beyond faith, assertion, and "illustrative case" (Cabot, 1931, as cited in Bloom, Fischer, & Orme, 1999, p. xiii). As one of the basic prerequisites in helping people to help themselves, social workers are expected to justify the efficiency and effectiveness of their service efforts and intervention endeavors. *Effectiveness* is concerned with the accomplishment of client system goals, whereas *efficiency* seeks to assess the cost expenditures of services and interventions in money, time, and other resources. In general, the evaluation stage is a time of studying and measuring the results of the actions taken during intervention. It is expected to (1) increase social workers' knowledge base, (2) facilitate informed decisions about service quality, (3) demonstrate accountability, and (4) determine that client goals are being met (Gabor & Grinnell, 1994).

Reasons for Evaluation

Ongoing Assessment Process and Outcome

Although the evaluation stage follows the intervention stage, evaluation is a continuous endeavor throughout the problem-solving process of the General Method. In a sense, the evaluation process commences during the engagement stage when the social worker and the client system begin exploring problems and goals, collecting data about the preliminary state of events, and evaluating the initial severity of the concerns presented. During assessment, evaluation becomes formalized in the client system contract, which records the social worker's and the client system's agreement to pursue particular goals while employing specific interventive strategies. The client system and the social worker agree to track and measure any changes throughout the planned intervention process. The actual evaluation stage, which follows the intervention stage, seeks to assess client system changes in their entirety. The client system and the social worker become continually involved in an evaluation of their experiences in trying to produce change. Their evaluation may indicate a need to redefine the problem (or define an entirely new problem), reassess goals and objectives (or develop new ones), reassess goal-related activities, or alter the intervention plan. Thus, evaluation is not only a linear process with a beginning and end but also a cyclical process that continues throughout the problem-solving approach of the General Method:

Engagement	The client system and the social worker develop a preliminary contract for problem and goal identification.
Data Collection	With the client system's agreement, the social worker gathers information to facilitate problem and goal prioritization. They decide whether it is possible and feasible to collect baseline information for each goal chosen.
Assessment	The social worker and the client system define the problem in view of the client system's needs, strengths, and resources. They choose goals, objectives, and tasks. They select criteria and make a time plan for goal accomplishment. The social worker presents options for intervention strategies and their potential consequences. They make a plan for evaluation, agree, and sign a contract.
Intervention	The client system and the social worker participate in contracted intervention activities. They track changes, monitor goal accomplishment, and discuss whether desired changes are occurring or whether intervention needs to be modified.
Evaluation	The social worker and the client system analyze goal accomplishment. They discuss the meaning of observed and measured changes. As goals are accomplished, the

| | client system's problems, strengths, and intervention strategies are reassessed and recontracted with three anticipated potential outcomes: (1) the client system being satisfied with goal accomplishment and deciding to move toward termination, (2) the client system desiring further change and retaining agency services but with modified or intensified interventions, or (3) the client system needing specialized services and being referred. |

Termination The social worker and the client system revisit the change process and the client system's progress toward goals for the final time. They discuss maintenance of gains, possible follow-up, and plan for the last contact.

Quality Assurance

Knowing how to help requires social workers to possess both relevant knowledge and practice skills. For example, in child welfare, achieving permanency for children who have been removed from their homes requires knowledge and practice skills that are specific enough to address the needs of the individual child who has been removed for reasons of child abuse yet broad enough to address the various needs of most children who lack a permanent home. A central reason for doing an evaluation is to maintain service quality in a way that informs not only the client system receiving services but also practitioners, program directors, funders, policymakers, and the general public. For example, client systems typically want to know that they have, indeed, benefitted by their program participation and whether the obtained services were worth the time, effort, and money expended. Practitioners want to know which interventions are likely to help with what types of problems for which clients, under what conditions, and with what kind of intervention methodology. Program directors want to know how well specified interventions serve particular client systems and whether they are effective and cost efficient. Policymakers, governmental bodies, and other administrative groups want to know comparative information about overall program efficiency and cost effectiveness in serving various client systems.

Accountability

Another reason for evaluation is to demonstrate accountability in meeting client system needs through the appropriate kind and amount of service and in assuring that specified client systems are the appropriate beneficiaries of the service delivered. Evaluation is often used to document that service funds are being appropriately spent. In addition, evaluation may be established to assure that delivery of services follows the relevant laws concerning client confidentiality, privacy of records, occupational and health safety, and affirmative action.

Goal Attainment

Last but not least, evaluation allows the social worker to document the attainment of the client system's goals. Client systems want to know if things have changed for the better by having their goals met through the General Method.

Types of Evaluation

The social worker may plan a practice evaluation that calls for an assessment and measurement of the intervention and its impact on a specific client system (be it an individual, family, group, organization, or community). This process may include a *formative evaluation*, which is used to inform and guide practice decisions throughout the service offered. As such, evaluation is a tool for ongoing monitoring of the intervention and changing it as necessary. In the General Method, a formative evaluation typically examines one client system at a time through monitoring changes before, during, and after the intervention. Practice evaluation also includes a *summative evaluation*, in which the practitioner attempts to assess client system outcomes while identifying the factors (or specified reasons) that contributed to the success (or failure) of the intervention. In the General Method, a summative evaluation examines one client system at a time, uses a more experimental research structure in its design and measurement approach, and is concerned about reasons for final outcome results.

The social worker may also pursue *program evaluation* to assess the effectiveness and efficiency of the entire program serving a number of client systems, be they individuals, families, groups, organizations, or communities. Program evaluation usually includes both formative and summative components. Formative program evaluation is used for assessing an ongoing program and changing aspects of its functioning to better serve client systems in their environments. Summative program evaluation is pursued to document program results for program planning, a funding source, or the agency's board of directors.

In this chapter, a model is suggested in which research tools and procedures are used by the social worker in formative and summative (outcome) evaluation. In addition, a research tool for ongoing evaluation throughout the General Method is presented.

During the evaluation process, the generalist not only uses research skills such as data collection, measurement, and analysis but also relies on individualized criteria to fit the particular client system and his or her professional observation and judgment. The social worker bears in mind that using measurable goals and systematic procedures are important for good documentation and sound outcome evaluation. However, if the evaluation process becomes too technical or impersonal, the system of contact may lose interest and disengage from the process.

Typically, these evaluations utilize a blend of quantitative and qualitative methodologies and are exemplified in single-system designs (Bloom, Fischer, & Orme, 1999), goal attainment scales (Gabor & Grinnell, 1994; Shepard, 1997), and

other practice outcome inventories (Kirk, 1999). All of these approaches are readily found in various current social work research texts (such as Rubin & Babbie,
1997; York, 1998). In this chapter, however, a different model for evaluation will be
presented. It is similar to that of the previously mentioned approaches in that it
uses the concept of a baseline starting point, measures goal accomplishment, and
tracks practice outcomes along a graph. It differs from other approaches in that it
focuses mainly on descriptive analysis for gauging quantitative and qualitative
changes and is viewed as a guiding framework—a tool that reflects a balance
between research and practice techniques for evaluation in the General Method.

This approach, which was developed out of the evaluation procedures commonly used by generalist practitioners, includes:

- Specifying the client system's needs, problems, and goals in the context of
  their environment (e.g., their amount and severity)
- Prioritizing targets for intervention, including short- and long-term goals
- Developing a strategy for monitoring and evaluating outcomes (e.g., deter-
  mining how a change in a client system's targeted goal would be known and
  judged as acceptable
- Contracting with the client system about who will do what, where, when,
  how, and by when
- Selecting a qualitative or quantitative design or a mixed method design for
  evaluation that includes both qualitative and quantitative approaches
- Deciding whether baseline information is necessary and/or appropriate
- Collecting data
- Analyzing results by monitoring progress and assessing goal/outcome
  attainment
- Providing feedback and reevaluating client systems' contractual needs and
  satisfaction
- Planning for termination and/or follow-up services

Through the process of blending practice and research tasks, the General
Method evaluation framework places emphasis on objectifying information and
procedures and attempting to avoid biases. Evaluation that contains documented,
unbiased information is less deniable as a reality. Realizing the professional desire
to be scientific while at the same time being sensitive to each client system's needs
sets the stage for practice evaluation.

Goal Analysis

Developing a clear definition and description of the intervention goals is always
the essential first step in all forms of evaluation. The social worker has to help the
client system develop specific goals in the early phase of the change process
(through goal refinement in engagement, data collection, and assessment contract).
Otherwise, the social worker will not be able to measure the desired outcome

effects during the evaluation stage. Evaluation also always involves some type of measurement. The social worker has to select criteria by which to measure client system goal targets (e.g., client behaviors, group knowledge, and community beliefs) that are expected to change during the intervention. The social worker has to possess a knowledge of research that organizes measurable entities into *dependent variables* or goals (outcomes or targets). When deciding what procedures to use to measure change in a client system, the social worker needs to bear in mind the following research tenets (Bloom, Fischer, & Orme, 1999; Kerlinger & Lee, 2000):

- The procedure or specific measuring device sought should be *valid*. It should measure what it is believed to measure and not something else. If a standardized instrument is used, care needs to be taken to examine the instrument's reported validity and whether the instrument was intended for use with a particular client system. If a measuring device developed by the social worker or agency is used, expert judges should assess whether the instrument actually measures what it purports to measure prior to its use with client systems.
- The chosen procedure should be *reliable* or yield similar results when the measurement is repeated under similar circumstances. If a standardized instrument is used, care needs to be taken to examine the instrument's reported reliability (typically presented as a correlation coefficient). An instrument that is judged reasonably reliable should have achieved a reliability correlation coefficient of at least 0.70. A reliability of less than 0.70 is considered suspect, as it may produce inconsistent responses to the same questions under similar conditions.
- The procedures should be *brief* (15 to 20 minutes maximum time), *easy to use* by the client system, and not require a specialist for administration or interpretation.
- The procedure should be able to detect *relatively small levels of change* as well as differences in the types of change achieved.
- The procedure should be *nonreactive* (i.e., able to detect differences without modifying or influencing the phenomena being measured).
- The design of measuring should lend itself to *tracking, monitoring, and evaluating change* using single subject designs. If the ongoing measuring is too complicated because it takes too long or requires special knowledge and/or training, *pre- and posttest measurements* may be more useful.

It needs to be emphasized here that practice evaluation measures only those things that are relevant and central to the provision of service to client systems and to understanding what happened as a result of that service.

To begin the fifth stage of the General Method, the social worker asks the following question: Has the goal been accomplished? For every task or set of tasks, a goal was stated on the contracted plan. That goal related directly to the problem listed in the column that preceded it. If the goal has been accomplished, the problem should now be resolved or modified, depending on how the goal was originally stated.

To answer the basic question cited, an intensive consideration is made of the change or progress that has taken place since the beginning of the social worker–client system interaction. First, the starting point is recalled; the social worker and system of contact ask: What was the problem when we first met? The description that follows the starting point (which may be referred to as the *baseline*) should be as precise and factual as possible. For example, if the presenting problem was Mr. and Mrs. S's constant quarreling, the social worker will try to be more specific by recalling that Mrs. S said every time she and her husband spoke to each other, they quarreled and that this was at least six times a week. On the contract that was agreed to by both Mr. and Mrs. S, the stated goal read, "To be able to talk and to listen to each other without quarreling." The social worker and client system would therefore ask: Has the communication between Mr. and Mrs. S improved? Are they speaking together without quarreling? Can they go a whole week without quarreling?

Answers to such questions may be received from different sources. The primary respondents are the client system receiving service and the social worker. In addition, information for goal analysis may be requested from other knowledgeable resources, such as family members, teachers, employers, and others. If a social worker does not think that the perception of a system of contact joined with the observations of the social worker is sufficient, reliable, or accurate, then outsiders may be brought into the evaluation process. As with data collection in the second stage of the General Method, the use of outside resources during evaluation with client systems should be discussed with and be sanctioned by the clients prior to contacting the resources.

If the answer to the basic question of goal accomplishment is not a clear 100 percent yes, a study is made to determine to what extent the goal has been accomplished. Beginning at the baseline starting point, the question is asked: From where you started when we first had contact, how much closer to or further from the goal have you moved? A scale may be used to help the social worker and the client system become more specific in answering this question (see Figure 8.1). It is a nine-point bipolar scale with an equal number of categories for progression and for regression. The midpoint on the scale (0) indicates the starting point. Descriptive criteria for this point should indicate the problem that led to the stated goal under study. The extreme right of the scale is numbered +4, and the anchoring description for this point is 100 percent "goal accomplished." More specifically, this score indicates that the problem at the starting point has been eliminated or reduced, according to the way it is spelled out in the stated goal. Conversely, the opposite end of the scale is numbered –4, and the descriptive criterion is "goal given up," with no attainment. The intermediate points on either side of the 0 are balanced to reflect movement to a little, some, or a large extent better or worse than the starting point.

FIGURE 8.1   Goal-Accomplishment Scale

−4	−3	−2	−1	0	1	2	3	4
Goal given up	Large extent worse	Somewhat worse	Little worse than starting point	Starting point	Little better than starting point	Somewhat better	Large extent better	Goal accomplished

The number of scale points to be used depends on the individual goal in each situation. Sometimes the goal may be a single activity that cannot be broken down into a measurable sequence. For example, a goal may be to get food stamps for a family or tutoring for a child. It may be sufficient here to have a simple 3-point scale (−1 = goal given up, 0 = starting point, +1 = goal accomplished). If any movement, even slight, can be detected, it is important to have a scale that can show this. Too few scale points may prevent the recognition of some progress, which could increase hope and motivation. Even the identification of going backwards and a consideration of how the situation may end if regression continues may cause sufficient anxiety to promote greater effort and involvement.

With each individual situation, an attempt is made to use objective descriptors, including numbers or times and events. For example, in the situation presented earlier, the problem at the starting point was Mr. and Mrs. S's repeated quarreling whenever they tried to communicate (at least six times a week). The long-range goal was to have the couple speak and listen to each other without quarreling. During intervention, techniques were used to help them listen to each other and try to understand each other's viewpoints. A sensitivity to nonverbal communication was encouraged, and words were suggested to help them express their feelings. After the social worker and Mr. and Mrs. S worked together for the period of time indicated in the contracted plan, they began to evaluate goal accomplishment. The scale in Figure 8.2 was developed under the guidance of the social worker.

In finding regressive descriptors, the social worker and the client system discern what have been or could be ways in which the situation would grow worse than when the problem was first identified. In the case of Mr. and Mrs. S, they said that at one time they had started to physically fight, and they feared this might happen again. Therefore, the negative indicators reflect the typical pattern of regression for this system. If they had feared an increasing withdrawal from any interaction with each other, then withdrawal would be indicated in the negative descriptors.

What needs to be emphasized is that during the evaluation stage of the General Method, there must be an opportunity to identify possible deterioration as well as growth in a situation. Even with general intervention, the communication between Mr. and Mrs. S, for example, could have become worse than when they

FIGURE 8.2 Mr. and Mrs. S

-4	-3	-2	-1	0	+1	+2	+3	+4
Goal given up; injury and separation	Large extent worse; no communication without fighting	Somewhat worse; quarrels moving into physical fights half the time they talk	Little worse; quarrels moving into physical fights once or twice a week	Start; no communication without quarreling (at least six times a week)	Little better; communicating without quarreling once or twice a week	Somewhat better; communicating without quarreling half the time they talk	Large extent better; communicating without quarreling most of the time (may be one quarrel a week)	Goal accomplished; open communication without quarreling

first set the goal. The cause of this deterioration would need to be considered as the evaluation progresses. It could be that the intervention was inappropriate because the relationship was too pathological or because Mr. and Mrs. S lacked sufficient motivation or capacity to work on it. The regression in the relationship could be caused by other factors, including those outside of the social worker's control, such as influences from individuals or systems unknown to the social worker. Before asking why the goal has or has not been attained, however, social worker and client system need to take time to judge what movement, forward or backward, has taken place on the goal-accomplishment scale. After this appraisal, they proceed to an analysis of why they have arrived at the particular point on the scale. Here again, the contracted plan is a helpful guide to social worker and system of contact as they analyze causation.

Contract Review

An evaluation does not stop at this point, even when the first question in the process is answered with a 100 percent yes. Although a goal has been attained, it is important to find out why this has happened. The question to be asked is: Has the goal been accomplished through the planned interventions identified by social worker and client system in the contracted plan? An honest appraisal of causality can build a stronger working relationship, and it can give direction for further interactions between social worker and client system. It is possible that a goal's accomplishment is due to negative circumstances that may have to be addressed with a reformulation of goals. For example, a goal of getting someone off welfare may have been accomplished because the person was imprisoned rather than because of the interventions of the social worker. More immediate goals may emerge, such as providing care for the children of the person incarcerated. If it appears that the goal has been accomplished as a result of the tasks identified in the contracted plan, then social worker and client system may move on to other problems and goals, or they may move into the process of termination (to be developed in the next chapter).

If a goal has not been accomplished by the date anticipated for the completion of tasks in a plan, the question must be asked: Why not? Again, the response may point to some unexpected circumstances; for example, a death or sudden tragedy may have caused the failure in goal accomplishment. If such circumstances are not readily identifiable, the social worker and the client system begin a systematic review of the planned contract, starting with the last column on the right, to find out why the goal has not been attained. Why has the goal not been accomplished? is the obvious question, but it is also important to ask: Why has movement toward goal accomplishment reached the point identified on the goal-attainment scale?

The last column on a contracted plan indicates the dates when planned tasks have or have not been accomplished to date. After recognizing which tasks have not been completed, focus should move over to the next column to find out when it was expected that these tasks would be accomplished. Questions to be asked at this point are: Was there an error in date anticipation? Is more time needed? Why was our timing off? If it appears that what is needed is an adjustment in the date anticipated, this can readily take place, and intervention will be continued. For example, a social worker may have worked out a contracted plan with a group of citizens in which it was anticipated that they would meet with a member of Congress by a certain date. It was found out later that the politician's schedule was fully booked until two weeks after the anticipated date on the plan. If the reason for a failure to accomplish a goal on the date expected is something other than insufficient time for task completion, evaluation continues by moving over to the "contract" column (the third column from the right) of the plan.

In analyzing the "contract" column, a review is made of the people or system responsible for carrying out the identified tasks. Questions include: Did the persons or system designated to carry out a task in the plan complete that task? If not, why not? There are several possible reasons for a failure in task execution. Basically, a review of motivation, capacity, opportunity, and understanding of expectations should be made. The failure could be due to work overload, insufficient resources, or environmental pressures greater than anticipated. A change or redistribution in task responsibilities may be all that is needed to move forward toward goal accomplishment. Perhaps a social worker or resource will have to withdraw from carrying out tasks in order to have a client system become more directly involved in problem resolution. Perhaps the social worker or a new resource will have to become directly involved in collaborating with a client system to accomplish certain tasks. For example, a social worker and Mr. M may have planned that Mr. M would go to the Vocational Rehabilitation Office to complete a set of tests. He was then expected to call the social worker to let her know how he made out. What actually happened was that Mr. M changed his mind as the date for the testing drew closer, because he was afraid to hear the results of his testing. When he called the social worker, he told her he didn't keep the appointment because he didn't feel well. The social worker asked Mr. M to come in to talk with her, and as they evaluated the plan they had made, Mr. M shared the fact that he couldn't face going for the tests and hearing the results by himself. The contract had to be changed so that the social worker would go with Mr. M to the Vocational Rehabilitation Office.

Through analysis of the "contract" column, it may become apparent that, even when everyone carries out the tasks as agreed to in the plan, goals may still not be accomplished. The next area to be considered, then, would be the "tasks" column, to see if there could be an error in identifying what tasks had to be performed to fulfill the stated goals. When the tasks outlined in the contracted plan are studied, the question to be asked should call for an evaluation not only of the identified task but also of the sequencing of the tasks as listed in the plan. The social worker asks: Were the tasks appropriately selected, clearly described, and properly sequenced in order to achieve the goal? Perhaps some steps were omitted in the process. There may have been resources or influences in the environment that needed to be contacted but were overlooked in the planning. The nature of the task itself may have been inappropriate for a particular system. For example, Mrs. L did not follow through with a plan to take her mother to visit a nursing home. Although Mrs. L passively agreed with the social worker that a nursing home would be good for her mother, and Mrs. L said that she would take her on a certain date, she never completed the task. Placing an elderly parent in a nursing home might in some cases be a successful plan to achieve the goal of providing needed care for a parent or of getting relief for a family strained by caring for an elderly person. In this situation, however, sending an elderly parent to a nursing home was not an acceptable or possible option for the family, because it was contrary to their basic cultural beliefs and customs.

Occasionally, tasks are identified, sequenced, and implemented and the stated goals are accomplished, but the problem may continue to be present. At this time, the social worker and the client system would have to review carefully the "goal" column to see whether the stated goal actually related to or reflected the opposite of the identified problem or need. The social worker asks: Did the accomplishment of this goal resolve, reduce, or prevent further growth of the problem? If not, why not? It could be that the goal indicated the outcome desired by the social worker but not by the client system. The needs of the client may continue to be unmet until the social worker clearly understands and expresses the goal of the client. For example, Mrs. F may have expressed strong dissatisfaction with her apartment, complaining about rats and cockroaches, and the social worker may have thought that Mrs. F was identifying the goal of extermination of rats and cockroaches from the apartment. When the problem of rats and cockroaches decreased after much activity involving the landlord and the Housing Code, Mrs. F was still dissatisfied with her apartment. Her true goal was to be relocated with the social worker's help.

If there is not an overall improvement in a situation even after a contracted plan has been fully implemented, another reason could be an inappropriate identification of the problem or need in the first place. In the case just cited, for example, the worker thought that the client system was presenting the problem of infested housing when, in fact, she was trying to give reasons for the social worker to help her move. She felt isolated and did not get along with her neighbors. She hoped the social worker would be able to arrange for her to move to the south end of town, where some of her relatives lived. As the generalist reviewed the case during evaluation, the question would be asked: What, in fact, was the problem? With hindsight, the social worker would be able to see that the real problem with Mrs. F was a lack of social adjustment. The goal she really wanted to accomplish was relocation.

It is apparent, then, that a social worker may use the contracted plan for evaluation in the General Method. There are six areas or columns that can be analyzed to locate possible causes for failure in problem resolution. At any step in the evaluated process, an understanding may take place that highlights the error in planning and pinpoints where reformulation must take place in the contracted plan.

Contract Reformulation

The General Method is a cyclical, ongoing process. It is more common than exceptional to have the helping process in social work move three steps forward and two steps backward all along the way. By the time the social worker and system of contact move into evaluation, however, they are often sensitive to the possibility that the next phase in their working together may be termination. If the evaluation leads to an awareness that little or no progress has been made and that the contracted plan has to be reformulated, there may be resistance or expressed frustration on the part of both social worker and client system. This is particularly true when it becomes apparent that there is regression in a situation after much time and energy has been invested by both social worker and client system. A social worker may need special support from his or her supervisor and a system of contact may need to receive special support from the social worker, if they are to find the energy necessary to persevere in the process of plan reformulation. A social worker needs to maintain a flexible, realistic attitude throughout the General Method, and this attitude must be conveyed to the client, action, and target systems with which he or she is working.

As problems, goals, tasks, contract, or dates are reformulated during the evaluation period, it is imperative that the system of contact play a major role in the revision. Learning to recognize and accept setbacks, to try again without giving up, to change expectations and plans when necessary, and, finally, to see results from planned and persistent action can be extremely valuable to the growth of any human being or system of contact.

When the evaluation has taken place that leads to a reformulation of some aspect of the contracted plan, the social worker records the dates of the evaluation and the planned revisions on the contracted plan. As shown in Table 8.1, in the "date identified" and "problem/need" columns, the social worker indicates the dates when the evaluation took place and the problems that were being evaluated. In the "problem/need" column, the social worker also states what reformulations are necessary. In the columns where reformulations are to be made, the social worker describes the changes or additions and then proceeds to fill in the other columns of the plan to reflect the revisions.

As shown in Table 8.1, the social worker had originally set the goal of having Mr. M grow in awareness of his intellectual potential and marketable skills. He was to complete a battery of tests and learn the results at the Vocational Rehabilitation Office. After he completed the tests and learned their results, he was to call the social worker. Mr. M failed to keep the appointment because he was afraid to hear the results. When Mr. M called to say he didn't go for the testing, the social worker arranged to meet with him. During this meeting, they evaluated how far they had come and identified where the plan was incomplete. The difficulty was in Mr. M's not being able to carry out task 7 on his own. After much discussion, the social worker offered to go with Mr. M for the testing. He agreed, and they also planned to meet again for a follow-up session. The evaluation, with reformulations of tasks and contract, is shown in Table 8.1.

TABLE 8.1 Contracted Plan

Date Identified	Problem/ Need	Goal	Task	Contract	Date Anticipated	Date Accomplished
2/6	1. Lack of self awareness of potential— Mr. M	1. To grow in awareness of potential (intelligence, skills)	1. Talk with Mr. M.	1. Social worker and Mr. M	2/13	2/13
			2. Talk with Mrs. M.	2. Social worker and Mrs. M	2/15	2/15
			3. Talk with Mr. and Mrs. M.	3. Social worker and Mr. and Mrs. M	2/22	2/22
			4. Call Vocational Rehabilitation.	4. Social worker	2/23	2/23
			5. Discuss Vocational Rehabilitation with Mr. M.	5. Social worker and Mr. M	2/28	2/28
			6. Call Vocational Rehabilitation for appointment.	6. Mr. M	3/1	3/1
			7. Go to Vocational Rehabilitation.	7. Mr. M	3/14	
			8. Call social worker.	8. Mr. M	3/15	3/15
3/17 Evaluation	Evaluation of problem 1 (as cited above)	Goal 1 (as cited above)	1. Recall goal 1; evaluate why not accomplished; reformulate contract.	1. Social worker and Mr. M	3/17	3/17
3/17 Contract reformulation	Change in contract 7 and in task 8 and contract 8		7. Go to Vocational Rehabilitation.	7. Social worker and Mr. M	3/25	3/27
			8. Meet to review contract 7.	8. Social worker and Mr. M		

Evaluation Questions

In essence, evaluation may be described as a process. In addition to those questions already identified that relate to the different areas of the contracted plan, the social worker raises questions about external and internal circumstances that may have affected goal accomplishment. As stated earlier, the social worker first considers the possibility that planning did not anticipate outside factors that may have caused failure or success in goal attainment. After considering outside factors and after reviewing the contracted plan, the social worker and system of contact should also ask if any internal factors or dynamics within their relationship have prevented progress. This would include an assessment of the level of trust, openness, and honesty within the relationship. If it is agreed that there has been some resistance or holding back in their interactions, this should be explored. A direct discussion about the social worker–client system relationship, its progress, and its setbacks can be a powerful source for movement during evaluation.

Basically, the essential questions to be asked during evaluation may be summarized as follows:

Has the goal been accomplished? (yes or no)
- If yes, has the goal been accomplished as a result of circumstances outside of the contracted plan? (external causes)
- If no, the following questions should be asked:
  1. From when the problem was first identified, how much closer to or further from the goal has the client, action, or target system moved? (goal-accomplishment scale)
  2. Has the goal not been accomplished as expected because of circumstances outside of the contracted plan? (external causes)
  3. Was there an error in date anticipation? (timing)
  4. Did a person or system of contact designated to complete a task fail to accomplish it? (contract)
  5. Were the tasks inappropriately selected, sequenced, or described? (tasks)
  6. If the goal has been accomplished, but the problem continues, was the goal inaccurately identified? (goal)
  7. If the goal has been accomplished, but the problem continues, was the problem inaccurately identified? (problem)
  8. Was there anything in the social worker–client system relationship that inhibited goal accomplishment? (internal causes)

As these questions are answered, the causes for failure in goal attainment become increasingly evident. The reason a goal has not been accomplished to the extent anticipated may be pinpointed to some area on the contracted plan or to external or internal circumstances. When there has been clarification of what prevented goal accomplishment, the social worker and the client system then begin to ask: Why did this happen? and What can be done to remedy the situation and make goal accomplishment feasible? A reformulation of the plan takes place.

Not all of the evaluation questions have to be asked if it becomes clear that a goal has not been attained for a reason suggested in earlier questions. Instead of proceeding with further questioning, the social worker and the system of contact move into an analysis of why the particular drawback existed and a consideration of what modifications or additions need to be made in the contracted plan. With a reformulation of identified problems, goals, tasks, contract, or dates, the social worker and the client, action, or target system return to the intervention stage for further action. After the newly developed plan has been enacted, another evaluation takes place. If goals have been attained at this time, the social worker and the system of contact are then ready either to work on other problems and needs or to move into the final stage of the General Method, called *termination*.

Ongoing Evaluation

As stated, the formal stage of evaluation begins with this question: Has the goal been accomplished? This question is asked at the time when it was anticipated on the contracted plan that a particular goal would be attained. In addition to this formal evaluation stage, it is possible to integrate a systematic evaluation throughout the entire General Method. Increasingly, efforts and instruments for ongoing evaluation in social work practice are being described in the professional literature (Fischer & Corcoran, 1994; Kirk, 1999). The value of a concentrated ongoing evaluation is that it helps the social worker and the client system to be sensitive to movement and to the long-range goals throughout the process.

A tool may be used to assist a social worker and system of contact in an ongoing evaluation process. The tool is a two-dimensional graph, which may begin to be constructed during any stage of the method. The zero point on the graph represents the starting point when a problem is identified and a goal is first established. The vertical line of the graph intersects the zero point midway, and the line has an equal number of plus and minus points above and below the zero point. The vertical line is the goal line, which is used to chart movement toward or away from the goal as the problem gets better or worse. The highest point at the top of this line indicates goal accomplishment; the midpoint (0) identifies where the problem is when the goal is set; and the lowest point represents total failure in goal accomplishment. Each intermediate point should have some measurable descriptive criterion that indicates progression or regression. Whenever possible, all points should be described in behavioral terms that can be objectively measured.

The horizontal line of the graph is a time indicator. It may represent weeks, days, or months, depending on the nature of the problem. (For a crisis, the intervals may represent days or hours.) The line to the left of the midpoint indicates time intervals prior to the starting point, when there was no contact between social worker and client system (i.e., the baseline time frame). The right side of the line indicates time intervals during the course of service delivery.

Generally, the graph has four points from the midpoint on each line (see Figure 8.3). More intervals may be added as work progresses, if this appears to be

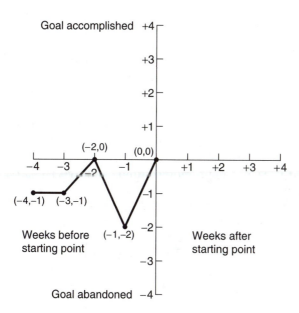

FIGURE 8.3   Ongoing Evaluation Graph: Mr. and Mrs. S

appropriate for a particular situation. During the data-collection stage of the General Method, information may be obtained for plotting dots on the left side of the graph. The social worker inquires about the severity of the problem prior to social worker–client system contact. Usually, this inquiry goes back to at least the previous four weeks. If it is a long-standing problem, a review may be made of the last four months or years. If it is a crisis that just recently began, the inquiry might cover the last four days or four hours. As the problem and goal become clear, the lines of the graph are drawn. As information is gathered about the history of the problem, person, and situation, dots are plotted on the left side of the graph. For example, if the intervals represent weeks, the social worker would ask what the situation was like one week, two weeks, three weeks, and four weeks before the system began to have contact with the generalist. As the situation for each time interval is described, an effort is made to locate a point on the goal line which matches the description. A dot is plotted where the time interval and goal indicator meet. In Figure 8.3, for example, one week before contact, the problem was assessed at the –2 point; two weeks before, it was at the 0 point (same as first contact with social worker); three weeks before, it was at the –1 level; and four weeks before, it was at the –1 level also. When the points are connected, it is apparent that the problem was at its worst one week before the system began to have contact with the social worker. In the case of Mr. and Mrs. S, this would mean that a week before they contacted the social worker, their quarrels were moving into physical fights half the time they talked.

If the tool in Figure 8.3 is used as an ongoing evaluation instrument, each time the social worker and the system of contact meet, they would plot a point on the graph to show what movement has taken place each week. During the assessment stage, the graph is refined with clear descriptors to measure movement toward or away from clarified goals within an expected time frame as indicated on the contracted plan. As points are plotted and connected, the social worker and the client system begin to envision the direction in which they expect to see the connecting line move, according to time intervals and dates anticipated on the contracted plan.

Plotting and charting movement could continue as the social worker and the client system go through the intervention, evaluation, and termination stages of the General Method. During the formal evaluation stage, a thorough analysis is made of the reasons why movement has been in the directions shown on the graph. The goal-accomplishment scale and the contracted plan may still be used as described earlier to pinpoint the extent of goal accomplishment at the evaluation stage and to locate causal factors that resulted in arriving at the identified point. These tools may be complemented by the ongoing evaluation graph, which could provide a general perspective of movement throughout the process of service delivery.

Continuing to use the graph during termination helps the social worker detect any regression that may take place as the client, action, or target system begins to realize that contacts with the social worker will be terminated. As shown in Figure 8.4, for example, when Mr. and Mrs. S first began to express their problems to the social worker, tensions mounted between them. They accused each other of betraying confidences by talking with the social worker. The problem increased (point 1, −1). Through further contacts with the social worker, Mr. and Mrs. S began to grow in being able to listen to and understand each other. Progress toward the stated goal became evident. They were able to go for three weeks with open communication without quarreling. During the next two weeks of contact, some regression became apparent. The direction of the movement line went slightly downward. This regression was due to the fact that the social worker began to talk about termination with Mr. and Mrs. S. They began to talk about the anxiety they were feeling as they thought about having to work on their goals without the help of the social worker. A conscious awareness of the way they were responding to termination, with strong support from the social worker, helped them experience relief and find strength to move to goal accomplishment.

The intervals at the right side of the graph on the horizontal line are extended as long as may be needed to indicate length of time receiving service. Although the social worker may have gathered data only on the 4 weeks prior to the starting point (left side of line), the service may continue even beyond a year, and thus the horizontal line on the right would be extended. In Figure 8.4, for example, Mr. and Mrs. S were seen by the social worker for 12 weeks. Although there was some regression at the time of termination, they did not go back to where they were during the month before they contacted the social worker. The extended graph shows that their goal was attained by the time termination was finalized.

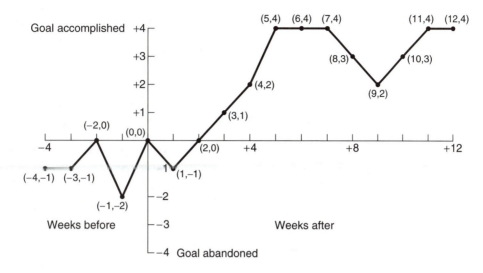

Descriptive criteria for goal line
+4 = Goal accomplished: open communication without quarreling
+3 = Communicating without quarreling most of the time (maybe one quarrel a week)
+2 = Communicating without quarreling half the time we talk
+1 = Communicating without quarreling once or twice a week
 0 = Starting point: no communication without quarreling (at least six times a week)
−1 = Quarreling moving into physical fights once or twice a week
−2 = Quarreling moving into physical fights half the time we talk
−3 = No communication without fighting
−4 = Goal abandoned: injury and separation

FIGURE 8.4   Ongoing Evaluation Graph: Mr. and Mrs. S at Termination

When the ongoing evaluation graph is used in working with a client system, it is very helpful to ask the client to keep a daily log from the time the goal is first established. If a client is asked to recall what happened over a week or a month (depending on frequency of contacts), it is very likely that there will be some error in what is said. Often, a person's memory of what happened is influenced by how the person is feeling at the time of recall. A daily log can be introduced when the graph is first formulated. The social worker asks the system to indicate briefly in the log each day the extent to which the problem and the goal were present. More specifically, the system may be asked to record the number of times or the length of duration of a particular behavior or event. For example, Mr. and Mrs. S would have been asked to jot down at the end of the day in their log how many times they quarreled and also how often they communicated with each other without quarreling during each day. If they bring the log with them each time they meet with the social worker, a more accurate plotting of points on the graph can take place. The social worker and the client system need to articulate as exactly as possible the measurable behaviors that are to be recorded and used to indicate movement in goal accomplishment.

One of the main drawbacks in using the ongoing evaluation graph is the possibility that goals may change during the course of work with a client system. With a multiple-problem family, for example, a goal in one area may become abandoned or at least shifted in priority because of a crisis that arises in another area. Progress for the family is then recognized as movement toward a different goal. If more than one goal is being worked on at one time, a number of graphs may be used simultaneously. For example, a child's health problem may be the working goal for a family, when suddenly they receive eviction papers. This new problem has to be addressed immediately. The new goal is to relocate the family within 30 days. A new graph indicating progression and regression in movement toward this goal would have to be developed.

The use of groups and scales as depicted in Figures 8.3 and 8.4 is similar to that used in a single-subject research design. The research methodology includes measurement processes and statistical techniques for testing the significance of results. The short baselines and time frames of many interventions make the use of these techniques infrequent. The graphic visual presentation of results, however, is extremely beneficial in the course of charting progress.

The ongoing evaluation process used in single-subject design and in the related variation found in Figure 8.3 is applicable to work with a variety of problems, including those of a psychosocial nature. Examples include issues of adolescence, identity, alcoholism, loss or separation, and child abuse (Dean & Reinherz, 1986; Kirk, 1999; Salladin & Timberlake, 1995).

Working with Different Client Systems

No matter what type of system a social worker has been working with for goal accomplishment, a time is needed to evaluate how far the system of contact has moved toward or away from the goal. A deliberate, objective study—which includes an analysis of change, identification of impediments to goal accomplishment, and planning or reformulating contracts—may help break through resistances and provide direction for future interactions between social worker and system of contact.

The tools and processes described in this chapter are general in nature; they may be used in evaluation with individuals, families, groups, organizations, or communities. The evaluation questions, the goal-accomplishment scale, the contracted plan, and the ongoing evaluation graph may be adapted for use with any system of contact. Even when working with teams or target systems, the generalist takes time to involve the system of contact in an evaluation, during which the tools and processes suggested may be utilized.

When working with a team, for example, evaluation questions are asked about the goals that the team identified collectively. The contract the team members developed is used to locate causal factors when goals are not accomplished. The timing, contract, tasks, problems, and goals found on the team contract are considered, along with external circumstances not anticipated by the team in planning. Internal circumstances are also considered as possible causal factors. A study would be made not only of the relationships of team members with the client or target system but also of the relationships among the team members themselves (trust, openness) and how these relationships have affected the process of goal attainment. The goal-accomplishment scale may be used to show how much movement the team believes has taken place for each of the goals it stated. The ongoing evaluation graph may also be used to monitor direction over a period of time toward or away from the goals.

To cite an example of evaluation in teamwork, a vocational counselor from the State Department of Vocational Rehabilitation, a social worker from the East Side Women's Center, and a child-welfare worker from the Department of Children's Services formed a team to coordinate service delivery for Mrs. Judy E and her 5-year-old daughter, Betty. Mrs. E had been reported three months previously for suspected child abuse. The child-welfare worker was monitoring the home situation. She had helped Mrs. E reach the point where the client was asking for skill training to become employed. Mrs. E and the social worker developed a plan in which Mrs. E could be referred to the Women's Center and the Department of Vocational Rehabilitation. Mrs. E agreed also to have the social workers from the three resources form a team to provide ongoing, coordinated services for herself and her daughter.

Once the team was formed, goals were identified and tasks were distributed among the members of the team and Mrs. E. The vocational counselor had the task of arranging for Mrs. E to receive skill training. After completing the skill-training program, Mrs. E was to be helped by the vocational counselor to locate employment. The social worker from the East Side Women's Center was at that time leading a support group for unemployed women who needed to develop a sense of self-worth and self-confidence. Mrs. E was to be added to this group. The child-welfare worker was to help Mrs. E locate day care for Betty. This social worker also had the task of case management. She initiated the first meeting of the team and served as the team leader when it began. Rotating leadership was later used.

The main goals, tasks, and contracted responsibilities that were collectively identified by the team are summarized as follows:

1. To help Mrs. E become employed by her going through a process of testing, training, job locating, and being hired (assigned to vocational counselor and Mrs. E)
2. To help Mrs. E grow in self-worth and self-confidence by her attendance at a weekly women's support group (assigned to social worker at the Women's Center and Mrs. E)
3. To help Mrs. E locate appropriate, available day care for Betty through searching for a resource and completing the application process (assigned to child-welfare worker, Mrs. E, and Betty)
4. To have Mrs. E participate in the coordinated team effort by encouraging her to accept the invitation to join and become involved in all team meetings

The contracted plan also stated the anticipated dates for completing each of the identified tasks. As interventions were carried out, the team moved into the evaluation stage. If a goal and its planned tasks were apparently the direct responsibility of one social worker on the team (as in goals 1 through 3), this member was the one responsible for developing the ongoing evaluation graph and/or the goal-accomplishment scale for the particular goal. This team member was asked to lead the team as members took time to assess the extent to which that goal has been accomplished. Collectively, the team reviewed the evaluation questions and the contracted plan. This analysis was conducted with input from the client system.

The fourth goal in the team example is one of shared responsibility by all team members. Each member was expected to encourage Mrs. E to attend and to participate in team meetings. Together, the team designed a goal-accomplishment scale and an ongoing evaluation graph for this goal. Because the goal has the distinct dimensions of (1) attendance and (2) participation in team meetings, the team decided to draw up two graphs and two scales for clarity in assessment of goal 4. For example, in Figures 8.5 and 8.6 (goal accomplishment scales) and Figures 8.7 and 8.8 (ongoing evaluation graphs), the team members—it is hoped including Mrs. E as a member—discussed and identified what they saw as criteria for identifying movement in goal accomplishment. The dual scales and graphs help highlight the multiple options that may exist when the two variables (attendance and participation) are considered necessary to achieve the one goal (Mrs. E's participating in the coordinated team effort). In Figure 8.5, Mrs. E is seen as attending the team meetings regularly (4 is checked on Figure 8.5), but she is not yet participating fully at the meetings (1 is checked on Figure 8.6). Both Figures 8.5 and 8.6 would have to reach a +4 if the goal is to be accomplished totally, according to the criteria developed by the team.

It should be noted that in the scales of Figures 8.5 and 8.6 and in the goal lines of the graphs of Figures 8.7 and 8.8, there are no minus numbers and line. This is because there is no degree to which the goal of attendance and participation at team meetings can be less than the starting point (0). The 0 on the scales means zero attendance and participation.

The ongoing evaluation graphs in Figures 8.7 and 8.8 shows that there was 0 attendance and participation in team meetings prior to the starting point when

FIGURE 8.5   Attendance at Team Meetings

				X
0	1	2	3	4
Starting point: no attendance	Little attendance: one out of four meetings a month	Some attendance: two out of four meetings a month	Frequent attendance: three out of four meetings a month	Goal accomplished: regular attendance

FIGURE 8.6   Participation in Team Meetings

	X			
0	1	2	3	4
Starting point: no participation in meetings	Little participation: speaking up once or twice during a meeting or only when spoken to	Some participation: speaking up three or four times during a meeting	Frequent participation: speaking up and sharing five or six times	Goal accomplished: active—fully participating in flow of meetings

Mrs. E was first invited to attend. The graphs also show the progress that took place as Mrs. E began to feel more in control of her life, more confidence in herself, and more comfortable with the other team members.

In work with a target system rather than a team or a client system, the evaluation process may be somewhat different. Although a generalist may interact with a target system for goal accomplishment, the two may never arrive at a point where they develop a contracted plan together. A social worker alone, or with a client system or other resource, may initiate contact with a target system to request some assistance or change in service. The social worker and other members of the action system may state clearly at that time their purpose or goals in making the

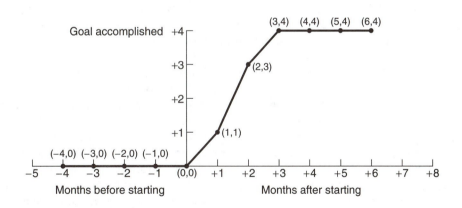

Descriptive criteria for goal line 4a
+4 = Goal accomplished: regular attendance at team meetings
+3 = Attending three out of four meetings a month
+2 = Attending two out of four meetings a month
+1 = Attending one out of four meetings a month
 0 = Starting point: no attendance at team meetings

FIGURE 8.7   Attendance at Team Meetings

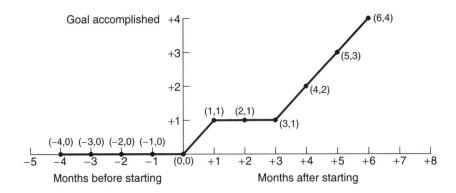

Descriptive criteria for goal line 4b
+4 = Goal accomplished: active participation in flow of meetings
+3 = Speaking up and sharing five or six times during a meeting
+2 = Speaking up three or four times during a meeting
+1 = Speaking up once or twice during a meeting or only when spoken to
 0 = Starting point: no participation in team meetings

FIGURE 8.8   Participation in Team Meetings

contact. The target system, however, may not respond favorably. If the social worker continues to try to change the target system through repeated contacts and pressures, there may be a time when the social worker evaluates with the target system what movement toward or away from the stated goal has taken place since their first contact. Here, a goal-accomplishment scale or an ongoing evaluation graph may be helpful as the social worker tries to make an objective presentation to confront the target system with the reality of the situation.

For example, on behalf of her tenants, a generalist may speak to the landlady of an apartment complex to try to get her to improve the conditions of the apartment. A list is presented indicating repairs, renovations, and improvements needed. To have all 12 items on the list taken care of is the ultimate goal. The generalist and the tenants involve a Housing Code Inspector and the Housing Court in efforts to pressure the landlady to make the improvements. Periodically, the generalist meets with the landlady to continue to bring to her attention the unattended needs of the tenants. As conditions improve or deteriorate, the social worker may choose to use an ongoing evaluation graph or a goal-accomplishment scale to demonstrate what has taken place since the problems and needs were first presented to the landlady (starting point). This evaluative approach may help create sufficient feelings for progress to be made.

As depicted on the graph in Figure 8.9, the conditions at the apartment complex had deteriorated during the weeks prior to the social worker's contact with the landlady. Through various pressures and continued contacts, some improvements were made. After the fifth week of contact, however, there was a tapering off of efforts to improve conditions, and problems increased. The social worker

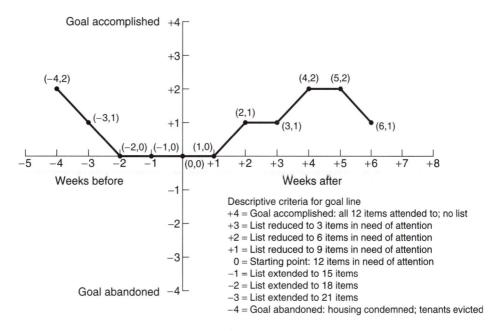

FIGURE 8.9   **Target System: Landlady**

used the graph (Figure 8.9) to point out to the landlady what progress had been made, how conditions were starting to get worse, and how far they were from accomplishing the original goal (+4).

Using Social Work Foundation Knowledge in Evaluation

The holistic foundation for generalist practice, as diagrammed in Chapter 1 (Table 1.3), identifies the fundamental values, knowledge, and skills used during evaluation. The social worker demonstrates care for a system and a commitment to quality service by taking time to analyze movement toward or away from goals. Throughout the evaluation process, the principles of *individualization* and *self-determination* are emphasized. Any assessment of movement or change is strongly dependent on input from the system of contact. Any reformulation of a contract takes place only after a client system, an action system, or, if possible, a target system has spoken with the social worker and has given input and consent.

In practice, the social worker inquires about changes in feelings and attitudes as well as behaviors. He or she recognizes and encourages *purposeful expression of feelings* during evaluation. If progress has not taken place, the social worker conveys a *nonjudgmental attitude* toward the client system, as focus is directed to exploring possible causal factors and a reformulation of the plan.

From scientific research, the generalist uses knowledge and skills for measuring, graphing, and scaling during evaluation. In addition to research skills, it may be necessary to use relationship, problem-solving, and political skills. Frequently, the social worker guides, clarifies, and confronts as goals are analyzed. Within the evaluation period, such problem-solving skills as problem and need identification, data collection, assessment, and contracting may be reviewed and repeated.

Foundation knowledge used during evaluation varies according to the problem or goal that is being evaluated. In order to identify indicators of improvement or regression in a problem, the nature and dynamics of the problem must be understood.

Through holistic knowledge, the generalist is enabled to conduct a comprehensive study of causal factors. As the evaluation questions are raised and internal and external circumstances are considered, the social worker is aided by the foundation knowledge base, which is integrated within the ecological-systems perspective of *person in environment*. The generalist is sensitive to the complex and multiple factors that interact and influence a client system.

Human Diversity in Evaluation

Core human diversity issues also need to be recognized and incorporated in evaluation. As noted earlier, these issues include institutional racism, cultural diversity, gender-role expectations, sexual orientation, and socio-economic status.

As the social worker and system of contact move into the evaluation stage of the General Method, they begin with the question: Have the goals been accomplished? The social worker must distinguish between long-range goals and short-range goals. Core human diversity issues may be readily identified as basically causing a client system to have unmet needs. Long-range goals may be the eradication of these two problems. Although the long-range goals may not be accomplished at the time of evaluation, the efforts made to work toward them should be evaluated. The identified immediate or short-range goals are usually articulated in more precise terms that can be measured for accomplishment. If they have not been fully accomplished, the contract review (described in Chapter 7) may help highlight the reason why plans are not carried out successfully. Again, the timing projected for goal accomplishment may not have been in line with the time orientation of the culture of the client system. The persons or resources expected to carry out the planned tasks, or the tasks themselves, may have been culturally inappropriate. It may be that the goals or the problems were not correctly understood or articulated.

As pointed out, a final question to raise during evaluation is: Was there anything in the social worker–client system relationship that inhibited goal accomplishment? To answer this question, a social worker needs to ask himself or herself: How sensitive and accepting was I toward this person, family, group, organization, or community? Self-awareness is necessary. If a social worker has come to understand and appreciate his or her own ethnicity, it is often easier to recognize and accept the ethnicity of others. As with the systems receiving service, a social worker also brings to any new relationship his or her ethnic history and personal experiences with certain cultural, social, and socio-demographic groups. Although, admittedly, it may be natural to transfer or stereotype, a working relationship can be very inhibited when those receiving help, or even those providing help, sense that they are not being treated as unique individuals. If goals are not being accomplished, the reason could be related to an absence of cultural sensitivity or of any shared cultural elements, with a resulting stereotyping by both the social worker and the client system receiving service. When stereotyping is present, studies have shown that participants begin to feel discomfort, and that they retreat into exaggerated behaviors that depict and confirm the ethnic-group stereotype. For example, during an interethnic study between Japanese Americans and Caucasian Americans, it was found that in time the Japanese Americans became increasingly quiet and aloof, whereas the Caucasian Americans became loud and aggressive (Fong & Mokuau, 1994; Sue & Sue, 1990; Tamura & Lau, 1992). An honest evaluation of the social worker–client system relationship can promote an increase in self-awareness for both social worker and client system, and it may help break through some of the discomfort or resistance in the relationship.

In the evaluation stage, while making an appraisal of the extent of goal accomplishment and a comprehensive evaluation to locate possible reasons for any lack of accomplishment, a social worker who is knowledgeable about multiculturalism, social pluralism, and socio-demographic diversity can better recognize dynamics and factors that may affect or prevent the attainment of goals. In reviewing the contract, it may become apparent that service providers or other persons who were expected to complete certain tasks may have taken longer than planned or may have changed their minds as the anticipated date arrived. The change on their part could be due to fears, threats, or insincere commitments that surfaced as the plan unfolded. Clients themselves may have changed their minds and plans as they began to experience pressures from family members, lawyers, judges, or others. An individual who seemed interested in joining a support group, for example, may have failed to show up for meetings because of increased fears of being identified with the group. And finally, here, too, it is possible that the social worker or the client system may be uncomfortable with the working relationship itself and that this discomfort has interfered with goal accomplishment. Perhaps the openness or support needed did not develop, owing to hidden biases or fears. Again, an honest evaluation of the social worker–client system relationship at this time may result in a breakthrough so that progress can begin.

When it is time to evaluate goals that relate to gender-role changes, progress in personal and environmental goals should be considered realistically. Both the social worker and those receiving service need to realize that only with continued efforts and much time and patience can there be any lasting change in prejudicial attitudes, practices, and policies. If a goal was to eliminate prejudice in a target system and this has not been accomplished, progress may have been made if at least some conscious awareness of its presence has begun to develop in the target system. On a personal level, to have an individual become aware of his or her self-image and bias may be a major accomplishment, even though the person may not change his or her behavior or life situation.

Here, too, a major factor to be reviewed when goals have not been accomplished is the expectations and attitudes of the social worker toward those receiving service. A social worker who is finding it difficult to support efforts to overcome bias and prejudice may be contributing to the failure in goal attainment.

Evaluation in Micro, Mezzo, and Macro Practice in Diverse Field Areas

In the following section, the application of knowledge and skills during the *evaluation stage* of the General Method will be demonstrated by entry-level generalists in seven diverse field areas.

I. **Field Area: Child Welfare**

   A. **Agency: State Department of Children's Services**
   B. **Client System**
       K, a 15-year-old female, was placed in a group home three months ago. (For more background information, see Chapter 4, Engagement in Micro, Mezzo, and Macro Practice in Diverse Field Areas, I. Child Welfare.)
   C. **Summary of Preceding Stages**
       The problems, goals, and tasks identified and implemented in earlier stages are found in Table 6.6 in Chapter 6 and Table 7.1 in Chapter 7. The social worker's interventions included direct work with K, the client; a referral to the group home and a court petitioning for custody continuance; and teamwork with personnel from the shelter, the group home, and the school K is attending.
   D. **Evaluation**
       Goal analysis: The primary goals of (1) obtaining and maintaining a permanent placement, (2) reentering school, and (3) personal growth were analyzed by K and the social worker. They agreed that a placement had been found and was being maintained (goal 1). K was also attending school regularly (goal 2). Her personal problems (3a–3d) were beginning to surface in casework and group sessions at the home, though she was still finding it difficult to believe that she was of any worth and to talk about her sexuality. Goal 4, to obtain continuance of custody, was achieved on 3/30.

       Scales were developed to assess the extent to which the first two goals were accomplished. The two dimensions of goal 1 (obtaining placement and maintaining placement) were separated for greater clarity in evaluation (see Figures 8.10 and 8.11). The goal of school reentry was expanded at this time to include optimal school performance. Two scales were also used then to evaluate goal 2 (see Figures 8.12 and 8.13). The goal regarding personal growth (goal 3) had four subheadings (a–d). Because the child-welfare worker was not working directly on this goal with K, the four parts were reviewed in discussion and evaluated in

FIGURE 8.10 Goal 1a: To Obtain a Permanent Placement

				X
-2	-1	0	+1	+2
Goal abandoned	No place located	Starting point at shelter	Place located	Goal accomplished; placement obtained

FIGURE 8.11 Goal 1b: To Maintain a Permanent Placement

						X		
-4	-3	-2	-1	0	+1	+2	+3	+4
Goal abandoned: removal from placement	Marked problems: high conflict level	Increased problems	Beginning problems in adjustment	Starting point; beginning placement at new group home	Beginning to adjust	Satisfactory adjustment, but room for improvement	Marked improvement, high comfort level	Goal accomplished; stabilized adjustment

FIGURE 8.12   Goal 2a: To Reenter School

				X
-2	-1	0	+1	+2
Goal abandoned	No School located	Starting point—out of school	School located	Goal accomplished—returned to school

FIGURE 8.13   Goal 2b: To Achieve Optimal Level of Academic Performance

						X		
-4	-3	-2	-1	0	+1	+2	+3	+4
Goal abandoned: school dismissal or dropping out	Marked persistent problems	Increasing problems	Beginning to have problems in academic achievement	Starting point; beginning new school	Beginning to achieve academically	Stabilizing academic achievement, but room for improvement	Marked improvement in academic performance	Goal accomplished, optimal level of academic performance

general, on the basis of input from K, from the social worker who was seeing K individually, and from the group-home social worker who attended the peer-group meetings.

Goal 1a was evaluated by K and the social worker as accomplished (+2). K was placed in a group home where she could stay until adulthood.

According to K and the group-home staff, K was adjusting well to the placement. They thought, however, that she could try to participate more fully in group activities. She was completing her chores and getting along satisfactorily with the other residents. Because K had only been in the home for three months and said she was not completely comfortable there yet, the social worker and K evaluated the extent of accomplishment for goal 1b as +2 on the scale.

K was accepted into the local school; therefore, goal 2a was accomplished, as indicated with a +2 on the scale in Figure 8.12.

K and the social worker considered ways in which they could objectively assess her progress in school. They agreed that they would look at her grades and report card from school and that they would ask for verbal assessments from K's teachers through the school social worker. At the time of this evaluation, K's performance was described by her teachers as "satisfactory." They thought she could do better, especially in her writing and class participation. They expected that K would perform at a higher achievement level as she became more familiar with the school. K said that she liked school and her teachers and thought she was learning a great deal. She knew she could try harder and bring up her grades by the end of the semester. K did not believe that she needed a tutor or any additional help with her schoolwork at this time. The social worker and K assessed the extent of accomplishment for goal 2b as +2 on the scale (Figure 8.13).

K said she continued to find it hard to talk about herself and her personal problems (goal 3). She enjoyed the group meetings because the other residents were able to say things she couldn't. Deep down inside she knew she was feeling happier but was afraid it was "too good to be true." She said she would try harder to talk with her social worker about herself and her feelings. K's social worker at the group home thought that K was beginning to relax more during individual sessions and that more time was needed before K would be able to talk freely about herself, her past, or her future.

Contract review and reformulation: *During contract review, the social worker and K recognized the need for more time before goals 1, 2, and 3 (especially goal 3) could be accomplished. In reviewing contracted tasks, the social worker and K agreed that the social worker did not have to continue to follow up with K every two weeks. K knew that she could always call the social worker if she needed her. They agreed that the social worker would begin to visit K once a month, unless there was some reason for additional contact. The social worker recorded the process of evaluation that occurred at this stage, indicating the reformulation of contract, as found in Table 8.2.*

Ongoing evaluation: *At this point, the social worker and K developed graphs to assess ongoing progress in (1) maintenance (adjustment) in the group home and (2) school performance. The graphs they designed are found in Figures 8.14 and*

TABLE 8.2 Contracted Plan: State Department of Children's Services (Continued from Tables 6.7 and 7.1)

Date Identified	Problem/ Need	Goal	Task	Contract	Date Anticipated	Date Accomplished
4/25 Evaluation	Evaluation of problems 1, 2, 3, 4	Goals 1, 2, 3, 4	1. Recall each goal. 2. Assess extent of accomplishment. 3. Reformulate contract.	Social worker and K (with input from school and group-home personnel)	4/25	4/25
Contract reformu-lation	Change in 1. Date antici-pated for task 4, goal 1; task 3, goal 3	Goal 1	Task 4—follow-up	Social worker, K, group home staff	5/25 and once a month thereafter	
		Goal 3	Task 3—follow-up	Social worker, K, social worker at group home	5/25 and once a month thereafter	
	2. Goal statement for problem 2; contract and date antici-pated for task 2, goals 2a and 2b	2a. To reenter school b. To achieve an optimal level of academic performance	Task 2—follow-up	Social worker and school social worker	5/25 and once a month thereafter	

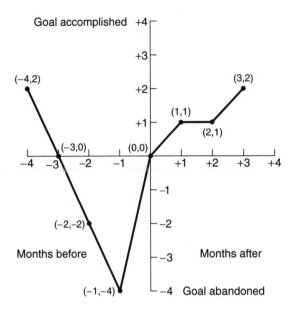

Descriptive criteria for goal line (Y— vertical line)
+4 = Goal accomplished: permanent placement maintained (stabilized)
+3 = Marked improvement: participation in group, high comfort level
+2 = Stabilizing adjustment: satisfactory, but room for improvement
+1 = Beginning to adjust
  0 = Starting point: beginning placement — insecure, withdrawn
−1 = Beginning problems
−2 = Increased problems
−3 = Marked problems in adjustment, high conflict level
−4 = Goal abandoned: removal from placement
Line X — horizontal line = Months in residence
  Plus numbers   = Months in new group home
  0   = Beginning placement in new group home
Minus numbers   = Months before placement in new group home
  0 to −1   = Placement in shelter
  −1 to −3   = Months in foster home
  −3 and before   = Months in first group home

FIGURE 8.14   Goal 1b: To Maintain Permanent Placement

8.15 (page 286). The social worker and K planned to use the graphs each month when they met for ongoing evaluation and charting of progress.

II. Field Area: Gerontology

A. Agency: Seaside Nursing Home
B. Client System
Mrs. J, an 80-year-old Portuguese woman, is in a skilled-nursing facility. (For additional information, see Chapter 4, Engagement in Micro, Mezzo, and Macro Practice in Diverse Field Areas, II. Gerontology.)

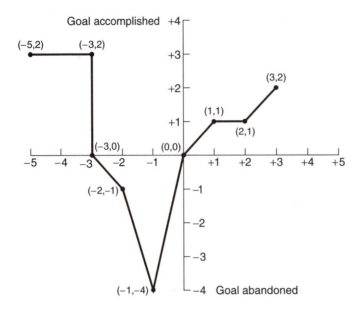

Descriptive criteria for goal line (Y— vertical line)
+4 = Goal accomplished: optimal level of academic performance
+3 = Marked improvement in academic performance (writing and class participation)
+2 = Stabilizing academic achievement, room for improvement
+1 = Beginning to achieve academically
 0 = Starting point: beginning new school — insecure, withdrawn
−1 = Beginning problems in academic achievement
−2 = Increasing problems
−3 = Marked, persistent problems in academic performance
−4 = Goal abandoned: school dismissal or dropout
Line X — horizontal line = Time
   Plus numbers   = Months attending new school
   0   = Beginning new school
   Minus numbers   = Months before attending new school

FIGURE 8.15   **Goal 2b: To Achieve an Optimal Level of Academic Performance**

C. Summary of Preceding Stages

The contracted plan indicating the problems, goals, and tasks identified in earlier stages is found in Table 7.2 in Chapter 7. The social worker's interventions were direct work with Mrs. J and teamwork with the staff of the nursing home and the pastor of the church Mrs. J used to attend. The prioritized goals for Mrs. J were the following: (1) to get to know the staff and the resources of the nursing home; (2) to work out a mutually satisfactory bath schedule with the nurses; (3) to leave her room alone (at least once a day) and to attend a house activity (at least once a week); (4) to stop name calling and yelling at residents; and (5) to share her culture with others.

D. Evaluation

Goal analysis: After three months, the social worker and Mrs. J analyzed the extent of goal accomplishment for the five prioritized goals. Goals 2 and 4 had clearly been accomplished. Mrs. J's bath was scheduled earlier, and she no longer fought with the nurses. She also stopped calling the residents names and was beginning to feel more comfortable in the home as she got to know the staff and the resources available (goal 1). She met with the program planner, the director of volunteers, the head nurse and other nurses, the chaplain, and staff members from recreational therapy. Although there were occasional days when she did not leave her room, she was attending nursing-home activities with her roommate (goal 3) and appeared less fearful of having her possessions stolen. Regarding goal 5, Mrs. J's pastor and two members of the congregation came to see her. They took her to their church for a Christmas prayer service and a concert. A volunteer who spoke Portuguese visited Mrs. J for three weeks in November but then dropped out of the program.

Scales to assess the extent of goal accomplishment for goals 3a and 3b were developed and drawn on a large sheet of paper (see Figures 8.16 and 8.17). The

FIGURE 8.16   Goal 3a: To Leave Room Alone (at Least Once a Day)

				X		
−3	−2	−1	0	+1	+2	+3
Total refusal to go out of room—goal dropped	Increased refusal to leave room (once a day)	Occasional refusal to leave even when someone offers to take her (about once a week)	Starting point: only leave when someone takes her for meals	Occasional going out of room alone (about once a week)	Increased going out of room alone (once a day)	Going out of room alone freely; maximum goal accomplished

FIGURE 8.17   Goal 3b: To Attend House Activity (at Least Once a Week)

	X		
0	1	2	3
Starting point: attending no house activities (program or meeting)	Attending house activity with social worker or staff member (once a week)	Attending house activity with other residents once a week	Attending house activities with residents more than once a week; maximum goal accomplished

scale for goal 3a was expanded into an ongoing evaluation graph, which the social worker reviewed with Mrs. J each succeeding week (see Figure 8.18). The nurse at the head station agreed to help Mrs. J and the social worker keep track of the days when Mrs. J was able to leave her room on her own. A small calendar was kept at the head station, and the date was circled when Mrs. J came to the station to say "hello" to the nurse on duty.

The goal does not extend to Mrs. J's going outside the institution on her own. At this time, it is not seen as a possibility. The maximum goal accomplishment considered, therefore, was Mrs. J's being able to freely and frequently go out of her bedroom on her own. The graph in Figure 8.18 demonstrates that Mrs. J was able to live alone up to 3 weeks before she was hospitalized. She was in the hospital for 2 weeks prior to her placement in the nursing home. During her first 2 weeks at the home, she regressed. At the time of evaluation (12 weeks in residence), she progressed to occasionally leaving her room independently (averaging once a week), which is shown at point +1 on the goal line of Figure

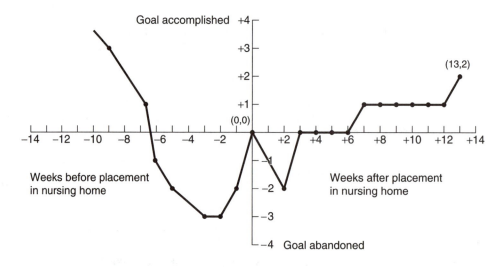

Descriptive criteria for points on goal line (Y— vertical line)
+4 = Goal accomplished: going out of room freely
+3 = Increased going out of room alone (three times a day average)
+2 = Increased going out of room alone (once a day average)
+1 = Occasionally going out of room alone (once a week average)
 0 = Starting point: placement in nursing home; leaving room only when taken to meals
−1 = Occasional refusal to leave room even when someone offers to accompany her (once a week average)
−2 = Increased refusal to leave room even when someone offers to accompany her (once a day average)
−3 = Repeated refusal to leave room even when someone offers to accompany her (more than once a day)
−4 = Goal abandoned: total refusal to leave room
Line X = horizontal line = Weeks before and after placement in nursing home

FIGURE 8.18   Goal 3a: To Leave Room by Herself

8.18. With the added involvement of the nurses at the station on Mrs. J's floor, the goal reached the point +2 by one week after the evaluation, as shown in point 13,2 of Figure 8.18.

<u>Contract reformulation:</u>   The evaluation conducted by Mrs. J and the social worker 12 weeks after she began residency in the nursing home was recorded on the contracted plan (Table 8.3). As indicated, the task for goal 3a was expanded to include Mrs. J's saying "hello" to the nurse at the station on her floor at least once a day after leaving her room on her own. The task of having the nurse chart on the calendar Mrs. J's visit to the station was also added to the contract. In addition, the head nurse and the social worker planned to meet once a week to review Mrs. J's progress, using the charted calendar. The social worker would use this information when she met with Mrs. J to chart progress in goal 3a on the evaluation graph each week. As shown in Table 8.3 (page 290), the contract reformulation and the three-month evaluation were indicated on the contracted plan.

III.   **Field Area: Public Social Worker**

A. **Agency: State Social Services**

B. **Client System**

Mr. and Mrs. P and their two children (ages 2 and 4) were placed in emergency shelter (Center City Motor Inn) for 44 days and are currently living in an apartment. (For additional background information, see Chapter 4, Engagement in Micro, Mezzo, and Macro Practice in Diverse Field Areas, III. Public Social Welfare.)

C. **Summary of Preceding Stages**

The problems, goals, and tasks identified and enacted in earlier stages are listed in Table 6.10 in Chapter 6 and Table 7.3 in Chapter 7. The interventions of the social worker were primarily (1) referral to several resources, (2) direct work with the P family, and (3) teamwork with the income-maintenance technician and Mr. P's psychiatrist.

D. **Evaluation**

<u>Goal analysis:</u>   After 10 weeks of service, the social worker and Mr. and Mrs. P evaluated the extent to which the goals of the contracted plan were accomplished. They agreed that goals for problems 1, 2, 3, 4, 6, 7, 8, and 9 were accomplished. These goals are the following: (1) to obtain an emergency food supply, (2) to move into emergency shelter, (3) to receive a food supply until AFDC check and food stamps arrive, (4) to move into an apartment for long-term residence of family, (6) to have children examined at the health center, (7) to obtain fuel assistance, (8) to receive AFDC check and food stamps, and (9) to have the refrigerator repaired.

Goals 10, 11, and 12 were not accomplished by the time of the evaluation. These goals are (10) to receive Supplemental Security Income, (11) to receive a Thanksgiving food basket, and (12) to receive Christmas gifts for the children.

No goal was ever stated on the contracted plan for problem 5 (poor money management) because Mr. and Mrs. P refused to recognize this problem. They

TABLE 8.3   Contracted Plan: Seaside Nursing Home (Continued from Tables 6.9 and 7.2)

Date Identified	Problem/ Need	Goal	Task	Contract	Date Anticipated	Date Accomplished
12/8 Evaluation	Evaluation of problems 1–5	Goals 1–5	1. Review each goal. 2. Evaluate extent of accomplishment for each goal. 3. Reformulate contract.	Mrs. J and social worker	12/18 and 12/20	12/18 and 12/20
Contract reformu- lation	Change in tasks, contract, and dates anticipated for goal 3a	3a. To leave room alone (at least once a day)	(3a)1. Leave room alone and walk down to nurse's station and say "hello" to nurse on duty.	1. Mrs. J	12/21 and each day thereafter	
			2. Circle date of visit on calendar.	2. Nurse on duty	12/21 and each day thereafter	
			3. Meet to discuss Mrs. J's progress.	3. Head nurse and social worker	12/27 and each Thursday thereafter	
			4. Evaluate progress toward goal 3a using graph.	4. Social worker and Mrs. J	12/27 and each Thursday thereafter	

continued to blame others and to deny that their evictions from past apartments were related to their poor management of money.

<u>*Contract review:*</u>   *In reviewing the goals that were accomplished, the social worker asked if the attainment of goals was a result of the plan contracted. With the exception of goals 4 and 9, goal attainment directly followed the completion of planned tasks. The contract for goal 4 stated that the Ps and the social worker would collaborate on locating an apartment. For goal 9, the social worker and the Ps planned that Mr. P would contact the Salvation Army for financial assistance to pay for repairs. Instead, the Ps contacted their income-maintenance technician directly, and she arranged for them to receive a new refrigerator.*

In analyzing goals that were not accomplished (goals 10, 11, and 12), the social worker noted that the arrest in the process of goal accomplishment for each of these goals could be pinpointed to tasks contracted to Mr. P that he failed to complete. He did not follow up on his application for Supplemental Security Income, nor did he contact churches for a Thanksgiving food basket or the Salvation Army for Christmas presents for the children.

Even with goal 9 (refrigerator repair), instead of Mr. P's getting estimates on repair costs and contacting the Salvation Army, he and Mrs. P called the income-maintenance technician and requested a new refrigerator. (The social worker and the income-maintenance technician realized that they should have communicated with each other about this new request before either one enacted a plan thus avoiding teamwork breakdown.)

The social worker did not use scales to assess the extent of goal accomplishment during the evaluation stage because of the basic nature of the identified goals and the interventions utilized. Although the primary needs for housing and food were being met for the present, the social worker realized that there were two continuing problem areas: (1) poor money management and (2) excessive dependency on others to meet their needs. At the time of the evaluation, the Ps were not recognizing these problems and did not want to work on either of them. When the social worker pointed out that the tasks assigned to Mr. P had not been accomplished, he said he planned to do them when he felt up to it.

Since the Ps were not asking for help from the social worker with the two cited problems or with any additional problems or needs at the time of the evaluation, and because the social worker did not want to continue unnecessary dependency, he began to talk about terminating with the family. Both the Ps and the social worker agreed that they would begin the process of termination.

E. Charted Progress

The social worker recorded the evaluation process on the contracted plan as found in Table 8.4.

In the social worker's discussions with the Ps, their income-maintenance technician, and Mr. P's psychiatrist, the social worker shared his continued concern regarding the family's management of money and dependence on outside resources to meet their needs. The problem of the family's poor money management had been recorded on the problem list earlier. During evaluation, the family's problem of dependency became more obvious to the social worker, and it was

TABLE 8.4 Contracted Plan: State Social Services (Continued from Tables 6.11 and 7.3)

Date Identified	Problem/ Need	Goal	Task	Contract	Date Anticipated	Date Accomplished
12/4 Evaluation	Evaluation of problems 1–12	Goals 1–4 and 6–12 (no goal for problem 5)	1. Review goals.	1. Mr. and Mrs. P and social worker	12/4	12/4
			2. Assess extent of accomplishment.	2. Mr. and Mrs. P and social worker	12/4	12/4
			3. Analyze progress.	3. Mr. and Mrs. P and social worker	12/4	12/4
			4. Reformulate contract or begin termination.	4. Mr. and Mrs. P and social worker	12/4	12/4
Contract reformu- lation	Add problem 13: family's depen- dence on outside resources					

added to the problem list when he recorded the evaluation (see Table 8.4). The social worker expected that the case of the P family would possibly need to be reopened at a later date, and he thought it would be helpful to have the basic problem of dependency highlighted in the summarized chart.

IV. **Field Area: Community Services**

A. **Agency: Clayton Neighborhood House**

B. **Client System**

Four Hispanic families needed heat in their apartments on the second floor of 33 T Street. (For more background information, see Chapter 4, Engagement in Micro, Mezzo, and Macro Practice in Diverse Field Areas, IV. Community Services.)

C. **Summary of Preceding Stages**

The problems, goals, and tasks as identified and contracted in earlier stages are outlined in Table 6.12 in Chapter 6 and Table 7.4 in Chapter 7. The social worker's interventions were direct and indirect with residents and their landlord. By the third meeting of the social worker with the residents, they were ready to move into the evaluation stage of the General Method.

D. **Evaluation**

Goal analysis: After the residents monitored the heat in their apartments for a week, they met to share their findings with the social worker. Each family reported that the heat was adequate, ranging from 65° to 70° each day. At night, the heat went down to 63° to 65°, and this was acceptable to the families. The residents expressed relief and gratitude to the social worker. They were hopeful that the heating would continue throughout the winter.

As the social worker and the residents began to recall their identified goal, she presented a scale (as found in Figure 8.19) for goal analysis.

The families agreed that at this time their heating during the day is checked as averaging 68° (see the X in Figure 8.19). The goal of adequate heating was being accomplished. The continuation of heating throughout the winter remained in question. They wanted to continue monitoring the heat throughout the winter and asked how they could show it on the scale each week. The social worker introduced the ongoing evaluation graph found in Figure 8.20. She explained that the horizontal line represented weeks and that the vertical line indicated temperature. She showed them when and how to plot their findings on the graph. They agreed to meet again the following week to plot their findings.

FIGURE 8.19   **Goal 1: To Obtain Consistent, Adequate Heating**

								X	
30	35	40	45	50	55	60	65	70	
				Starting					

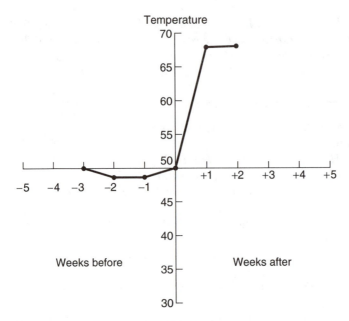

FIGURE 8.20 Temperature Monitoring

Contract review and reformulation: *In reviewing the contracted plan, the social worker reminded the residents that she had never met with the janitor (no entry in "date accomplished" for Task 1, Goal 1, in Table 6.12 in Chapter 6). They agreed that there was no need for anyone to say anything to him now that the upstairs was being heated adequately. The residents knew that they continued to have a problem communicating with the landlord, but they didn't want to do anything about it for the present.*

At this time, the social worker and the residents agreed to extend their contact for another week. If there was no further problem with the heating and if the residents had nothing else they wanted to work on with the social worker, she would terminate with them during the next meeting.

E. Charted Progress

The evaluation and contract reformulation by the social worker and the residents was recorded on the contracted plan as indicated in Table 8.5.

V. Field Area: Education

A. Agency: Keeney Elementary School

B. Client System

Jim G, an 8-year-old third-grader, was showing regressive behavior in school and at home in reaction to his parents' strained relationship. (For additional background information, see Chapter 4, Engagement in Micro, Mezzo, and Macro Practice in Diverse Field Areas, V. Education.)

TABLE 8.5 Contracted Plan: Clayton Neighborhood House (Continued from Tables 6.12 and 7.4)

Date Identified	Problem/ Need	Goal	Task	Contract	Date Anticipated	Date Accomplished
12/12 Evaluation	Evaluation of problems 1 (heating) and 2 (communication with landlord)	1. Adequate, consistent heating (no goal set for problem 2)	1. Review goal and problems.	Social worker and residents	12/2	12/12
			2. Evaluation extent of goal accomplishment.			
			3. Reformulate contract.			
Contract reformulation	Drop task 1, of goal 1, add tasks 6 and 7 for goal 1		6. Continue to monitor heat daily.	6. Mr. T, Mrs. V, Mr. A, and CR	12/12–12/19	
			7. Meet to review findings (and possible termination).	7. Social worker and residents	12/19	

295

C. Summary of Preceding Stages

The problems, goals, and tasks that were identified in earlier stages are outlined in the contracted plan found in Table 6.14 in Chapter 6. After the joint session with Mr. and Mrs. G, Jim, and the social worker at school, Mr. and Mrs. G followed through with going for marital counseling at a local family counseling center, and Jim began to show improvement in his school work.

D. Evaluation

Progress in school performance was evaluated by Jim and the social worker as they met twice a week in her office. When the social worker called Mrs. G each week, they would evaluate what progress had been made. During the last home visit, the social worker, Jim, and his parents reviewed the contracted plan and analyzed the extent of goal accomplishment for all four problem areas.

Goal analysis: As the social worker and Jim met together and focused on his school performance, they looked mainly at the extent to which Jim was (1) paying attention (showing interest in learning), (2) participating in class (raising hand to give answers or ask questions), and (3) bringing his grades up in math and spelling. These were specific areas in need of improvement identified by Jim's teacher. Each week, the social worker met briefly with Jim's teacher to receive a report on his progress in the classroom. The teacher showed the social worker Jim's weekly test scores in math and spelling. When Jim met with the social worker, the teacher's report was reviewed, and scales to evaluate goal accomplishment were used (see Figure 8.21).

By the end of the second week after the meeting with Jim and his parents, Jim's academic performance was assessed as +3 on the interest scale ("much interest") and as +3 on the scale for class participation ("much raising hand—five or six times a day"); his grades in math jumped from an average of 40 to 90, and his spelling grades went from 50 to 100 (see Figure 8.21). There was obvious progress in Jim's investment in school. His school attendance was no longer a problem. He arrived on time each day and was back to walking to school with the neighborhood children. Mrs. G also reported that he was sleeping better at night. When talking with Mrs. G on the phone, the social worker learned that Mr. and Mrs. G were not finding the counseling sessions easy, but Mrs. G did think that they were helpful.

Contract review and reformulation: In the last planned visit with Mr. and Mrs. G and Jim, the social worker and the family recognized that all of their goals were being accomplished. More time was needed for Mr. and Mrs. G to work on their relationship, and they planned to continue in counseling for as long as was needed. Jim's problems had apparently subsided and he was back at his earlier functioning level (above average academically). Mr. and Mrs. G agreed that there was no reason for them to meet with the school social worker again unless additional problems developed with Jim.

Jim said he liked to meet with the social worker in her office and he didn't want to stop seeing her each week. They agreed that their visits would be reduced to once a week (instead of twice) for two more weeks (once before Christmas and

FIGURE 8.21   Goal 3: To Improve School Performance

INTEREST LEVEL (PAYING ATTENTION)

			X	
0	**1**	**2**	**3**	**4**
Starting point; no interest	Little interest	Some interest	Much interest	Totally interested

CLASS PARTICIPATION

			X	
0	**1**	**2**	**3**	**4**
Starting point; not raising hand	Little raising hand (once or twice a day)	Some raising hand (three or four times a day)	Much raising hand (five or six times a day)	Frequent raising hand (seven or more times a day)

MATH GRADES

0	10	20	30	40	50	60	70	80	90	100
				Starting point					X	

SPELLING GRADES

0	10	20	30	40	50	60	70	80	90	100
					Starting point					X

---

once after he came back from vacation). During these sessions, they said they would talk about ending their work together.

Ongoing evaluation: Since the social worker and Jim would meet to review his progress, ongoing evaluation graphs were drawn and hung on the social worker's wall (see Figures 8.22 and 8.23). The graphs indicated Jim's progress in math and spelling from the time he began school in the fall. Each point on the horizontal line indicated weeks before or after he started working with the social worker.

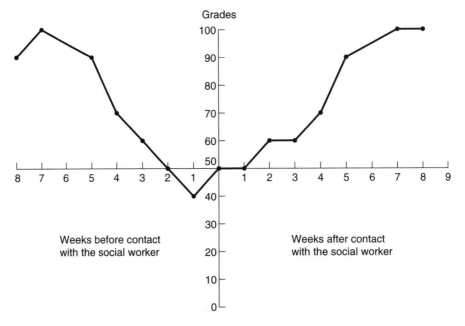

FIGURE 8.22   **Spelling**

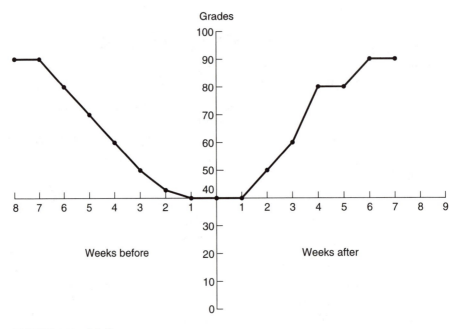

FIGURE 8.23   **Math**

TABLE 8.6 Contracted Plan: Keeney Elementary School (Continued from Table 6.14)

Date Identified	Problem/ Need	Goal	Task	Contract	Date Anticipated	Date Accomplished
12/4, 12/6, 12/13 Evaluation	Evaluation of problems 1, 2, 3, 4	Goals 1, 2, 3, 4	1. Review and evaluate goal 3 (school performance).	1. Jim and social worker	11/27, 11/29 12/4, 12/6	11/27, 11/29 12/4, 12/6
			2. Review and evaluate goals 1, 3, 4 (Jim's school functioning and sleeping).	2. Mr. and Mrs. G, Jim, and social worker	12/17	12/17
			3. Review goal 2 (Mr. and Mrs. G's relationship).	3. Social worker, Mr. and Mrs. G	12/17	12/17
			4. Reformulate contract or terminate.	4. Social worker, Mr. and Mrs. G, and Jim	12/17	12/17
Contract reformu- lation		To change task and date anticipated for task 4, problem 3 (see contracted plan, Table 6.13 in Chapter 6)	4. Meet once a week.	4. Social worker and Jim	12/20 and 1/8	

The vertical lines indicated grade averages each week, with the center point at the grade Jim was averaging when he first met the social worker.

E. Charted Progress

The evaluation of grades and the additional tasks planned at this time were recorded by the social worker on the contracted plan as shown in Table 8.6.

VI. Field Area: Corrections

A. Agency: Juvenile Court

B. Client System

A group of six male youths, all age 14, are on probation and attending weekly group meetings led by co-workers at Juvenile Court. (For further background information, see Chapter 4, Engagement in Micro, Mezzo, and Macro Practice in Diverse Field Areas, VI. Corrections.)

C. Summary of Preceding Stages

The problems, goals, and tasks contracted in earlier stages are outlined in Table 6.15 in Chapter 6 and Table 7.5 in Chapter 7. Attendance and participation in group meetings and weekly behavior reports from home and school were charted on graphs from every member of the group at the end of each meeting. Issues of interest or "changes" for the members were selected and discussed each week. After three and one-half months (14 weeks), the social workers began to go through a formal goal analysis with the youths. They also talked about the group process and progress. The ongoing evaluation graphs and weekly charts that were developed and used earlier (Figures 6.1, 6.2, 6.3, and 6.4 in Chapter 6 and Figures 7.6 and 7.7 in Chapter 7) were helpful in the evaluation process.

D. Evaluation

<u>Goal analysis:</u>   Since the four-month probationary period would be over in two weeks, all of the youths were eager to know if they would be getting off probation and if the group would be ending at that time. In evaluating goal 1 ("to get off probation in four months"), the members were reminded by the social workers of the criteria that had been stated earlier for achieving this goal: (1) to maintain a score of 2 for group attendance—present each week unless excused, (2) to maintain an average score of 3 ("much") or higher for group participation, (3) to maintain an average score of 3 ("good") or higher for behavior at home, (4) to maintain an average score of 3 ("good") or higher for behavior at school, and (5) to obey the rules of society (no further law breaking).

Each of the group members was asked to look over his graphs and to assess the extent to which he met the criteria for accomplishing goal 1. It was obvious that four of the youths (MK, ML, B, C) could be recommended for a reduction in probation from six to four months. One member (A) had already left the group and had been sent to a correctional center. The other two (J and T) had failed to attend and to participate in meetings regularly. J's home reports averaged "poor" to "fair," and T had "poor" school reports because he continued to get into fights at school. J and T realized that they had not accomplished goal 1 and would there-

fore need to continue to meet with the social workers each Monday. They were told that if they brought their scores up in all areas during the next six weeks, they could have their probation reduced by one month. They also knew that if they continued to do poorly, their probation period would be extended.

In evaluating goal 2 ("to control tempers"), each of the youths reviewed his scores on the weekly chart (Figures 7.23 and 7.24 in Chapter 7). All agreed that they had grown in recognizing when they were beginning to feel angry and it was time to "cool it." They verbalized ways they had learned to handle their feelings instead of "blowing up." In looking at the progression of their weekly scores, improvement in temper control was apparent for all of the youths except T.

In analyzing the third goal (to learn more about "the changes" of teenagers), the youths reviewed the topics that had been covered during group meetings. They indicated which issues or speakers they thought were the most interesting. They described the film on human sexuality as "kind of stupid," but the talk by the ex-prisoner and the trip to the vocational training school were "great." They all agreed that they had grown in understanding some of the changes they were going through.

After the evaluation, it was clear that four of the group members would probably be leaving the group in two or three weeks. Although the co-workers would continue to meet with J and T, the plan was made to begin to discuss in the following meetings "what it is like when you're off probation and there's no more group."

E. Charted Progress and Contract Reformulation

The social worker recorded the group evaluation and contract reformulation as outlined in Table 8.7 (page 302). The outline indicates that the anticipated dates for group meetings would be extended to at least six additional weeks for J and T. Also indicated in the record is the plan made by the group to begin to discuss group termination and being off probation at the next meeting.

VII. Field Area: Homeless Shelter

A. Agency: West End Community Shelter
B. Client System

Mr. Romano, a 37-year-old Hispanic male, is homeless and HIV positive. (For additional background information, see Chapter 4, Engagement in Micro, Mezzo, and Macro Practice in Diverse Field Areas, VII, Homeless Shelter.)

C. Summary of Preceding Stages

Mr. R came to the shelter on May 7 feeling afraid and abandoned. During engagement, he informed the social worker that he had completed a drug detoxification program over six years ago and had tried to get his life in order ever since. Mr. R wanted to go back to work and to get more information about his illness. During assessment and intervention, the social worker and he developed and carried out a plan that included Mr. R's going to the free health clinic, getting involved with the Harmony, Inc. program, seeking employment, and returning to church.

TABLE 8.7 Contracted Plan: Juvenile Court (Continued from Tables 6.15 and 7.5)

Date Identified	Problem/ Need	Goal	Task	Contract	Date Anticipated	Date Accomplished
1/14 Evaluation	Evaluation of problems 1, 2, 3	Goals 1, 2, 3	1. Review goals. 2. Evaluate goal accomplishment. 3. Reformulate contract or introduce termination.	Members and co-workers	1/14	1/14
Contract reformulation	1. Add goal 1a, task 1, contract date anticipated to reflect plan to extend group meetings for J and T for at least 6 more weeks	1a. To get off probation by March 1	1. Attend weekly group meetings.	J and T and co-workers	Up to 2/25	
	2. Add beginning termination plan, tasks 1 and 2		1. Introduce termination. 2. Discuss being "off probation."	1. Co-workers 2. Co-workers and group members	1/14 1/22	

D. Evaluation

Goal analysis: Two days after Mr. R applied for residence at Hope Home, the shelter received a call from the social worker at Hope Home, who stated that they were anticipating an opening for Mr. R around the first of the month. They were making arrangements to move a resident to hospice in Florida where he could be near relatives. Mr. R could come over for a preplacement visit. The social worker and Mr. R decided it was time to evaluate what progress had been made in achieving goals and to plan for the future. In using the goal-accomplishment scales, it was apparent that the goals of obtaining emergency shelter, reunion with the church, gaining information regarding HIV/AIDs, obtaining medical care, and getting social support had been accomplished. The goal of locating housing after staying 60 days at the shelter was progressing (+3), but there was some regression in the goal of getting income (1.5) (see Figures 8.24 and 8.25). The reason for the regression was due to Mr. R's having to drop to part-time employment and his not being able to obtain social security and social services until his condition became worse (see Figure 8.24). The social worker recalled that during data collection she learned that even when Mr. R's testing indicates that he has AIDS

FIGURE 8.24 Goal 4: To Earn Steady Income

					X			
−4	−3	−2	−1	0	+1	+2	+3	+4
Goal abandoned								Goal accomplished

FIGURE 8.25 Goal 5: To Locate Residence

							X	
−4	−3	−2	−1	0	+1	+2	+3	+4
Goal abandoned								Goal accomplished

(250 white T-cell count), and he is accepted for social security, there will be a 120-day wait before the first check is received. Mr. R could apply for general assistance during the interim period. During evaluation, Mr. R returned to the health clinic and learned that his white T-cell count was at 250. The doctor discussed with Mr. R the medications that would be prescribed.

Ongoing evaluation: While working with Mr. R, the social worker used the ongoing evaluation graphs for goals 4 and 5 (see Figures 8.26 and 8.27). These goals were selected because they appeared to be more complex and in need of more time than the other goals identified on the contracted plan.

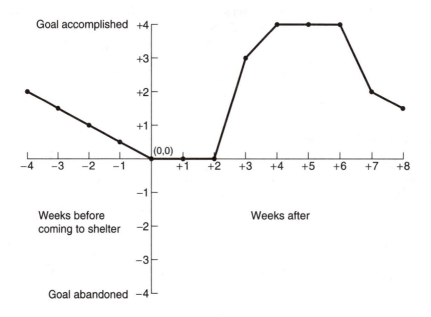

Descriptive criteria (Y line)
+4 = Goal: steady income (employment or SS/SSI)
+3 = Almost steady income or more than part-time employment
+2 = Some income or part-time employment
+1 = Little income or brief (one-time) jobs
 0 = Starting point: no income
−1 = Beginning to go into debt
−2 = Increasing debt
−3 = Major debts
−4 = Goal abandoned: no work and denied assistance or SS/SSI

FIGURE 8.26   Steady Income

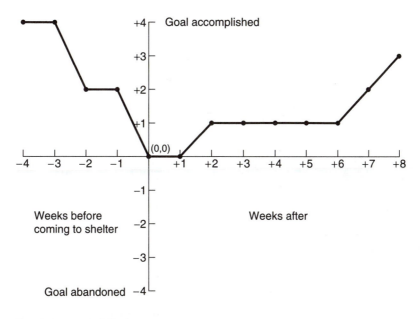

Descriptive criteria (Y line)
+4 = Goal: permanent residence
+3 = Going for placement visit for permanent residence
+2 = Applying for place or temporary residence
+1 = Identifying possible places
 0 = Starting point: only home is shelter (60 days max.)
−1 = 40 days left/no place located
−2 = 20 days left/no place located
−3 = No days left/no place to go
−4 = Goal abandoned: homeless

FIGURE 8.27   Permanent Residence after Shelter

<u>*Contract review and reformulation:*</u>   *The only recognized contract reformulations that were needed at the time of the evaluation were additions to the tasks for goals 4 and 5. Mr. R needed to plan his move to Hope Home and apply for social security, SSI disability, and general public assistance. The contracted plan was augmented to reflect these anticipated developments for Mr. R (see Table 8.8).*

E. Charted Progress
Progress in goal accomplishment was indicated on the contracted plan and the scales and graphs were placed in the record. The social worker entered information obtained from the Hope Home social worker and the doctor at the clinic in summary recordings.

TABLE 8.8 Contracted Plan: West End Community Shelter (Continued from Tables 6.17 and 7.6)

Date Identified	Problem/ Need	Goal	Task	Contract	Date Anticipated	Date Accomplished
6/26	Evaluation of problems 1–7	Goals 1–7	1. Recall each goal. 2. Assess extent of accomplishment. 3. Reformulate contract.	1. Mr. R and social worker	6/26	6/26
Contract reformulation	1. Change task 4, date anticipated, and add tasks 5–8 for problem 4	Goal 4	4. Request doctor's report. 5. Get report. 6. Apply for SS and general assistance. 7. Get general assistance. 8. Get SS.	4. Mr. R 5. Mr. R 6. Mr. R 7. Mr. R 8. Mr. R	6/26 6/27 6/27 7/5 10/25	
	2. Add tasks 3 and 4 to problem 5	Goal 5	3. Go for preplacement visit. 4. Decide about placement.	3. Mr. R 4. Mr. R and Home social worker	7/1 7/2	

Conclusion

In this chapter, the meaning and process of evaluation in general practice were presented. Evaluation was recognized as a particular stage in and as an ongoing dimension of the General Method. The need and values of evaluation in social work practice were emphasized.

Tools and processes were introduced that may be used during evaluation with any type of system. Various examples were given to demonstrate their applicability. The art and the science of practice are very apparent as a social worker objectively and sensitively tries to assess progress and direction in each individualized situation.

As pointed out earlier, evaluation may lead to a reformulation of the contracted plan with additional interventions, or it may serve as a bridge to cross into the final stage of the General Method. Evaluation is a necessary prelude to termination.

CHAPTER

9

Termination

When a social worker begins to disengage with a client system, time, skill, and understanding are needed for an effective closure of services. The art of termination involves skillful interactions and procedures with honest sharing in an atmosphere of realistic hope. Although each client system is unique with its own individual pace and method of responding to both achievement and loss, some general reaction patterns are often present during termination and need to be identified.

In this chapter, the knowledge, values, and skills utilized during termination will be presented. The need for a social worker to develop the art of termination cannot be overemphasized. A poorly timed or poorly executed termination may result in marked regression or failure in goal accomplishment. By contrast, a meaningful, growth-promoting termination experience can stabilize progress and serve as a support and model for a client system as it faces new attachments, separations, and losses in the future.

The Meaning of Termination

At its best, this sixth and final stage of the General Method of social work practice is much more than simply breaking off contact with a client, action, or target system. As referred to in this chapter, *termination* comprises the time taken and the process used in planning to cease contact. Symbolically, termination has double-edged meanings—ending yet beginning anew, losing yet gaining. Affectively, these symbolic meanings elicit feelings of sadness, anxiety, ambivalence, pleasure, and excitement. Even when there has been little contact and sharing, time is needed for the social worker and the client, action, or target system to recall their purpose in coming together, review their progress in fulfilling this purpose, clarify the reasons for ending, and plan the termination. Together, these actions serve to:

- Integrate the earlier work and consolidate gains.
- Support personal and collective resourcefulness.
- Create a sense of accomplishment, mastery, and hope.
- Strengthen the client system's ability to function within an enhanced environment.
- Build a bridge linking present and future.

Thus, this final stage is a culmination of all the work that has gone before and a pathway into an enhanced future.

Reactions to Termination as Ending and Loss

Central to an understanding of termination is an awareness of the possible feelings and reactions that may take place as client systems and social workers separate. For some client systems, the recognition and expression of these feelings may come quite easily at this time. For others, however, strong reactions against these feelings may come into operation. Disguised reactions to particular feelings can make termination a time of confusion and frustration for both client systems and social workers.

Children, for example, have been found to experience such feelings as fear, anxiety, sadness, loss, rejection, guilt, helplessness, and cultural shock when they are separated from significant others or familiar surroundings. Instead of being able to express these feelings, some react with such behaviors as hostility, acting out, lack of trust, bed-wetting, poor schoolwork, destructiveness, lying, and running away. Rather than acting out, some children become extremely withdrawn and refuse to form new attachments. In studying this reaction, Littner (1981, p. 22) writes:

> To the degree that he cannot master these feelings and must repress them, the child will need to fend off close relationships, using the various techniques previously mentioned, and suffer the painful consequences of this self-imposed emotional isolation. He will keep bottled up within him an enormous desire for closeness, which he cannot allow himself to really satisfy. It is noteworthy, too, that his impaired ability to relate to people may also influence his capacity to be close to his own children, and therefore sometimes directly affects their ability to be close to others.

Child, adult, and family client systems seen by social workers have often experienced painful separations and terminations in their lives. Many times, they are guarded and fearful of forming a trusting relationship with a social worker. If an attachment is formed, when it comes time to terminate, strong feelings from past separations may emerge along with feelings over the anticipated loss of the social worker. Thus, it is not surprising that they may display a variety of coping styles to ward off past and present hurts and anxieties. The feelings that are avoided often include a sense of abandonment, fear of being unable to cope alone, helplessness, guilt, failure, and holding oneself responsible for the felt rejection. These feelings may be covered up through one, several, or a sequence of reactive behaviors.

The coping styles and reactions of individuals, families, and small treatment groups during termination may fall within a five-stage termination sequence that is similar to the stages of the grieving process (Hess & Hess, 1994; Kubler-Ross, 1969; Timberlake & Cutler, 2001). Although not necessarily in every case, nor in the exact order described here, reactions to termination are often identified as falling within one or all of the following stages:

1. *Denial:* The client may ignore what the social worker is saying or avoid any discussion of termination. This may extend to failing to keep appointments and/or coming late or leaving early. In a group, individual members or the group as a whole may isolate themselves, refuse to participate in the conversation, or attempt to change the topic of discussion.
2. *Anger:* There may be outbursts of verbal or physical assaults. These may be directed toward the social worker, toward other members of the system, or toward a person who is expected to take over the social worker's role after termination. Anger may also be turned inward as the client displays a lack of concern or care for self, including possible personal injury. There may be regression to earlier problematic behavior in order to be punished or to punish the social worker.
3. *Bargaining:* The client tries to negotiate an extension of time or a modified cutback in contacts. Promises of "being good if" are presented. Gifts or rewards may be offered.

4. *Depression:* The client manifests listlessness, little energy, withdrawal, sadness, helplessness, despair, and/or no motivation to go on. Pain is real and evident. There is regression in accomplishments. Time is needed to mourn. Beginning resignation is apparent.

5. *Acceptance:* With the acceptance of the termination, there is an increase in energy. The client is able to talk about the good and the bad times and to think about the future. There is a quiet expectation as the client begins to show interest in forming new attachments. The client returns to the level of functioning prior to the depression and moves away from self-pity or self-centeredness.

Small, closed groups with service time limits also react to the loss elements in termination. The group's feelings about the loss of the social worker and the services provided are compounded by their feelings about losing the shared experience and interpersonal history created within the group. Thus, groups also need time to recall their purpose in coming together, review their progress in fulfilling this purpose, clarify the reasons for ending, and plan the termination. The group termination process includes an examination of the important life space events and general support that occurred during the group's existence. As members face the reality that the treatment group as a problem-solving resource will cease to exist, they also work through feelings and stages of denial, anger, bargaining, depression, and finally acceptance. The social worker facilitates members' awareness that their individual growth and change goes beyond the shared group activity and works to stabilize these individual changes in everyday social functioning.

The larger client, action, and target systems of organizations and communities also need time to process the termination experience and react to the loss elements of ending. It is, however, important to note that the professional relationship elements of the social services provided are purposively different. These elements are also diluted by the sheer size of larger client, action, and target systems. Yet, members of organizations and communities collectively benefit from sharing in the termination stage processes of recalling their purpose in coming together, reviewing their progress in fulfilling this purpose, clarifying the reasons for ending, and planning the termination. A major difference, however, is that these macro systems will continue their existence beyond the life of this service period with the social worker. Therefore, it is important that the social worker and the macro system process residual feelings about change and loss, celebrate enhanced or acquired community resources, stabilize change by developing leadership indigenous to the organization and community, institutionalize socially just policies and procedures for the macro system's future beyond the work completed, and envision the future planning and problem-solving process of the macro system in response to forthcoming issues and challenges.

During termination with individuals, families, groups, organizations, and communities, there may not be a clear transition from one stage of the sequence to the next. Frequently, there are signs of regression in the process, and a discussion of fears and feelings will have to be repeated. A social worker who is aware of the natural process and reactions of micro, mezzo, and macro client systems found during termination is less likely to take what is happening personally or literally and then react inappropriately.

Reactions to Termination as Celebration and Beginning

As noted earlier, termination involves more than the needs and feelings triggered by ending and loss. It also involves a celebration of work well done, goals achieved, problem-solving skills attained, and beginning an autonomous existence in a newly enhanced environment. Thus, in a sense, termination—like graduation—is a rite of passage that involves looking backward to take stock of where one has been, integrate goal achievements and consolidate the gains made today, mobilize resourcefulness, and strengthen the sense of mastery and hope while moving from the present toward a more autonomous future with enhanced personal and collective resources.

When the focus is on celebration and beginning anew, it conveys the social worker's perception of the client system's strengths and resourcefulness as well as the expectation of the client system's ability to maintain the gains in problem solving and well-being. In other words, termination becomes an empowering experience as it shifts from the initial reactions of loss and ending toward celebration and renewed beginning.

The Decision to Terminate

After a social worker and a system of contact have completed an evaluation of goal accomplishment, they may conclude that the purpose for their coming together has been attained. The scales and graphs suggested in Chapter 8 may have helped demonstrate the movement and progress that have been made. In addition to these indicators, a social worker can assess the appropriateness of moving into termination with a client system by (1) reviewing with his or her supervisor the work that has taken place with the client system, (2) observing and talking with the client system itself, and (3) talking with other knowledgeable sources about the client system's readiness to terminate with the social worker (with informed consent of system).

If there is some hesitancy to move into termination on the part of the client system or the social worker, the cause for holding back needs to be identified. A supervisor can help a social worker let go of a system when there may be strong attachment because there has been progress and the social worker gets much satisfaction in working with the client system, or because progress has been minimal and the social worker has feelings of failure.

If the system of contact is holding back from facing termination, this could be caused by the feelings identified earlier or by other problematic areas that the system would like to face with the social worker, even though there has been avoidance and fear up to this time. The supervisor might help detect this and might suggest that the social worker explore this possibility with the client system before moving on to termination.

It may be that a social worker wants to terminate with a client system even when there is insufficient evidence that goals have been accomplished. Through supervision, the social worker may be helped to recognize feelings of anger or helplessness in working with the system of contact that are causing the desire to terminate prematurely. If a client system wants an early termination with a social worker, it may be (1) because the social worker is beginning to touch on conflict areas that the client system does not want to face, (2) because the client system is anticipating the social worker's leaving and wants to be in control by initiating the termination, or (3) because the client system is taking flight from having to face any of the other feelings already identified (rejection, anger, grief, etc.). Here, too, the social worker may need help through supervision to discern the dynamics of the particular situation.

In observing and talking with a client system or other resources about possible termination, the social worker assesses the extent of goal accomplishment as well as the current functioning level of the client system. The questions to be asked are:

1. Have the goals been accomplished according to the contracted plan?
2. Can the client system go on functioning at least at the level attained at this time without continued contact with the social worker?
3. Although the identified problems may have been resolved and the goals accomplished, if a similar need or problem develops, will the client system be able to handle it, or at least know how to get help?
4. If additional supports will be needed after the social worker terminates, are they available?

A social worker continues to work with a client system beyond the point of achieving contracted goals only for the length of time needed to stabilize goal accomplishment and to go through the process of termination. If the preceding questions are answered affirmatively, then the client system is ready for termination to begin.

Sometimes a client system gives the message to a social worker indirectly that it is ready to terminate. Perhaps even before a social worker begins to discuss the issue, a client system may give indicators that it is able to handle problems on its own. Since client systems often internalize the coping patterns a social worker has demonstrated and, with experience, develop problem-solving skills that are transferable, there may be an apparent decrease in dependency and a desire to handle things independently. When the system of contact is a group or community, attendance may become irregular as members no longer feel the need to meet with the social worker or with one another. New sources of support and involvement may have been found by members of the system of contact. Indirectly, the client system may be showing a readiness for termination. These behaviors are different when a client system reacts to termination by breaking off in anger or as a means to regain control. There is little affect connected with behaviors that suggest a readiness to terminate. Even when a client system demonstrates this readiness, some of the feelings and reactions to loss described earlier may become apparent as the social worker begins to talk about termination. The thought of not having the social worker available for ongoing support may stir up earlier feelings of loss of a significant person. There may be some regression in functioning in order to keep the social worker involved and to avoid dealing with fears or feelings of loss. The social worker and the client system may both recognize that it is time to terminate, but opportunity will be needed to identify and express feelings and to plan for termination.

Occasionally, a social worker has to terminate with a client system before goals have been accomplished. This could happen because of the social worker's lack of skills to help the particular client system, because of an inappropriate emotional involvement, or because the social worker is leaving the agency. When the decision to terminate is not based on evaluation evidence of the client system's readiness, but on reasons related to the social worker's professional performance or life circumstances, the social worker and his or her agency have the responsibility to see that the client system continues to receive help from an appropriate resource. Also, time should be given to explain to the client system why there has to be a termination and to give the client system the opportunity to react to the unexpected closure.

A Life-Cycle Approach to Termination

Throughout the process of terminating with a client system, the social worker may use a life-cycle approach. Basically, the social worker tries to help the client system step back and review the life cycle of their work together. Initially, as the concept of termination is first introduced and early reactions of the client system to the idea may include denial, anger, or bargaining, the social worker helps the client system express the feelings underneath these reactions through a review of the *past*. They recall why they first came together and consider how they have moved to the present point in time. Recalling what they have been through together can help to bring out feelings of fear, anger, closeness, or loss. It can also help identify the nature and strength of the current relationship.

As the social worker and the client system move from focusing on the past to the *present*, it can become clearer that goals have been accomplished and that the earlier needs or problems that necessitated help from the social worker no longer exist. The instruments used earlier to evaluate progress during the stage of evaluation may be recalled. As the system begins to face the reality that termination is imminent, an attempt may be made to bargain for more time or to locate new problems. The social worker may sensitively point out that the client system has demonstrated an ability to handle such problems at this time and then begin to talk about the feelings that are making it difficult for the client system to terminate. Signs and feelings of depression may begin to appear as the client system becomes resigned to the termination. Strong feelings of fear, loss, or grief may emerge. Independently, the client system may begin to ask about the *future* and what will happen when he, she, or they will have to manage without the social worker. At this point, a plan for termination may begin to be formulated. Much time may be needed before the client system has the energy ready to invest in planning for the future. Feelings may need to be expressed repeatedly before a plan is completed. If the client system is not ready to move into considering the future, the social worker will need to stay with the present, even though this may call for great patience on the part of the social worker. In time, a client system will move from mourning over the anticipated loss to an acceptance of termination.

When the client system begins to accept the termination, more investment in developing and implementing a termination plan can be expected. As the social worker discusses the future with the client system, frequent reference is made to the needs that were identified in the *past* and to the strengths that are apparent in the *present*, in order to give hope for the *future*.

The life-cycle approach is a dynamic process used throughout the termination stage. Although the three focus points of *past*, *present*, and *future* are not necessarily addressed in an exact sequence, the framework offers some direction and guidance for the social worker to help a client system move through the process of termination.

Planning the Termination

As soon as possible, an ending date for the final planned contact between social worker and client system should be set. Ideally, both the social worker and the system of contact should mutually agree on this date and on the extent and times of contacts they will have prior to the termination date. Meetings between social worker and client system may be gradually tapered off until the closing date, or they may continue on a regular basis until final termination. The termination plan developed by social worker and client system should be individualized according to the needs and circumstances of the particular system. The point to be emphasized is that for an effective termination, a plan has to be articulated, understood, and implemented. If it is apparent that a client system is ready to terminate with a social worker but will need additional supports or services, the process of referral, transfer, and mobilization of environmental resources should be included as an essential dimension of the termination plan.

As brought out in Chapter 7 in the discussion on referral, when resources are being mobilized for a client system, every effort should be made to have the client system initiate and follow through on contacting the resource on its own. During termination, unless direct involvement by a social worker is absolutely necessary, the social worker should try to negotiate a plan in which the client system itself establishes linkages with the resources needed. This is particularly the case when resources are informal, such as is the case with family members, church, or neighborhood. Having the client system make its own contacts is empowering, fosters self-confidence, and provides the social worker with an opportunity to see if the client system can develop new relationships independently.

If a social worker is terminating with a client system that is unable to sustain itself without continued professional help, the social worker first tries to transfer the client system to another social worker in the same helping agency. If the agency already in contact with the client system has no social workers with the time or skills needed, then the social worker locates an appropriate outside resource and makes a referral (see the process for referral in Chapter 7). If a referral (outside resource) or a transfer (inside resource) is needed, a client system may have feelings about being referred or transferred that need to be expressed, and there are ways to proceed that can help to ensure a smooth transition as a system moves from an old social worker to a new social service provider.

When a client system experiences the loss of a social worker, particularly if a trusting relationship has developed, it can be very difficult for the client system to begin to bond with a new provider of services. The former social worker can help facilitate the transition process. Generally, only after having expressed some of the reactions to termination—such as denial, anger, bargaining, and depression—can the social worker and the client system begin to rationally consider establishing contact with a new resource. The client system in need of continued service may have strong feelings of loyalty to the former social worker. There may be a fear of appearing ungrateful or disloyal if the client system begins to relate positively to a new resource. The former social worker needs to sanction clearly the client system's involvement with a new social worker. This can be demonstrated in meetings that should be planned for all three parties (former social worker, client system in need, and new social worker) prior to the final termination date. At these meetings, the former social worker participates in a hopeful and supportive manner. He or she conveys a sense of trust in the abilities of the new social worker and of the client system in need of continued service to work constructively with each other.

It is necessary for all three parties to know exactly when the former social worker is going to terminate with the client system and if there is any plan for a follow-up. If there is some expectation of contact after the final termination date, it needs to be clear whom the former social worker will contact, when the contact can be expected, and why it is necessary. If the door is left open for the client system to reestablish contact with the former social worker, there may be a holding back from investment with the new social worker. The client system itself may contact the former social worker unexpectedly by a phone call or a letter. The former social worker can be most helpful by acknowledging the contact when received but then directing the client system back to the new social worker for continued help.

Even when a new resource has entered the termination process, there should be time on the final date for only the former social worker and the client system to meet together. During their last contact, there is often a planned expression of the significance of the meeting. If the client system is a group or community, there is generally a party or some type of ceremony. Pictures may be taken or exchanged. This time provides the opportunity for the final expression of feelings and hopes.

Stating the termination plan in writing helps avoid manipulation or misunderstanding. A separate format or instrument does not have to be drawn up. The contracted plan that was introduced and developed during assessment, intervention, and evaluation may continue to be used. As the social worker and the client system arrive at a final date and make plans for the intervening period, entries are made in the contracted plan to indicate the what (tasks), who (contract), and when (dates anticipated) of the plan. If it is agreed that new resources will be needed to support the system after the social worker leaves, the plan for initiating contact with these resources is included in the written statement. As the termination plan is carried out, dates of accomplishment for each of the tasks are entered on the contracted plan. An example is given in Table 9.1 of a termination plan for a group of young adolescent girls called "the Angels." This group was one of many offered at a neighborhood center each year. All groups terminated at the end of June and began again in September. The social worker knew who was expected to take "the Angels" the following year; therefore, the new social worker was invited to meet with the group as part of the termination plan.

Reactions of Service Providers

As human beings, providers of service become attached to others. Social workers, teachers, child-care workers, nurses, and other professionals suffer from feelings of loss when they are separated from client systems that have been meaningfully involved in their lives. If there has not been the opportunity to anticipate the loss, move through the reactions, and express the related feelings prior to final termination, a service provider may demonstrate depression, withdrawal, or burnout after one or several terminations of this nature.

In addition to the need for client systems receiving services to have time to express feelings and plans prior to termination, social workers and those in collaborative service provision need time to anticipate and express their possible emptiness when a system no longer needs their assistance. A double energy is often used by a service provider in termination: (1) that of helping a client system move away and (2) that of moving away himself or herself. A provider may deny, become angry, or become depressed during or after the energy drain. Through supportive supervision, peer meetings, and other available environmental supports, a provider may find a place, persons, and convenient time to work on what is happening inside of him or her.

When a service provider is employed in an emotionally charged service, such as child protection or work with the terminally ill, the need for supportive outlets is especially apparent. For example, in a residential setting for disturbed children, the child-care director became the main significant other for a 5-year-old boy. The child progressed remarkably and was moved into a foster home. Following his

TABLE 9.1 Contracted Plan: The Angels

Date Identified	Problem/Need	Goal	Task	Contract	Date Anticipated	Date Accomplished
5/3	21. Funding for trip to beach	21. To raise $50 for trip	1. Explore ways to raise funds; begin to plan. 2. Finalize plans for bake sale.	1. Group and social worker 2. Group and social worker	5/3 5/10	8/3 5/10
			3. Have bake sale. 4. Critique bake sale; set date and plan for beach trip; begin to discuss year-end evaluation.	3. Group and center 4. Group and social worker	5/15 5/17	5/15 5/17
5/24 Evaluation	Year-end evaluation of problems/needs 1–21, as cited above	1–21 as cited above	1. Recall goals. 2. Evaluate extent of goal accomplishment.	1. Group and social worker	4/24 and 6/1	5/24 and 6/1
6/1	Termination process	Satisfactory termination (progress stabilized)	1. Introduce termination. 2. Discuss feelings and reactions to ending the group; clarify final termination date.	1. Group and social worker 2. Group and social worker	6/1 6/7	6/1 6/7
			3. Identify present strengths, discuss the future; plan termination.	3. Group and social worker	6/14	6/14
			4. Invite new social worker (who will have the group after summer vacation) to the next meeting.	4. Mary C (for the group)	6/15	6/15
			5. Meet with new social worker.	5. Former social worker, group, and new social worker	6/21	6/21
			6. Go on beach trip.	6. Former social worker, group, and new social worker	6/26	6/26
			7. Conduct closing session and have party.	7. Former social worker and group	6/28	6/28

placement, the director became obviously antagonistic toward the social worker and increasingly irritable toward the other children. It was not until the social worker and the director took time to look painfully at what was happening that the director began to touch her feelings of depression due to the loss of the young boy. If the social worker or others at the facility had been more sensitive to the natural feelings of the director, more time could have been given to deal with termination prior to the child's discharge—a step that would have prevented some of the reactions that followed.

A social worker who serves as a case manager for a team that is about to terminate with a client system can show sensitivity to the needs of the team members by building in a time to talk about the feelings they might have as they anticipate closing the case. Supervisors and administrators also have a major responsibility to help prevent burnout in their employees. If they understand the significance of termination in the provision of services, they can find various ways to assist their social workers. For example, in a hospice facility where service providers were repeatedly experiencing the deaths of their patients, an administrator not only set aside times for peer support meetings but also designated a room on the top floor as "the Tower," where staff could go whenever they felt the need "to yell, cry, or pray." Unless a service provider can reach a point of acceptance with a termination, he or she will not be able to have the anticipation, hope, and energy necessary to invest in new client system work assignments.

Developing Sensitivity and Skills

The ideas about termination that are presented in this chapter are often rejected as an overexaggeration. New social workers, in particular, find it difficult to believe that their leaving a client system can have an impact on the system or on their own selves. A verbal presentation on the dynamics of termination may be only an intellectual consideration unless some aspect of experiential learning can be included. Three basic exercises (Exercises 9.1, 9.2, and 9.3) may be used to help students or service providers grow in sensitivity and skill for working with termination.

By using these three exercises, social workers can become more aware of the following central ideas:

1. Terminations may cause a variety of feelings and reactions that lead to a need for help from others.
2. Departures may cause disorientations and frustration, leading to an arrest in progress or to withdrawal or anger toward the person who initiated the separation.
3. There are ways to respond to client, action, or target systems who are facing terminations that can help let them know that you understand what they are going through.
4. Social workers themselves may have feelings and reactions that they need help with during terminations.

EXERCISE 9.1
Using Imagery

All the individuals participating in this experience are asked to close their eyes and picture a significant person in their lives. They are then asked to imagine that this person is talking with them and saying that he or she is going away and does not plan to return. Participants are then asked to identify their immediate feelings. They are next asked to imagine that they express these feelings to the person, but that the person repeats his or her plan to leave. They then imagine the person getting up and walking out. They are asked to let themselves enter into what they would feel when the person has left, and to try to find words to express these feelings. Finally, the participants are asked: What would you do next? The individuals are then asked: What do you need at this time?

This exercise helps a person sense some of the feelings that often emerge as one perceives the loss of a meaningful other. Talking about the experience may also lead to a discussion about what actions a person may take in trying to cope with such a loss and what resources might help the person through the experience.

EXERCISE 9.2
Small Group Experience

Participants are divided into small groups to discuss a topic, such as "timing needed for termination" or "writing up a termination plan." The facilitator moves around to different groups and eventually asks a member of one group to leave and join another identified group. After a few minutes, the facilitator moves to the next group and again directs a member to leave and join a different group, with no explanation for the move. This procedure is continued until every group has lost one of its original members.

In the discussion that follows, participants are asked to describe any thoughts or feelings they had when one of their members was asked to leave. They usually say that they wondered why the person was removed from the group and that they felt some frustration over the departure. They are then asked how they felt about another person joining the group. Here, too, feelings of anger and frustration were often experienced over having to adjust to the entry of a new person. The leaving or entering may have slowed down or stopped the group process. In addition, participants may share feelings of anger toward the facilitator for interrupting the group. Those that were directed to leave a group may disclose that they felt disoriented, isolated, rejected, or perhaps withdrawn as they entered a new group.

EXERCISE **9.3**

Role-Play

In this role-play between a social worker and a client system, there is a partial script that is given only to the actor who plays the role of the client system. The person in the role of the social worker is directed to begin the play by saying, "I will be leaving the agency in May." To what the social worker says, the person playing the client system is directed to feel free to respond as he or she feels like responding. Eventually, however, the "client system" is expected to make the statements (in whatever order seems appropriate) identified in the script.

Termination Script

SW: I will be leaving the agency in May.

CLIENT SYSTEM: Will I be seeing someone else?

SW: (?)

CLIENT SYSTEM: I had a fight with that neighbor again.

SW: (?)

CLIENT SYSTEM: What did I bother coming here for anyway? You're not really helping me.

SW: (?)

CLIENT SYSTEM: I'll come to see you where you are going—maybe just for a few months.

SW: (?)

CLIENT SYSTEM: Nobody cares about what happens to me anyway.

SW: (?)

CLIENT SYSTEM: May I take your picture before you leave?

SW: (?)

CLIENT SYSTEM: Thanks for everything.

SW: (?)

This exercise may also be done as a "fishbowl" experience. Here, anyone watching the role-play who believes he or she may have a more appropriate way to respond to the client may come in back of the person playing the role of the social worker and tap him or her on the shoulder. The social worker then exchanges places with this person, and the new response is given.

In the discussion that follows the role play, the facilitator asks the participants to consider what both actors were feeling as they made different statements. A basic question asked is: Was the social worker responding to the content literally, or was he or she tuning into the feelings of the client system? Participants are asked to consider other responses the social worker could have made to particular statements by the client system. The most important question is: What does the client system need to hear at this time?

There are other exercises and activities that can enhance a social worker's knowledge and skills in the process of terminating with a particular client system. For example, recording an individual interview on termination and then reviewing the recording by oneself or with one's supervisor or peers can help a social worker to better understand the dynamics that are taking place and to locate where the client system and the social worker are in the termination process. During this last stage of the General Method, a social worker's feelings may be so intense that it is difficult to maintain an objective perspective. Using such exercises as recording, role-play, and imagery can help strengthen the social worker's comprehension and self-control.

Working with Different Client Systems

Feelings and concerns of client, action, and target systems at the micro, mezzo, and macro practice levels during termination differ according to the unique circumstances and perspective of each system. Feelings of loss may extend beyond the loss of a social worker to the loss of a support group and its members (group), the loss of an external control system (institution), or the loss of a secure nurturing environment (agency). In trying to identify the feelings a client system is experiencing during the termination process, a social worker needs to be aware of these variations and other types of feelings frequently felt by client systems of particular size or purpose.

When a social worker is terminating with a community, for example, members may be planning to continue working together on issues by themselves, or they may be breaking up because they were a short-term organization with a task focus. Continuing without the social worker may be somewhat fearful for them because they depended on the social worker's leadership and support. Dissolving this organization may also cause some fears over losing a structure that gave them a sense of power and protection. These feelings will need to be clarified and expressed.

Diversity in reactions to termination also depends on the extent of investment made by each client system in the relationship with the social worker. This may present a challenge to a social worker when the client system is a family, group, organization, or community and the extent of investment differs among the individual members of the same client system. Although those with little investment may have minimal feeling about ending contacts, others in the client system may have strong feelings, with much difficulty in accepting the termination. In this situation, it may be helpful for the social worker to plan to meet with each member individually, as well as with the whole client system, to work on termination. It is probable that the meetings with the less invested may be light and brief, whereas the meetings with those more invested may be intense and lengthy. Planning to meet with every member individually avoids singling out certain members and yet allows more time for those who need it. Even when an individual has developed no attachment, the social worker and this person need to discuss an overview of the past (purpose for beginning contact), the present (extent of goal accomplishment), and the future (plans for when all contacts are over).

In addition to a review of past, present, and future with members of a client system individually and collectively, the social worker may ask all the members to share together how each one perceives the termination. Many times, members are surprised to hear, perhaps for the first time, that they have meant something to one another. Individuals who are hesitant to admit that they have some feelings about the termination may begin to feel freer to talk about them when they hear others openly express their feelings. Also, the sharing may bring about some final efforts to clarify and heal any misunderstandings the members may have had with each other or with the social worker.

Using Social Work Foundation Knowledge in Termination

As stated earlier, there is an art to termination that calls on the values, knowledge, and skills of a social worker. The social work generalist demonstrates this art as various elements from the holistic foundation for social work practice (Table 1.3 in Chapter 1) are selected, integrated, and applied throughout the termination process.

As a social worker and a client system begin to bring their relationship to an end, all of the value principles of individualization, acceptance, self-determination, nonjudgmental attitude, controlled emotional involvement, purposeful expression of feelings, and confidentiality are utilized. The timing, planning, and processing of termination have to be *individualized* according to each client system's unique circumstances. If a client system is avoiding or denying the termination, the social worker patiently *accepts* the reaction pattern. Keeping in mind the principle of *controlled emotional involvement*, the social worker honestly shares his or her feelings about terminating and artfully encourages the *purposeful expression of the client system's related feelings*. If a client system does not choose to identify new problem areas or to be referred for additional support, the social worker maintains a *nonjudgmental attitude* and respects the client system's right to *self-determination*. When a referral or transfer is made or data are collected from an outside resource, all information about the client system is treated as *confidential* and released only with the informed consent of the client system.

Knowledge of human development, group dynamics, organizations, and ecological systems are among the concepts and perspectives that give direction and understanding to a social worker in the termination stage. In human development theory, the social worker learns about the natural needs all human systems have for attachments throughout the life cycle. The trauma of separation and the impact of an abrupt termination on a human system is also presented. Through theories of group dynamics and organizations, the social worker learns about the conflicts, tasks, and processes a group, community, or organization undergoes when a person who was seen as the leader (or someone with power and control) leaves the client, action, or target system.

Using an ecological-systems perspective, the social worker perceives the interdependence that develops between a client system and its service-providing environment. This perspective helps social workers understand that it may not be feasible to expect an organism to maintain its functioning level when a major nurturer and sustainer in its environment is removed. Therefore, the need for a careful assessment of a client system's available internal and external resources after termination with a social worker is highlighted.

In addition to values and knowledge from the holistic foundation, a social worker uses a range of general skills, particularly problem-solving skills, during the termination process. For example, as a social worker begins to introduce the idea of termination to a client system, skill is needed for a clear identification of what it means to terminate (need-identification skills). In reviewing the past, data collection and evaluation skills are used. As focus is given to the present, a social worker uses assessment skills in appraising the strengths and readiness of a client system for termination and in locating appropriate supportive resources in the environment. Planning skills, including the sequencing of tasks and contracting, are used as a social worker and a client system begin to plan for the future. Recording skills are needed for writing the termination plan. A variety of interventive skills, including referral and transfer, may be needed in the implementation of the plan. Listening, responding, and clarifying are among the communication skills that are demonstrated repeatedly throughout the entire termination process.

Essentially, the three primary skills needed during termination may be described as (1) sensing skills (recognizing feelings and reactions), (2) timing skills (knowing when to identify, wait, or stop), and (3) processing skills (moving from past to present to future). The art of termination rests in a social worker's demonstrated sensitivity to the time and movement needed for a client system to be ready to accept termination. All of the actions of a social worker, throughout the process, reflect an artful integration and application of values, knowledge, and skills.

Human Diversity in Termination

The core human diversity issues to be understood at termination include institutional racism, cultural diversity, gender-role expectations, sexual orientation, and socio-economic status. That is, their ongoing impact on client, action, and target systems at the micro, mezzo, and macro levels needs to be understood and addressed during the ending period if gains are to be maintained.

Basic questions asked include the following: (1) Can the client system go on functioning at the level attained at this time without continued contact with the social worker? (2) Although the identified problems may have been resolved and the goals accomplished, if a similar need develops will the client system be able to handle it, or at least know how to get help? (3) If additional supports are needed after the social worker terminates, are they available? In working with minority ethnic groups, a central need has been described as empowerment. Rather than doing for a client system, the social worker tries to prevent dependency and to encourage self-help and autonomy. The reality is, however, that the needs of oppressed groups are often multiple and pervasive. A social worker and a client system may frequently feel overwhelmed or discouraged because little progress is apparent. The social worker or the client system, or both, may have a strong inclination to terminate, even when goals have not been accomplished and when regression will obviously take place after the social worker leaves. Particular care has to be taken by the social worker when planning a termination to ensure the stabilization of change efforts and the availability of ongoing supports as needed.

Termination, as brought out in this chapter, is a stage when skills in timing and sensing of feelings are especially needed. Again, knowledge of a culture's orientation toward the expression of feelings and the meaning of time is imperative. If a social worker has played a meaningful role in the life of a client system, he or she will naturally have some feelings and a sense of loss when the worker terminates. The reactions of the client system will be culturally derived. A skilled social worker will understand and enable the client system to find the time and the opportunity to express feelings and to prepare for the termination. Expressions of denial, bargaining, anger, or depression may vary according to cultural orientation toward separation and death. The process of moving from past to present to future may also be influenced by the time orientation of one's cultural background. As indicated earlier, members of Asian/Pacific American, Native American, and African American cultures lean toward emphasizing the past, whereas Mexican Americans are more concerned with the present and Anglo-Saxon Americans are more future oriented. Recognizing such differences enables a social worker to have more realistic expectations of the pace needed by a client system to move to the point of acceptance in the process of termination.

After an evaluation, the social worker and the client system may decide to terminate, even though long-range goals for social change have not been achieved. With personal, interpersonal, or short-range goals attained, they may decide to continue to address the need to change target systems on their own or in other ways. The social worker may continue to advocate equal opportunities and services for vulnerable client systems through introducing or supporting related legislation, policies, programs, or practices. When the decision to terminate is reached by both social worker and client system, it is important for the client to feel that he or she is welcome to return to the social worker or the agency for additional services after termination, if needed.

If a client group is terminating at an agency, individual members generally need to have other formal or informal networks available. Planning for the future should include thoughtful consideration and efforts to build in appropriate resources for these individuals.

As with any working relationship, a deep attachment may develop between social worker and client system in the course of their working together. For client systems, it may be the first time they have met someone who has been able to listen to their questions and concerns and been able to accept and respect them as unique individuals. For social workers, it may be the first time they have had the opportunity to get to know and work with a particular cultural, social, or socio-demographic group. Terminating the relationship may evoke feelings for both social worker and client system that are difficult to face and to express. Again, time is needed for them to review the life cycle of their relationship and to honestly discuss their feelings, such as anger, fear, loss, and love. It will be easier for both the social worker and the client system to accept termination if a sense of acceptance has existed throughout the time they have been together. If there has not been acceptance, either one may continue to feel a need to try to prove something to or to change something in the other.

As a social worker and a system of contact move into the termination stage of the General Method, a key question to be asked is: Will the progress that has been made be sustained and developed after the social worker leaves? The tendency to regress to roles that existed for years before the social worker became involved is very strong after the social worker terminates. Again, if change is to remain stabilized, it may be imperative that support networks be located and activated before final termination.

As stated earlier, during termination, individuals are encouraged to express their feelings and fears surrounding the anticipated loss of the social worker and perhaps other members of a group. Here, too, client systems who hold back from expressing feelings may not be able to admit that they will miss the social worker or the client group. If a bonding of mutual respect and support has developed between the client system and the social worker or other group members, this experience may serve as a model for the client system in future relationships and interactions.

Thus, each stage of the General Method calls for a sensitive application of values, knowledge, and skills as a social worker interacts with systems of diverse cultures, sexual orientation, or gender. As brought out in Chapter 3, a social worker is sensitive also to diversity in age and stages, gender and sexual orientation, endowment and personality, value system, social class, and geographic location. A knowledge of human diversity and an awareness of one's own human responses to various individuals, cultures, lifestyles, roles, and environments are essential for an effective application of the General Method.

Termination in Micro, Mezzo, and Macro Practice in Diverse Field Areas

In the following section, the application of knowledge and skills during the *termination stage* of the General Method will be demonstrated by entry-level generalists in seven diverse field areas.

I. Field Area: Child Welfare

A. Agency: State Department of Children's Services

B. Client System

K, a 15-year-old female, was placed in a group home six months ago. (For more background information, see Chapter 4, Engagement in Micro, Mezzo, and Macro Practice in Diverse Field Areas I. Child Welfare.)

C. Summary of Preceding Stages

The problems, goals, and tasks identified and implemented in earlier stages are found in Table 6.7 in Chapter 6 and Table 7.1 in Chapter 7. A summary of the evaluation of goals and contract reformulation may be found in Table 8.2 in Chapter 8. Basically, progress was identified during evaluation for all of the stated goals. The goal related to personal growth was the slowest in achievement, and more time was recognized as needed for progress in this area. The contract was reformulated to extend goal 2 to include optimal academic performance and to change the frequency of social worker contact to once a month rather than once every two weeks.

D. Termination

After K had been in her group home for six months, the social worker began to terminate because she was leaving the Department of Children's Services. K's first reaction to the termination was total indifference. She said she didn't "need the state any more," and hoped she would not have to get another state social worker. She was helped to express anger and fear of being abandoned. She admitted that she liked the social worker and would miss her very much. She was assured that the social worker would miss her also.

As the social worker and K began to review the life cycle of their work together, the ongoing evaluation tools described in Chapter 8 (Figures 8.14 and 8.15) were used. Her academic performance and group home maintenance were assessed as +3. They recalled what the past was like for K and how far she had progressed, particularly in her present group home and in school. K knew that she continued to need help with her personal problems (goal 3).

In considering the future, K said she wished to remain in her present group home and school for at least another few years. Her long-range goals included returning to live with her real mother some day. K knew that this was not possible in the near future.

K's case was transferred back to a social worker (recently returned from sick leave) who had originally worked with her. K remembered her original social worker and said she was glad she didn't have to start all over with someone new. Two weeks before termination, K and the two state social workers had a meeting, at which time goals and progress were reviewed. For their last meeting, K and her social worker went for a walk. They took and exchanged pictures of each other. K asked if she could write the social worker after she left Children's Services, but this continued contact was discouraged.

E. Charted Progress

The termination plan that was developed and implemented by the social worker and K is found in Table 9.2. In recording, this plan was added to the contracted plan that was used during assessment and evaluation.

TABLE 9.2   Contracted Plan: State Department of Children's Services (Continued from Tables 6.7, 7.1, and 8.2)

Date Identified	Problem/ Need	Goal	Task	Contract	Date Antici- pated	Date Accom- plished
7/26	Termination process	Satisfactory termination	1. Introduce termination.	1. Social worker	7/26	7/26
			2. Discuss feelings and termination.	2. Social worker and K	7/26 and 8/5	8/5
			3. Do life-cycle review.	3. Social worker and K	8/15	8/15
			4. Meet with transfer social worker.	4. K, social worker, and transfer social worker	8/22	8/22
			5. Conduct final session.	5. Social worker and K	8/30	8/30

II. Field Area: Gerontology

A. Agency: Seaside Nursing Home

B. Client System

Mrs. J, an 80-year-old Portuguese woman, is in a skilled-nursing facility. (For additional information, see Chapter 4, Engagement in Micro, Mezzo, and Macro Practice in Diverse Field Areas, II. Gerontology.)

C. Summary of Preceding Stages

The problems, goals, and tasks identified and contracted in earlier stages may be found in Table 7.2 in Chapter 7. The evaluation process and contract reformulation of the preceding stage are outlined in Table 8.3 in Chapter 8. At the time of evaluation, progress was noted for all of the stated goals. The least amount of progress was shown for goal 3a (to have Mrs. J go out of her room on her own at least once a day). Additional efforts to work on goal 3a were developed and contracted during the evaluation stage. These included the creation of an ongoing evaluation graph (Figure 8.18 in Chapter 8) and more involvement by nursing staff in helping to chart the frequency of Mrs. J's leaving her room by herself. Mrs. J and the social worker agreed to assess progress in goal 3a weekly.

D. Intervention

After working with Mrs. J for seven months, the social worker began the process of termination because she was leaving the agency. When the social worker informed Mrs. J that she would be working at the nursing home for only four more weeks, Mrs. J repeated, "No, you won't" or "You won't go" and refused to discuss it any further. Mrs. J would turn on her television whenever the social worker tried to talk about her leaving. One day, the social worker went to see Mrs. J at their regular meeting time and Mrs. J was not in her room. She was later located walking on the floor downstairs by herself. She said she didn't know why she was there.

The social worker told Mrs. J that she could see that she was upset and angry with her because she was leaving. Mrs. J said she could not understand why the social worker had to go. The social worker tried to review the progress Mrs. J had made, but Mrs. J said she didn't want to talk about it. She became very silent and refused to speak at all after the social worker said she would not be coming back, even to visit Mrs. J. Mrs. J was told that the social worker's supervisor would come to see her occasionally and would be available if Mrs. J needed to talk to a social worker. Mrs. J did not respond and remained withdrawn throughout the remainder of the time the social worker was at the home.

Realizing that Mrs. J was finding it difficult to accept the termination, the social worker's supervisor agreed to see Mrs. J at least once a week for a while after the social worker left. During the second-to-last meeting of the social worker and Mrs. J, the supervisor dropped in, but Mrs. J said very little to her.

E. Charted Progress

The termination plan was drawn up by the social worker, who kept trying to get Mrs. J involved in the process. The plan was recorded as found in Table 9.3.

As apparent in Table 9.3, tasks 2 and 3 (discuss feelings, review life cycle of working relationship) of the termination plan were not accomplished. No dates are entered in the last column ("date accomplished") for tasks 2 and 3. The social worker was not able to engage Mrs. J either in a discussion of feelings about the termination or in a life-cycle review. Thus, in the termination summary left in the record, the social worker emphasized the fact that the termination process had not been attained. The social worker's supervisor planned to focus on tasks 2 and 3 when she met with Mrs. J after the social worker's termination.

TABLE 9.3   Contracted Plan: Seaside Nursing Home (Continued from Tables 6.9, 7.2, and 8.3)

Date Identified	Problem/ Need	Goal	Task	Contract	Date Antici- pated	Date Accom- plished
4/29	Termination process	Satisfactory termination	1. Introduce termination.	1. Social worker	4/29	4/29
			2. Discuss termi- nation and feelings.	2. Social worker and Mrs. J	5/1 and 5/6	
			3. Do life-cycle review.	3. Social worker and Mrs. J	5/1 and 5/6	
			4. Meet with supervisor.	4. Social worker, Mrs. J, and supervisor	5/15	5/15
			5. Conduct final session.	5. Social worker and Mrs. J	5/22	5/22

III. **Field Area: Public Social Welfare**

A. **Agency: State Social Services**

B. **Client System**

Mr. and Mrs. P and their two children (ages 2 and 4) were placed in emergency shelter (Center City Motor Inn) for 44 days and then relocated in an apartment. The family was receiving AFDC because of Mr. P's mental incapacity. (Additional background information may be found in Chapter 4, Engagement in Micro, Mezzo, and Macro Practice in Diverse Field Areas, III. Public Social Welfare.)

C. **Summary of Preceding Stages**

The problems, goals, and interventions of earlier stages are outlined in Table 6.10 in Chapter 6 and Table 7.3 in Chapter 7. A summary of the evaluation that was completed is charted in Table 8.4 in Chapter 8. The basic goals for food, housing, medical examination, fuel assistance, AFDC payment, and a functioning refrigerator were accomplished mainly through extensive involvement by resources outside of the family. The goals of obtaining Supplemental Security Income, a Thanksgiving food basket, and Christmas gifts for the children were not accomplished (to date) because of Mr. P's failure to complete contracted tasks. The problems of poor money management and excessive dependence on outside resources were identified by the social worker but left unresolved because Mr. and Mrs. P refused to recognize them as problems in need of attention. The evaluation culminated with both the social worker and the family agreeing to begin the process of termination.

D. **Termination**

Although the Ps said they had no immediate need for continued social services, they appeared a little angry with the social worker when the idea of termination was first introduced. They were able to admit that they were disappointed when the social worker did not take care of fixing their refrigerator and also when the social worker didn't get them a food basket for Thanksgiving. They knew that they should try to do more for themselves and said it was easier for a social worker to deal with other programs and services. The social worker reminded them that when they really had to get something done, they were able to work it out (such as locating an apartment). At this point, they admitted that Mrs. P's father was actually the one who found the apartment for them. They asked if the social worker couldn't come by at least once every month to see how they were getting along. The social worker did not agree to this, because he felt it was better for the family to try to solve their problems as they arose and not to hold them until the social worker came each month. Again, the social worker cautioned them about their need for careful planning in money management and said that if they ever wanted help in developing their skill in this area, they could bring this to the attention of their income-maintenance technician or they could call the Social Services Department directly.

The social worker planned to meet three additional times with the family before their final termination. During these last visits, the family continued to complain about how hard it is to maintain a home and raise children these days. They repeated their desire for Christmas presents for the children, and the social worker reviewed the tasks identified in the contracted plan. Mr. P did call the Salvation Army (task 2, problem 12, Table 7-3, Chapter 7) on the day of the social worker's last visit.

E. **Charted Progress**
   The termination plan carried out by the social worker and the Ps is recorded in Table 9.4. In the closing summary for the record, the social worker emphasized that although problems 5 (poor money management) and 13 (excessive dependency) were never recognized by the Ps, these were assessed as continuing and serious by the social worker.

IV. **Field Area: Community Services**

   A. **Agency: Clayton Neighborhood House**
   B. **Client System**
   Four Hispanic families needed heat in their apartments on the second floor of 33 L Street. (For more background information, see Chapter 4, Engagement in Micro, Mezzo, and Macro Practice in Diverse Field Areas, IV. Community Services.)
   C. **Summary of Preceding Stages**
   The problems, goals, and tasks identified and enacted during early stages are described in the contracted plan found in Table 6.12 in Chapter 6, Table 7.4 in Chapter 7, and Table 8.5 in Chapter 8. Although the families initially felt victimized and helpless, they expressed feelings of relief and gratitude during the evaluation stage. There was adequate heating in their apartments, and they were actively monitoring the temperature daily. They knew that they continued to have a problem in communicating with their landlord, but they did not want to try to improve their communications at this time.

TABLE 9.4   Contracted Plan: State Social Services (Continued from Tables 6.11, 7.3, and 8.4)

Date Identified	Problem/ Need	Goal	Task	Contract	Date Anticipated	Date Accomplished
12/4	Termination process	Satisfactory termination	1. Introduce termination.	1. Social worker	12/4	12/4
			2. Discuss termination and feelings.	2. Social worker and Ps	12/11	12/11
			3. Do life-cycle review.	3. Social worker and Ps	12/11	12/11
			4. Conduct final session.	4. Social worker and Ps	12/21	12/21

D. Termination

When the social worker returned to meet with the families and review the heating situation, she learned that consistent heat had been provided throughout the week. This finding was charted on the ongoing evaluation graph given in Figure 8.20 in Chapter 8. The social worker had mentioned to the families the previous week that if there didn't seem to be any remaining problems to work on when she came for this meeting, she would talk with them about terminating her contacts with them.

Residents first expressed a wish that the social worker would continue to visit with them at least once a week. Comments were made, such as "Don't you like us any more?" One tenant said that he had heard that the landlord was selling the apartment building and that maybe they all would be put out on the street. The social worker assured the residents that if they received notice that they had to leave the building, they could contact Clayton House for assistance with relocation.

In reviewing the life cycle of their working together, the social worker recalled their first meeting and the way in which they worked on the heating problem. The families were happy to know that they could drop into Clayton House if they ever wanted help with any problem. They were also informed of the regular community meetings and activities that went on at Clayton for children and adults.

The tenants decided that they wanted to continue their daily monitoring of the heat in their apartments throughout the winter. Mrs. T offered to keep track of their findings by marking temperature points on the graph (Figure 8.20 in Chapter 8) once a week. If there was any marked regression, she would contact the social worker and call a meeting.

The social worker shared how much she had enjoyed working with them, even though their contact had been brief. She was invited to drop in any time she was in the neighborhood.

E. Charted Progress

The termination plan was carried out and recorded as outlined in Table 9.5.

V. Field Area: Education

A. Agency: Keeney Elementary School

B. Client System

Jim G, an 8-year-old third-grader, was showing regressive behavior in school and at home in reaction to his parents' problems with their relationship and Mrs. G's threat to abandon the family. (For additional background information, see Chapter 4, Engagement in Micro, Mezzo, and Macro Practice in Diverse Field Areas, V. Education.)

C. Summary of Preceding Stages

The contracted plan developed and implemented by Jim, his parents, and the social worker is found in Table 6.14 in Chapter 6. During evaluation, progress was noted for all four identified goals. The goal to improve Mr. and Mrs. G's marital relationship was recognized as needing more time before its accomplishment.

TABLE 9.5 Contracted Plan: Clayton Neighborhood House (Continued from Tables 6.12, 7.4, and 8.5)

Date Identified	Problem/ Need	Goal	Task	Contract	Date Antici- pated	Date Accom- plished
12/19	Termination process	Satisfactory termination	1. Introduce termination.	1. Social worker	12/12	12/12
			2. Discuss termination and feelings.	2. Social worker and residents	12/19	12/19
			3. Do life-cycle review.	3. Social worker and residents	12/19	12/19
			4. Conduct final session.	4. Social worker and residents	12/19	12/19

Mr. and Mrs. G were motivated to remain in counseling at the family counseling center.

D. Termination

During the last interview with Mr. and Mrs. G and Jim, termination was introduced and discussed. Although it was agreed that the social worker did not need to meet with Mr. and Mrs. G again, the contract with Jim was extended to include two additional sessions at school.

As the social worker and the Gs recognized the progress that had been made, Mr. and Mrs. G expressed gratitude to the social worker for her interest in Jim and in them. They said it was good to know that the social worker was at the school to help the children and their families. They admitted that they probably would not have gone for help for themselves if it hadn't been for the social worker. They were reminded by the social worker that it was Jim who was feeling their pain and reacting to the situation. It was Jim who led them to look closer at what was happening to them and to their family. Using the life-cycle approach, the social worker moved from the past to the present and then to the future. In considering the future, the social worker strongly encouraged Mr. and Mrs. G to continue their work at the family counseling center, even if it got rough at times. They were assured also that they could contact the social worker at school if she could be of any further assistance.

When the social worker began to talk with Jim about termination during their last two meetings, he said he didn't want to stop coming. He liked to play with the toys in the office and he liked talking about his grades and keeping track of his improvement on the graphs.

During these sessions, Jim repeatedly asked if the social worker had started to see some other child in his place. He was assured that no one could take his place. Jim said he was happy about home, but he was sad that he couldn't continue to see the social worker. He told her that he might "surprise" her and drop in to see her on his own sometime. Before leaving, he took the graphs that were

TABLE 9.6   Contracted Plan: Keeney Elementary School (Continued from Table 6.14)

Date Identified	Problem/ Need	Goal	Task	Contract	Date Antici- pated	Date Accom- plished
12/13	Termination process	Satisfactory termination	1. Introduce termination.	1. Social worker	12/17	12/17
			2. Discuss termi- nation and feelings.	2. Social worker, Mr. and Mrs. G, and Jim	12/17	12/17
			3. Terminate with Mr. and Mrs. G.	3. Social worker	12/17	12/17
			4. Further discus- sion of termi- nation and feelings.	4. Social worker and Jim	12/20 and 1/8	12/20 and 1/8
			5. Conduct final session.	5. Social worker and Jim	1/8	1/8

hanging on the wall with him. He brought the social worker a drawing he had made of himself and his family and hung it on her wall. He said that she could keep it—for a while.

E. **Charted Progress**

The plan for termination was recorded on the contracted plan as outlined in Table 9.6.

VI. **Field Area: Corrections**

A. **Agency: Juvenile Court**

B. **Client System**

A group of six (originally seven) male youths, all age 14, are on probation and attending weekly group meetings led by co-workers at Juvenile Court. (For addi- tional background information, see Chapter 4, Engagement in Micro, Mezzo, and Macro Practice in Diverse Field Areas, VI. Corrections.)

C. **Summary of Preceding Stages**

The group met weekly and focused on the three prioritized goals of (1) to get off probation in four months, (2) to control tempers at home and at school, and (3) to learn more about "the changes" they were facing as teenagers. After three and one-half months, the group evaluated their progress in goal accomplishment. Four of the members were achieving the stated goals as planned. They were being recommended for termination of probation. One youth was sent to a correctional center after he had attended six meetings, because he was found breaking into a store. The remaining two members were not meeting the requirements for a reduction in probation. Group meetings were extended for at least an additional six weeks for these two members. After the evaluation, the group began to focus on termination.

D. Termination

As the group began to discuss what it would be like to be off probation, MK and B said that they were glad they were getting off probation but that they would miss seeing everyone in the group. They asked the group leaders to let them know about any upcoming trips in which they could join the group. J and T expressed anger over having to come back for group meetings. They began to blame the co-workers for not recommending that they get reduced time, but other group members reminded J and T that they themselves didn't keep up their scores.

As the group discussed the life cycle of their working together (i.e., past, present, and future), they began to recall what it was like when they first started attending. Most of the youths admitted that they didn't think that they could trust the social workers and doubted that they would give them time off. C reminded the group about A, saying he was sorry A didn't make it but that A should have listened to the probation officers. C also shared how excited he was because his mother and little sister and brother were coming from Puerto Rico to live with him and his father.

All of the youths said that they thought they were doing better than when they first were put on probation. They didn't know if they would be able to stay out of trouble once they were off probation. J and T said they probably would never get off probation. They knew that if they began to do better, they still could have a probation reduction of one month (rather than two). In looking toward the future, J and T were told by the social workers that if they continued to fail to meet the requirements, the group would stop at the end of its fifth month, but J and T would be expected to meet individually with a social worker each week for as long as they remained on probation.

In talking about the future for those who were leaving in two weeks (MK, B, ML, and C), the leaders encouraged each of them to try to get active with local churches or recreational centers. Specific places were identified for each of the youths. They were encouraged also to ask to see the school social worker if they started to have any problems in school.

At the end of the last meeting with all six members, the group had a pizza party. In the following weeks, J's behavior markedly improved at meetings, at home, and in school. He was recommended to be removed from probation one month early. T continued to come late to meetings. His fighting at school continued, and he was not obeying his grandmother. His probation period was extended beyond five months, and he was required to come to see the male social worker once a week.

E. Charted Progress

The termination plan was recorded as outlined in Table 9.7 (page 336).

VII. Field Area: Homeless Shelter

A. Agency: West End Community Shelter

B. Client System

Mr. Romano is a resident at the homeless shelter and he has AIDS. (For further background information, see Chapter 4, Engagement in Micro, Mezzo, and Macro Practice in Diverse Field Areas, VII, Homeless Shelter.)

TABLE 9.7 Contracted Plan: Juvenile Court (Continued from Tables 6.15, 7.5, and 8.7)

Date Identified	Problem/ Need	Goal	Task	Contract	Date Anticipated	Date Accomplished
1/14	Termination process	Satisfactory termination	1. Introduce termination.	1. Social workers	1/14	1/14
			2. Discuss termination and feelings.	2. Members and social workers	1/21, 1/28	1/21, 1/28
			3. Do life-cycle review.	3. Members and social workers	1/21, 1/28	1/21, 1/28
			4. Conduct final session for MK, ML, B, and C—pizza party.	4. Members and social workers	1/28	1/28
			5. Continue weekly meetings for a month.	5. J, T, and social workers	2/4, 2/11, 2/18, 2/25	2/4, 2/11, 2/18, 2/25
			6. Evaluate progress of J and T.	6. J, T, and social workers	2/11	2/11
			7. Conduct final session for J.	7. J, T, and social workers	2/25	2/25
			8. Continue to meet once a week.	8. T and social worker (M.S.W.)	3/4 and each week until off probation	

C. Summary of Preceding Stages

When Mr. R came to the shelter in May, he was unemployed, homeless, and test-ing HIV positive. During his stay at the shelter, he found a job and worked full and part time on a chicken farm. He has become active with the Harmony Pro-gram and with Saint John's Church. He started and continues to be seen at the free clinic located near the shelter. Recently, the doctor informed Mr. R that test results indicate that he has AIDS. Mr. R is not able to continue working. He has applied for public assistance and social security. He applied also for residence at Hope Home and was invited for a preplacement visit.

D. Termination

The decision was made by Mr. R and the staff at Hope Home that Mr. R would move to Hope Home on July 8. The shelter social worker and Mr. R took time to plan his termination from the shelter. Mr. R recalled how hopeless he felt that first night when he came to the shelter and signed in for a bed. He expressed deep appreciation for the help he received from the social worker and said he would like to come back if he could to visit everyone sometimes. They recognized that Mr. R has been going through a lot of changes in his life and that the road ahead may not be easy. Mr. R said that the doctor helped him to understand the virus better and what he might expect. He said that he was very glad that he had "made peace with God" and his church. He still was afraid but not as much as when he first learned he was HIV positive. He said that he thought he would like the people at Hope Home. He was looking forward to sharing a room with only one person.

E. Charted Progress

A termination plan was added to Mr. R's contracted plan as found in Table 9.8.

TABLE 9.8 Contracted Plan: West End Community Shelter (Continued from Tables 6.17, 7.6, and 8.8)

Date Identified	Problem/ Need	Goal	Task	Contract	Date Antici-pated	Date Accom-plished
7/2	Termination process	Satisfactory termination	1. Discuss termi-nation past/ present/future.	1. Social worker and Mr. R	7/3	
			2. Plan move.	2. Social worker, Mr. R, and "buddy"	7/3	
			3. Have last meeting.	3. Social worker and Mr. R	7/7	
			4. Move to Hope Home.	4. Mr. R with help of buddy	7/8	

Conclusion

In reviewing the content of this chapter, it may be perceived that the process of termination includes all of the stages of the General Method. The six-stage nature of the method (engagement, data collection, assessment, intervention, evaluation, termination) is contained within the last stage. During termination, the social worker and the client system begin with an identification of the meaning of termination (engagement). They proceed to gathering information as they move from past to present (data collection). They move on to assessing and planning for the future (assessment). The plan is then implemented (intervention) and evaluated (evaluation). Finally, there is closure (termination). The General Method is a cyclical process. In the termination cycle, the process is repeated and completed.

The opportunity for the identification and expression of feelings has been emphasized as essential to the termination process. In this chapter, approaches and exercises for understanding and working with termination feelings have been suggested. The reactions of a client system to ending a relationship were described in terms of the five-stage sequence of denial, anger, bargaining, depression, and acceptance. A life-cycle approach containing the three focal points of past, present, and future was offered as a guiding framework for social workers during the termination process. Attention was also given to the possible feelings and reactions of service providers as they go through repeated termination experiences. Examples were included to demonstrate a social worker's sensitivity to human diversity in the final stage of the General Method and to show how termination is carried out in diverse areas of practice.

New social workers frequently say that the most difficult part of working with a client system is getting started. In time, social workers generally say the most difficult part is the ending. At the beginning, there may be some fears and emptiness because of little experience or knowledge of a system. Seasoned social workers know, however, the awesome reality that the emptiness after termination may be filled with memories of the experience, particularly the final stage, that live on.

10 The Generalist Practitioner

Identity and Integration

The General Method: A Purposeful Procedure

As discussed throughout this book, the General Method of social work practice involves a purposeful procedure. Respecting the right of a human system to self-determination, the generalist follows the lead of the client system receiving service and offers an approach that is a planned problem-solving procedure. A sensitivity to human diversity enables the social worker to be skillful in timing the process and in selecting interventions, tools, and techniques. With the identification of mutual goals, the social worker and the system of contact proceed with interactions that have the purpose of goal accomplishment.

The method presented in this book is not actually new to social work. When enacting the traditional methods of casework, group work, and community organization, social workers have often used a problem-solving approach. As articulated and organized in this text, however, the General Method incorporates an ecological-systems perspective, an open selection of theories and interventions, a strengths orientation, and a multilevel approach. The method is a problem-solving process consisting of six identifiable stages.

The process is dynamic in nature and does not restrict a social worker to following a set sequence according to a fixed pattern. The stages of the method are presented sequentially for conceptualization, but, in practice, they are often cyclical. As pointed out earlier, elements of each stage are often observable in every stage. Frequently, there is a returning to an earlier stage as problems or needs evolve. In addition, the general nature of the method does not restrict a social worker to working with client systems of a particular size. It may be used with individuals, families, organizations, groups, and communities. Interventions are selected to match the individualized needs of the client system receiving service at a given time. A plan to work with members of a client system, for example, may include seeing them individually, as a family, and in groups. The method blends general and individual conceptualizations. A holistic perspective that recognizes individuality and interrelatedness is therefore fundamental to the method.

For beginning social workers, the General Method is a guiding framework. Rather than learning about a variety of skills to be applied eclectically, the social worker who learns the method has an organized body of skills. He or she is enabled to be process minded and to recognize movement in problem solving. The method guides the generalist and the client system receiving service in their collaborative effort for goal attainment.

Classification of Methods in Human Services

The terms *methods, models, approaches, modes,* and *processes* are frequently used interchangeably to refer to the organized use of techniques and skills by helping professionals. In addition to the General Method of entry-level social workers and the traditional methods of advanced social workers, numerous other methods may be used by advanced practitioners from social work or other helping disciplines. Depending on theory and value foundations, different interventions are enacted; these are described in the professional literature. Various methods may be different or essentially similar. Frequently, diverse helpers use the same techniques and skills as well as the same terminology and theories. Some approaches, however, are based on contrasting theories and therefore do not work well together. To avoid confusion and to increase comprehension, a means of categorizing various helping methods is needed. A systematic framework for distinguishing methods would not only provide a broad overview of different approaches but would also provide greater clarification of the place of the General Method in relation to other methodologies.

There is a way to cluster methods according to their essential characteristics. Basically, all methods may be seen as falling under one of three major headings: client focused, problem focused, or social worker focused. *Client* may be defined as *client system,* meaning "people who sanction or ask for the change agent's services, who are the expected beneficiaries of service, and who have a working agreement or contract with the change agent (Pincus & Minahan, 1973). The word *problem* means the issue, need, question, or difficulty facing the client system and being brought to the attention of the social worker or other change agent. And the *social worker* or other change agent may be any member of the helping professionals within the field of human services. The central consideration in the classification is the role of the social worker in the triplex of client system, problem, and social worker.

In the first category of methodologies, the *client-focused* cluster, the social worker assumes a limited role, giving support mainly through listening and reassuring the client systems of their potential for coping with difficulties. There is minimum structure, leadership, and control on the part of the social worker. The social worker's direct intervention with the problem itself is minimal, if present. The client system is seen as strong and well able to deal with problems with a little help from the social worker. Consultation and some community locality development may fall into this category. Developmental, client-centered, and other basic counseling approaches are the types of interventions appropriately clustered in this grouping. As shown in the "Methods A" representation in Figure 10.1, the social worker using these methods may be depicted as working directly with client systems, who in turn are enabled to work out their problems or needs by themselves.

In the second major category of methodologies, the *problem-focused* cluster, the social worker and the client system work in a more balanced and collaborative effort. Structure, leadership, and control are shared. The nature of the problems or needs is recognized as calling for the involvement of both the professional social worker and the client system. Although there is belief in the potential of the client

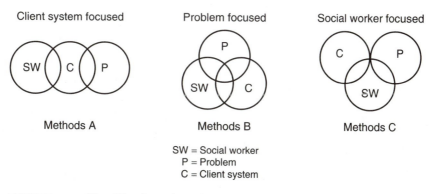

FIGURE 10.1   **Classification of Methods**

system and the hope of eventual withdrawal of the social worker, the method is identified as initially calling for some direct intervention by the social worker as well as the client system. These methods convey the notion of teamwork, as both client system and social worker focus on the problem in need of resolution. The methods of intervention described in the works of William Glasser or William Reid and Laura Epstein come under this category. Task-centered, problem-solving, functional, and rational approaches and some locality development may be identified in this group, as illustrated in "Methods B" of Figure 10.1.

The third and final cluster of methods describes the *social worker-focused* category. In these interventions, the social worker plays a major directive role, assuming clearly the responsibility for bringing about goal accomplishment. Modifying models and aggressive change models calling for specialized interventions by social workers are classified here. Behavior modification, class advocacy, Gestalt therapy, psychoanalysis, psychotherapy, and social planning may be among the models of this group. As represented in "Methods C" of Figure 10.1, the social worker carries the burden of planning, directing, coaching, and structuring for the client system.

For further understanding, the categories of methods may be conceptualized as falling at different points on a circle. Usually, in the process of helping, social workers move along the line, depending on the progress of the service. Ideally, a social worker who begins with a social worker-focused method would work toward developing a more problem-focused or collaborative relationship and eventually a more client-focused approach followed by termination, with the client system becoming self-actualized (see Figure 10.2). Unfortunately, at times the social worker who begins with a less directive approach may see the need for greater social worker involvement. If he or she is not qualified for more advanced or specialized interventions, a referral may be necessary.

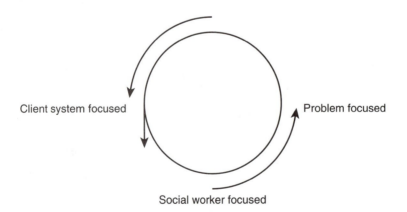

FIGURE 10.2   **The Methodological Process**

The General Method in the Classification

In considering the range of methods and the three basic categories, it is easy to find the place of the General Method as a problem-focused methodology. The social worker and the client system cooperate together at each stage of the General Method. The skills of the generalist may also allow for the use of a client system-focused method when the client has the strengths, with support from a professional, to work out his or her own problem. Moreover, the generalist has skill and knowledge to use the General Method when direct problem intervention by the social worker in collaboration with the client system is needed (see Figure 10.3). If the method needed is of the social worker-focused type, the generalist has the skill to refer or transfer the client system to a graduate-level social worker. The entry-level generalist, however, is not expected to have developed in his or her generalist education the knowledge and skills for social worker-focused interventions. The entry-level generalist, therefore, is not eclectic when it comes to choosing specialized methods. To practice with these approaches, the entry-level generalist would need further education and supervised experience.

For B.S.W. generalists to have the competence to use client system-focused and problem-focused methods, their professional programs would have to include content and field experiences for the development of both types of methods. For graduate-level social workers to have expertise in all three types of methodologies, curriculum content on the three types would have to be addressed in their graduate programs. Presently, skills and techniques used in client system-focused and problem-focused methods are found in accredited baccalaureate programs and may also be found in the foundation of graduate social work programs.

The Generalist Practitioner: A Basic Identity

This book prepares the new social worker for entering generalist practice. This person is a human service provider with broad-based skills and foundation knowledge of persons, environments, and the interactions that take place at the interface between person(s) and environment(s). He or she has a commitment to social work

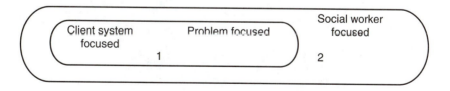

1 = Entry-level generalists   2 = Advanced social workers

FIGURE 10.3   **The Scope of Methodology**

values, as well as basic competence for working with individuals, families, groups, organizations, and communities. As described in this text, the generalist is a person grounded in the use of the General Method of social work practice.

According to the Curriculum Policy Statement of the Council on Social Work Education (1994), entry-level social workers are prepared primarily for direct practice with a variety of client systems. In addition to direct interventions with client systems, the generalist may use indirect interventions with various client systems in the extended environment. As stated earlier, indirect interventions refer to the efforts made by a social worker to interact with a client system that has the power or potential to respond to problems or needs and to contribute to goal attainment, even though that client system itself may be neither experiencing the problem or need nor asking for help from the social worker. The indirect interventions of a generalist relate to the needs and goals of particular client systems receiving services (as described in Chapter 7).

The work environment of the generalist includes the five major systems of (1) client, (2) agency of employment, (3) client resources, (4) the social work profession, and (5) society at large. As depicted in Figure 10.4, generalist practitioners (GP) function within an agency structure and as such interface primarily with

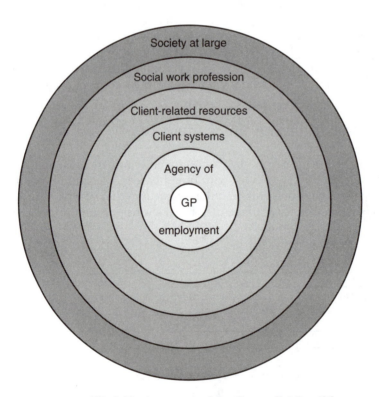

FIGURE 10.4   Work Environment of the Generalist Practitioner

client systems in direct service. The scope of their work, however, as seen in the diagram, includes moving out to related resources, the social work profession, and organizations or institutions in society at large. To be true to their identity, generalist practitioners see and respond to the interdependence that exists among the systems in their work environment. Although most of their formal work time (agency hours) may be used in providing direct services for client systems, generalists take time to be politically and professionally active. Involvement with the extended environment may include advocating for the poor, serving on boards or committees, giving testimony, having personal contact with legislators, and participating in political campaigns or political action groups. Unless generalist practitioners maintain an awareness of and some involvement in the development of policy and services in their extended environment, they run the risk of losing their basic identity.

A Forgotten Commitment to People in Need

As a profession, social work has a history of demonstrated commitment and concern for the poor and the underprivileged. Today, social work generalists and specialists continue to be needed to speak out against social injustices and unmet human needs. As the numbers of people without employment or adequate housing, food, and care increase, social workers are greatly needed to be present once again in the extended environment to stand in solidarity with the underprivileged and to advocate for social change. Unfortunately, some social workers have moved away from active societal involvement outside of direct work responsibilities. The "social" dimension of their name and profession has become obscure and perhaps forgotten.

A growing shortage in social work personnel to work with and for the poor, particularly in public welfare, has become increasingly evident in the profession (Keith-Lucas, 1992; Walz, 1989). After studies showed that a majority of social workers in public welfare services had little or no professional preparation for their jobs, CSWE and NASW recognized the B.S.W. level of practice. It was intended that B.S.W. practitioners would fill public welfare positions and enable the profession to continue to serve the needy in public social services. Unfortunately, few current B.S.W. programs and graduates prepare for or enter public welfare services. B.S.W. practitioners move quickly into M.S.W. programs or into private services. There are several reasons why social workers may avoid working in the public welfare system. These may include low pay, large caseloads, limited supervision and number of available professionally trained colleagues, and insufficient or inadequate resources. The results of these circumstances and pressures often include low staff morale and high staff burnout and job turnover. Special support and recognition should be given to those who persevere in the system because of a strong commitment and dedication to serving those without resources and with multiple needs in what is frequently the most degrading and impoverished of service systems.

Addressing the broad and multiple needs of the poor often calls for political skills and strategies. Although basic political skills have been identified as fundamental to practice at the entry level (see Table 1.3 in Chapter 1), new social workers will need to have models and supervisors in their agencies who promote and demonstrate the use of these skills. If there is little mezzo or macro practice activity by graduate-level generalist social workers, new generalists may lose sight of their commitment and identity.

Current changes taking place in social policy and programs call for an updating of curriculum and learning opportunities for social work students. As the implications of new legislation and policy changes are being studied, social work educators, students, and practitioners need to have ongoing communication, with opportunities for observation and validation of what is happening in the field.

For legislators, decision makers, and groups with needs, social workers with research and political skills can assist in identifying and documenting priorities. In addition, a social worker with an understanding of policy development and with relevant political skills can contribute to the introduction and passage of legislation that reflects human priorities.

Thus, curriculum content for social work students could include political science in their liberal arts curriculum as well as guidelines for giving testimony and other techniques and tactics for legislative advocacy. Because their professional knowledge, values, skills, and identity are embedded in the human diversity, ecological-systems, and problem-solving paradigms, generalist social work practitioners understand and can help explain the strong correlations that are emerging between program cutbacks and increasing social problems. They are also in a position to advocate for funding and programming to meet the current and emerging needs of this nation's vulnerable populations.

The Generalist Practitioner: Our Future Challenge

The same forces that have shaped the profession's development in the United States in the last century will continue to influence social work in the twenty-first century. Issues such as immigration and migration, race and ethnicity, changing family forms and gender roles, the welfare state and capitation practices in social and health care programs, housing and transportation, and job demands and work force changes will continue to evolve. They will also continue to create tensions that call for effective social work responses to newly emerging variations of these complex and often interdependent problems (Simon, 1998). As social workers move more into direct work with individuals and families and as direct-practice social workers become more involved (by choice or necessity) with political or power systems, the quest for holism is becoming an apparent reality in the profession. Social workers are extending their activities to include a broader range of skills and systems. Generalist practice for entry- and graduate-level social workers is becoming more clearly understood and appreciated. Social work knowledge, values, and skills must be embedded in the human diversity, ecological-systems, strengths-oriented, and problem-solving paradigm so that, together, these various components may create a unified practice framework.

In addition to breadth, there is an ongoing search for greater depth and sophistication in the profession—striving for an understanding and mastery of concentrations and specializations in practice. As pointed out in Chapter 1, further work is needed to develop and articulate the knowledge and skills for advanced practice in areas of concentration. The holistic foundation (Chapter 1) and the generalist perspective and the General Method (Chapters 2 through 9) described in this book serve as a base on which to build, refine, and extend the profession's efforts to arrive at a holistic conception of all of social work practice. To complete the picture and move beyond conceptualization and anecdote, more work is needed in empirically testing and documenting the applicability of the General Method in social work to diverse micro-, mezzo-, and macro-level problems experienced by diverse populations across multiple levels of practice. As the profession continues to grow in sensitivity to and knowledge about the variations of human diversity, interdependence of persons and environments, and the complexities inherent in daily living, social workers will continue increasing their awareness of the interdependence and complementarity of practice knowledge, values, and skills among the different levels of practice in the profession.

Conclusion

To complete this book, it is important to articulate how the beginning generalist practitioner in social work will change with practice and experience. Specifically, what professional growth might one expect to experience years after completing social work education for generalist practice? Because changing societal factors (economy, employment, income, housing, education, and health), advancing technologies, and the global economy will differentially impact on client system's problems and needs, role-position pressures will lead general practitioners to modify and deepen their knowledge about best practices for the populations-at-risk they have chosen to serve (see Figure 10.5). Through their professional practice experience, collaborative teamwork, staff development training, and the professional literature, the generalist practitioner will become well informed about the political, legal, administrative, programmatic, and evaluation issues that affect people and service programs in their area of practice expertise. Their client systems will be understood more clearly and with a breadth, depth, and sophistication that increases their ability not only to use but also to develop best practices for particular populations. Thus, the experienced generalist practitioner will have grown by deepening his or her professional knowledge about the people, populations, and environmental conditions that are crucial to an enhanced environment and the client systems' highest level of social functioning.

Concurrently, there will be much greater dexterity in the generalist practitioner's role-enactment skills. The experienced social worker will have greater

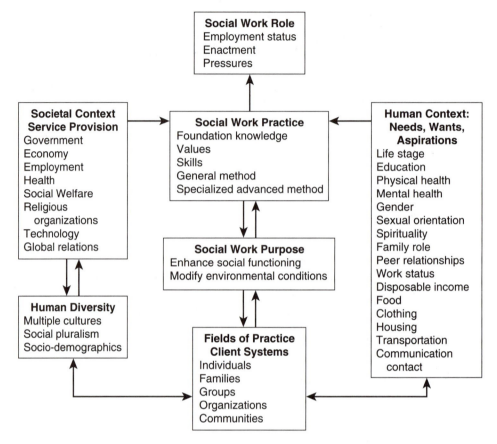

FIGURE 10.5   Social Work Role

knowledge about the micro, mezzo, and macro risk and protective factors associated with their client systems in their environments. He or she will also implement sophisticated multiple strategies that enable the client system to reap the full benefits of the holistic generalist practice method as it is designed and intended. Finally, the seasoned generalist practitioner will bring greater self-awareness, confidence, and power to bear on whatever person-in-environment situation presents itself.

Today, complex problems and powerful systems challenge social workers. There is great need for "whole" social workers—those with a vision of what could be as well as what is and has been; those with knowledge, values, and skills for generalist practice; and, last but not least, those with sensitivity, warmth, hope, and professional purpose.

It is clear that the seasoned generalist practitioner will move into contemporary action as holistic conceptualizations and relevant methodologies continue to be developed and refined through their ongoing practice experience. Therefore, entry-level professionals are encouraged to take what is here as a proposed guide and not as definitive. Newly developed frameworks will continue to be in process as long as there is a dynamic, responsive profession. We in the social work profession need you, ecological generalist practitioners, with your vitality, creativity, and unifying perspective. We welcome you and encourage your full participation in our vital and growing profession.

BIBLIOGRAPHY

Addams, J. (1910). *Twenty years at Hull House.* New York: Macmillan.

Anderson, J., & Brown, R. (1980). Life history grid for adolescents. *Social Work, 25,* 321–323.

Anthony, W. (1993). Recovery from mental illness: The guiding vision of the mental health system in the 1990s. *Psychosocial Rehabilitation Journal, 14,* 11–23.

Applewhite, S. (1995). Curanderismo: Demystifying the health beliefs and practices of elderly Mexican Americans. *Health and Social Work, 20,* 247–253.

Axinn, J., & Levin, H. (1997). *Social welfare: A history of the American response to need* (4th ed.). New York: Longman.

Baer, B., & Federico, R. (1979). *Educating the baccalaureate social worker* (Vols. 1, 2). Cambridge, MA: Ballinger.

Bailey, D. (1994). Organizational empowerment from self to interbeing. In L. Gutierrez & P. Nurius (Eds.), *Education and research for empowerment practice* (pp. 37–42). Seattle: University of Washington Press.

Bardill, D. (1997). *The relational systems model for family therapy.* New York: Haworth.

Bartlett, H. (1958). Toward clarification and improvement of social work practice. *Social Work, 3,* 5–8.

Bean, F., & Tienda, M. (1987). *The Hispanic population of the United States.* New York: Academic Press.

Beck, A. (1979). *Cognitive therapy and the emotional disorders.* New York: Meridien.

Belenky, M., Clinchy, B., Goldberger, N., & Tarule, J. (1986). *Women's ways of knowing.* New York: Basic Books.

Belle, D. (1982). *Lives in stress.* Beverly Hills: Sage.

Berkowitz, E. (1987). *Disabled policy: America's programs for the handicapped.* London: Cambridge University Press.

Berl, F. (1979). Clinical practice in a Jewish context. *Journal of Jewish Communal Service, 55,* 366–368.

Bertalanffy, L. von. (1968). *General systems theory* (Rev. ed.). New York: Braziller.

Biestek, F. (1957). *The casework relationship.* Chicago: University of Chicago Press.

Bisman, C. (1994). *Social work practice: Cases and principles.* Pacific Grove, CA: Brooks/Cole.

Bloom, M., Fischer, J., & Orme, J. (1999). *Evaluating practice* (3rd ed.). Boston: Allyn and Bacon.

Blount, M., Thyer, B., & Frye, T. (1992). Social work practice with Native Americans. In D. Harrison, J. Wodarski, & B. Thyer (Eds.), *Cultural diversity and social work practice* (pp. 102–118). Springfield, IL: Charles C. Thomas.

Boyd-Franklin, N. (1989). *Black families in therapy: A multisystem approach.* New York: Guilford.

Braeger, G., & Holloway, S. (1978). *Changing human service organizations: Politics and practice.* New York: Free Press.

Brice-Baker, J. (1996). Jamaican families. In M. McGoldrick, J. Pearce, & J. Giordano (Eds.), *Ethnicity and family therapy* (2nd ed.). New York: Guilford.

Brieland, D., Briggs, T., & Luenberger, P. (1973). *The team model in social work practice.* Syracuse, NY: Syracuse University, School of Social Work.

Brieland, D., Costin, L., & Atherton, C. (1985). *Contemporary social work: An introduction to social work and social welfare* (3rd ed.). New York: McGraw-Hill.

Brill, N. (1995). *Working with people: The helping process* (5th ed.). White Plains, NY: Longman.

Bronfenbrenner, U. (1999). Environments in developmental perspective: Theoretical and operational models. In S. Friedman & T. Wachs (Eds.), *Measuring environment across the life span: Emerging methods and concepts.* Washington, DC: American Psychological Association.

Brown, E., & Shaughnessy, T. (1979). *Education for social work practice with American Indian families.* American Indian Projects for Community Development. Tempe: Arizona State University, School of Social Work.

Brown, J. (1984). Group work with low income black youths. *Social Work with Groups, 7,* 111–124.

Brown, N. (1992). *Teaching group dynamics.* Hartford, CT: Praeger.

Browne, C., & Broderick, A. (1994). Asian and Pacific Island elders: Issues for social work practice and education. *Social Work, 39,* 252–259.

Brueggeman, W. (1996). *The practice of macro social work.* Chicago: Nelson-Hall.

Buechner, F. (1983). *Godric.* San Francisco: HarperCollins.

Bullis, R. (1996). *Spirituality in social work practice.* Washington, DC: Taylor & Francis.

Campbell, R. (1985). Crisis on the farm. *American Demographic, 7,* 30–34.

Canda, E. (1983). General implications of Shamanism for clinical social work. *International Social
Work, 26,* 14–22.

Canda, E. (1998). *Spirituality and social work: New
directions.* Binghamton, NY: Haworth Pastoral
Press.

Canda, E., & Furman, L. (1999). *Spiritual diversity in
social work practice: The heart of helping.* New
York: Free Press.

Caplan, N., Choy, M., & Whitmore, J. (1992). Indochinese refugee families and academic achievement. *Scientific American,* February, 36–42.

Carkhuff, R., & Anthony, W. (1979). *The skills of helping: An introduction to counseling skills.* Amherst,
MA: Human Resource Development Press.

Castex, G. (1994). Providing services to Hispanic/
Latino populations: Profiles in diversity. *Social
Work, 39,* 288–297.

Center for Visionary Leadership, in cooperation
with Milton Eisenhower Foundation. (1998). *A
guide to best practices: Practical information for
developing and implementing programs to enhance
the safety and security, personal empowerment, and
economic self-sufficiency of public housing residents.*
Washington, DC: U.S. Department of Housing
and Urban Development, Office of Public and
Indian Housing, Office of Public and Assisted
Housing Delivery.

Chao, C. (1992). The inner heart: Therapy with
southeast Asian families. In L. Vargus & J. Koss-
Chioino (Eds.), *Working with culture: Psychother-
apeutic interventions with ethnic minority children
and adolescents* (pp. 157–181). San Francisco:
Jossey-Bass.

Chestang, L. (1982). The delivery of child welfare
services to minority group children and their
families. In L. Chestang (Ed.), *Working with
Black families and children.* Richmond, VA:
Region III Child Welfare Training Center.

Chin, R., & Benne, K. (1969). General strategies for
effecting changes in human systems. In W. Ben-
nis, K. Benne, & R. Chin (Eds.), *The planning of
change.* New York: Holt, Rinehart and Winston.

Ching, J., McDermott, J., Fukunaga, C., Yamagida,
E., Mann, E., & Waldron, J. (1995). Perceptions
of family values and roles among Japanese
Americans: Clinical considerations. *American
Journal of Orthopsychiatry, 65,* 216–224.

Chung, D. (1992). Asian cultural commonalities: A
comparison with mainstream American culture. In S. Furuto, R. Biswas, D. Chung, K.
Marase, & F. Ross-Sheriff (Eds.), *Social work
practice with Asian Americans* (pp. 27–44). Newbury Park, CA: Sage.

Cnaan, R. (1999). *The newer deal: Social work and religion in partnership.* New York: Columbia University Press.

Coggins, K. (1991). *Cultural considerations in social
program planning among American Indians.*
Unpublished manuscript. School of Social
Work, University of Michigan, Ann Arbor.

Compton, B., & Galaway, B. (1999). *Social work
processes* (6th ed.). Belmont, CA: Brooks/Cole.

Conger, R., & Elder, G. (1994). *Families in troubled
times: Adapting to change in rural America.*
Hawthorne, NY: Aldine de Gruyter.

Cornett, C. (1982). Toward a more comprehensive
personology: Integrating a spiritual perspective
in social work practice. *Social Work, 17,* 1–10.

Council on Social Work Education (CSWE). (1994).
*Handbook of accreditation standards and proce-
dures.* Alexandria, VA: CSWE Commission on
Accreditation.

Coward, R., & Dwyer, J. (1993). The health and well-
being of rural elderly. In L. Ginsberg (Ed.),
Social work in rural communities (2nd ed., pp.
164–182). Alexandria, VA: Council on Social
Work Education.

Cowger, C. (1997). Assessing client strengths:
Assessment for client empowerment. In D.
Saleebey (Ed.), *The strengths perspective in social
work practice* (2nd ed., pp. 59–74). New York:
Longman.

Davis, L., & Proctor, E. (1989). *Race, gender, and class:
Guidelines for practice with individuals, families,
and groups.* Englewood Cliffs, NJ: Prentice-Hall.

Dean, R., & Reinherz, H. (1986). Psychodynamics
practice and single-system design: The odd
couple. *Journal of Social Work Education, 22,*
71–81.

DeAnda, D. (1984). Bicultural socialization: Factors
affecting the minority experience. *Social Work,
29,* 172–181.

De Hoyos, G. (1989). Person-in-environment: A
tri-level practice model. *Social Casework, 70,*
131–138.

DeJong, G., Batavia, A., & McKnew, L. (1992). The
independent living model of personal assistance in long-term-care policy. *Generations, 16,*
89–95.

Derezotes, D. (1995). Spirituality and religiosity:
Neglected factors in social work practice. *Arete,
20,* 1–15.

Devore, W., & Schlessinger, E. (1999). *Ethnic-sensi-
tive social work practice* (5th ed.). St. Louis, MO:
Mosby.

Dominelli, L., & McLeod, E. (1989). *Feminist social
work.* New York: New York University Press.

Doyle, R. (1998). *Skill and strategies in the helping process* (2nd ed.). Pacific Grove, CA: Brooks/Cole.

Drower, S. (1996). Social work values, professional unity, and the South African context. *Social Work, 41,* 138–151.

Duhl, F., Kantor, D., & Duhl, B. (1973). Learning, space, and action in family therapy: A primer of sculpture. In D. Bloch (Ed.), *Techniques of family therapy: A primer.* New York: Grune & Stratton.

Dunst, C., Trivette, C., & Deal, A. (1994). *Supporting and strengthening families: Methods, strategies, and practice* (Vol. 1). Cambridge, MA: Brookline.

Duryea, M., & Gundison, J. (1993). *Conflict and culture: Research in five communities in Vancouver, British Columbia.* Victoria, BC: University of Victoria, Institute for Dispute Resolution.

Dybwad, G. (1970). Treatment of the mentally retarded: A cross-cultural view. In H. Haywood (Ed.), *Cross-cultural aspects of mental retardation* (pp. 560–575). New York: Appleton-Century-Crofts.

Egan, G. (1998). *The skilled helper* (6th ed.). Pacific Grove, CA: Brooks/Cole.

Epstein, L. (1985). *Talking and listening: A guide to the helping interview.* St. Louis, MO: Times Mirror/Mosby.

Erikson, R., & Goldthorpe, J. (1993). *The constant flux: A study of class mobility in industrial societies.* Oxford: Clarendon Press.

Everett, J., Chipungu, S., & Leashore, B. (1991). *Child welfare: An Africentric perspective.* New Brunswick, NJ: Rutgers University Press.

Farley, J. (1994). *Sociology* (3rd ed.). Englewood Cliffs, NJ: Prentice-Hall.

Farley, O., Griffiths, K., Skidmore, R., & Thackeray, M. (1982). *Rural social work practice.* New York: Free Press.

Fischer, J., & Corcoran, K. (1994). *Measures for clinical practice* (Vols. I, II). New York: Free Press.

Fisher, R., Ury, W., & Patton, B. (1991). *Getting to yes: Negotiating agreement without giving in.* New York: Penguin.

Fitchen, J. (1981). *Poverty in America: A case study.* Boulder, CO: Westview.

Fong, R., & Mokuau, N. (1994). Not simply "Asian American": Periodical literature review on Asians and Pacific Islanders. *Social Work, 39,* 298–312.

Franklin, D. (1985). Differential clinical assessments: The influence of class and race. *Social Service Review, 59,* 44–61.

Fraser, M., & Galinsky, M. (1997). Toward a resilience-based model of practice. In M. Fraser (Ed.), *Risk and resilience in childhood: An ecological perspective.* Washington, DC: National Association of Social Workers.

Fraser, M., Nelson, K., & Rivard, J. (1997). Effectiveness of family preservation services. *Social Work Research, 21,* 138–153.

Freeman, E. (1990). Theoretical perspectives for practice with black families. In S. Logan, E. Freeman, & R. McRoy (Eds.), *Social work practice with black families: A culturally specific perspective* (pp. 38–52). New York: Longman.

Friedman, S., & Wachs, T. (1999). *Measuring environment across the life span: Emerging methods and concepts.* Washington, DC: American Psychological Association.

Gabor, P., & Grinnell, R. (1994). *Evaluation and quality improvement in the human services.* Boston: Allyn and Bacon.

Gallesich, J. (1982). *The profession and practice of consultation.* San Francisco: Jossey-Bass.

Gans, H. (1979). Symbolic ethnicity: The future of ethnic groups and cultures. *American Ethnic and Racial Studies, 2,* 1–20.

Garcia-Preto, N. (1996). Puerto Rican families. In M. McGoldrick, J. Giordano, & J. Pearce (Eds.), *Ethnicity and family therapy* (2nd ed., pp. 183–199). New York: Guilford.

Garland, D., & Conrad, A. (1990). The church as a context for professional practice. In D. Garland & D. Pancoast (Eds.), *The church's ministry with families.* Dallas, TX: Word Publishing.

Gary, L., & Leashore, B. (1982). High-risk status of black men. *Social Work, 27,* 55–56.

Gerhart, U. (1990). *Caring for the chronic mentally ill.* Itasca, IL: Peacock.

Germaine, C. (1973). An ecological perspective in casework practice. *Social Casework, 54,* 323–330.

Germaine, C. (Ed.). (1979). *Social work practice: People and environments—An ecological perspective.* New York: Columbia University Press.

Germaine, C., & Gitterman, A. (1979). The life model of social work practice. In F. Turner (Ed.), *Social work treatment: Interlocking theoretical approaches* (2nd ed., pp. 361–384). New York: Free Press.

Germaine, C., & Gitterman, A. (1995). Ecological perspective. *Encyclopedia of social work* (19th ed., pp. 816–824). Washington, DC: National Association of Social Workers Press.

Germaine, C., & Gitterman, A. (1996). *The life model of social work practice: Advances in theory and practice.* New York: Columbia University Press.

Ginsberg, L. (1998). *Social work in rural communities* (3rd ed.). Alexandria, VA: Council on Social Work Education.

Goldberg, G., & Kremen, E. (1990). *The feminization of poverty.* New York: Greenwood.

Goldberg, H. (1978). *The new male.* New York: New American Library.

Goldstein, H. (1990). The knowledge base of social work practice: Theory, wisdom, analogue, or art? *Families in Society: The Journal of Contemporary Human Services, 71,* 32–43.

Gordon, W. (1962). A critique of the working definition. *Social Work, 7,* 3–13.

Gordon, W. (1969). Basic concepts for an integrative and generative conception of social work. In G. Hearn (Ed.), *The general systems approach: Contributions toward an holistic conception of social work* (pp. 5–11). New York: Council on Social Work Education.

Graham, M., Kaiser, T., & Garrett, K. (1998). Naming the spiritual: The hidden dimension of helping. *Social Thought, 18,* 49–61.

Granvold, G. (Ed.). (1994). *Cognitive and behavioral treatment.* Pacific Grove, CA: Brooks/Cole.

Green, J. (1999). *Cultural awareness in the human services: A multiethnic approach* (3rd ed.). Boston: Allyn and Bacon.

Griffith, J., & Villavicencio, S. (1985). Relationship among acculturation, sociodemographic characteristics, and social support in Mexican American adults. *Hispanic Journal of Behavioral Sciences, 7,* 75–92.

Guarnaccia, P. (1993). Ataques de nervios in Puerto Rico: Culture-bound syndrome or popular illness? *Medical Anthropology, 15,* 157–170.

Gutierrez, L. (1990). Working with women of color: An empowerment perspective. *Social Work, 35,* 149–153.

Gutierrez, L. (1994). Beyond coping: An empowerment perspective on stressful life events. *Journal of Sociology and Social Welfare, 21,* 201–219.

Gutierrez, L. (1995). Understanding the empowerment process: Does consciousness make a difference? *Social Work Research, 19,* 229–237.

Gutierrez, L., Alvarez, A., Nemon, H., & Lewis, E. (1997). Multicultural community organizing: A strategy for change. In P. Ewalt, E. Freeman, S. Kirk, & D. Poole (Eds.), *Social policy: Reform, research, and practice.* Washington, DC: National Association of Social Workers Press.

Gutierrez, L., & Cox, E. (1998). *Empowerment in social work practice: A source book.* Pacific Grove, CA: Brooks/Cole.

Gutierrez, L., & Lewis, E. (1999). *Empowering women of color.* New York: Columbia University Press.

Hallowitz, D. (1979). Problem-solving theory. In F. Turner (Ed.), *Social work treatment: Interlocking theoretical approaches* (2nd ed., pp. 93–122). New York: Free Press.

Hardcastle, D., Wenocur, S., & Powers, P. (1997). *Community practice: Theories and skills for social workers.* New York: Oxford University Press.

Hartman, A., & Laird, J. (1983). *Family-centered social work practice.* New York: Free Press.

Hawkins, B. (1997). Hostile environments: Reducing applications to medical schools nationwide. *Black Issues in Higher Education, 14,* 18–20.

Hearn, G. (1969). *The general systems approach: Contributions toward an holistic conception of social work.* New York: Council on Social Work Education.

Hearn, G. (1979). General systems theory and social work. In F. Turner (Ed.), *Social work treatment: Interlocking theoretical approaches* (2nd ed., pp. 333–360). New York: Free Press.

Hepworth, D., Rooney, R., & Larsen, J. (1997). *Direct social work practice: Theory and skills definition* (5th ed.). Belmont, CA: Brooks/Cole.

Hess, H., & Hess, P. (1994). Termination in context. In B. Compton & B. Galaway (Eds.), *Social work processes* (pp. 529–539). Pacific Grove, CA: Brooks/Cole.

Hollis, F. (1965). Casework and social class. *Social Casework, 46,* 466–469.

Homan, M. (1999). *Promoting community change: Making it happen in the real world* (2nd ed.). Pacific Grove, CA: Brooks/Cole.

Horwitz, A., & Scheid, T. (1999). *A handbook for the study of mental health: Social contexts, theories, and systems.* New York: Cambridge University Press.

Huang, K. (1991). Chinese Americans. In N. Mokuau (Ed.), *Handbook of social services for Asian and Pacific Islanders.* New York: Greenwood.

Jenkins, L., & Cook, A. (1961). The rural hospice: Integrating normal and informal helping systems. *Social Work, 26,* 415–416.

Jiobu, R. (1988). *Ethnicity and assimilation.* Albany: State University of New York Press.

Johnson, W. (1993). Rural crime, delinquency, substance abuse, and corrections. In L. Ginsberg (Ed.), *Social work in rural communities* (2nd ed., pp. 203–217). Alexandria, VA: Council on Social Work Education.

Jones, S., & Zlotnik, J. (1998). *Preparing helping professionals to meet community needs: Generalizing from the rural experience.* Alexandria, VA: Council on Social Work Education.

Jordan, J., Kaplan, A., Miller, J., Stiver, I., & Surrey, J. (1991). *Women's growth in connection.* New York: Guilford.

Joseph, V. (1975). The parish as a social service and

social action center: An ecological systems approach. *Social Thought, 13,* 12–23.

Joseph, V. (1987). The religious and spiritual aspects of social work practice: A neglected dimension of social work. *Social Thought, 13,* 12–23.

Joseph, V. (1988). Religion and social work practice. *Social Casework, 69,* 443–452.

Joseph, V. (1997). Toward the future: Call, covenant, mission. *Society for Spirituality and Social Work Newsletter, 4,* 1–5 & 11–12.

Karger, H., & Stoesz, D. (1990). *American social welfare policy. A structural approach.* White Plains, NY: Longman.

Keith-Lucas, A. (1972). *Giving and taking help.* Chapel Hill: University of North Carolina Press.

Keith-Lucas, A. (1985). *So you want to be a social worker: A primer for Christian students.* St. Davids, PA: North American Association of Christians in Social Work.

Keith-Lucas, A. (1992). A socially-sanctioned profession? In P. Reid & P. Popple (Eds.), *The moral purposes of social work.* Chicago: Nelson-Hall.

Kerlinger, F., & Lee, H. (2000). *Foundations of behavioral research.* Fort Worth, TX: Harcourt College Publishers.

Kilpatrick, A., & Holland, T. (1995). *Working with families: An integrative model by level of functioning.* Boston: Allyn and Bacon.

Kirk, S. (1999). *Social work research methods.* Washington, DC: National Association of Social Workers.

Kirst-Ashman, K., & Hull, G. (1999). *Understanding generalist practice* (2nd ed.). Chicago: Nelson-Hall.

Kochman, T. (1981). *Black and white conflicts.* Chicago: University of Chicago Press.

Kretzman, J., & McKnight, J. (1993). *Building communities from the inside out.* Evanston, IL: Northwestern University, Center for Urban Affairs and Policy Research.

Kubler-Ross, E. (1969). *On death and dying.* New York: Macmillan.

Kumabe, K., Nishida, C., & Hepworth, D. (1985). *Bridging ethnocultural diversity in social work and health.* Honolulu: University of Hawaii Press.

Laborde, P., & Seligman, M. (1991). Counseling parents of children with disabilities. In M. Seligman (Ed.), *The family with a handicapped child* (2nd ed., pp. 337–369). Boston: Allyn and Bacon.

Lake, R. (1983). Shamanism in northwestern California: A female perspective of sickness, healing, and health. *White Cloud Journal of American Indian Mental Health, 3,* 31–42.

Land, H., & Hudson, S. (1997). Methodological considerations in studying Latina AIDS caregivers: Issues in sampling and measurement. *Social Work Research, 21,* 233–246.

Lazerson, M. (1975). Educational institutions and mental subnormality: Notes on writing a history. In M. Begab & S. Richardson (Eds.), *The mentally retarded and society: A social science perspective* (pp. 33–52). Baltimore, MD: University Park Press.

Lee, M. (1996). A constructivist approach to the help-seeking process of clients: A response to cultural diversity. *Journal of Clinical Social Work, 24,* 187–202.

Lefley, H., & Pedersen, P. (1986). *Cross-cultural training for mental health professionals.* Springfield, IL: Charles C. Thomas.

LeResche, D. (1992). Comparison of the American mediation process with Korean American harmony restoration process. *Mediation Quarterly, 9,* 323–339.

LeVine, E., & Padilla, A. (1980). *Crossing cultures in therapy: Pluralist counseling for the Hispanic.* Monterey, CA: Brooks/Cole.

Levy, C. (1973). The value base of social work. *Journal of Education for Social Work, 9,* 34–42.

Lewin, K. (1951). *Field theory in social science.* New York: Harper and Row.

Lewis, E. (1991). Social change and citizen action: A philosophical exploration for modern social group work. *Social Work with Groups, 14,* 23–34.

Lie, G. (1999). Empowerment: Asian-American women's perspectives. In L. Gutierrez & E. Lewis (Eds.), *Empowering women of color* (pp. 187–207). New York: Columbia University Press.

Lineberry, R. (1975). Suburbia and metropolitan turf. *The Annals of American Academy of Political and Social Science, 422,* 3–11.

Linzer, N. (1999). *Resolving ethical dilemmas.* Boston: Allyn and Bacon.

Lippett, R., Watson, J., & Westley, B. (1958). *The dynamics of planned change.* New York: Harcourt, Brace, & World.

Littner, N. (1981). *Some traumatic effects of separation and placement.* New York: Child Welfare League of America.

Loewenberg, F. (1988). *Religion and social work practice in contemporary American society.* New York: Columbia University Press.

Lum, D. (1996). *Social work practice and people of color* (3rd ed.). Pacific Grove, CA: Brooks/Cole.

Lum, D. (1999). *Culturally competent practice.* Pacific Grove, CA: Brooks/Cole.

Lum, D., & Lu, E. (1999). Skill development. In D. Lum (Ed.), *Culturally competent practice* (pp. 113–144). Pacific Grove, CA: Brooks/Cole.

Lundblad, K. (1995). Jane Addams and social reform: A role model for the 1990s. *Social Work, 40,* 661–669.

Mackelprang, R., & Salsgiver, R. (1996). People with disabilities and social work: Historical and contemporary issues. *Social Work, 41,* 7–14.

Mackelprang, R., & Santos, D. (1992). *Educational strategies for working with persons of disability.* Faculty Development Institute presented at the Annual Program Meeting of the Council on Social Work Education, Kansas City, MO.

Mahaffey, M. (1976). Sexism and social work. *Social Work, 21,* 419.

Maluccio, A. (1981). *Promoting competence in clients.* New York: Free Press.

Marin, G. (1993). Defining culturally appropriate community interventions: Hispanics as a case study. *Journal of Community Psychology, 21,* 149–161.

Marin, G., & Marin, B. (1991). *Research with Hispanic populations.* Newbury Park, CA: Sage.

Marmor, J. (1980). *Homosexual behavior: A modern reappraisal.* New York: Basic Books.

Marsella, J. (1993). Counseling and psychotherapy with Japanese Americans: Cross-cultural considerations. *American Journal of Orthopsychiatry, 63,* 200–208.

Marsh, D. (1992). *Families and mental retardation.* New York: Praeger.

Marshak, L., & Seligman, M. (1993). *Counseling persons with disabilities: Theoretical and clinical perspectives.* Austin, TX: ProEd.

Martens, W., & Holmstrum, E. (1974). Problem-oriented recording. *Social Casework, 55,* 554–561.

Martinez-Brawley, E. (1990). *Perspectives on the small community.* Silver Spring, MD: National Association of Social Workers.

Martinez-Brawley, E. (1980). Historical perspectives on rural social work: Implications for curriculum development. *Journal of Education for Social Work, 16,* 49–52.

Martinez-Brawley, E. (1987). *Social work and the rural crisis: Is education responding?* Paper presented at the Invitational Session Council on Social Work Education Annual Program Meeting, St. Louis, MO.

Martinez-Brawley, E., & Blundell, J. (1989). Farm families' preference toward the personal social services. *Social Work, 34,* 513–522.

Maslow, A. (1968). *Toward a psychology of being.* New York: Van Nostrand.

Maslow, A. (1970). *Motivation and personality* (2nd ed.). New York: Harper and Row.

Mattaini, M., Lowery, C., & Meyer, C. (Eds.). (1998). *The foundations of social work practice* (2nd ed.). Washington, DC: National Association of Social Workers.

McAdoo, H. (Ed.). (1993). *Family ethnicity: Strength in diversity.* Newbury Park, CA: Sage.

McCormick, M. (1954). *Diagnostic casework in the Thomistic pattern.* New York: Columbia University Press.

McGoldrick, M., Garcia-Preto, N., Hines, P., & Lee, E. (1989). Ethnicity and women. In M. McGoldrick, C. Anderson, & F. Walsh (Eds.), *Women in families: A framework for family therapy* (pp. 169–199). New York: Norton.

McGoldrick, M., & Gerson, R. (1985). *Genograms in family assessment.* New York: Norton.

McGoldrick, M., Giordano, J., & Pearce, J. (Eds.). (1996). *Ethnicity and family therapy* (2nd ed.). New York: Guilford.

McMahon, M. (1996). *The general method of social work practice: A generalist perspective* (3rd ed.). Boston: Allyn and Bacon.

McMillen, J. (1999). Better for it: How people benefit from adversity. *Social Work, 44,* 455–467.

McMiller, W., & Weisz, J. (1996). Help-seeking preceding mental health clinic intake among African American, Latino, and Caucasian youths. *Journal of American Academy of Child and Adolescent Psychiatry, 35,* 1086–1094.

McNaught, B. (1981). *A disturbed peace.* Washington, DC: A Dignity Publication.

Mechanic, D. (1978). *Medical sociology* (2nd ed.). New York: Free Press.

Merton, R. (1957). *Social theory and social structure.* New York: Free Press.

Merton, R., & Nisbet, R. (1971). *Contemporary social problems.* New York: Harcourt.

Meyer, C. (1966). The changing concept of individualized services. *Social Casework, 47.*

Meyer, C. (1993). *Assessment in social work practice.* New York: Columbia University Press.

Miley, K., O'Melia, M., & DuBois, B. (1998). *Generalist social work practice: An empowering approach* (2nd ed.). Boston: Allyn and Bacon.

Mizrahi, T., & Rosenthal, B. (1993). Managing dynamic tensions in social change coalitions. In T. Mizrahi & J. Morrison (Eds.), *Community organizations and social administration* (pp. 11–40). New York: Haworth.

Morales, R. (1976). *Asian and Pacific American curriculum in social work education.* Los Angeles:

Asian American Community Mental Health Training Center.

Mueller, E., & Murphy, P. (1965). Communication problems: Social workers and lawyers. *Social Work, 10*, 97–103.

Mulroy, E. (1997). Building a neighborhood network: Interorganizational collaboration to prevent child abuse and neglect. *Social Work, 42*, 255–264.

National Association of Social Workers. (1996). *Code of ethics.* Washington, DC: NASW.

Nelson, K., & Landsman, M. (1992). *Alternative models of family preservation: Family-based services in context.* Springfield, IL: Charles C. Thomas.

Newman, J. (1991). Handicapped persons and their families: Philosophical, historical, and legislative perspectives. In M. Seligman (Ed.), *The family with a handicapped child* (2nd ed., pp. 1–26). Boston: Allyn and Bacon.

Nichols, M., & Schwartz, R. (1995). *Family therapy: Concepts and methods.* Boston: Allyn and Bacon.

Norton, D. (1978). *The dual perspective: Inclusion of ethnic minority content in the social work curriculum.* Washington, DC: Council on Social Work Education.

Norton, D. (1993). Diversity, early socialization, and temporal development: The dual perspective revisited. *Social Work, 38*, 82–90.

O'Hare, W. (1992). America's minorities—The demographics of diversity. *Population Bulletin, 47.* Washington, DC: Population Reference Bureau.

O'Neil, M. (1980–83). Small group discussions with inmates at Somers Maximum Security Prison, Somers, CT.

O'Neil, M., & Ball, J. (1987). *The general method of social work in rural environments.* Paper presented at Council on Social Work Education Annual Program Meeting, Saint Louis, MO.

Opirhory, G., & Peters, G. (1982). Counseling intervention strategies for families with less than a perfect newborn. *Personnel and Guidance Journal, 60*, 451–455.

Ordaz, M., & DeAnda, D. (1996). Cultural legacies: Operationalizing Chicano cultural values. *Journal of Multicultural Social Work, 4*, 57–68.

Parsons, R., Jorgensen, J., & Hernandez, S. (1994). *The integration of social work practice.* Pacific Grove, CA: Brooks/Cole.

Patterson, O. (1995). Affirmative action on the merit system. *New York Times,* August 9, p. 13.

Pearl, W., Leo, P., & Tsang, W. (1995). Use of Chinese therapies among Chinese patients seeking emergency department care. *Annals of Emergency Medicine, 26*, 735–738.

Pedersen, P. (1997). *Culture-centered counseling interventions.* Thousand Oaks, CA: Sage.

Perez, J. (1979). *Family counseling: Theory and practice.* New York: Van Nostrand.

Perlman, H. (1957). *Social casework: A problem-solving process.* Chicago: University of Chicago Press.

Piccard, B. (1988). *An introduction to social work: A primer* (3rd ed.). Homewood, IL: Dorsey.

Pincus, A., & Minahan, A. (1973). *Social work practice: Model and method.* Itasca, IL: Peacock.

Pinderhughes, E. (1989). *Understanding race, ethnicity, and power: The key to efficacy in clinical practice.* New York: Free Press.

Pinderhughes, E. (1995). Empowering diverse populations: Family practice in the 21st century. *Families in Society, 76*, 131–140.

Pray, J. (1991). Respecting the uniqueness of the individual: Social work practice within a reflective model. *Social Work, 36*, 80–85.

Reamer, F. (1993). *The foundations of social work knowledge.* New York: Columbia University Press.

Reid, P., & Popple, P. (Eds.). (1992). *The moral purposes of social work: The character and intentions of a profession.* Chicago: Nelson-Hall.

Reid, W. (1996). Task-centered social work. In F. Turner (Ed.), *Social work treatment* (4th ed., pp. 617–640). New York: Free Press.

Reid, W., & Epstein, L. (1972). *Task-centered casework.* New York: Columbia University Press.

Richmond, M. (1917). *Social diagnosis.* New York: Russell Sage.

Rivera, F., & Erlich, J. (1998). *Community organizing in a diverse society* (3rd ed.). Boston: Allyn and Bacon.

Robbins, S., Chatterjee, P., & Canda, E. (1998). *Contemporary human behavior theory: A critical perspective for social work.* Boston: Allyn and Bacon.

Romero, D. (1977). Biases in gender-role research, *Social Work, 22*, 214.

Ross, M. (1995). *Community organization: Theory and principles.* New York: Harper & Brothers.

Rubin, A., & Babbie, E. (1997). *Research methods for social work.* Belmont, CA: Wadsworth.

Rubin, H., & Rubin, I. (1992). *Community organizing and development* (2nd ed.). New York: Macmillan.

Sabatino, C. (1999). School social work consultation and collaboration. In R. Constable, S. McDonald, & J. Flynn (Eds.), *School social work: Practice, policy, and research perspectives* (4th ed., pp. 334–355). Chicago: Lyceum.

Saleebey, D. (1994). Culture, theory, and narrative: The intersection of meanings in practice. *Social Work, 39*, 352–361.

Saleebey, D. (1996). The strengths perspective in social work practice: Extensions and cautions. *Social Work, 41,* 296–305.

Saleebey, D. (1997). *The strengths perspective in social work practice.* New York: Longman.

Salladin, L., & Timberlake, E. (1995). Assessing clinical progress: A case study of Daryl. *Child and Adolescent Social Work Journal, 12,* 289–316.

Salsgiver, R. (1993). The Americans with Disabilities Act, ableism, and social work. *NASW California News,* March 4.

Sandau-Beckler, P., Salcido, R., & Ronnau, J. (1993). Culturally-competent family preservation services: An approach for first-generation Hispanic families in an international border community. *Counseling & Therapy for Couples & Families, 1,* 313–323.

Schultz, S. (1982). How Southeast Asian refugees in California adapt to unfamiliar health care practices. *Health and Social Work, 7,* 148–156.

Schwartz, I., & AuClaire, P. (Eds.). (1995). *Home-based services for troubled children.* Lincoln: University of Nebraska Press.

See, L. (1998). *Human behavior in the social environment from an African American perspective.* New York: Haworth.

Seligman, M., & Darling, R. (1997). *Ordinary families, special children* (2nd ed.). New York: Guilford.

Shardlow, S. (1989). Changing social work values: An introduction. In S. Shardlow (Ed.), *The values of change in social work* (pp. 1–8). London: Tavistock/Routledge.

Sheafor, B., Horejsi, C., & Horejsi, G. (1997). *Techniques and guidelines for social work practice* (4th ed.). Boston: Allyn and Bacon.

Shepard, M. (1997). Site-based services for residents of single-room occupancy hotels. *Social Work, 42,* 585–592.

Shulman, L. (1999). *The skills of helping individuals, families, groups, and communities* (4th ed.). Itasca, IL: Peacock.

Simon, B. (1994). *The empowerment tradition in American social work.* New York: Columbia University Press.

Simon, B. (1998). The profession of social work. In M. Mattaini, C. Lowery, & C. Meyer (Eds.), *The foundations of social work practice* (2nd ed., pp. 317–325). Washington, DC: NASW Press.

Siporin, M. (1975). *Introduction to social work practice.* New York: Macmillan.

Siporin, M. (1990). Welcome to the *Spirituality and Social Work Communicator. Spirituality and Social Work Communicator, 1,* 3–4.

Siporin, M. (1993). The social worker's style. *Clinical Social Work Journal, 21,* 257–270.

Smith, E. (1995). Addressing the psychospiritual distress of death as reality: A transpersonal approach. *Social Work, 40,* 402–412.

Spencer, S. (1956). Religion and social work. *Social Work, 1,* 19–26.

Substance Abuse and Mental Health Services Administration. (1995). *Cultural competence series: A guide for alcohol and other drug abuse prevention practitioners working with ethnic/racial communities.* Rockville, MD: U.S. Department of Health and Human Services, Office of Substance Abuse Programs.

Sue, D., & Sue, D. (1990). *Counseling the culturally different.* New York: Wiley.

Sullivan, P. (1994). Should spiritual principles guide social policy? No. In H. Karger & J. Midgely (Eds.), *Controversial issues in human behavior in the social environment* (pp. 69–74). Boston: Allyn and Bacon.

Sullivan, W. (1992). Spirituality as social support for individuals with severe mental illness. *Spirituality and Social Work Journal, 3,* 7–13.

Swenson, L. (1993). *Psychology and law for the helping professions.* Pacific Grove, CA: Brooks/Cole.

Tamura, T., & Lau, A. (1992). Connectedness versus separateness: Applicability of family therapy to Japanese families. *Family Process, 31,* 319–340.

Taylor, J. (1997). Niches and practice: Extending the ecological perspective. In D. Saleeby (Ed.), *The strengths perspective in social work practice* (2nd ed., pp. 217–227). New York: Longman.

Timberlake, E., & Cutler, M. (2001). *Developmental play therapy in clinical social work.* Boston: Allyn and Bacon.

Timms, N. (1983). *Social work values: An inquiry.* London: Routledge & Kegan Paul.

Towle, C. (1957). *Common human needs.* Washington, DC: National Association of Social Workers.

Tropman, J. (1989). *American values and social welfare: Cultural contradictions in the welfare state.* Englewood Cliffs, NJ: Prentice-Hall.

Tropman, J. (1999). *The Catholic ethic in American society: An exploration of values.* San Francisco: Jossey-Bass.

Tropman, J., Erlich, J., & Rothman, J. (1995). *Tactics and techniques of community intervention* (3rd ed.). Itasca, IL: Peacock.

Turner, J., & Jaco, R. (1996). Problem-solving and social work treatment. In F. Turner (Ed.), *Social work treatment: Interlocking theoretical approaches* (pp. 503–522). New York: Free Press.

U.S. Bureau of the Census. (1995). Population profile of the United States. *Current Population Reports, Series P23-189*. Washington, DC: U.S. Government Printing Office.

Valentine, C. (1971). Deficit, difference, and bicultural models of Afro-American behavior. *Howard Educational Review, 41*, 137–157.

Vourlekis, E., & Greene, R. (1992). *Social work case management*. New York: Aldine de Gruyter.

Wakefield, J. (1993). Is altruism part of human nature? Toward a theoretical foundation for the helping professions. *Social Service Review, 67*, 406–458.

Wall, S., Timberlake, E., Farber, M., Sabatino, C., Liebow, H., Smith, N., & Taylor, N. (2000). Needs and aspirations of the working poor: Early Head Start applicants. *Families-in-Society, 81*, 412–421.

Walz, T. (1989). The mission of social work revisited: An agenda for the 1990s. William R. Hodson Lecture, quoted in the Public Social Services: The Social Work Role, *School of Social Work Alumni Report*. Minneapolis: University of Minnesota.

Webster's desk dictionary of the English language. (1990). New York: Portland House.

Weed, L. (1971). *Medical records, medical education, and patient care*. Cleveland, OH: Case Western Reserve University Press.

Weick, A., Rapp, C., Sullivan, P., & Kisthardt, W. (1989). A strengths perspective for social work practice. *Social Work, 34*, 350–354.

Wijnberg, M., & Colca, L. (1981). Facing up to the diversity in rural practice: A curriculum model. *Journal of Education for Social Work, 17*, 91–101.

Williams, E., & Ellison, F. (1996). Culturally informed social work practice with American Indian clients: Guidelines for non-Indian social workers. *Social Work, 41*, 147–151.

Williams, J. (1983). *The state of black America—1983*. New York: National Urban League.

Wilson, S. (1978). *Confidentiality in social work: Issues and principles*. New York: Free Press.

Wilson-Coker, P. (1982). *Working effectively with attorneys in the adversary system: Observations and suggestions for protective service social workers*. Unpublished paper, Saint Joseph College, West Hartford, CT.

Wolfensberger, W. (1972). *Normalization*. New York: National Institute on Mental Retardation.

Wolin, S., & Wolin, S. (1993). *The resilient self: How survivors of troubled families rise above adversity*. New York: Villard.

Wood, G., & Middleman, R. (1989). *The structural approach to direct practice in social work*. New York: Columbia University Press.

Worden, M. (1999). *Family therapy basics* (2nd ed.). Pacific Grove, CA: Brooks/Cole.

Wright, E. (1985). *Classes*. London: Verso.

Yamashiro, G., & Matsuoka, J. (1997). Help-seeking among Asian and Pacific Americans: A multiperspective analysis. *Social Work, 42*, 176–186.

York, R. (1998). *Conducting social work research*. Boston: Allyn and Bacon.

Zastrow, C. (1999). *The practice of social work* (6th ed.). Pacific Grove, CA: Brooks/Cole.

INDEX

Human diversity, *continued*
  help-seeking behaviors, 50–51
  in intervention, 230–231
  minority status, 43–45
  nationalities, 41
  perceptions of illness and health, 72–73
  personalities, 61–62
  physical and mental abilities, 73–75
  races, 41–42
  religions, 47–50
  sensitivity to, 75–78
    in data collection stage, 140–141
  sexual orientation, 69–71
  social classes, 53–56
  well-being, 45–47

I

"I" statements, 215
Illness and health, various perceptions of, 72–73
Imagery exercise, 320
Indirect intervention, 217–219, 225
  and emotional involvement, 229
Indirect practice vs. indirect intervention, 217
Individuality, principles of, 68, 277
  in assessment stage, 175
  and direct intervention, 229
Information:
  confidentiality, 126–129
  providing to clients, 208–212
  release of, 120–121
Informed consent by client, 121–122, 126–127
Integrated service delivery, 212–217
Intergenerational differences in identifying with national origin, 41
Interrelationships of professionals, 3
Intervention, 201–252
  case applications, 231–252
    for clients in homeless shelters, 250–252
    for clients on state social services, 235, 238–240, 241–242

  in child welfare field, 232–233, 234
  in community services, 240, 243
  in education field, 243–246
  in gerontology, 233–235, 236–237
  in juvenile court, 246–249
  case management, 212–217
  cultural sensitivity in, 230–231
  direct, 205–208
  human diversity issues in, 130–231
  indirect, 217–219, 225
  roles of social worker, 202–203
  selections of, 29–31
  for social change, 219–223
  by social work generalist, 4
  teamwork, 212–217
Involving significant others in problem-solving process, 31

J

Juvenile court:
  case applications:
    assessment of, 190, 192–196
    data collection on, 151–153
    engagement with, 111–113
    evaluation in, 298–299, 301, 302
    termination, 334–335, 336
  intervention for, 246–249

K

Knowledge base of social worker, 3, 9–12
  in data collection, 139–140
  in engagement stage, 100–101
  in evaluation, 277–278
  in intervention stage, 229–230
  in termination, 323–324

L

Lawyers and social workers, tensions between, 218
Least restrictive environment principle, 74